DIAGNOSING FROM A DISTANCE

Ever since the rise of Adolf Hitler, mental health professionals have sought to use their knowledge of human psychology to understand – and to intervene in – political developments. Psychiatrists have commented, sometimes brashly, on the mental health of public figures from Barry Goldwater to Donald Trump. But is the practice ethical? While the American Psychiatric Association prohibits psychiatric comment on public figures under its "Goldwater Rule," others disagree.

Diagnosing from a Distance is the first in-depth exploration of this controversy. Making extensive use of archival sources and original interviews, John Martin-Joy reconstructs the historical debates between psychiatrists, journalists, and politicians in an era when libel law and professional standards have undergone dramatic change. Charting the Goldwater Rule's crucial role in the current furor over Trump's fitness for office, Martin-Joy assesses the Rule's impact and offers a more liberal alternative. This remarkable book will change the way we think about psychiatric ethics and public life.

John Martin-Joy, MD, is a psychiatrist in Cambridge, Massachusetts, and a part-time instructor in psychiatry at Harvard Medical School.

DIAGNOSING FROM A DISTANCE

*Debates over Libel Law, Media, and Psychiatric Ethics
from Barry Goldwater to Donald Trump*

John Martin-Joy, MD

Harvard Medical School

CAMBRIDGE
UNIVERSITY PRESS

CAMBRIDGE
UNIVERSITY PRESS

University Printing House, Cambridge CB2 8BS, United Kingdom

One Liberty Plaza, 20th Floor, New York, NY 10006, USA

477 Williamstown Road, Port Melbourne, VIC 3207, Australia

314–321, 3rd Floor, Plot 3, Splendor Forum, Jasola District Centre,
New Delhi – 110025, India

79 Anson Road, #06–04/06, Singapore 079906

Cambridge University Press is part of the University of Cambridge.

It furthers the University's mission by disseminating knowledge in the pursuit of
education, learning, and research at the highest international levels of excellence.

www.cambridge.org
Information on this title: www.cambridge.org/9781108486583
DOI: 10.1017/9781108761222

First published 2020

Printed in the United Kingdom by TJ International Ltd, Padstow Cornwall

A catalogue record for this publication is available from the British Library.

Library of Congress Cataloging-in-Publication Data
Names: Martin-Joy, John, author.
Title: Diagnosing from a distance : debates over libel law, media, and psychiatric ethics
from Barry Goldwater to Donald Trump / John Martin-Joy.
Description: Cambridge ; New York, NY : Cambridge University Press, 2020. | Includes
bibliographical references and index.
Identifiers: LCCN 2019049174 (print) | LCCN 2019049175 (ebook) | ISBN
9781108486583 (hardback) | ISBN 9781108707985 (paperback) | ISBN
9781108761222 (epub)
Subjects: LCSH: Goldwater, Barry M. (Barry Morris), 1909–1998 – Mental health. |
Trump, Donald, 1946– Mental health. | Mental illness – Diagnosis – Moral and ethical
aspects. | Mental illness – Diagnosis – Political aspects. | Psychiatric ethics.
Classification: LCC RC469 .M368 2020 (print) | LCC RC469 (ebook) | DDC 616.89/
075–dc23
LC record available at https://lccn.loc.gov/2019049174
LC ebook record available at https://lccn.loc.gov/2019049175

ISBN 978-1-108-48658-3 Hardback
ISBN 978-1-108-70798-5 Paperback

to
Robert Coles

Contents

CONTENTS

About the Author

John Martin-Joy, MD, is a psychiatrist in Cambridge, Massachusetts. A part-time instructor in psychiatry at Harvard Medical School, he teaches at the BIDMC Harvard Psychiatry Residency Training Program in Boston and at Mt. Auburn Hospital in Cambridge. He is also a candidate at the Boston Psychoanalytic Society and Institute. Dr. Martin-Joy has worked in both inpatient and outpatient settings and has testified extensively as an expert psychiatric witness in court. He has written about activism in psychiatry, has published scholarly articles on the Goldwater Rule, and has published empirical research documenting the maturation of defense (coping) mechanisms over the adult life span. A former book editor in history and sociology, he is the coeditor of *Conversations with Donald Hall* (forthcoming from University Press of Mississippi).

Acknowledgments

I am grateful to the many people who assisted in the completion of this book. First and foremost, I would like to thank the participants in the events recounted here, as well as their families, for granting me interviews that helped clarify and expand my understanding of my topic. Thanks go to Lark Ginzburg Kuhta and Bonnie Ginzburg Erbe, who were cooperative and provided beneficial insights into their father, publisher Ralph Ginzburg; to psychiatrist Gail Barton, whose interview shed light on her father, Walter Barton, the medical director of the American Psychiatric Association (APA) in the 1960s and early 1970s; to psychiatrists Judith Herman, Bandy Lee, and Leonard Glass for speaking with me about their concerns about President Donald Trump and the APA's Goldwater Rule; to current APA medical director Saul Levin and Ethics Committee chair Rebecca Brendel, who spoke with me about the APA's point of view; and to two former APA presidents, Anita Everett and Jeffrey Lieberman, who shared their perspectives on their involvement in the debate over the Goldwater Rule.

Staff members at several libraries and archival collections generously helped me to locate and understand archival material. Grateful acknowledgments go to the staff of the Harvard University Libraries, including at Widener Library and at Houghton Library, home of Walter Langer's annotated copy of his report on Adolf Hitler to the Office of Strategic Services. In Laramie, Wyoming, John Waggoner, archivist at the University of Wyoming's American Heritage Collection, provided access to and permission to quote from the Ralph Ginzburg papers; at Arizona State University, Rob Spindler and Renee D. James of the special collections staff made the Barry Goldwater Papers accessible; at the LBJ Library in Austin, Texas, Liza Talbot and Chris Banks provided useful material on Lyndon Johnson's response to Ralph Ginzburg. At the Melvin Sabshin Library of the American Psychiatric Association in Washington, DC, archivist Deena Gorland and APA general counsel Colleen Coyle welcomed me and graciously granted me access to and perspective on the organization's extensive archives. At the Oscar Diethelm Library of Weill Cornell Medicine in New York City, special collections archivist Marisa Shaari located and sent material on the *Fact* episode from the archives of the American Psychoanalytic Association.

At the Boston Psychoanalytic Society and Institute (BPSI), executive director Catherine Kimble graciously reviewed portions of the manuscript and provided helpful comments, as did analyst Julia Matthews, fellow candidates Chris Leich and Jane Keat, and historian Elizabeth Lunbeck. Archivist Olga Umansky provided valuable assistance in locating material on psychoanalytic history as well as information on Walter Langer in particular, including permission to reproduce a photograph of Langer from the BPSI archives. Boston Psychoanalytic Institute teachers and supervisors Anna Ornstein, Jane Hanenberg, Steve Bernstein, Tony Kris, Steven Cooper, my fellow third-year classmates, and many others showed timely interest in the project, for which I am most grateful.

I learned much over several years from former APA president Paul Appelbaum, who commented on drafts of my early articles on the Goldwater Rule. Former APA president Alan Stone provided a brief comment that I much appreciated.

Lifelong friend Jon Carey and expert on journalistic ethics Meredith Levine helped me think through my early work. Former presidential candidate Michael Dukakis agreed to share his thoughts about the Goldwater Rule from the point of view of the public figure; Jon Carey and Sagar Vijapura helped to conduct an interview with Governor Dukakis. Research assistant Barbara Bogart helped me find my way in the Ralph Ginzburg papers, especially in the enormous transcript of *Goldwater* v. *Ginzburg*, and helpfully commented on the manuscript.

I owe a special debt to historian Larry Friedman of Harvard University, who over an extended period of time provided me with a role model for historically and psychologically sensitive biography. Larry enlivened many a lunch with his perceptive comments and guidance. For in-depth comments, very special thanks go to Jay Hamilton of Stanford University's Communications Department; to attorney Elmer Ward of the Sauk-Suiattle Indian tribe in Washington State; to historian Matt Linton, then at Brandeis University; to the anonymous reviewers at Cambridge University Press; and to Susan Martin-Joy. At Cambridge University Press, editor Janka Romera understood early the vision I held for the book, shared her enthusiasm, and turned it into a reality; Emily Watton, Ilaria Tassistro, Chloe Bradley, Bethany Johnson, Sunantha Ramamoorthy, Ami Naramor, and Eric Anderson attended to copyediting, indexing, and the myriad other professional tasks that allowed the book take shape. Chris and Jeff Hyde, Carole and Tom Pauls, Janet Lowe, Kevin Hill, Kevin and Kathy Sheehan, Martin LaRoche, and many others provided much encouragement and support. Jeremy and Susan Martin-Joy deserve special thanks for their interest and their support.

Early versions of material presented in this book appeared as the brief introduction to an invited forum at the annual meeting of the American Psychiatric Association in 2015; in "Images in Psychiatry: *Goldwater v. Ginzburg*" in the *American Journal of Psychiatry* in 2015; in "Introduction to the Special Section on the Goldwater Rule" and "Interpreting the Goldwater Rule" in the *Journal of the American Academy of Psychiatry and the Law* (*JAAPL*) in 2017; and in a panel presentation on the Goldwater Rule at a meeting of the New York County Psychiatric Society in 2018. I am grateful to the panel organizers for the chance to think through the Goldwater Rule together, as well as to *JAAPL* for granting permission to use material that originally appeared there.

The late Christopher Bullock, a psychiatrist and candidate at BPSI, enabled me to discover the liberating power of a personal psychoanalysis. Psychiatrist Robert Coles, to whom this book is dedicated, has been an inspiring teacher and mentor. Beginning in 1979, when I first heard him speak, I have been inspired by Dr. Coles's decades-long effort to understand the lives of Americans who are caught up in the midst of historic crises. "He is a doctor," as novelist Walker Percy once wrote, "to the worst of our ills."

Abbreviations

APA: American Psychiatric Association

APA Archives: American Psychiatric Association Archives, Melvin Sabshin, MD Archives and Library, 800 Maine Avenue, SW, Washington, DC

APsaA: American Psychoanalytic Association

APsaA Papers: American Psychoanalytic Association Papers. Record Group 15, Series 7, Literature and Publications, Articles/Theses/Various Publications/APsaA Position Statements, 1964 *Fact* Magazine Survey. Oskar Diethelm Library, Dewitt Wallace Institute for the History of Psychiatry, Weill Cornell Medicine, New York, NY

BG Papers: Personal and Political Papers of Senator Barry M. Goldwater, Arizona Historical Foundation Collection, Arizona State University Libraries, Tempe, AZ. Box 52. References in the notes refer to box number: folder number (e.g., 52:11 is box 52, folder 11)

GG Transcript: *Goldwater* v. *Ginzburg* transcript. Copy of official stenographer's transcript of the district court trial, Southern District of New York, May 6–22, 1968. In Ginzburg Papers, boxes 32–34

Ginzburg Papers: Ralph Ginzburg papers, Accession number 7755, American Heritage Center, University of Wyoming, Laramie, WY

House Subcommittee on Intelligence Report (1973): *Inquiry into the Alleged Involvement of the Central Intelligence Agency in the Watergate and Ellsberg Matters: Report of the Special Subcommittee on Intelligence of the Committee on Armed Services, House of Representatives, 93rd Congress, First Session, October 23, 1973.* Washington, DC: US Government Printing Office. Accessed on July 7, 2019, at https://babel.hathitrust.org/cgi/pt?id=uc1.31210017809086&view=1up&seq=7

House Subcommittee on Intelligence Hearings (1975): Inquiry into the Alleged Involvement of the Central Intelligence Agency in the Watergate and Ellsberg Matters: Hearings before the Special Subcommittee on Intelligence of the Committee on Armed Services, House of Representatives, 94th Congress, First Session [Hearings of 1973–4] (1975). Washington, DC: US Government Printing Office. Accessed on July 23, 2019, at https://babel.hathitrust.org/cgi/pt?id=m dp.39015082037170&view=1up&seq=45

Joint Senate Hearing (1977). Project MKUltra, the CIA's Program of Research in Behavioral Modification. Joint Hearing before the Senate Committee on Intelligence and the Subcommittee on Health and Scientific Research of the Committee on Human Resources, US Senate, 95th Congress, First Session. August 3, 1977. Washington, DC: US Government Printing Office. Accessed on November 9, 2019, at https://babel.hathitrust.org/cgi/pt?id=md p.39015013739290&view=1up&seq=1

LBJ Library: LBJ Library [formerly Lyndon Baines Johnson Presidential Library and Museum], Austin, Texas

Senate Foreign Relations Committee (1975): Hearing before the Committee on Foreign Relations, United States Senate, 94th Congress, First Session, on Activities of the Central Intelligence Agency in Foreign Countries and in the United States. January 22, 1975. Washington, DC: US Government Printing Office. Accessed on July 7, 2019, at www.cia.gov/library/readingroom/docs/CIA-RDP91-00901R000500170001-7.pdf

An Ethical Dilemma

THE ELECTION OF DONALD TRUMP IN 2016 RAISED PROFOUND ethical questions for many psychiatrists. Is it ethical to diagnose a public figure without examining him or her? If so, why? If not, why not? Are there compelling reasons for a psychiatrist to comment on a president's mental health if nuclear warfare or the conduct of an unjust war is at stake? Is the media the right place for such comment? Under what circumstances, and in the name of what higher principles, may a psychiatrist violate the ethical code of her own professional organization?

In *Diagnosing from a Distance*, I explore and reflect on these ethical questions using a historical and philosophical lens. This book is a study of the development of professional ideas in a political context – and ultimately an argument about how we might approach the ethics of psychiatric comment on public figures.

HOW DID WE GET HERE?

As a psychiatrist myself, and one with a long-standing interest in history, politics, and ethics, I became interested in the question of what a professional owes to the larger society some time after I graduated from my psychiatry residency at the Harvard Longwood psychiatry training program in Boston. During college, I had learned about psychoanalyst Erik Erikson and his efforts in "psychohistory" from a teacher and mentor, psychiatrist Robert Coles. Later, I read and admired Erikson's influential book *Young Man Luther* (1958). The book is a deeply humane consideration of the relation between a developing religious thinker's inner conflicts and his emerging role in a historical movement. Erikson remained a favorite after my residency, as I joined the faculty at Harvard Longwood and began to teach adult development (the unfolding of psychological strengths over the life span) to psychiatry residents there. Along the way, a colleague enthusiastically recommended psychoanalyst John Mack's biography of T. E. Lawrence, *A Prince of Our Disorder* (1976), and it proved to be a remarkable book. But I had not formally studied history beyond college, and I had never really given much thought to the ethics of speaking about *living* figures.

In 2008, I saw a series of articles in the *New York Times*. These explained that the American Psychiatric Association (APA), an organization to which I belonged, was reviewing section 7.3 of *Principles of Medical Ethics with Annotations Especially Applicable to Psychiatry*. Section 7.3, the portion of the psychiatric ethics code that deals with comment on public figures, is better known by its informal name: the Goldwater Rule. In 1973, I learned, the APA had first adopted the Rule and had stuck to the principle ever since. In wording that was puzzling to me, the Rule said that when psychiatrists are asked by members of the media to comment on public figures, they should refrain, because it is unethical to offer a professional opinion unless one has interviewed the person and obtained his or her consent:

> On occasion psychiatrists are asked for an opinion about an individual who is in the light of public attention or who has disclosed information about himself/herself through public media. In such circumstances, a psychiatrist may share with the public his or her expertise about psychiatric issues in general. However, it is unethical for a psychiatrist to offer a professional opinion unless he or she has conducted an examination and has been granted proper authorization for such a statement.[1]

Was the Goldwater Rule a ban on comment to the media, as its framing in the first sentence seemed to suggest? Or was it intended as a ban on any professional comment without interview and consent, as the ringing principle enunciated in the final sentence seemed to imply? In my uneasy rereading of section 7.3, I concluded that the APA believed it is always unethical to comment on a person without interview and consent – a procedure that my title for this book calls, for convenience, "diagnosis from a distance." By this term I mean not only diagnosis, but a variety of ethically debated activities undertaken by psychiatrists without a personal interview with the subject, authorization from an appropriate institution, and/or the consent of the subject herself, including offering professional comment on a subject's leadership style, on his or her personality, reactions to stress, or what psychoanalytic clinicians call "psychodynamics" – how an individual's thinking, feelings, and behavior change according to emotional circumstances and according to little understood (unconscious) forces within himself. A more formally elaborated version of such comment is psychological profiling or psychobiography. In the text, I generally refer to these various activities simply as psychiatric "comment" or "comment without interview and consent."

The tone of the Goldwater Rule, as I read it, was strikingly different from the tone the APA used in other areas of psychiatry and ethics. In many clinical settings, ethics principles conflict and must be reconciled or resolved through close reasoning about the risks involved in the case. In emergency settings, for example, concern about safety often conflicts with the otherwise central principle of respect for privacy. In my psychiatry residency training, I had learned that a psychiatrist is sometimes compelled to violate a patient's confidentiality in order to keep the patient herself safe or to protect a patient's potential victim: if there is no safe alternative, one calls the police or an ambulance and ensures that the patient is taken to an emergency room for an evaluation, even if this intervention is against the patient's wishes. On a regular basis, my co-residents and I had learned to use our judgment in just such difficult circumstances. Under the doctrine known as *parens patriae*, the patient's safety – and sometimes the public's – required it.

The Goldwater Rule, in contrast, seemed to say that it is *always* unethical to comment on a person's mental health without interview or consent. But did the APA really mean always? There were, it turned out, even further circumstances where diagnosis from a distance happened all the time – not only in the common case of the emergency room, where patients often declined to be interviewed, but in forensic (court) settings, where defendants often saw only hazards in speaking to a psychiatrist, and in the case of the psychological profiling of world leaders by psychiatrists in the Central Intelligence Agency (CIA). In the ordinary course of our learning as residents, we were encouraged to seek opinions from knowledgeable colleagues, supervisors, and local experts in the daily course of our work. Was a "curbside" consultation, in which we briefly asked a knowledgeable peer for an opinion on a diagnosis or treatment, ethically supportable?

The Rule turned out to be more complicated than I had realized. I did not know it at the time, but the APA had addressed each of these issues but continued to endorse the seemingly absolute wording of the Rule. Why?

During the presidential campaign of 1964, a provocative publisher named Ralph Ginzburg – who figures prominently in this book – put together and publicized a special issue of his hip, independently funded *Fact* magazine (which he advertised as "not for squares"). The issue consisted of a psychological profile of candidate Barry Goldwater and the results of a survey of the nation's psychiatrists. Complete with *Mad* magazine–style cartoons lampooning Goldwater, the issue hit the stands a little more than a month before the election. *Fact*'s back cover included numerous sample comments from psychiatrists: "I find myself increasingly thinking of the early 1930s and the rise of another intemperate, impulsive, counterfeit figure of a masculine man, namely, Adolf Hitler." If elected, said another, Goldwater would lead the country straight into nuclear war and "obliteration."[2]

The incident had led the APA to form a new ethics rule on the issue – and no wonder. But did that mean that CIA profilers could not opine on foreign leaders like, say, Saddam Hussein? Was Erik Erikson's book *Young Man Luther*, and, for that matter, the whole field of psychohistory that I had so admired, unethical to pursue?

I was puzzled but very curious, and I wanted to know more. In 2015, I invited experts on each side of the issue to participate in a panel, held at the APA's annual meeting in Toronto, on the ethics of the Rule. I was not interested in soliciting their comments on public figures, but I did want to know their reasoning about the Rule: Is section 7.3 an important ethics guideline or a hindrance to sound ethical practice, and why? For presentation at the conference, two colleagues and I conducted a videotaped interview with 1988 presidential candidate Michael Dukakis and sought *his* opinion on the Rule. He strongly supported it as an important protection for the profession as well as for public figures. At the panel, journalist and ethicist Meredith Levine agreed with Dukakis and argued that the Rule protects the quality of the public discourse on politics and psychiatry. Yet Jerrold Post, a psychiatrist and former CIA profiler, had strong doubts about the Rule. He recounted his experience with profiling and with the APA and concluded that the Rule interferes with important contributions that psychiatrists could otherwise make to the conduct of foreign policy and to public safety. Psychiatrist Paul Appelbaum, a former APA president, gave the most balanced assessment of anyone on the panel, concluding that section 7.3 is imperfect but too valuable to do without.[3]

In the next year or two, I decided to look further into the history and background of the Rule. How had the odd framing and phrasing of the Rule come into being? What exactly is prohibited under it? Given the Rule's seeming ban on all psychiatric comment without interview, did the APA view psychological profiling for the CIA (for example) as ethically appropriate? Or did it mean only to ban individual psychiatrists from making comments in the media? How had the APA decided to put this Rule in place, and how did the organization interpret its own Rule? I published the first results of my inquiries in the *Journal of the American Academy of Psychiatry and the Law* in 2017. By then I had concluded that the Rule is unclear, that its wording makes it appear more general in scope than it actually is, and that it needs to be revised in the interest of clarity and fairness. Adopting this unclear Rule as a central ethics principle, I argued, could itself lead to problems – including misunderstanding by APA members and by the general public.[4]

HISTORY, ETHICS, AND PSYCHIATRIC COMMENT: A CLOSER LOOK

This book represents the next stage of my curiosity. I have tried to deepen my understanding not only of how the Rule developed but also of its antecedents in history: psychoanalysts' efforts during World War II to profile Adolf Hitler (about which there was no controversy), the controversy over Barry Goldwater in 1964, the role of the CIA in profiling over decades, and the current bitter debate about Donald Trump's mental health and whether it is ethical or an ethics violation to comment on him in the absence of an interview and consent. I looked more deeply into archives for this project than I had done before, and I interviewed a number of the antagonists in my narrative. The APA and its critics disagreed with each other, but each side spoke with me.

The resulting study, I hope, has several virtues to recommend it. By presenting original material and reassessing clichés about my topic, I hope *Diagnosing from a Distance* will illuminate the various political and media contexts in which psychiatric comment, and the ethics debates over it, have taken place. In other words, I intend *Diagnosing from a Distance* to be an original investigation of the psychiatrist's relationship to society from the 1930s to the present. I also hope the historical material I present will add perspective to our era's debate over the ethics of commenting on public figures. For example, I spend much time reconstructing the history of changes in libel law in the 1960s, where the controversy over Goldwater first played itself out fully. In recent years, Supreme Court justices Antonin Scalia and Clarence Thomas, and President Trump himself, have shown great interest in reversing *Sullivan* and thereby making libel law more restrictive again. Such changes would undo the progressive evolution in libel law that protected reporters and publishers and allowed ordinary citizens wide latitude to criticize government officials.[5]

I hesitate to say, with Santayana, that history repeats itself (in his words, those who cannot remember the past are condemned to repeat it). I much prefer two other sayings – Wilfred Sheed's remark that anyone who has ever discovered Santayana's remark is condemned to repeat it, and the concise saying attributed to Mark Twain: history rhymes. Sheed's witticism reminds me that clichés have a destructive power of their own, while Twain's alleged remark (it is not clear that he ever actually said it) highlights how historical parallels are intriguing yet can never be exact. Sometimes apparent repetitions are in fact very different phenomena.[6]

In Chapter 1, I examine American psychoanalysts' effort to profile Hitler for the Office of Strategic Services (OSS) during World War II. Partly conducted in secret and largely uncontroversial at the time, this effort is in many ways the progenitor of modern psychological profiling. Here American psychoanalysts, including a highly sophisticated refugee from Nazism, tried to understand and undermine the worst form of totalitarianism Europe has ever seen. The effort to profile Hitler and to understand him in a cultural and leadership context remains an indispensable reference point for the controversies over psychiatric comment on public figures that would follow in the years ahead.

I next take an in-depth look at the controversy that gave rise to the Goldwater Rule itself. As Chapter 2 shows, Ralph Ginzburg devoted a special issue of his *Fact* magazine to the alleged dangerousness and lack of fitness for office of 1964 Republican presidential candidate Barry Goldwater. Like many liberals of his era, Ginzburg turned to psychoanalytic thinking (in his case, a much-debased version of it) to deal with the fear of fascism and nuclear war that came over him as he watched Goldwater announce on television that "extremism in the defense of liberty is no vice." The provocative Ginzburg, I argue, has seldom been taken seriously as a free speech advocate or as a liberal opponent of repression. His career as a publisher, little understood today, deserves to be revisited in a fresh light despite the ethics problems his publications raised. Hitler, Jewishness, masculinity, professionalism, and the need to prevent nuclear war were central in the furious ethics debate that ensued.

Barry Goldwater, target of the special issue of *Fact*, was understandably outraged by it. Ahead of his time politically, Goldwater was also ahead of his own conservative movement in grasping that a lawsuit could be used as a political weapon. Goldwater chose to pursue the point, bringing a libel suit against Ralph Ginzburg and *Fact* in 1966. In an era of expanding civil liberties, Goldwater argued that public figures need to be protected from vilification. As Chapter 3 demonstrates, Goldwater's capable attorney Roger Robb faced off against Ginzburg in the Foley Square courthouse in New York in *Goldwater* v. *Ginzburg*. Ginzburg contended that *Fact* was motivated by genuine concern for the country's welfare and was covered by the doctrine of free speech; Goldwater and Robb argued that *Fact* had committed an outrageous violation of journalistic and medical ethics as well as libel law. This was a complicated question at the time, because both Ginzburg and Goldwater were operating within a new space cleared by a revolutionary new doctrine of libel announced in 1964 by the Supreme Court in *New York Times* v. *Sullivan*. Before *Sullivan*, public figures could bring libel actions fairly easily; while technically the burden of proof was on the plaintiff, the substantial difficulty rested with defendants. Under traditional libel law, "defamatory state-ments were presumed to be false"; the defendant had to prove otherwise. After *Sullivan*, newspapers could publish much more freely, and the burden of proof was now on plaintiffs to prove that libel had been committed. But what were the limits of the new doctrine?[7]

Chapters 2–4 of this book, then, largely relate the story of how journal-ists and public figures adjusted to the new legal reality of *Sullivan* and argued bitterly over its limits. Inevitably, the media descended on the courtroom and covered all three weeks of the contest in *Goldwater* v. *Ginzburg*. This media scrutiny – with major newspapers, wire services, radio, and *Time* magazine covering the proceedings in detail – provided the equivalent of a gigantic microphone for each side to use as it saw fit.

As I document in Chapter 4, after the district court was decided, the losing side tried to get the Supreme Court to accept the case for further review. (I prefer not to disclose too early who won the case.) The moment proved to be an occasion for an eloquent statement by Justice Hugo Black, a liberal icon of First Amendment jurisprudence. The depth of Goldwater's support and the value he gained from media exposure in the case may be traced in his correspondence with his often passionate supporters.

If the 1964 *Fact* debacle had stopped at the Supreme Court and only influenced libel law, it would still be noteworthy. But there was much more. In the second part of this book, I look at the next iteration of the debate: how the country's largest organization of psychiatrists also was deeply shocked by Ralph Ginzburg's publication, and how it responded in an era of growing specialization and professionalization. At a time when psychiatry was gaining wide acceptance but still felt insecure about its status, the American Psychiatric Association was preparing its first formal ethics code. The Goldwater Rule – a direct response to the *Fact* episode – was enshrined in the organization's first formal code of ethics in 1973. There was no shortage of disagreement either then or later, as the Rule gradually hardened into established doctrine.

I next explore psychological profiling in the CIA and the White House, especially during the Nixon administration. The saga is too little known by psychiatrists today, but it represents perhaps the most egre-gious ethical violation involving psychological profiling ever to occur within a government agency. As I document, the Nixon White House aimed to discredit antiwar activist Daniel Ellsberg in the media by commissioning a psychological profile from the CIA. Agency psychiatrists had done sophisticated profiles of foreign leaders for years. But profiling an American citizen was outside the domestic mandate of the CIA's charter. The uncomfortable response of the CIA psychiatrists, who agreed to create the profile but then raised objections and used delay tactics, is sadly instructive rather than inspiring. These professionals were caught between a president and their sense of what was proper.

The CIA's story also shows that profiling has proceeded unimpeded over the decades. Given the existence of the Goldwater Rule, how can this be? As the reader of the Rule will note, profiling for government agencies is not mentioned in the text of section 7.3; it turns out that government profiling is elsewhere specifically *exempted* from the Rule's purview. In the APA's view, profiling for the CIA (i.e., *for* a president) is ethically acceptable, but it is unethical for an individual psychiatrist of conscience to comment *on* an American president. This ethics stance, I argue, is insensitive to the risks of profiling when undertaken for the government and can place government psychiatrists in a precarious ethical position.[8]

It has been during the Trump administration that the controversy over the ethics of psychiatric comment has grown most bitter and most personal. Since Donald Trump's election and inauguration, a large group of psychiatrists has concluded that it is in the national interest to warn the public about what it sees as the president's dangerousness. Bandy Lee's best-selling book *The Dangerous Case of Donald Trump* (2017) illustrates both the strength of this movement and its limits, and the strong backlash against it. The APA listened to the Lee group's argument but then rigidly reasserted its prohibition on media comment. Here I try, as much as it is possible in recounting contemporary events, to understand what is at stake for both sides in the debate. This latest iteration of the ethics debate has played out against the backdrop of a constitutional crisis nearly as dramatic as the Watergate crisis of 1973–4.

In important ways, issues of civil rights, ethnicity, and immigration are central to this book. In the 1930s and 1940s, the effort to defeat Hitler involved many Jewish psychoanalysts and at least one media executive who understood personally what was at stake in the war and who sought to use the then-considerable power of psychoanalysis and the media to the greatest possible advantage in that effort. Ralph Ginzburg, Jewish himself, saw Barry Goldwater not only as similar to Hitler in his authoritarianism and mental instability but also as a threat to the welfare of African Americans and the civil rights of all Americans. Like many left-leaning Jewish activists in the 1960s, he imaginatively identified with the civil rights and antiwar movements. Daniel Ellsberg, whose parents were of Jewish descent, was similarly drawn to protest over what he saw as an unethical war in Vietnam. Justice Hugo Black, once a Ku Klux Klan member himself but now the nation's leading advocate for the First Amendment, would voice his views in cases involving the actions of both men – as Ginzburg clashed with Goldwater, and as the *Washington Post* (to whom Ellsberg leaked antiwar information) clashed with Nixon. *Sullivan* itself had grown from a case involving Martin Luther King and the Southern effort to quash coverage of the civil rights movement – what Anthony Lewis calls the "strategy of intimidation by civil libel suits."[9] Thus my story is inseparable from the story of civil rights and social justice.

By the time immigration reemerged as an issue during the Trump presidency, the political beliefs of left-leaning European refugees or the rights of African Americans were no longer central issues in the debate, as they had been in the 1950s and 1960s. The rights of marginalized citizens remained an issue, however, as the debate over the treatment of immigrants at America's southern border showed. Once marginalized in the discussion themselves, women were now well represented in the debate over psychiatric comment on public figures and over public policy. Bandy Lee, a Korean-American female psychiatrist, took the lead in challenging the public to confront what she saw as the dangerousness of Donald Trump. Many of the mental health professionals who contributed to Lee's *Dangerous Case* were appalled by Trump's statements and policies concerning women and immigrants, and the APA itself assertively fought Trump's policy on the separation of children from their parents at the border.[10]

In my Conclusion, I review themes that emerge from the history I have presented and use this foundation to reconsider the ethics of the Goldwater Rule. The reader need not agree with me in all of my conclusions. But I hope that by that point, the history and ethical considerations explored in this book will have provided the reader with material for her own examination and reexamination of psychiatric ethics in a divided society.

SOURCES AND METHODS

I have tried to write an accessible narrative – to tell a story. But in doing so, I draw on a wealth of specialized scholarly sources, contemporaneous newspaper accounts, original interviews, and archival research in several different fields. I hope the result is both readable and original. To my knowledge no one has previously written a scholarly book – or any book – devoted to the *Fact* episode, to the Goldwater Rule, or to the history and ethics of psychiatric comment on public figures. I could have approached this book as a narrow contribution to any number of the fields it touches on – the history of psychoanalysis, the development of libel law in America, the growth and perpetual crises of the mass media, the culture wars of the 1960s, the history of the professions, or the problem of government ethics and the abuse of power. It was tempting to frame this book entirely as an account of psychiatric comment during the Trump years. I decided instead to trace, as more or less one sequence, the prehistory, history, and ongoing legacy of the issues raised by *Fact*'s 1964 special issue on the mental health of Barry Goldwater. The result is a study that follows a particular thread of interest – the ethics of psychiatric comment on public figures from a distance – through all of the fields listed earlier and through the entire period from the late 1930s to the present. I hope readers will find much of interest in my interdisciplinary story of professionals in combat over time.

Several historians have influenced my approach. Those whose work perhaps most resembles my own are American historians who chronicle and analyze legal doctrine in its historical and social context. For example, Michael Klarman's work on *Brown* v. *Board of Education* and the movement for same-sex marriage shows that courts often move forward carefully, issuing progressive decisions at a particular moment when the court believes society may be ready to accept change. Klarman documents how often such decisions are followed by a bitter backlash and by numerous unintended consequences. Laura Kalman's *The Long Reach of the Sixties* (2017) similarly sets Supreme Court history firmly in the context of the nomination wars and political upheavals of that decade and the early 1970s. In the realm of libel law and privacy law after *Sullivan*, Samantha Barbas's *Newsworthy* provides a socially and biographically sensitive account of the evolution of the law in context. In the popular narrative tradition, Anthony Lewis's *Gideon's Trumpet* (1964/1989) has seldom been equaled as a dramatic exposition of the development of progressive legal doctrine.

As is evident in what follows, I rely on primary sources whenever possible. I also quote from the many voices involved in my story and try to consider multiple points of view. This approach reflects my wish to connect the reader as directly as I can with the lived experience of history. Debates over professional ethics are not dry exchanges. They are debates conducted by real people – variously noble, misguided, self-interested, admirable, or a mix of all these qualities. I hope that including a variety of colorful viewpoints in context will help the reader see things in three dimensions rather than two. To that end, I examined Walter Langer's letters and memoirs of the Nazi arrival in Vienna; I considered psychoanalyst Erik Erikson's work from a fresh viewpoint. I looked closely at the mostly unexplored papers of publisher Ralph Ginzburg of *Fact* magazine and of his antagonist Barry Goldwater, who meticulously saved his records of the case for future historians. I interviewed Warren Boroson, *Fact*'s managing editor and thus a colleague of Ginzburg; I spoke with surviving family members of Ralph Ginzburg on the one hand and of Walter E. Barton, the medical director of the APA in the 1960s and 1970s, on the other. I explored the archives of the American Psychiatric Association (APA) and the American Psychoanalytic Association (APsaA), organizations that took contrasting positions on the ethics question in 1964. I read the memoirs of the White House Plumbers, scrutinized a recently declassified CIA internal report on the Daniel Ellsberg profile, and worked through the reports and hearings of congressional subcommittees on the case. I was fortunate to be able to interview many of the antagonists in the controversy over Donald Trump. These included psychiatrists Judith Lewis Herman, Bandy X. Lee, and Robert Jay Lifton; Leonard Glass, who resigned from the APA in protest; and former APA presidents Jeffrey

A. Lieberman and Anita Everett, both proponents of the Rule. I also spoke with current APA medical director Saul Levin and APA ethics committee chair Rebecca Brendel about the organization's stance and reasoning. I have ultimately reached my own conclusions on the ethics questions involved, but whenever possible I first made a primary effort to speak with and understand the point of view of the major antagonists in the debate.

When controversies arise in the mental health field, professional interests are at stake. In these circumstances, organizational differences matter a great deal. In 1973, it was the American Psychiatric Association (a group of physicians with mental health training) that imposed a firm ban on comment on public figures and began a seemingly endless controversy in ethics. Psychologists (PhDs who have extensive training in mental health but are not physicians), by contrast, took a more relaxed position. One result is that most media comment on public figures since 1973 has been provided by psychologists rather than psychiatrists. (There have been ongoing disagreements since then, over what ethical standards are appropriate in psychiatry and psychology – not only on the mental health of public figures but also on issues such as participation in torture.) Organizational and professional differences also informed the political stances of psychiatrists and their medical colleagues. In 1964, many members of the American Psychoanalytic Association (at the time, mainly physicians who had training in psychoanalysis) disliked Goldwater intensely. Many of them contributed to Ralph Ginzburg's survey about Goldwater's mental health. The psychoanalysts' organization never formally banned the practice of comment as the American Psychiatric Association did. On the opposite end of the political spectrum, the American Medical Association (AMA) (surgeons, general physicians, and medical specialists, including psychiatrists) had a much more conservative membership. The AMA actually supported Goldwater publicly in the 1964 campaign, and the AMA's public relations office was in frequent, fawning contact with Goldwater as *Goldwater* v. *Ginzburg* unfolded. The medical organization was deeply embarrassed that its mailing list had been used against its reliable political ally.[11]

Making use of an organizational perspective has allowed me to attend to some mistakes that seem to creep into discussions of my topic with some regularity. The otherwise excellent historian Bruce Schulman, for example, reports that Nixon's Plumbers burglarized the office of Daniel Ellsberg's psychologist. In fact, Ellsberg had been seeing a psychiatrist and psychoanalyst, Dr. Lewis Fielding; in 1971, psychologists in the United States were not yet generally allowed to train at psychoanalytic institutes. Conversely, John Heidenry reports that Ralph Ginzburg got the mailing list for his survey of psychiatrists from the American Psychoanalytic Association, a report Rick Perlstein repeated in his popular biography of Barry Goldwater. As Goldwater's letter and the trial records make clear, however, Ginzburg actually got the list from a contractor to the AMA – without informing the AMA itself. Just how Ginzburg obtained the list became the occasion for a friendly but pointed exchange between Goldwater and the AMA in the pretrial discovery phase of *Goldwater* v. *Ginzburg* and probably played a role in the AMA's decision to denounce the survey.[12]

By the 1960s, a split had emerged between the adherents of the "duty to warn" viewpoint and the advocates for what might be called a "duty to refrain." The duty to warn adherents, often individual psychiatrists or journalists who worked with them, started the ethics debate by warning the public. Those psychiatrists who argued for professional responsibility – most often proudly affiliated with the APA or serving in APA administrative positions – reacted critically. Though each side also had institutional and professional interests that complicated its reasoning, neither argument was frivolous or without merit. We need a dialogue between both points of view if we are to do justice to the complex and still conflicted nature of the psychiatrist's position in society.

I have not attempted to trace all comment by all mental health professionals on public figures during the period from World War II to the present. That would require a much larger book. To make my task more pointed and more manageable, I have focused on psychiatrists, who are the only mental health professionals directly affected by the prohibitions of the Goldwater Rule. In Chapter 1, I do discuss the work of two psychologists, Walter Langer and Erik Erikson, who set the terms for much of what followed. Importantly, however, Langer and Erikson were both psychoanalysts (and, unusual for psychologists, honorary members of APsaA). They offered state-of-the-art thinking about the rise of Fascism and ways to combat it. Langer influenced the future field of psychohistory and leadership profiling, while Erikson had a powerful influence on developmental, historical, and cultural thinking in psychiatry.[13]

In this book, I am not interested in offering a diagnosis of anyone. Where my subjects are no longer living, I try to convey through narrative a sense of the personality style of the combatants in the ethical contest; wherever possible, I do this by using ordinary language, by describing behavior in context, and by helping the reader to "see" the antagonists in action, not by using psychiatric terminology. In this way I hope to evoke a person's complex role in the debate over the ethics of profiling. For living persons, the psychiatric writer's ethical terrain is much trickier to assess. With living persons, my goals are also to provide a readable narrative, to understand points of view and weigh ethical positions, and to portray the debate in political and media contexts, not to establish a diagnosis or psychopathology. The task is complicated and has required a certain kind of tact. My aim is to ask how we got here, to show the many intricacies of our current dilemma, and to understand both sides in this recurring debate – in a word, to explore the Goldwater Rule without breaking it.

CHAPTER 1

Psychoanalysis, Media, and Politics from the Rise of Hitler to the 1950s

What we need . . . is a realistic appraisal of the German situation. If Hitler is running the show, what kind of a person is he? What are his ambitions? How does he appear to the German people? What is he like with his associates? What is his background? And most of all, we want to know as much as possible about his psychological make-up – the things that make him tick. In addition, we ought to know what he might do if things begin to go against him. Do you suppose you could come up with something along these lines?

General William J. Donovan of the US Office of Strategic Services
speaking to psychoanalyst William C. Langer, 1943[1]

It started with a newspaper article. Leafing through the newspaper while recovering from a hernia operation in 1941, Cambridge, Massachusetts, psychoanalyst Walter Langer saw a notice that a new government agency had just come into existence. The Office of Coordinator of Information would pool intelligence information and "organize and conduct psychological warfare."[2] Thinking psychoanalysis could be of help in this effort, Langer contacted William Donovan, the head of the new agency. Donovan was interested. Langer went on to write a detailed psychological study of Adolf Hitler, whom he had never met but whom he felt it was urgent to defeat.

Between the rise of Hitler and the cultural upheavals of the 1960s, American psychiatry and psychoanalysis lived a tumultuous existence. Many European psychoanalysts, trained in Vienna and Berlin in Freud's methods, fled to the United States in the 1930s. Sophisticated intellectuals and social critics, they had seen the rise of Hitler firsthand. Many were welcomed enthusiastically into American universities; some were consulted by a US government that was eager to learn. Unlike Langer, however, the refugee psychoanalysts soon met the skeptical eye of the American public – and of American politicians. In the late 1940s and early 1950s, just as psychoanalysts were gaining national prestige as psychological experts, Wisconsin senator Joseph McCarthy and others began their quest to expose Communists in America.

PSYCHOANALYSIS AND THE RISE OF NAZISM

In November 1937, Adolf Hitler held a dramatic meeting in Berlin with his foreign policy minister and the assembled heads of the German army, navy, and air force. With increased demand for food and better living standards, and the vagaries of the international market, the Führer told the group, Germany had only a tenuous ability to feed its people. This ability had to be strengthened. For this purpose, Hitler said, Germany needed to acquire "greater living space." Germany was faced with Britain and France, its "two hate-inspired antagonists," and a complex international situation. Stressing the virtues of quick military action, Hitler announced that it was crucial to use force while Germany had the advantage of strength – by 1943–5 "at the latest," and perhaps sooner. While leaving the timing open and specifying many strategic contingencies, Hitler ominously referred to his foregone conclusion: "our attack on the Czechs and Austria." If he died, Hitler said, the decisions of this meeting should be viewed as his "political testament."[3]

Austria was first. In February 1938, Hitler met with the Austrian chancellor at the Berghof, the Fuhrer's mountain retreat near the town of Berchtesgaden in the Bavarian Alps. It was only a few miles from the Austrian border and had a stunning view of the mountains. Hitler, having stacked the meeting with German generals, exploded at the chancellor, threatened to invade Austria, and finally intimidated the chancellor into making formal concessions. The arrangement gave Hitler a prominent pro-Nazi member of the Austrian government. The Austrian negotiating party, "browbeaten and depressed after subjection to such merciless bullying" in Berchtesgaden, returned to Vienna. There the chancellor unexpectedly called a plebiscite on independence that he hoped would show Austrians' wish to stay independent and thus avoid an invasion. But it only made Hitler furious. In March 1938, Nazi troops crossed into Austria.[4]

On Vienna's Ringstrasse in the Ninth District, crowds watched as Nazi troops moved in. At first, there was silence except for an occasional shout of "Heil Hitler!" But then the shouts and the Nazi salutes became overwhelming, as they did when Hitler himself later entered the city and began giving his "long, monotonous and fiery speeches." Vienna's churches, said one historian, "pealed their bells in Hitler's honour and flew swastika banners from their steeples." "One had to be there and see it in order to believe it," recalled Walter C. Langer. Langer, then a young American psychoanalytic candidate, had traveled from Boston so that he could have the experience of training with Anna Freud.[5]

Anna's father, the ailing Sigmund Freud, had long had his consulting room near the Ringstrasse. Freud had predicted that the Nazi threat would pass, as other anti-Semitic threats had. Now, however, the pogroms began. The Nazis searched his home, confiscated the Vienna Psychoanalytic Institute's library, and took Anna Freud in for questioning, events that convinced Freud to belatedly accept help in escaping.[6]

On June 5, 1938, in what became a famous tableau in psychoanalytic history, Sigmund Freud boarded a train and left for England with Anna Freud and a few other members of his family. With Freud's approval, Walter Langer accompanied the Freuds in order to observe the Nazis' treatment of them. It was the beginning of a long exile for psychoanalysis. Future self-psychologist Heinz Kohut, a Vienna native, later described forced immigration as an "incomprehensible rupture." Kohut recalled that though he did not speak to Freud, he was on the train platform at the time and tipped his hat to the 82-year-old founder of psychoanalysis.[7]

* * *

It was a frightening moment in a forced intellectual migration. In 1938, the American Psychoanalytic Association (APsaA) helped almost 150 analysts escape Europe; more came to the United States than to any other country. Langer himself, with Anna Freud's support, had made a trip to the United States and had tried to persuade friends to sign blank affidavits for the émigrés. The affidavits would guarantee financial support to an émigré if necessary once he or she entered the United States. Langer hoped to bring the signed affidavits back to Vienna. Langer found many friends and acquaintances who were willing to help. At Harvard, a Jewish professor heard Langer's story and said: "What do you want me to sign and how many?" Future Supreme Court justice Felix Frankfurter invited four prominent friends to hear Langer's report on conditions in Vienna; Langer recalled that he "came away with fifteen blank affidavits and a promise of more." On the other hand, the president of the New York Psychoanalytic Society declined to help, even after Langer told him it was a matter of life and death. The president first said he would have to take it up with the Society's governing board, then explained that in fact the Society had no room for more analysts in New York City. In all Langer gathered 40 to 50 affidavits and was pleased.[8]

Fanning out to analytic institutes in New York, in Boston, in Chicago, in Los Angeles, and in San Francisco, the émigré psychoanalysts worked hard to spread psychoanalytic thought to America. They had an enormous impact on their new home country. But soon enough, the rupture from Europe was followed by encounters with significant prejudice in the United States. Analyst Helen Deutsch had grown up in Poland and lived in Vienna during the height of the hostilities toward Jews there. But it was in America, she said, that she experienced "personal anti-Semitism for the first time."[9]

* * *

Walter Langer's knowledge of Vienna and Freud, and of psychoanalysis, would prove invaluable to the US government. In the early 1940s, Langer, by now fully trained as a psychoanalyst, had returned to Cambridge and obtained a PhD in psychology. Langer saw a newspaper story about a new agency that was forming in the American government. As the country faced the possibility of war, the Office of the Coordinator of Information (COI) – a precursor of the Office of Strategic Services (OSS) and the Central Intelligence Agency (CIA) – was planning to gather and coordinate information that could be useful if war developed in Europe. Why not, thought Langer, include psychoanalysts in the project? He contacted William ("Wild Bill") Donovan of the COI, who encouraged him to form a group of psychoanalysts that could advise the agency. The psychoanalytic organization was enthusiastic about what it called an "exceptional opportunity" for the organization to "show its mettle." Langer, who consulted for the OSS between 1942 and 1945, said in memos that about 100 APsaA members were collaborating with him and his Psychoanalytic Field Unit on various intelligence projects. That number represented nearly half of the psychoanalytic organization's 204 members.[10]

Langer, a World War I veteran who had suffered a lung injury in the war and was ill enough afterward to qualify for partial disability, had breathing problems for the rest of his life. At Harvard after the war, he had sought psychiatric help and benefited from psychoanalysis. During his time in Vienna, it became obvious to him that Austria "was to be the next victim." Langer watched the Nazis march into Vienna in 1938. Having fled with the Freuds, Langer had insider credentials within the psychoanalytic movement despite the fact that as a psychologist he was considered a lay analyst, that is, a nonphysician. He clearly inspired Donovan's trust at the OSS.[11]

By 1943, Langer's work at the OSS was focused on the effort to profile Adolf Hitler. Could a profile be created from a distance? As far as Langer knew, "no such study had ever been attempted." He developed a staff of consulting psychoanalysts to help him develop the profile of Hitler. At that point, psychoanalysis, with its individualistic focus and its interest in motivation, was seen as "particularly well suited to a war against a totalitarian enemy." Langer, employed as a consultant, worked with several associates on his project, including Henry A. Murray, MD, of the Harvard Psychological Clinic and psychoanalysts Ernst Kris and Bertram Lewin of New York City. Langer also hired several psychoanalytically trained assistants to go to the New York Public Library and assemble all the published material they could find on Hitler. An early draft by Murray is available and may have been subsumed into Langer's final version for the OSS, though reports suggest that this was because Murray withdrew from participation in the project. Langer provided the OSS with 100 copies of his typewritten report, prominently marked "SECRET" and replete with photos of Hitler, his mother, and his father.[12]

Langer conscientiously indicated the limits of his effort. Foremost among these was the lack of firsthand data. He had no personal interview or therapeutic relationship to rely on. Conducting an evaluation from a distance, Langer said, meant that the psychoanalyst lacked his usual ability to correct hypotheses by observing the effect of interpretations on the patient. It also forced him to rely on a mass of non-firsthand material, "superficial and fragmentary," that would almost inevitably prove "untrustworthy and irrelevant." "There was no firm ground on which to stand," he emphasized, making for an unhappy situation for the analyst. But in the emergency conditions of war, he felt there was no alternative. Langer "decided to accept the challenge and do the best we could." He gathered a group of analysts and interviewed or made use of information from Hitler's niece and others who knew Hitler. It helped that Langer was of German descent himself, but more crucial was his personal experience directly observing Nazi rule in Berlin, in Vienna, and in Nuremberg. Langer had been able to witness one of the gigantic annual Nazi rallies at Nuremberg.[13]

First, was Hitler sincere? Many had raised the question, but Langer's review of the evidence suggested strongly that he was: Hitler saw himself as an immortal, the founder of a new world order. Assembling evidence and impressions, Langer first addressed Hitler's view of himself, then Hitler "as the German people know him," then Hitler as seen by his associates. Langer then delivered his comprehensive analysis and predictions.

Langer's observations about Hitler were many, but they clustered around a portrayal of Hitler as having a disturbed childhood that led to bigotry and to a messiah complex. Langer noted the confusing relationship Hitler had with his alcoholic father, the close relationship he had with his mother, and the putative trauma of discovering his parents having intercourse and then of finding that his mother was pregnant. These discoveries, Langer asserted, raised themes of assault and submission that proved lasting in their influence on Hitler: he had a lifelong fear of domination, which related to his anti-Semitism. In part, this development was due to Hitler's experiences with his father, especially the fact that Hitler could not look up to him. Hitler's father was often full of propriety but when drunk could become "brutal, unjust, and inconsiderate," not to mention assaultive toward his defenseless wife and children. The young Hitler had to turn elsewhere for guidance. Henry Murray, in his more impressionistic and more dramatic report, described Hitler as paranoid, said that the German leader projected objectionable aspects of himself onto others, and predicted that he would go insane or commit suicide. Langer agreed with the prediction.

Of special interest is the attention Langer gave to Hitler's sexual development. Langer documented the "rather stringent" toilet training presumably insisted on by Hitler's mother: her traits included "excessive cleanliness and tidiness." For Langer, this early experience left the boy with unresolved tensions and aggressions that centered on the anal zone. Themes of feces, dirt, and disgust can be seen in the adult Hitler's imagery; in *Mein Kampf*, he expresses a horror of syphilis, which Langer took as straightforward evidence of a poorly resolved Oedipus complex, with its fear of genital injury. (Hitler's autopsy later revealed that he had an undescended or missing left testicle, a point that Langer could not have known at the time he wrote.) These early experiences, for Langer, set the stage for an alleged perversion in the adult Hitler: an eroticization of the gaze and of the buttocks, developed as a way to master a childhood puzzlement about where babies come from. "In her description of sexual experiences with Hitler, Geli [his niece] stressed the fact that it was of utmost importance to him that she squat over him in such a way that he could see everything." Langer presented anecdotes suggesting that when Hitler "is smitten with a girl he tends to grovel at her feet." "As soon as such [warm or intimate] feelings are aroused, he feels compelled to degrade himself in the eyes of the loved object and eat their dirt figuratively." Downplaying the possibility that Hitler was an overt homosexual, Langer was struck nonetheless by his alleged femininity in manner.[14]

Many of these themes – which would contribute to the stock portrayal of the authoritarian personality – would be taken up in different contexts by Theodor Adorno and other philosophers and psychologists of the Frankfurt School in the 1950s. Pioneered by Erich Fromm in Germany and then in America in his book *Escape from Freedom*, the notion of susceptibility to authoritarianism would be revived by journalist Ralph Ginzburg in the 1960s and again by the dissenting mental health professionals in the age of Trump. Many if not all of these later commentators would reference Hitler and some version of Fromm or Adorno's sadomasochistic (authoritarian) personality. For his part, Langer restated Fromm in relatively simple, orthodox form, emphasizing traditional Freudian sexual themes more than had Fromm, who was an innovator in thinking about culture and personality.

Langer says little about how Hitler functioned in the context of German society or history.

What was to be done? Murray suggested to the OSS that a "propaganda" effort was needed and should be developed. There was much optimism here, perhaps too much. Years later, Langer himself said that the study "came too late" to affect either the conduct of the war or postwar American foreign policy. Yet, Langer said, he would like to believe that if similar studies of leaders had been conducted earlier, disasters like the appeasement at Munich, the Yalta Conference, the Cuban Missile Crisis of the 1960s, and the Vietnam War could have been prevented. He soberly conceded that such outcomes "would be too much to expect" but on balance thought that some international blunders that had resulted from psychological naïveté could have been avoided.

Despite the study's acknowledged limitations, reviewers found Langer's analysis plausible in many respects. When the study was published as a book in 1972, psychiatrist Robert Jay Lifton called it "adventurous, intelligent, and risky."[15]

* * *

At about the same time as Langer was doing his work, the OSS had the wisdom to recruit another émigré psychoanalyst, the young Erik H. Erikson. Erikson, who grew up in Germany as Erik Homburger, was of Danish origin. An artist and then a teacher, he taught in a progressive school run by Dorothy Burlingham in Vienna, then entered analysis with Anna Freud. When he came to the United States, the peripatetic psychoanalyst, psychosocial theorist, and cross-cultural researcher realized that his last name sounded comical to Americans. Erikson – soon to become famous for his work on the identity crisis – decided to change his name. In place of his step-father's name, his own appeared: it was as if he had given birth to his new American self. Despite lacking a college degree and a degree in either psychology or psychiatry, Erikson was welcomed first at Harvard (in Henry Murray's clinic), then at Yale, and then at the University of California, where he studied childhood, adult develop-ment, and the interaction of personality and culture. According to

Robert Jay Lifton, Erikson was "the first among psychoanalysts to take historical circumstances (and history itself) seriously." More original in his thinking than Langer and more familiar with German language and society, Erikson brought an artist's eye to his work. In time, Erikson would become one of the most famous psychoanalysts in America.[16]

As the war approached, it dawned on American authorities that the new émigré analysts had special knowledge and expertise to share. Thus the outbreak of the war itself gave the refugee psycho-analysts a new, more valued identity in America. Karen Horney had already stressed the fit between culture and personality in her popu-lar book *The Neurotic Personality of Our Time* (1937). Fromm made conformity and authoritarianism central themes in his work. Erikson had been studying native American cultures and would later publish influential work on how repressive societies affected identity and life stages such as adolescence. All were viewed with suspicion by ortho-dox Freudians, but all became famous and influential in America as they explored emerging issues of the individual in relation to social norms and practices. "Erikson's rise," says Paul Roazen, "was meteoric."[17]

In his sophisticated report for the OSS, written in approximately 1942 and then published in the journal *Psychiatry*, Erikson detailed his view of Hitler and his role in German culture. In Erikson's account, it was not just that the Führer had sexual conflicts or a remarkable ability to bond with his followers. It was that Hitler's personal struggles dovetailed with the culture around him. Germany itself had always believed in its own "metaphysical uniqueness"; the nation had been able to overcome persistent divisions of its collective identity by the use of "common symbols." These symbols resonated in Germany's history, in its geographical situation in Europe, and in the imagination of its citizens: for landlocked and humiliated Germany, for example, "encircle-ment" and "inner disunity" had become important symbolic ideas. In the Nazi era, the images Hitler used to describe his own childhood – what Erikson terms Hitler's "best tune for German ears" – became one such symbol in the culture. Unlike Langer, who focused on Hitler's personality in relative isolation, Erikson wanted to understand and analyze the specific ways Hitler appealed to his followers: "It is the tune, not the man, which

I intend to analyze." Erikson surveyed Hitler's imagery as it drew upon, played with, and then developed further the cultural identities of father, mother, adolescent, Jew, and soldier in Germany.[18]

This complex exploration of Fascism starts by tracing the narrative Hitler offers in his autobiographical book *Mein Kampf.* For Erikson, the story told in this document is not only "young Adolf's stubborn opposition" to his tyrannical father and the boy's warm attachment to his young mother but also the way Hitler talks to his culture: the passionate way, for example, that Hitler sees the German-speaking minority in Austria as longing to return to the arms of Germany, "the beloved mother." Erikson notes the Oedipal configuration but finds this common general pattern less than useful for his purpose of understanding Hitler's appeal to German culture. Instead, Erikson explores the images of mother and father in *Mein Kampf* as both personal revelation and "shrewd propaganda," the statements of an adventurer and an actor who needed an audience. Erikson postulates an "*inner affinity*" between Hitler's parental imagery and the childhoods of those young Germans who became his followers. To them, Hitler showed decisively that "no old man" need "stand in the way" of the adolescent's "love for Germany." Instead of a despised tyrannical father, the youth of Germany had Hitler to look up to – Hitler the "*adolescent who never gave in*," the "*glorified older brother,* who replaces the father."

At just the right moment Germany itself, says Erikson,

> ... meets a leader and a gang who proclaim that the neighbors are senile imbeciles, that the adolescent is always right, that aggression is good, conscience an affliction, adjustment a crime. He seems to throw off his conscience. He closes up against the people he had loved and the values he had recognized.

Such a decline of conscience could only happen in a culture, Erikson asserts, when parents, especially fathers, lack true authority. On the social level, Fascism's adolescent world could only come into existence because of what Erikson calls the presence of "senile systems which would neither learn nor die." Seeing Germany in this way as a kind of "delinquent adolescent" lacking in superego, Erikson asserts that there may be ways to break "the spell of these magic ideas." But he stops at the threshold of recommending action, saying modestly if somewhat disingenuously: "How this can be accomplished is not for the psychologist to say."

It remains unknown what the OSS staff made of Erikson's complex readings of identity and culture, or how, if at all, they affected the pursuit of the war. Unlike Langer's profile, which remained secret for decades, Erikson's was published quickly in a professional journal. Based largely on the publicly available *Mein Kampf* rather than on government sources, Erikson's contribution may have been best suited for sophisticated professionals. In the issue of *Psychiatry* where the profile appeared, the editors were convinced that psychiatrists and other mental health professionals "have a great and unavoidable part to play in the postwar reconstruction" – if first they can help in the task of "COMPLETING OUR MOBILIZATION." In that way, efforts like Erikson's were assumed to be part of the war effort, broadly conceived. As Peter Mandler has suggested, the "neo-Freudians" – psychoanalysts Erikson and Fromm, anthropologist Margaret Mead, and other culturally sensitive psychological observers working to expand the Freudian tradition – faced a wartime task more complex than simply characterizing or denigrating German or Japanese national character. For Erikson and his colleagues, it was important to differentiate between Germany in general and Germany under Hitler specifically, as well as between Germany under Hitler's influence and an anticipated Germany that would have to be rehabilitated after the war. These shifting cultural considerations made the neo-Freudians subtle in their formulations but may have rendered their profiles less pragmatically useful for the OSS. Director William Donovan was known for ineffective lobbying and for giving President Roosevelt masses of unfiltered and sometimes unreliable information, an approach that may have hampered his usefulness to the president.[19]

Erikson's work, which tried to strike a balance between his innovations in psychoanalysis and a loyalty to traditional Freudian concepts, was elegant and accessible. *Young Man Luther* (1958), Erikson's first venture in psychologically sensitive historical biography, attracted wide acclaim and led in part to his appointment as a professor of human development at Harvard. A few years after he wrote the Hitler study for the OSS, Erikson revised it and included it in his *Childhood and Society* (1950). Issued in revised form as a paperback in 1963, the book became one of the best-selling college textbooks of the era. The chapter "The Legend of Hitler's Childhood" thus played a part in the formation of Erikson's own legend. Students and civil rights activists came to idolize him as teacher and sage in an era when authority figures were widely mistrusted.

As Erikson noted in 1963, in the nuclear age it was unwise to forget the lessons of Hitler too quickly. "Rather, it is our task to recognize that the black miracle of Nazism was only the German version – superbly planned and superbly bungled – of a universal contemporary potential."[20]

* * *

Neither Langer nor Erikson made extensive comments on the ethics of what they were doing for the government. Langer, it is true, commented on the limitations of profiling without an interview, but he took this limitation as inherent in his task and plunged ahead. Erikson did not mention ethical considerations at all. In the consensus of the war years, it is likely that such efforts were viewed as simply psychiatry and psychology's contribution to the war effort – and that the value of fighting Hitler was self-evident. Reviewing Langer's book in 1972, Robert Jay Lifton said: "Given what Hitler represented, Langer's ethical position as a psychohistorian had an enviable moral clarity."

Langer and Erikson were not alone among psychoanalysts in their degree of comfort with the war effort. By 1941, the American Psychoanalytic Association (APsaA) had already formed its Committee on Morale, separate from Langer's unit, that was "tasked with facilitating contributions to national morale." According to psychoanalyst Knuth Müller, APsaA's newsletter and psychoanalysts' contemporaneous memos document the activities the organization envisioned:

> One of its [the Committee on Morale's] first tasks was to gather material from analytic patients who held "fascist, communist or similar attitudes" in order to "discover and tabulate all mechanisms typical of such cases." … The aim was to identify patterns deemed typical of anti-democratic attitudes and to counteract these through psychoanalytically informed propaganda strategies. … The Chicago Psychoanalytic Institute, under the directorship of Franz Alexander, began a "[p]sychoanalytic study of civilian morale through pooling of observations made on about 150–200 patients while under daily observation."

One analyst wrote papers such as "Psychoanalytic Study of a Communist" and "Analysis of a Potential Nazi" for the American government; these papers included patient information. Presumably these efforts, like Langer's and Erikson's diagnoses from a distance, were intended as a contribution to the fight against Hitler or against subversion. As far as I can determine, ethical questions about the project were not raised until generations later.

What Robert Jay Lifton said in 1972 about the moral clarity of Walter Langer's effort on the Hitler profile could have been said of Erikson, Alexander, and APsaA as well – and perhaps of all psychoanalytically inclined commentators on public figures of concern. These psychoanalytically inclined observers were involved in what they saw as the task of defeating a moral monster. Lifton reflected that he could not imagine another situation in which a psychoanalyst or psychohistorian could feel so ethically justified in writing a profile for the American government:

> He must have had the sense that his investigative work could have immediate usefulness in combating a grotesque evil, a sense rarely given to scholarly investigators. Hence he could accept, with no more than "a feeling of frustration," the investigative self abnegation [sic] required of him by his sponsor, General Donovan, who "never said what he planned to do with the analysis." That might well have been the last situation in which an American scholar could surrender his product so unquestioningly without surrendering his integrity as well.[21]

* * *

After the war, organized psychiatry and psychology boomed. The number of mental health professionals grew faster than either the general population or other health professionals. Psychoanalysis itself grew rapidly yet at the same time became more regimented and medicalized. Walter Langer, who had so much enjoyed the informal training atmosphere of Vienna in 1936–8, found that he felt alienated from much of postwar psychoanalysis in America, which was dominated by bureaucracy instead: many procedures, committees, and a hostility to lay analysts.[22]

The work psychological experts had done in the war – "psychological warfare, intelligence classification, training, clinical treatment," and the engineering of military equipment with an eye to "human factors" – was made permanent in the military bureaucracy of the 1950s. Mental health experts moved fluidly between jobs in the Department of Defense and civilian agencies such as the National Science Foundation and the booming National Institutes for Mental Health. One psychologist commented after the war that his service in government had established "one of the best old-boy (or old-girl) networks ever." Walter Barton, a psychiatrist and administrator in the Massachusetts state hospital system, served as a captain in the army, organizing army psychiatric hospitals and directing reconditioning programs (this work would now be called psychiatric rehabilitation). Barton would put the leadership lessons he gained to good use first as the president and then as the medical director of the American Psychiatric Association.[23]

Psychologists, psychiatrists, and psychoanalysts who were involved in the war effort discovered or invented templates for postwar efforts. The vision was to apply the lessons gained in the war's modern, large-scale organizational effort to the problems of mental health in a growing society. Mental health professionals thus discovered the power of national networks and vision – and were eager to share that vision with a country that appeared anxious to see and to hear what the new experts had to say.

AMERICAN MEDIA AFTER WORLD WAR II

During the war, radio and newspapers were the dominant means by which professionals and politicians could communicate with the public at large. But it was clear that a new era was about to begin. The technology behind television was developed in the 1930s and early 1940s and was of immediate interest to the heads of the major radio networks. But at the request of the US government, the radio networks delayed the development of commercial television in favor of wartime uses of the new technology.[24]

Like psychiatrists, radio executives developed much organizational experience and many national contacts while they waited and planned for the new era. David Sarnoff of RCA and William S. Paley of CBS both served in communications roles during the war. Both were of Russian Jewish origin and felt strongly about the war against Hitler. During the D-Day campaign, Paley served as the head of radio broadcasting in the psychological division of Dwight Eisenhower's staff. Once demobilized, Sarnoff and Paley returned to New York to oversee the postwar boom and to capture what Sarnoff called the "vast market out there" in television.[25]

Between 1949 and 1955, the percentage of American households with a television rose from a mere 2 percent to almost two-thirds, representing 30.5 million TV sets. At first, television had a pronounced regional differentiation. It began mostly on the East Coast and in big cities: at the start of 1947, one could watch television mainly in "New York, Schenectady, Philadelphia, Chicago, Baltimore, Washington, D.C., Cleveland, Detroit, Milwaukee, St. Louis, and Los Angeles." In 1948, half of American television sets were located in the New York City area. "National hookup," or coast-to-coast TV, was not available until 1951; the first major national talk show, the *Tonight Show*, did not debut until 1953. In that year television reached 60 percent of households, but that number concealed a spectrum ranging from 84 percent on the populous East Coast to a mere 33 percent in Texas and to only 15 percent in Arkansas and other rural states.[26] The difference between the rural and urban experiences would soften by the end of the 1950s, but the regional differentiation remained – and in some ways would play out as a factor in the content of television programming. The 1962 CBS comedy *The Beverly Hillbillies*, watched by almost a third of the American population, spun ratings gold from the contrast between the ways of simple rural folk and those of the sophisticated, commercialized big city.[27]

Politicians adapted with alacrity to the new medium. In 1948, few TV stations existed, but public figures proved more prescient than the amused newspapermen who attended the political conventions of the time. Both the Democrats and Republicans agreed to hold their 1948 conventions in the same eastern city, Philadelphia, so that television coverage would be easier technically. Fourteen early TV stations, all located in eastern states, broadcast the proceedings to an audience of 10 million viewers. By the mid-1950s, television news, and coverage of the presidential conventions in particular, was maturing.[28]

Radio, once the dominant electronic news and entertainment media, declined rapidly with the advent of television – at least in urban areas. In 1949 in the enormous New York City market, the city's total television viewing audience was about the size of the listening audience for top-ten radio; two years later, the TV audience was four times larger than radio's. Like other traditional media, radio had to adapt. When transistor radios became available in the 1960s, there was a renaissance in the content and the financial success of radio: "locally oriented," the boom was "little short of phenomenal." These local radio markets, spread across thousands of cities and towns, were easy to overlook at first glance. But they allowed media owners to develop alternative points of view that quietly – or noisily – flourished beyond the national monoliths of network TV and the *New York Times*.[29]

* * *

If television was the country's wonder child, the newspaper industry after the war was something of a fabulous invalid. At first newspaper editors and publishers thought TV posed little threat to them or to their advertising revenue. Newspaper circulation had already declined during the Depression as many papers closed. During the war itself, the rationing of newsprint, voluntary censorship, and a diminished domestic audience made it hard for newspapers to reach the American public in the usual way. Then, as birth rates rose and the American economy expanded, observers began to note that newspaper circulation was rising dramatically. As Americans – especially white Americans – moved to the suburbs, newspapers appeared to have a commanding position in American life. Total daily newspaper circulation stood at 48 million in 1945, had passed 56 million by 1955, and rose steadily to more than 60 million by 1965.[30]

Circulation, as students of the newspaper industry have noted, is not only an indication of commercial value. It is a marker of influence. If a newspaper is read by public figures and noticed often enough by citizens, its coverage and its editorial support can "help to shape public discussion, formulate public policy, and develop public opinion." This kind of influence in turn can increase circulation further and can serve as evidence for a newspaper's sense of itself as providing a public service. Thus newspapers educated the public, tried to foster discussion, and ran human interest stories about public figures. Depending on the paper's politics, these could be powerful contributions. No wonder politicians and government officials hoped to shape how newspapers portrayed them.[31]

But the profitability of newspapers and their rising circulation after the war masked problems that were initially hard to recognize. As readers and advertisers moved to the suburbs, they tended to lose interest in the issues most pertinent to big cities, where newspaper production costs were highest. Suburban newspapers, often local in focus, boomed. Thus the overall modest growth in newspaper circulation from 1945 to 1965 concealed two trends: a dramatic decline in the circulation of urban newspapers and a rise in the circulation of suburban ones. "The smaller the city of publication," said *Editor and Publisher*, "the faster the rate of circulation growth." Nationally, the growth in newspaper circulation rates, while reasonable, was not keeping up with the remarkable growth in population. Thus newspaper circulation per household actually dropped after the war.

The changes in the newspaper industry also had regionally differentiated implications. Daily newspaper readers tended to be older and well educated; they had higher incomes and were more likely than nonreaders to live in urban or suburban areas. But large papers could be insensitive to local needs and attitudes. Small, independently owned papers could focus on just one market, such as a less affluent and less educated niche not served well by the big urban dailies. By the 1950s, the smaller papers in the suburbs and in conservative small towns were taking advantage of cheaper printing methods such as offset printing. Lacking professional management but also lacking high fixed costs, these small-town papers could be flexible. They also could and did develop "eccentric" corporate cultures more reflective of local beliefs than of national trends. Politicians, especially on the right, would learn to exploit these advantages. Small papers became an important outlet not only for Senator Joseph McCarthy in the 1950s but also for Barry Goldwater and his message of traditionalism, free enterprise, and anticommunism in the late 1950s and early 1960s.[32]

As television came to dominate the news market, newspaper and newsmagazine editors had to differentiate their role from that of the

TV networks. Editor Ben Bradlee, who worked first for *Newsweek* and then for the *Washington Post*, was probably typical in asserting that perspective and context were the unique contributions of newspapers, in contrast to television's focus on immediate coverage of dramatic events. For their part, *Time* and *Newsweek* presented an easily digestible summary of the week's news, spiced with analysis, commentary, and reviews; they drew much highbrow criticism in the process. In the late 1930s, Edmund Wilson bemoaned the way the Henry Luce empire – *Time, Life,* and *Fortune* – hired liberal and radical writers, then proceeded to wreck their talent. It was, said Wilson, as if a group of schoolboy writers were suddenly "in a position to avail themselves of gigantic research equipment." One literary critic in the 1960s said that an adoring *Time* cover story, full of "blasé sanctimoniousness," was the worst possible development for any writer featured there. But the newsmagazines sold well – by the 1970s, *Time* had a circulation of 4 million – and they helped create a national audience. Among other things, the weeklies were able to reach those in the South, Midwest, and West who could not get the *New York Times.*

There was much criticism of the media as shallow, sensationalistic, and the servant of business interests. The most famous blast came from Federal Communications Commission chairman Newt Minow in 1961 (television, he said, is a "vast wasteland"), but Minow added the gratuitous boast that when TV is good, "nothing – not the theater, not the magazines or newspapers – nothing is better." As early as 1947, a special commission was formed to look into the traditional press. Headed by Robert Hutchins of the University of Chicago, the commission found the press fell short in its mission to serve the needs of the country. Journalism listened and to some extent began to professionalize. Accredited programs in journalism education and national organizations like the American Press Institute began to flourish.[33]

* * *

On October 25, 1948, *Time* magazine featured an avuncular-looking psychiatrist on its cover. "Will" Menninger, as the cover warmly called him, appeared in a suit and tie and gazed benignly at the reader. Behind him was a schematic illustration of the brain with a lock embedded in its surface. In the foreground, a free-floating key seemed to suggest that the solution to the brain's mysteries was close at hand. In that same year, Menninger himself reported that psychiatry "probably enjoys a wider popular interest at the present time than does any other field of medicine."[34]

During World War II, Menninger had directed the psychiatry consultation division of the US Surgeon General's Office. It was an enormously influential position, and Menninger then made his army service into a springboard for the growth of psychoanalytically oriented psychiatry – not only at his own Menninger Clinic in Topeka, Kansas, but throughout the postwar world. "Dr. Will, big, direct and straightforward, forceful and pragmatic," was a genial presence, an interpersonal genius, and a phenomenally hard worker with excellent political antennae. He understood how to help move psychiatry into the mainstream: he was devoted to "helping the public understand psychiatry." Like many others, future APA medical director Walter Barton was inspired by Menninger's leadership.

Publicity sometimes had a down side. The media paid so much attention to psychiatry that in 1947 the American Psychiatric Association's ethics committee felt compelled to consider whether many of the popular magazine articles that were appearing on the topic were appropriate. Articles of concern ranged from "Squeal, Nazi, Squeal" to glowing media portraits of mental health leaders. According to Jeremy Lazarus, the ethics committee's main concern was "how the profession would be viewed" if non-credible articles continued to appear. The APA ethics committee chairman even suggested that the organization set up criteria for what content an article should have if it was to be considered ethical. In 1949, the ethics chairman had what Lazarus describes as a "lively" correspondence with the ubiquitous William Menninger himself, who was then serving as APA president. Was it ethical for Menninger to let *Time* put his picture on its cover? The ethics chair wrote to Menninger that the committee's role was to say no when necessary but also to find a way of "protecting" colorful personalities from inappropriate praise and criticism. "I hope our Association," he said, "can work out some straight forward [*sic*] ethical principles to cover both of these points." It remains unclear what formal action the committee took, if any.[35]

POLITICS AND PSYCHOLOGY IN THE NUCLEAR AGE

In the aftermath of the war, as the Soviet Union declined to withdraw from Iraq and as Winston Churchill declared the existence of an iron curtain across Europe (1946), fears of Communism increased in America. Communist forces had won a victory in China and had emerged as the rulers of North Korea. The Korean War – technically a United Nation action – led to a new round of anxieties. Such fears were compounded by the moral crisis that developed around the atomic bomb, which, poet John Berryman said, had created "a widespread, violent condition of *bad conscience*" in Americans.[36] Architectural critic Lewis Mumford wrote in *Saturday Review* in terms that, for liberals at least, would resonate through the postwar years. In the atomic age, the world had been turned upside down: "Madmen govern our affairs in the name of order and security. The chief madmen claim the titles of general, admiral, senator, scientist, administrator, Secretary of State, even President." By 1950, to make matters worse, the Soviet Union had developed and deployed its own atomic bomb.

The United States had a new antagonist – worldwide communism – and federal agencies were quick to respond. This development was especially ominous for liberals and psychoanalysts, many of whom had viewed the Soviet experiment favorably until the mid-1930s or were liberal or even openly Marxist in their thinking. In 1950, FBI director J. Edgar Hoover wrote an editorial for the *Journal of the American Medical Association* asserting that doctors "must kill the infectious and deadly germs" of "an alien ideology." From these remarks and similar ones by President Harry Truman, the question of loyalty now had a new intensity. Hoover urged doctors to report "immediately any information which might come into their possession" that had a bearing on "subversive activities." The Committee on Social Issues of APsaA objected to Hoover's editorial, calling what he proposed an invasion of patients' privacy and a risk to the physician–patient relationship.[37]

In 1950, the state of California required its employees, including professors at the University of California, to sign a special loyalty oath.

The oath went beyond the already required oath of office, which involved a promise to support the US Constitution and to "faithfully discharge the duties of my office to the best of my ability." For those who had lived in Germany as Hitler rose to power, the similarity of the loyalty oaths to Hitler's demands for obedience was striking. Erik Erikson, who had only recently been appointed to a professorship, declined to sign, as did about 89 other faculty members. In a stirring statement to the Committee on Privilege and Tenure before which he was called, Erikson said that he had never been a communist himself. But as a teacher of the young and as a psychoanalyst who specialized in part in the study of hysteria and irrational fear, he told the committee that it would be not only an "empty gesture" but a dangerous one if he signed:

> I do not believe [the students] can remain unimpressed by the fact that the men who are to teach them to think and to act judiciously and spontaneously must undergo a political test; must sign a statement which implicitly questions the validity of their own oath of office . . . a dangerous rift may well occur between the "official truth" and those deep and often radical doubts which are the necessary conditions for the development of thought.

This analyst of Hitler's appeal to the German people said that if asked, University of California professors would gladly devote their resources to a study of communism and what could be done about it. He would find it difficult, Erikson said, to ask his students and research subjects to work with him "if I were to participate without protest in a vague, fearful and somewhat vindictive gesture" like the loyalty oath. "In this sense, I may say that my conscience did not permit me to sign the contract after having sworn that I would do my job to the best of my ability."[38]

A committee of the American Psychoanalytic Association praised Erikson's stance. In that same year, 81 percent of APsaA members voted to oppose special loyalty oaths in the academy because of their inhibiting effect on research. Hoping to educate the public, the organization also held a panel on mass hysteria and paranoia. Twenty APsaA members and candidates had signed the loyalty oath under protest; one psychiatrist-analyst who refused to sign did not regain his appointment. Erikson, an APsaA member himself, was able to keep his professorship but resigned soon thereafter.[39]

* * *

The elections of 1952 were intimately related to the Korean War and to the question of communism. Richard Nixon, running for vice president on the ticket with moderate and war hero Dwight Eisenhower, emphasized his firm opposition to the communist threat. In the Arizona Senate campaign of that year, so did conservative candidate Barry Goldwater. Goldwater attacked sitting president Harry Truman as a socialist and pledged to fight Truman's "appalling record of waste, inefficiency, dishonesty, and failure both at home and abroad." To Goldwater, this meant taking a strong stand against communism, not only in the Soviet Union but internationally and in the administration: "Now is the time to discharge those who have coddled the communists. Now is the time to defeat those who have ... failed to recognize the source and magnitude of this danger to our freedom." His later bestseller *The Conscience of a Conservative* (1960) also stressed the threat to freedom posed by labor unions, which he thought were oppressing the rights of workers. It was a career-long theme that resonated with Republicans. In the Senate, Goldwater would bitterly attack Walter Reuther, the president of United Automobile Workers, as corrupt.[40]

At 44, after a narrow victory, Goldwater took office and quickly became what his biographer calls "a salesman-at-large for conservatism." He himself confessed that he too often shot from the hip: "I wasn't the most patient politician in the world," especially when answering questions from the press. His asymmetrical smile could come across as a species of grimace. But Goldwater's advantages included a practical sensibility, a strong sense of integrity, and what a liberal journalist called an "easy, breezy Aw Shucks Western manner." Goldwater himself recalled that older Republican stalwarts like Robert Taft made dull copy for journalists. But his own willingness to "talk back" to the left and to reporters made him, by media lights, "hot stuff."[41]

* * *

Goldwater had known Senator Joseph McCarthy since the 1940s. The heavy-drinking Wisconsin senator brought a crude, flamboyant, publicity-hungry style to the national scene – along with a new intolerance. Starting in 1950, McCarthy alleged that he had a list of communists in the State Department. The exact numbers he claimed often varied, and their credibility was doubtful from the start, as Goldwater himself knew. But as commentators recognized at the time, dramatic headlines followed McCarthy. The senator understood when deadlines loomed for newspapers and wire services and was skillful at timing press releases "for maximum exposure." Goldwater himself attacked McCarthy's enemies as "people who coddle communists." On the campaign trail, he found that defending McCarthy even briefly led to "overwhelming applause," and he advised the Republican Senate Campaign Committee to keep speaking up in this way – "except, possibly, in the large industrial cities."

Many photos of McCarthy in action show him holding forth before a bevy of microphones. According to a 1952 book by Jack Anderson and Ronald May, McCarthy fed the press so much good copy that he was impossible to resist: "it was the press that kept the wheel turning." McCarthy would level new charges before his previous charges could be refuted, an effective technique in keeping attention. It was common for newspapers to repeat his accusations, even when reporters suspected the statements were false. This dynamic, however, drove McCarthy to expand the scope of his inquiries. He inspired terror until 1954, when for six weeks the Army–McCarthy hearings let 20 million viewers see him attack alleged communists in the military. Once McCarthy was censured by the Senate and was safely off the scene, the media acknowledged their role had been too servile. Many newspapers began to include more interpretative reporting as a way of countering McCarthy-like tactics. As a result of the debacle and the toxic cycle of false stories, the relationship between newspapers and government continued to deteriorate.[42]

* * *

In the age of the Red Scare, psychiatrists and psychological commentators with socialist sympathies often had to dissemble. But some found a way to speak out. Theodor Adorno et al.'s *The Authoritarian Personality*

(1950), perhaps the most influential exploration of factors that might lead Americans to prejudice and to sympathy with Fascism, is one example. In many cases refugees from Nazism themselves, Adorno and his colleagues in the Frankfurt School were deeply concerned about how to prevent a recurrence of Hitler. Adorno also had deep Marxist sympathies. But in the book he barely mentioned socialism except as an empirical category for studying his subjects; Marx and Stalin do not appear at all in the book's index. On the other hand, readers were likely to relate to the warning that history could repeat itself. Already, said Max Horkheimer and a colleague in their preface to the series, "the world scarcely remembers the mechanized persecution and extermination of millions of human beings." When it was successful, this delicate balancing act – criticizing American society from a Marxist-inspired viewpoint while avoiding endorsement of the Soviet Union and emphasizing a commitment to fighting fascism – could provide much credibility on the mainstream left and at times even lead to best-seller status. *The Authoritarian Personality* was listed as a *New York Times* most influential book of the decade and was quickly taken up by liberal historian Richard Hofstadter in his effort to understand the rise of the right.

Erich Fromm, who had conducted several of the studies that inspired Adorno, also had an outsized impact on American culture with (among other books) *The Sane Society* (1955). Here Fromm creatively reframed Marxist alienation as the idea that democratic society itself had become ill: "the pathology of normalcy" was the dominant theme of his book. More open than Adorno in his sympathies with Marxism, Fromm was nonetheless careful to defend socialism against the popular view that it was identical to Stalinism. For Fromm, Stalinism was a betrayal of Marx's ideas; he lumped Stalinism in with Nazism and Fascism as false refuges for alienated men frightened of freedom. He also framed his effort in part as a response to the threat of the atomic bomb and its unprecedented prospect of "mass slaughter." His books sold millions of copies and proved influential in postwar American society.[43]

* * *

In the 1950s, there were occasional if not frequent incidents involving psychological comment without interview or consent. When they did occur, these were often covered extensively by the media. The most controversial demonstrated that in the vitriolic mix of Cold War politics, there was no longer a consensus about psychiatric comment. In 1950, psychiatrist Carl Binger and psychologist Henry Murray (the same Murray who had helped Langer profile Hitler during the war) testified at the perjury trial of Whitaker Chambers. Chambers, a hero to the American right, was a staunch anticommunist and a vivid personality. Chambers had accused Alger Hiss of spying for the Soviets, but Hiss denied it. Hiss was then tried for perjury. In the trial, Binger and Murray testified as experts for Chambers's nemesis, Alger Hiss, but in fact directed much of their attention to Chambers's mental state. Murray "testified that belief in Soviet espionage was a sign of 'instability,'" while Binger testified that Chambers suffered from a "psychopathic personality." Binger at least had never met Chambers. Conservative thinkers were outraged and even today regard Binger's psychiatric testimony as part of a "smear campaign" against a conservative patriot.[44]

In the other incident, psychiatry showed the public not its partisan or demonic side but what seemed to be its almost magical predictive powers in helping the public. Psychiatrist and psychoanalyst James A. Brussel was the head of a state mental hospital in Queens, New York. He was consulted by the New York Police Department after an unknown person began detonating bombs in public places in New York City. "We'd appreciate any ideas you might have on this case," the police captain told Brussel. In 1956, Brussel developed a criminal profile that highlighted the dynamics of the unknown bomber's paranoia, haughtiness, and longing to be taken seriously. The bomber, Brussel thought, was likely a single former electric company employee of medium build and of Slavic descent. A collector of injustices and a believer in his own importance, he was nonetheless underemployed and lived with an older female relative. Brussel, a lover of attention himself, urged the police to "publicize the description I've given you. Spread it in the newspapers, on radio and television." He was convinced that publicity would help. The *New York Times* published the psychological profile on page one. The *New York Journal-American* then published an open letter to the killer, offering to let him air his grievances and to publish "the essential parts" of his story, and urging him to give himself up.

Despite the skepticism of many in law enforcement, events validated Brussel's prediction that the open letter would induce the killer to communicate further about his grievances. When George Metesky was arrested in 1957 and then confessed, his characteristics turned out to be much as Brussel had predicted. The *Journal-American*, which had been struggling financially, saw circulation rise by more than 100,000 after the arrest. The paper received congratulations from FBI director J. Edgar Hoover, the mayor of New York City, and the governor of New York State. For his part, Dr. Brussel was deluged with interview requests and received flattering coverage in newspapers, on television, and on radio.[45]

* * *

Senator Barry Goldwater rapidly caught the attention of William F. Buckley, the author, columnist, and organizer who was soon to found *National Review* (1955). Buckley too had admired and defended Joseph McCarthy. Unhappy with President Dwight Eisenhower and skeptical about Richard Nixon, the 28-year-old Buckley, already a best-selling author, believed the time was right for a movement that could bring together the often warring strands of right-wing thought: anticommunism, traditionalism, and libertarianism.[46] Buckley hoped his new magazine, emerging out of the tiny world of competing right-wing publications, could fuse the three strains and do for conservativism something like what the *Nation* or *The New Republic* had done for the left. It was always an uneasy coalition, but Buckley's journalism did much to hold it together. In 1955, from what associates described as his "shabby" offices on East 37th Street in Manhattan, Buckley launched *National Review*. (The offices later moved to East 35th Street.) The first issue made a suave promise to stand "athwart history, yelling Stop." It is not clear if the reality of the movement was ever as strong as its rhetoric, but *National Review* got attention and galvanized its readers.[47]

To achieve his conservative coalition, Buckley had to differentiate *National Review* and its readers from liberal and moderate magazines on the one hand and from what he called "mimeographed" newsletters "describing the Plot to Destroy America" on the other. Ultimately their need for mainstream credibility led Buckley and Goldwater to distance their movement from the John Birch Society and Robert Welch, who believed that Eisenhower and other prominent officials were outright communists.[48]

Starting in the late 1950s, Barry Goldwater was Buckley's favored candidate for the presidency. Buckley, who implied that he developed the conservative movement first and found Goldwater only later, nonetheless pushed him in the pages of *National Review*. Buckley's brother-in-law, L. Brent Bozell Jr., was soon ghostwriting the conservative manifesto published in 1960 under Goldwater's name, Regnery Press's influential *The Conscience of a Conservative*. *Conscience*, originally the brainchild of right-wing radio host Clarence Manion, benefited from the novel publishing idea that Manion presented to corporate subscribers of his radio show: they would finance the book, then sell copies to other businesses, an arrangement he called "conservative political action." Buckley was delighted with the response to the book as well as with its excellent sales: *Conscience of a Conservative* sold 85,000 copies in its first month and was on the *New York Times* bestseller list a month after that. By the end of the year, it had sold 500,000 copies.[49]

Buckley had occasional private misgivings about Goldwater, as did many more moderate Republicans. At one low point, Buckley described Goldwater as "perhaps not ... our man," "*not as well qualified to run or serve*" as one could hope. Of the three strands that made up the unstable mix of "fusion" conservatism, Goldwater was most sympathetic to libertarianism and not particularly strong on traditionalism (Karl Hess recalled that the senator was quietly and deeply religious but did not attend church regularly). But Buckley ultimately agreed with *National Review* staffers who felt that Goldwater was the movement's only real choice in 1960 or 1964. He finally saw Goldwater as "someone who would not bend with the spirit of the age" and a man of "candor and courage." In *Conscience of a Conservative*, Goldwater took a firm stand against the Supreme Court's 1954 decision in *Brown* v. *Board of Education* and encouraged readers to resist school integration by any nonviolent means. It was a position he would later regret and retract.[50]

* * *

By the late 1950s, Stalin was dead. Americans and their government had developed an interest in following a new generation of leaders that was emerging in the Communist world. Nikita Khrushchev in the Soviet Union and Fidel Castro in Cuba were posing new challenges. When Premier Khrushchev, in a speech in Hungary, "rubbed the noses of the battered Hungarian people" in the memory of the 1956 Soviet invasion, conservatives raised the alarm, as they were now doing with increasing frequency. The CIA also took notice. William F. Buckley, who had once briefly worked for the Agency, regarded Khrushchev as nothing less than "the butcher of Budapest."

In the first years of the new decade, former vice president Richard Nixon returned to the private practice of law, eventually working on cases involving libel and privacy. With Nixon sitting out the next presidential race, establishment Republicans were confident that one of their East Coast candidates, perhaps New York governor Nelson Rockefeller, would emerge to effectively challenge John F. Kennedy. Urban liberals reveled in the new era of civil liberties ushered in by liberal Republican Chief Justice of the Supreme Court Earl Warren. With a broad political consensus in so many areas, some observers wondered if there was any meaningful difference between the parties any more.[51]

In Arizona, the junior senator believed it was his duty to describe an alternative regardless of what the moderates were saying. Emphasizing the need to fight aggressively against the Soviet menace, he said the United States must achieve military superiority over the Communists. This included superiority in "small, clean" nuclear weapons. In some circumstances, a mobile unit, "equipped with appropriate nuclear weapons," could be sent to the scene of unresolved negotiations. To prevent the Soviets from launching a first nuclear strike, he said he would emphasize the certainty of mutually assured destruction. In this way, claimed Barry Goldwater, he would force the Soviets to choose between a local defeat and the "total destruction of the Soviet Union." President Kennedy looked forward to running against Goldwater in 1964 because he was sure he could easily beat him.[52]

In an office building in midtown Manhattan, an outspoken publisher with a flair for publicity had left *Esquire* magazine and had set up his own

FROM THE RISE OF HITLER TO THE 1950S

publishing operation. In order to speak truth to power, he decided he would not accept advertising; he would not make use of bookstores or newsstands either. Instead, he would use direct mail advertising to market his books and magazines to his hip readers. A master of promotion, Ralph Ginzburg was looking forward to having his say in the new era of civil liberties.

PART I

DIAGNOSIS FROM A DISTANCE AND LIBEL LAW IN THE 1960S: *GOLDWATER V. GINZBURG*

CHAPTER 2

Ralph Ginzburg

Provocateur

ROGER ROBB: ... I believe you stated that you were proud of the
article, have you not?

RALPH GINZBURG: I believe we made a very real public service,
contributed a very real public service on the publication side,
that I am indeed proud of the project.

ROBB: ... Getting back to your article, the caption on it is, "Goldwater:
The Man and the Menace." The dictionary defines a menace as
a threat of evil. Is that what you meant to convey by using the word
as you did?

GINZBURG: I meant that he was potentially a menace should he
become president.

Exchange in court during *Goldwater* v. *Ginzburg*, 1968[1]

*Liberalism, often viewed as triumphing in the 1960s, was in fact a precarious
achievement. As historian Alan Brinkley has argued, American liberalism was
never "a uniform or stable creed" and "in fact has never been uncontested."[2]
But after the humiliations of the McCarthy period in the 1950s, Democrats,
union members, and college professors could breathe at least somewhat more
easily. Psychoanalysts, though never free from internal divisions of their own,
found a growing acceptance of their ideas in the culture, and the refugee
analysts continued to grow in status. In 1962, literary critic Alfred Kazin
proclaimed Freud a hero and a conquistador. The paperback edition of Erik
Erikson's* Childhood and Society *(1963) became a bestseller on college
campuses.*

*Liberals were also able to celebrate a remarkable string of progressive decisions by
the US Supreme Court, all occurring after the fall of McCarthy:* Brown *v.* Board

of Education *on school desegregation (1954)*, Roth *v.* United States *on pornography (1958)*, Engel *v.* Vitale *on school prayer (1962), and* Gideon *v.* Wainwright *on the right to counsel (1963). Each of these decisions insisted in new ways on the rights of the oppressed or defined and protected a new space for free thought and free speech. For a time,* Brown *(known simply as "the Decision") and* Roth *became rallying cries for many in the South and West who were concerned about the rapid growth of federal power.*[3]

When the Court also loosened libel law in New York Times *v.* Sullivan *(early 1964), many on the left and in the media were proud. Ralph Ginzburg, a dramatic publicist for free speech, was an admirer of the Supreme Court's free speech absolutists, Hugo Black and William O. Douglas. Ginzburg hoped to push the Court even further in the direction of allowing free speech. By the middle of the sixties – in an era when Earl Warren headed the Supreme Court, Lyndon Johnson was president, and the civil rights movement was transforming the nation – it seemed a plausible enough hope.*

Editor, journalist, and publisher Ralph Ginzburg (1929–2006) is little remembered or understood today. Psychiatrists, it is true, know all too well that his *Fact* magazine ignited a libel suit by former presidential candidate Barry Goldwater in the 1960s, and histories of obscenity law sometimes briefly refer to Ginzburg and his *Eros* magazine. However, as Ginzburg himself recognized with disappointment toward the end of his life, he had ended up a mere footnote. He wanted more: "I might have become a major force in American publishing."[4]

For a time, some believed he had succeeded. Master of publicity in an era when mail-order business could circumvent conventional marketing channels, gain attention, and earn much money, Ginzburg could be described by one of his passionate defenders, not without some hyperbole, as "the most celebrated publisher of our time." *Time* magazine, in a 1968 article, acknowledged that "few individuals have been as influential as Ralph Ginzburg in pushing the courts toward a refinement of legal definitions." Two Supreme Court justices sided with him repeatedly in First Amendment matters that he – very much in character – tried to push to the highest levels.

Appalled by presidential candidate Barry Goldwater in 1964, Ralph Ginzburg used all the resources of publicity and provocation to challenge the mental fitness to serve of the Republican presidential candidate. The special issue of his *Fact* magazine, put together in great haste on the eve of the election, was entitled "1,189 Psychiatrists Say Barry Goldwater Is Psychologically Unfit to Be President!" The special issue continues to provoke and to shock today.[5]

Despite controversy over his aims, his political biases, and his sometimes slipshod methods, Ginzburg's legacy endures. He not only dared to challenge a powerful figure in print and then defend himself vigorously in public and on principled grounds. In response to his seemingly endless provocation, holders of power at every level – district court judges, appellate judges, a member of Congress, Supreme Court justices, a presidential candidate, a sitting president, and finally the nation's largest organization of psychiatrists – expressed their outrage and cited, enforced, or created conventional rules to contain him. But it has been in the domain of psychiatric ethics that Ginzburg had his longest-lasting impact. The Goldwater Rule, the ethics rule that the American Psychiatric Association (APA) put in place after the *Fact* controversy, bans all psychiatric comment on the mental health of public figures. Members of the APA have vigorously debated the Rule in the years since. Today, as many psychiatrists feel an obligation to speak out about the mental health and fitness of President Donald Trump, Ginzburg's legacy is as relevant as ever.[6]

* * *

Ralph Ginzburg was born in Brooklyn on October 28, 1929, just one day before the stock market crash. His parents had immigrated from Russia (or Lithuania, which was complexly related to Russia at the time), and they settled in Borough Park, a poor-to-middle-class Jewish neighborhood in Brooklyn. His father worked as a house painter. Like most talented boys in the crowded immigrant New York neighborhoods of the time, Ralph Ginzburg attended public school, in his case New Utrecht High School in Brooklyn. He got good grades and was president of his class there. Later supporters described him as glib, a "fast-talking, diamond-in-the-rough New Yorker" who kept his Brooklyn accent. However, he did not smoke, believed in monogamy, and only rarely took a drink. He was, they said, "decent" and "straightforward." In high school he dreamed of becoming a millionaire.[7]

Older Brooklyn natives, like literary critics Alfred Kazin and Irving Howe and memoirist and commentator Norman Podhoretz, had found the immigrant neighborhoods tight-knit but stifling. They made the journey across the Brooklyn Bridge to get educated at City College and to begin creating their careers in the exciting cosmopolitan world of Manhattan, then newly open to Jewish participation. As sociologist Daniel Bell recalled, a dawning political and historical awareness meant that "suddenly the whole world open[ed] up" for those reared in the immigrant neighborhoods. City College was a competitive place that was not easy to get into. But it was affordable, and there the radical discussions of politics, history, and literature that had begun in Brooklyn could be continued and intensified.[8]

Ginzburg graduated from high school at 16. Intelligent and dramatic, entering college in 1946 a generation after Kazin and Bell, Ginzburg planned to study accounting. For that reason he enrolled not at the main campus at 137th Street in Harlem, but at the business school campus downtown. Majoring in accounting and journalism, Ginzburg took summer classes and graduated magna cum laude after only three years. He then took additional coursework in literature and in economics. But a meeting with an influential professor at college had convinced him that his real calling was in journalism. Ginzburg later recalled that he began working nights at a newspaper during school. It is not clear, but he may have meant that he was editor of the school newspaper, *The Ticker*.

Impressions of Ginzburg's personality tend to converge on the phrase later used by Nat Hentoff in *Playboy*: "Brashly outspoken." Merle Miller, who was critical of Ginzburg's personality but interviewed him and his former colleagues in depth, reported that his nickname at City College was "Windy." A later chronicler was sympathetic but called him a "loudmouthed, left-wing, Jewish intellectual." Ginzburg himself later said to *Playboy*: "Look, I *am* a vigorous, energetic promoter and hustler, but that doesn't preclude my being a serious publisher, too."[9]

At some point after his graduation in 1949, Ginzburg married and had a daughter. Within a few years, Ginzburg's wife was killed by a New York subway train; at some point, possibly because of her death, Ginzburg entered psychoanalysis. He later described his treatment as successful. Before he was drafted into the army, Ginzburg worked as a copy boy and reporter at the *New York Daily Compass*. During the Korean War, he edited a newspaper at his army post in Virginia and worked nights as a copyeditor, reportedly at the *Washington Times-Herald*. Reitman, whose source is unclear, says Ginzburg worked in the Public Information Office in Washington, DC. He was given an honorable discharge.[10]

At this point Ralph Ginzburg began his real career. He worked first as a freelancer, publishing articles and photographs in *Harper's*, *Esquire*, *Reader's Digest*, *Look*, and elsewhere. He eventually took a job as a writer with NBC in New York; then a friend got him a job in an advertising agency on Madison Avenue. It wasn't enough. According to Bob Reitman, whose admiring *Freedom on Trial* (1966) is the only book ever written about Ginzburg, the 23-year-old employee yearned to work in magazine promotion so badly that from his office on the 17th floor he sent a note to *Look* magazine, whose offices were located on a lower floor of the building. He was promptly hired as a circulation promotions director at *Look*. Ginzburg worked in that job for three years, then as an articles editor for *Esquire*. According to the ever-vigilant Miller, a number of Ginzburg's colleagues found him annoying.[11]

Moving in the world of magazine journalism, Ginzburg discovered that he had a talent for writing "attention-grabbing promotional advertisements" that were well suited to the mail order business. An employee who worked for Ginzburg much later recalled the enormous impact Ginzburg had on him: Ginzburg explained to the neophyte his philosophy of "direct selling, through the ads, why certain words worked better than others to grab subscriptions." A former colleague more frankly termed him a "newsstand promotion hustler, and a damned good one, too." By 1958, Ginzburg had founded his own publishing venture, Helmsman Press, and established himself in an office at 110 West 40th Street, a narrow midtown office building near Bryant Park and the New York Public Library. There he brought out and marketed by direct mail advertising his *An Unhurried View of Erotica* (1958). The only title published by Helmsman, it had originated as an article for *Esquire* but was never published. Instead, Ginzburg expanded it into a book and undertook what Heidenry calls "a promotional blitzkrieg, virtually unlike anything ever seen before in the staid world of book publishing." The book sold more than 100,000 copies in hardback and 250,000 in paperback. *An Unhurried View* brought Ginzburg enough money that he could fund further ventures, this time in the magazine business. He had not yet turned 30.[12]

A later Ginzburg effort illustrates his publicity methods. Trying to prove and expose a possible mental disability in conservative presidential candidate George Wallace in 1968, Ginzburg wrote an open letter to Wallace, tried to take out ads in the *Montgomery Advertiser*, and wrote a typed memo to himself or his staff on how to proceed: "CALL NACHMAN LAWYER ... IF NO SOAP, FEED TO ALL WIRES ... TIME, NEWSWEEK, UPI, ETC." This was not enough for Ginzburg, so he added a handwritten postscript: "+ Get ACLU!!!"[13]

The books Ginzburg published during his early years featured attention-getting titles, but they were far from mere ephemera. In *An Unhurried View of Erotica*, in Rey Anthony's *The Housewife's Handbook on Selective Promiscuity* (1960), in *Eros* magazine (four issues, all in 1962), and in his own civil rights-oriented *100 Years of Lynchings* (1962), Ginzburg gained attention by tuning into and amplifying the zeitgeist as it evolved. Ginzburg's well-hyped publications before *Fact* spoke frankly of sex and race at a time when this approach was risky – and when it generated sales and made headlines. Because Ginzburg published his own books and advertised and sold them strictly by mail, he could evade the attention of more conventional outlets. As conservative columnist Ernest Cuneo complained in discussing Ginzburg, a booming industry had developed "which is selling with dirty word-pictures and through the mails what it can't legally sell" on street corners. This particular book industry was always marginal socially and vulnerable legally. But because it had the economic advantage of low fixed costs and few investors or advertisers to answer to, erotic publishers could function happily in their niche with only minimal editorial oversight. As Jay Hamilton has demonstrated, something like this same combination of factors is responsible for the uncontrolled bias in content that later accompanied the rise of Internet news. But the point also applies whenever low-budget information entrepreneurs try to exploit their marginal position in the marketplace. Other than his own employees, there was no one to supervise Ginzburg as he made his money. It was a lesson Ginzburg would eventually learn all too well.[14]

Ginzburg had a flair for finding the point where the provocative meets the highbrow. Hugh Hefner's *Playboy* magazine had appeared just five years earlier and had begun to move what had been considered pornographic into the mainstream. By 1963, the magazine had a circulation of 1.25 million readers.[15] In contrast, the reader of Ginzburg's *An Unhurried View* had to buy the title by mail order and do without illustrations. In place of photos, the reader could find a diverting if not quite scholarly discussion of highbrow erotic literature from Ovid to D. H. Lawrence.

The tone of *An Unhurried View of Erotica* was often grandiose and self-serving, but it was not salacious. The book's frontispiece runs as follows:

TO THE FURTHER LIBERATION
OF MAN'S HEALTHIER
INSTINCTS

Bolstering its highbrow credentials, the book included a lively introduction by lay psychoanalyst Theodor Reik and a short preface by playwright George Jean Nathan. Reik, a Jewish émigré who had studied with Freud – and who years earlier had taught analyst Erich Fromm in Berlin – acknowledged that the book's presentation was only fragmentary. But, he said, *An Unhurried View* was valuable for demonstrating the "powerful undercurrent of pornography that runs faithfully with the great stream of literature." Reik thought the book showed how sexuality, unconscious emotion, and disavowed impulses seek satisfaction. In this "age of psychoanalysis," he said, it is unnecessary "to state that this book has great scientific value," touching on "serious problems between its lines, problems intimately connected with the situation of our civilization." Reik welcomed "this courageous book that presents a valuable piece of conscientious research." Some, like Kazin, thought Theodor Reik was "long-winded and inconsequential," but he formed an important part of the literary-psychoanalytic scene in New York nonetheless.[16]

An Unhurried View quoted liberally from the texts of the books it surveyed during its short and somewhat grandiose tour of many centuries of "classic erotica in the English language." Aiming to show that great literature has often been considered obscene, Ginzburg discussed works as early as the Anglo-Saxon *Exeter Book*, as memorable as seventeenth-century poetry and fiction, and as recent as banned novels. He sprinkled in credible historical and literary judgments along the way. Of D. H. Lawrence's *Lady Chatterley's Lover*, for example, Ginzburg proclaimed, "[it] is not only the finest erotic novel ever written in the English language, but probably the best ever written in any language."[17]

Ginzburg's reference was timely. In 1957 in *Roth* v. *United States*, the Warren Court had narrowed substantially the grounds on which obscenity cases could be brought. To be considered obscene, *Roth* said, material not only had to be devoid of social importance; "taken as a whole," it had to be prurient, and it had to be at variance with current community standards. Around the time of *Roth* there was much excitement about the potential liberating impact of the new standard on literature. For some time, for example, Grove Press had been working on an unexpurgated edition of D. H. Lawrence's *Lady Chatterley's Lover* with the intent of challenging federal obscenity law. In 1956, Alfred Kazin, who would eventually testify along with Malcolm Cowley in Grove's obscenity trial, confided to his journal that *Lady Chatterley* fascinated and pleased him. Kazin twice exclaimed "O life" as the book inspired him to want to *be* Lawrence, to "know what you are, and so to fuck with all one's being, straight into the core." The word that thrilled Kazin was a particular point of controversy in the upcoming Grove trial and had great liberating potential at that moment.

The Supreme Court's *Roth* decision and the 1959 district court decision in *Grove Press Inc.* v. *Christenberry* both addressed the issue of sending obscene material through the mail. The trend, including the court's finding that Lawrence's book was literary and not obscene, seemed to be in a liberal direction; the *Grove* case was upheld in appeals court and never taken to the Supreme Court because it seemed so likely to be upheld there. These decisions, along with the success of *An Unhurried View*, encouraged Ginzburg to continue publishing provocative titles.[18]

His next title, which appeared as Rey Anthony's *The Housewife's Handbook of Selective Promiscuity* (1960), was not his own work. But his decision to publish it revealed both his continued preoccupation with free speech and his grasp of marketing. As Ginzburg now understood, readers were waiting. The sexual revolution, primed by the Kinsey Reports (1948 and 1953), by *Playboy*, by the Beat Poets, and then by the pill (1960), was just beginning its remarkable ascent. Ginzburg was aware of the forces of censorship but confident that they would yield to the movement toward increasingly free speech. Though he could inveigh intensely against conventional morality, he believed that history was on his side. He exemplifies Alan Brinkley's view that for liberals in the 1950s and 1960s, evidence for the triumph of their cause was everywhere. Conservatives might appear on occasion to spoil the party, as Ginzburg had already learned. But essentially the right seemed to liberals to be "a force at the margins of American life, without the resources to shake the great edifice of liberal achievement."[19]

A confidence in the marketplace also underlay Ginzburg's marketing efforts. The *Handbook*'s author, Maxine Serett, had published it privately under the pseudonym two years previously, and it had sold about 2,000 copies. (At various points Serett also went by the names Lilian Maxine Sanini and Maxine Savant; she was an advocate for sexual self-expression who was later described as "pro-abortion, pro-sexual pleasure and pro-equal rights.") In the *Handbook*, she narrated her own journey. Serett had garnered endorsements from Theodor Reik ("a work of admirable moral courage") and sex researcher Albert Ellis: "Belongs in the library of every serious researcher and professional worker concerned with sex, love, marriage, and family relations." Ginzburg thought the book had greater potential. He acquired the rights and put his direct-mail techniques to work. Ginzburg's edition of the *Handbook* sold 20,000 copies.[20]

* * *

Ginzburg has been called many things, including a pornographer. This part of his reputation comes mainly from his magazine *Eros*, which appeared in 1962 in four hardbound issues, and from the federal prosecution and the Supreme Court case that soon arose from it. William F. Buckley Jr., for example, referred to him in the *National Review* as "the pornographer Ginzburg" and "a pornographer-for-profit."[21] By that point, 1966, Ginzburg was already enmeshed in the controversy with Barry Goldwater, making it likely that Buckley had other reasons for his slurs. The simple basis for the claim by Buckley and others is that Ginzburg was in fact convicted of distributing obscene material by mail (the *Housewife's Handbook*, his highbrow erotic magazine *Eros*, and another publication). But it is a greatly oversimplified label and is badly in need of correction by historical context. In truth, in an era when laws on obscenity, libel, and race were changing rapidly, Ginzburg was not a smut peddler, but a superficial gadfly who deliberately provoked others in the name of free speech and a more liberated future. He was willing to risk prison for his trouble.

To look at Ginzburg's career before *Fact* is to grasp how innocuous the obscene material he created really was – yet what a flair he had for making his publications seem erotic and yet principled. *Eros*, issued in 1962 from the tower at West 40th Street, was a collaboration with innovative graphic designer Herb Lubalin. The *New York Times* later called *Eros* "stunningly designed." Its contents included a letter by poet Allan Ginsberg, a story by Ray Bradbury, an illustrated feature on love in the Bible, an investigation into Shakespeare's possible homosexuality, and a piece on bawdy limericks. In *Eros*, as critic Richard Corliss lovingly detailed in a memoir, the highbrow erotic element predominated over the purely sexual. *Eros*, he recalled, "had loads of literary and artistic value. What it lacked for me, frankly, was redeeming prurient interest." Appearing a year before *The Feminine Mystique* and Gloria Steinem's exposé of Hugh Hefner's Playboy Clubs, and well before Andrea Dworkin's essays on pornography, Ginzburg's highbrow provocations attracted little if any attention from early feminists. (Friedan, however, did think it was worthwhile to provide a critical assessment of the work of Erik Erikson, who was an influential figure at the time.) As Corliss summarized, Ginzburg "suggested his magazine was dirty when it wasn't."

A certain amount of dissembling about *Eros*'s contents was a reliable element in Ginzburg's publicity strategy in 1962. Another was his usual appeal to free speech and artistic innovation. As an advertisement for the new magazine proclaimed:

> *Eros* is a child of its times. . . . [It] is the result of recent court decisions that have realistically interpreted America's obscenity laws and that have given to this country a new breadth of freedom of expression. . . . EROS takes full

advantage of this new freedom of expression. It is the magazine of sexual candor.[22]

Decades later, the *New York Times* agreed. It credited *Eros* not only with a distinguished list of contributors but also with helping to "set off the sexual revolution." But the reader who opened an issue of *Eros* expecting to find arousing material must have been sorely disappointed.

Scantily clad women in *Eros* there were, typically presented within at least a nominal social, historical, or literary frame. A feature on "French Post Cards" expressed amusement at the older generation's taste for quaint photos of nude or near-nude women, then reproduced eight pages of them. Ralph Hattersley Jr.'s photo feature "Black and White in Color" defended interracial couples as heroes who had to endure the world's incomprehension. The photos showed a barely clothed couple, a black man and a white woman, kissing and embracing thoughtfully. The caption described the photos as a visual exploration of "the conviction that love between a man and a woman, no matter what their races, is beautiful." Elsewhere Ginzburg used photos to suggest the cost of sexual repression. In one full-page photo, a woman wearing only clingy underwear is standing in a corner, looking over her shoulder at the camera in a mistrustful way. The caption refers to an authoritarian society. Corliss compares *Eros* with *Playboy* and sees Ginzburg as a kind of Hugh Hefner – but "with a higher IQ." Ginzburg's claim was that he tried to make *Eros* an honest antidote to obscenity: the opposite of the usual portrayal of sex in "slimy, tawdry, mean, crude and inartistic" magazines.[23]

A comparison of *Eros* with Hefner's *Playboy* is instructive. (Hefner was a supporter of Ginzburg and later ran an interview with him in the magazine.) In 1953, *Playboy*'s first issue featured Marilyn Monroe on its cover, along with the not very subtle announcement: "FIRST TIME in any magazine" – "FULL COLOR" – "the famous MARILYN MONROE NUDE." Inside, as promised, were color photos of Monroe completely nude, a winning smile on her face as she stretches out for the camera. The article itself gushed about how "there is nothing else quite like Marilyn on this good earth. . . . She is natural sex personified." In 1962, *Eros* also ran color photos of Monroe, but with a difference. The photos by Bert Stern had been taken in that year in the last photo session

Monroe had before her death. In the *Eros* photos, unlike those in *Playboy*, her smile seemed forced; she appeared weary and broken down. Rather than selecting the most sexually alluring photos, Ginzburg included a great variety of shots and showed that Monroe herself had rejected many of the photos, which were in fact a set of preliminary proofs. On its cover and on several of its oversized pages, *Eros* showed how Monroe had marked firmly through with a vivid orange "X" the photos she did not want to be used. Some of the captions did rhapsodize about her beauty and impact. But they also discussed her tragedy. The effect was to highlight Monroe's exhaustion and debilitation by letting the reader see her imperfection and aging close up. Corliss accurately termed the effect "ghoulish and poignant."[24]

Sex magazines catering to straight and gay interests were displayed in such profusions at New York City newsstands at the time that one observer found it hard to imagine that any judges cared any longer. But federal officials in New York and Washington, DC, did. Representative Kathryn Granahan gave a speech in the House, attacking Ginzburg as a pornographer. In December, a US marshal arrived at the *Eros* office during the staff's Christmas party. The indictment listed *Eros*, the *Housewife's Handbook of Selective Promiscuity*, and another Ginzburg publication called *Liaison*; the charges placed special focus on volume 1, issue 4 of *Eros*, in which the photo-essay "Black and White in Color" had appeared. The counts alleged that Ginzburg had made illegal use of the US mail by sending these publications. Specifically, the 9 million copies he had mailed – an extraordinary total under any circumstances, about the size of the entire circulation of the Knight newspaper chain – had violated the Comstock Act. Ginzburg would have to suspend publication of *Eros* and to face trial out of town, in Philadelphia. According to Heidenry, *Eros* had grossed a total of $3 million, a prodigious revenue stream that suddenly stopped.[25]

It is unclear why prosecutors decided on Philadelphia as the venue for Ginzburg's trial. But in the Eastern District of Pennsylvania, officials were known to be harsh on obscenity issues. While prison had not been threatened against Grove Press in the *Lady Chatterley's Lover* case, Ginzburg's charges carried the potential for severe penalties: up to

$280,000 in fines and 280 years in federal prison.[26] The next several years would be occupied with the trial and its various appeals.

Ginzburg must have been surprised. He had reasonably expected any trouble to involve civil charges. Under ordinary circumstances these would come from the post office, as they typically had in similar cases. But Ginzburg's charges came from the Justice Department, where criminal charges would now be involved.

The district court trial took place in Philadelphia in June 1963. The prosecution made its presentation quickly, establishing the facts and asserting obscenity. Appearing for Ginzburg were a list of experts that included literary critic Dwight MacDonald, a psychiatrist, and a Baptist preacher; the ACLU and others filed amicus briefs on his behalf. Ginzburg was optimistic that the decision would be in his favor. But Judge Body, the district court judge, found little or nothing of value in Ginzburg's claims. Ginzburg's flair for marketing came back to haunt him: in the judge's decision, Body noted that *Eros* had mailed its issues from Middlesex, New Jersey, and had inquired about doing similar mailings from the cities of Blue Ball and Intercourse, Pennsylvania. He saw *Eros*'s contents as pornographic and Ginzburg's methods as simple pandering. Unlike *Lady Chatterley's Lover, Eros* "ha[d] no saving grace" and was therefore simply obscene. Body singled out "Black and White in Color," saying that the photo-essay "constitute[d] a detailed portrayal of the act of sexual intercourse between a completely nude male and female, leaving nothing to the imagination."

Judge Body acknowledged that at first he had not read all of the *Handbook* before making his preliminary rulings on it. The point was significant because *Roth* required examining the work "as a whole" in order to judge whether a work was obscene. Body defended himself by saying that the material was "extremely boring, disgusting, and shocking to this Court," then by saying that ultimately he had read every word.

Bail was set at $10,000, and Ginzburg was later sentenced to five years in prison and a $42,000 fine. According to Heidenry, the press largely ignored the trial except to gloat over the result. *Newsweek* alone saw the case as a kind of persecution. In time, however, Ginzburg won steadfast support from the American Civil Liberties Union (ACLU), the Authors' League of America, and authors such as Joseph Heller, James Jones, Christopher Isherwood, and Arthur Miller. Generally his support came from people and organizations on the left who had an interest in protecting dissenting opinion: Jones and Isherwood wrote about sex, while Miller had suffered for declining to name names at a House Committee on Un-American Activities hearing in the 1950s.[27]

* * *

Ginzburg produced two other works of note in 1962. Both had political implications. Neither gave him as much trouble as *Eros*.

"Portrait of a Genius as a Young Chess Master," which appeared in *Harper's* in January, profiled reclusive chess player Bobby Fischer. Eighteen years old, half Jewish by background, and living in a walkup in Brooklyn's Bedford-Stuyvesant neighborhood, Fischer was about to challenge "Russia's traditional hold" on chess championships. Ginzburg, in a profile still widely read today, skillfully brought out Fischer's eccentricity, his egocentricism, and his paranoia.

100 Years of Lynchings, inspired by the civil rights movement, focused on racial violence. The book earned Ginzburg respectful mainstream recognition and in many ways served as a warm-up for his battle with Goldwater. Designed as an anthology of newspaper articles and aiming to document racial atrocities in America, *Lynchings* contained a brief, lucid preface by Ginzburg but otherwise offered no commentary at all. It simply presented a series of brief newspaper reports on racial atrocities that had occurred from 1880 to 1962. Ginzburg included headlines and made effective use of capital letters, bold fonts, and black lines to separate the entries and give the reader the sense that she is reading breaking news:

NEW YORK TRUTH SEEKER
April 17, 1880

FIRST NEGRO AT WEST POINT KNIFED BY FELLOW CADETS
WEST POINT, N.Y., Apr. 15 – James Webster Smith, the first colored cadet in the history of West Point, was recently taken from his bed, gagged, bound, and severely beaten, and then his ears were slit. He says that he cannot identify his assailants. The other cadets claim that he did it himself.

While the awkward mix of history and sex in *Eros* can seem comic, the sober, cumulative effect of *Lynchings* is overwhelming. Ginzburg's heart is clearly with his lynching victims; the last piece in the book is an article reporting a statement by Attorney General Robert F. Kennedy that someday a black president will be elected.

The book also includes a simple but effective appendix. Organized by year, again without commentary, it lists the names and places of death of thousands of African Americans who died as a result of racial violence. Presented without Ginzburg's usual fanfare, this appendix quietly anticipates the understated power of Maya Lin's Vietnam Veterans memorial. The book has its flaws, but it has been considered valuable enough to be reprinted and to be described as "as relevant today as it was then."[28]

The documentary feel of *100 Years of Lynchings* is impressive, and its substance is significant. But when one reads in Ginzburg's introduction that "many" of the articles appear as published, this reader at least grows uneasy. It turns out that other articles in the book have been "drastically rewritten for the sake of clarity or conciseness." And in some cases where several newspapers accounts appeared, "the information from all sources has been synthesized into one story and attributed to the newspaper which provided most of the facts." No further elaboration is given on the unusual methods, which Ginzburg dismissed as mere "technical points."[29] The issue of fidelity to sources would shortly cast its shadow over *Fact* and lead to a courtroom in New York in *Goldwater* v. *Ginzburg*.

* * *

Ginzburg always saw himself as a free speech activist, a role that allowed him to push the limits of good taste and the law. In his high-minded yet dramatic way, he endlessly provoked law enforcement agencies and in the process dramatized himself, generating even further headlines. Publicity and entrepreneurship made him money and brought him fame. But for all his gifts, Ginzburg had trouble converting principle and notoriety into something longer-lasting. After *Fact* and *Eros*, he moved on to other preoccupations, and the world largely forgot him.

Ultimately the best term for Ginzburg, I think, is *provocateur*. He was neither driven solely by pure principle nor animated solely by sordid motives. Unlike Hefner, he was not interested primarily in publishing risqué photographs or promoting a lifestyle. Instead, Ginzburg had a talent for seizing the moment, presenting himself as a shocking advocate of intellectual freedom and civil liberties. He could be a dramatic advocate for free speech and social justice; his sweeping book on race, though flawed, has been widely cited as a resource on America's history of racial atrocities. But as the *Fact* case proved, his tragedy was that he was so often incapable of advancing his case thoughtfully, of mobilizing substance to support the drama, of getting the details quite right. Filled with the excitement of his free speech mission, Ginzburg could not quite refrain from putting his finger on the scale as he made his dramatic announcements.

* * *

In 1964, at the time Barry Goldwater was nominated for president, Ralph Ginzburg was 34 years old. Remarried and living in Manhattan, he was now the father of three children who ranged in age from about 3 to 10. He liked to go to the office very early, come home for breakfast with his family, and then return to work for a long day; Miller says he preferred to be in bed by 8 PM. Ginzburg wore distinctive round glasses that gave him an inquiring and serious look. In a photograph from the early sixties, he is clean-shaven, balding, and somewhat tentative looking as he holds a copy of his new publication.[30]

The tentative look was misleading. Ginzburg and managing editor Warren Boroson proudly described *Fact* as an independent journal dedicated to publishing "important, timely articles" that most media outlets would avoid for fear of offending advertisers "or other powerful institutions." *Fact* did not accept advertising and was financed by Ginzburg. Ginzburg was proud of publishing controversial articles – he thought of this as a public service – and he eagerly sought and promoted them, not always subtly. In January 1964, the newspapers reported his announcement that he would soon begin publishing a new journal. Already notorious as the publisher of *Eros*, Ginzburg could count on making headlines. The *New York Times*, for example, referred to his "pornography" conviction and duly reported Ginzburg's promise that the new journal would be "completely uninhibited." *Fact* would frankly explore issues such as police brutality, automobile safety, politicians' character, religious beliefs, and mental health, and other hot topics as they emerged or could be discovered.[31]

At 110 West 40th Street, *Fact*'s staff consisted of almost 20 people, in addition to Ginzburg, managing editor Warren Boroson, art director and innovator Herb Lubalin, and research director Rosemary Latimore. Boroson and the others played second fiddle to Ginzburg, who had a strong vision, had invested the money, and clearly ran the show. While Ginzburg could be difficult – employees had a running bet on how long new hires would last, with the typical wager being one week – Boroson spoke highly of *Fact* for decades and said that of all the jobs he had in journalism, he liked working there the best.

The *Fact* staff paid close attention to events in politics and in the city. Much had changed since Ginzburg had first begun publishing and since he had begun fighting obscenity charges. The rise of the interstate highway system had led rapidly to suburbanization, eroding the importance of many traditional urban institutions in America. The old Penn Station, just six blocks from Ginzburg's midtown office, had been demolished in 1963. Even closer to the *Fact* offices, Times Square had begun its decline into a seedy neighborhood of peep shows. In early July, Congress passed and President Johnson signed the 1964 Civil Rights Act, which John F. Kennedy had proposed before his assassination. Goldwater had voted against the legislation. Two weeks later in Harlem, an African American teenager was shot by an off-duty white police officer. Race riots broke out, spread from Harlem into poor sections of Brooklyn, and lasted for more than a week.[32]

The presidential campaign of that year had once been expected to involve John F. Kennedy and perhaps Barry Goldwater. In fact, Kennedy and Goldwater had discussed just that possibility, and the thought had pleased Kennedy. He was sure he could win. If Goldwater is nominated, said Kennedy, "people will start asking him questions, and he's so damn quick on the trigger that he will answer them. And when he does, it will be all over." Instead, Kennedy's assassination turned the race into a grossly unequal contest between Goldwater and incumbent Lyndon Johnson, whom many voters saw as carrying on the legacy of Camelot. As predicted by his onetime rival, Goldwater had a habit of making simplistic, provocative statements off the cuff, a quality that endeared him to many conservative followers but troubled moderates in both parties. In May 1964, asked on national television how he would break enemy supply lines in Vietnam, he said he would not use any of the methods that had been suggested so far. But, he asserted, "defoliation of the forest by low-yield atomic weapons could well be done. When you remove the foliage, you remove the cover." Goldwater repeated a version of the comment during a trip to Germany; reporters portrayed him as deliberately planning a visit to Berchtesgaden, near Hitler's retreat in the Alps, with the aim of appealing to the right wing in Germany. Thereafter, accusations of fascism against Goldwater were commonplace, as were concerns about his recklessness. As Warren Boroson later recalled, "Mr. Goldwater's mental stability was becoming more and more discussed during the campaign."[33]

Americans had only recently been through the Cuban Missile Crisis, a fact that gave an intense edge to debates about mental stability. During the crisis in 1962, Defense Secretary McNamara said in retrospect, the world faced "what many of us felt then, and what since has been generally agreed, was the greatest danger of a catastrophic war since the advent of the nuclear age." As Ginzburg's attorney later recalled, "nuclear warfare was not an idle dream or theory, it was something which was frighteningly real to all of us." In a nuclear age, who would hold the world's most powerful office? How would that person act under pressure? Since the crisis, memories of Hitler, and the debate over how to prevent another Holocaust, had been freshly revived by the publication in 1963 of Hannah Arendt's controversial book *Eichmann in Jerusalem.* As William Shirer reflected in 1960 in the foreword to his phenomenally popular 1,400-page history of the Third Reich: "In our new age of terrifying, lethal gadgets ... the first great aggressive war, if it should come, will be launched by suicidal little madmen pressing an electronic button. Such a war will not last long and none will ever follow it. There will be no conquerors and no conquests, but only the charred bones of the dead on an uninhabited planet."[34]

* * *

On July 17, 1964, watching television at home on the second day of the Harlem riots, Ginzburg watched Barry Goldwater accept the Republican presidential nomination in San Francisco. He was alarmed at what he heard. Goldwater saw the violence around him as signs of impending American collapse in the face of communism, and he was prepared to intensify rather than abandon the fight. "Tonight there is violence in our streets," Goldwater said in his acceptance speech.

> The growing menace in our country tonight, to personal safety, to life, to limb and property, in homes, in churches, on the playgrounds, and places of business, particularly in our great cities, is the mounting concern, or should be, of every thoughtful citizen in the United States.
>
> Security from domestic violence, no less than from foreign aggression, is the most elementary and fundamental purpose of any government, and a government that cannot fulfill this purpose is one that cannot long command the loyalty of its citizens.

History, said Goldwater, "demonstrates that nothing – nothing prepares the way for tyranny more than the failure of public officials to keep the streets from bullies and marauders." Members of the media, while covering the convention with a new intensity, were uneasy nonetheless. Some did not feel safe. Earlier in the week, former president Dwight Eisenhower had made a pointed attack on "sensation-seeking columnists and commentators." Some delegates and onlookers responded by shaking their fists at television anchormen and reporters who were present in the convention hall.

Goldwater mentioned civil rights only glancingly, by referring to "false notions" about equality. As his remedy for America's social ills, he emphasized the need to protect liberty by curbing government. And the United States had to be less timid in foreign affairs. Above all, said Goldwater, the United States had to fight collectivism and communism.

Goldwater had made inflammatory statements throughout the campaign, but on this evening he reached a new level of drama. From the platform, Goldwater uttered a memorable phrase, which he had underlined for emphasis: "*Extremism in the defense of liberty is no vice. Moderation in the pursuit of justice is no virtue.*"[35]

Liberals and civil rights activists were frightened by the speech and quickly mobilized. The *Chicago Defender*, a leading black newspaper that already viewed Goldwater's style as "demagoguery," said fascism was now oozing its way into the mainstream. But the phrase itself backfired even among Republicans. Former president Dwight Eisenhower summoned Goldwater for an explanation. Richard Nixon said he felt "almost physically sick as I sat there" and concluded that Goldwater had lost the election "that night with that speech." Some of Goldwater's staff also objected to the statement about extremism. Former Brooklyn Dodger Jackie Robinson, a Republican who had supported Nixon in 1960, wrote a column with the headline "Hitlerism is reborn."[36]

Incumbent Lyndon Johnson, coolly sizing up his election strategy after the speech, was not unhappy. He thought Democrats might be vulnerable if the election focused on civil rights. But playing on fears of Goldwater's impulsiveness, he recognized, would be a winning strategy. Other Democrats, more fearful than Johnson, quickly detected what California governor Pat Brown termed "the stench of fascism" in the speech. Norman Mailer, who was sizing up Goldwater in San Francisco, believed Goldwater could win and was appalled. In addition to feeling disgust for Goldwater, Mailer was thrilled by the prospect of playing an opposition role in what might be a coming age of totalitarianism and war: "For if Goldwater were President, a new opposition would form, an underground – the time for secret armies might be near again."[37]

The morning after the speech, in the *Fact* offices, Ginzburg conferred with his managing editor, Warren Boroson. In the aftermath of the convention, most reporters were bewildered by Goldwater and the new right. Ginzburg put his feelings more directly. "Warren," he said, "you know, I am scared because this guy does not seem all right." Boroson thought Goldwater was "out of his mind" and suggested a psychological profile. As the 29-year-old Boroson envisioned it, the profile would focus on Goldwater's reported history of nervous breakdowns and on his personality problems. Perhaps they could interview a few psychiatrists. Ginzburg liked the idea but was thinking bigger: "Why not poll every psychiatrist in the country?"[38]

Fact seemed to Ginzburg the ideal vehicle for the story. Ginzburg himself felt that the "well being and preservation of humanity" were at stake; his motive was "to bring public attention to the emotional instability of a man who would have the destiny of civilization under his control." He could not think of a more important task than determining if his and the public's anxieties about Goldwater were justified. In Ginzburg's view, *Fact* could play an important role in stopping the madness.

Ginzburg and Boroson divided up responsibilities. Boroson would walk the few blocks to the New York Public Library and find whatever he could in the public record on Goldwater's personality. Ginzburg, meanwhile, would conduct the survey to determine psychiatrists' views on Goldwater's psychological fitness for the presidency.[39]

* * *

The survey took shape quickly. Ginzburg obtained a mailing list of 12,356 psychiatrists that he told Boroson had come from the American Medical Association (AMA).[40] Ginzburg had not contacted the AMA directly, but had obtained the list from the Clark O'Neil Company, a firm that rented lists of AMA members to others. The survey – which consisted entirely of one question – was typed and ready to go by the end of July.

On July 24, Ginzburg put the *Fact* survey in the mail. "Do you think that Barry Goldwater is psychologically fit to serve as President of the United States?" it asked. There were only two possible answers, "no" or "yes"; the "no" option was listed first. To introduce the survey, Ginzburg wrote a cover letter that went out over Boroson's signature. The letter asked for comments on whether Goldwater "is stable enough to serve" and called attention to what it labeled Goldwater's potential aggressiveness, his callousness to the needy, his "public temper-tantrums," and his "occasional outbursts of profanity." Ginzburg and Boroson took the fact of two nervous breakdowns for granted (they had seen an article on Goldwater by Alvin Toffler that reported the breakdowns) and asked this leading question: "Finally, do you think that his having had two nervous breakdowns has any bearing on his fitness to govern this country?" Respondents were encouraged to supply additional comments.[41]

By the second week in August, most of the replies were in. Ginzburg and Boroson had received 2,417 responses, a number that Ginzburg thought was meaningful. Of the 2,417 psychiatrists who answered the survey, 571 said they did not have enough information to answer, 657 thought Goldwater was psychologically fit, and 1,189 thought he was not (these raw numbers represented 24 percent, 27 percent, and 49 percent of the survey responses, respectively). *Fact* later trumpeted the figure of

1,189 on its cover, with an exclamation point and without further context. In addition to the numbers, Ginzburg now had a wealth of individual comments to work with; he would eventually include 163 excerpts in the published version.[42]

Ginzburg could be pleased with the list of distinguished names he could show off. Jerome Frank, head of psychiatry at Johns Hopkins, was a valued teacher who had trained at Harvard and studied with distinguished psychiatrist Adolf Meyer; he would be involved in the burgeoning civil rights and antinuclear movements. But some of the responses were so strong that they concerned Ginzburg. He consulted attorney Sidney Dickstein of Dickstein, Shapiro, and Calligan, a Washington, DC, firm that had recently won a high-profile case against the New York Stock Exchange. Dickstein advised him to secure permission to quote any response by name, especially if the opinion expressed was strong. Based on his consultation with Dickstein, Ginzburg considered that he had permission to quote any response that *Fact* received. However, he did try to reach any respondent whose name he planned to use. Using this standard of consent, at Dickstein's advice he marked as "anonymous" any strong response from a psychiatrist who could not be reached.[43]

With the election approaching, Ginzburg felt strongly that time and space were limited. The survey responses were so numerous, so long, and so repetitious that they would require some management.[44] Using different colored pencils and crayons, he condensed some responses to heighten their effect, added words, and "rearranged sentences."[45] Sometimes, he acknowledged, he had even "conflated" two separate letters and presented them as one.[46] The procedure strongly resembled what he had done in *100 Years of Lynchings* – and it is quite possible that Ginzburg was emboldened by his success there. He saw these changes as fair and as within the scope of his valid role as editor. More than once Ginzburg said that his changes "made the point stronger" than they were in the original, but he also believed the changes were true to the spirit of the original. The result was a powerful if oversimplified and overdramatized set of responses.[47]

Thanks to the vigilance of several of its members, the APA got wind of the survey before it was published. The APA's medical director wrote to

Ginzburg and objected to the survey as invalid. The APA's responses are proudly quoted even today on the organization's website:

> "[S]hould you decide to publish the results of a purported 'survey' of psychiatric opinion on the question you have posed, the Association will take all possible measures to disavow its validity," wrote APA Medical Director Walter Barton, M.D., in a letter to the magazine's editors on October 1, 1964.
>
> APA President Daniel Blain, M.D., denounced the compilation as "a hodge-podge of the personal political opinions of selected psychiatrists speaking as individuals. . . . [T]he replies to the question have no scientific or medical validity whatsoever."
>
> Tying political partisanship to the psychiatric profession, continued Blain, "has, in effect, administered a low blow to all who would work to advance the treatment and care of the mentally ill of America."

Ginzburg read Barton's letter but decided not to print it in the issue. Feeling that space was limited, he dramatically wrote "Kill" at the bottom of the sheet that contained Barton's letter.[48]

* * *

As the survey took shape, Boroson and Ginzburg undertook their own evaluation of Goldwater's mental health. Their psychological profile, "Goldwater: The Man and the Menace," would appear as the lead article in the special issue "The Unconscious of a Conservative." The title of the piece was a play on the title of Goldwater's own book *The Conscience of a Conservative*, which was selling well and was in the hands of many young Republicans in 1964. Boroson and Ginzburg started the article "right after the convention" in August and finished it in early September.[49] The freewheeling article drew not on the survey results or on original research, but on published sources that were already available. The piece also depended on, and would ultimately test, a new standard of permissiveness about freedom of expression.

The permissiveness was new and still untested. In January 1964, just days after Goldwater announced his candidacy, the Warren Supreme Court heard arguments in a case that would change American libel law dramatically. In many respects, *New York Times* v. *Sullivan* began as a civil rights case. In 1960, the *Times* had published an advertisement written and paid for by a civil rights group that supported Martin Luther King; King had been indicted in Alabama for alleged perjury in connection with his state tax returns. The ad, signed by former baseball player Jackie Robinson, singer Harry Belafonte, former first lady Eleanor Roosevelt, and many others, praised civil rights protesters for affirming "the right to live in human dignity." When the ad mentioned hostile actions taken by Southern officials in Montgomery, Alabama, however, it got some of the facts wrong. L. B. Sullivan, the commissioner for public affairs in Montgomery, believed the ad referred to him, and he sued for libel.

Parallel lawsuits by the governor of Alabama, the mayor of Montgomery, and the current and former city commissioner of Montgomery dramatized the potential cost to the *Times* of publishing any reporting on the civil rights movement. Before *Sullivan*, the Supreme Court viewed false and defamatory statements as "completely outside the purview of the First Amendment," an approach that caused difficulty for the press. Traditional libel law in America had also included a notion called "seditious libel," a charge that could be brought when citizens made false statements against government officials. In this traditional framework, the burden of proof had rested with the accused. Libel law in Commonwealth countries has traditionally retained many aspects of this tradition, which is hostile to the idea that defamatory statements on public matters should be protected – unless the defendant can prove the statements are true. Before 2013, when British and Welsh law was partially reformed, libel suits were expensive to defend, and plaintiffs won as many as 70–95 percent of them. These are the same barriers that defendants in the United States faced before *Sullivan* – and that led the ACLU and others in 1964 to support the *New York Times* in *Sullivan*. The ACLU argued that laws allowing liability for inadvertent errors about public officials had a "chilling effect," especially on dissenting voices, and should be replaced by a standard of "actual malice."

In *Sullivan*, decided in March 1964, the Supreme Court overthrew the doctrine of seditious libel and adopted actual malice as the new standard for libel judgments. Actual malice – a confusingly phrased standard best understood as reckless or flagrant *disregard* of the truth rather than as malicious intent – now had to be established.[50] Significantly, with *Sullivan* the burden of proof shifted to the public official who had allegedly been wronged.

Justice William Brennan articulated in *Sullivan* what he and a unanimous Court saw as the "central meaning" in the First Amendment: a "profound national commitment to the principle that debate on public issues should be uninhibited, robust, and wide-open." This ringing expression of principle was followed by the Court's clear recognition that such debate "may well include vehement, caustic, and sometimes unpleasantly sharp attacks on government and public officials."

This was not all. Three of the nine Supreme Court justices – Hugo Black, William O. Douglas, and Arthur Goldberg – said they would have gone even further in protecting speech. For Black, joined by Douglas, the First and Fourteenth Amendments gave the *Times* an "absolute, unconditional constitutional right to publish" criticism of the Montgomery officials. Goldberg echoed this language in his concurrence, finding an "absolute, unconditional privilege to criticize official conduct" – again, regardless of the "harm which may flow from excesses and abuses." Legal historian Samantha Barbas says that *Sullivan* "was immediately recognized as a landmark case, the most important First Amendment decision of the twentieth century, if not all time."

Ginzburg, then, had every reason to be heartened by the permissive state of libel law in late 1964, when he asked Warren Boroson to do research and write a draft article about Goldwater's personality.[51]

* * *

Boroson's work at the New York Public Library and the New York Academy of Medicine unearthed many published pieces about his subject. These included articles from the *New York Times, Time* magazine, and the *New Republic* as well as books on Goldwater's military service and on the campaign. Boroson underlined key passages in the sources he considered most relevant, drafted early versions of the piece, and then passed the material along to Ginzburg. Ginzburg then reviewed Boroson's information, especially the underlined passages, and revised the draft accordingly.[52]

But it was in investigating why people affiliate with political parties that Boroson found what he said was his most important source of understanding: *The Authoritarian Personality* (1950). This influential if methodologically imperfect study by philosopher Theodore Adorno, psychologist Daniel Levinson, and others loosely affiliated with the social critics of the Frankfurt School (formally known as the Institute for Social Research), had grown from a sense of shock that Germans could have come to support Hitler in the 1930s. The concern and the search for future prevention were widely shared. Erich Fromm, an early participant in the Frankfurt School, delineated the social and psychological roots of authoritarianism in a 1930s project. Fromm saw the sadomasochistic character as a key factor in how families perpetuate deference to authority.

The Authoritarian Personality itself wove together a largely unacknowledged Marxism with innovative Freudian thinking, seeming to carefully avoid any discussion of the Soviet Union or Stalin. Adorno et al. tried to understand the social roots of authoritarianism – specifically, prejudice and anti-Semitism, much as Fromm had. But the project's methods were more varied than Fromm's had been, and its contributors were at least sometimes divided about its approach. The project tried to integrate several diverse research methods, including the methods of individual psychology (clinical interviews, projective tests), of social science (survey and quantitative measurement), and of social and psychoanalytic theory. Its subjects were not overt fascists but Americans whom the authors studied for their potential to support fascism. These were mostly found in convenient-to-study settings such as labor unions, suburbs, and college campuses.

Adorno et al. gave a complex portrait of some personality types, including the syndrome that "comes closest to the over-all picture of the high scorer as it stands out throughout our study": the authoritarian. These individuals, according to Adorno, typically have difficult relations with their fathers, struggle with sadistic and punitive trends as a result, and need to direct their conscious hatred outward onto Jews, "Negroes," and other purportedly dangerous minority groups who must under no circumstances be pitied. Reading Adorno at the New York Academy of Medicine, Boroson was struck by the "extraordinary similarity" he saw between Adorno's prototypical authoritarian and the personality of Barry Goldwater. As he later said about his insight:

> The basic conclusion [Adorno et al.] reached was that the authoritarian personality is a person that did not sufficiently identify with his father, that

his father was remote and distant as a child [*sic*], and, consequently, these people grew up having an ideal of masculinity which was beyond their reach … throughout their lives they would have to appear as tough as possible, and they couldn't allow themselves to sympathize with anybody who was weak; they would sympathize with big business, with the military, and they would not sympathize with minority groups or labor unions or anybody or anything that was considered weak, because this would threaten their picture of themselves.

Boroson, who had what he called a "crippled hand" that gave him a 4 F status, might have understood something about perceived weakness. For years, he had sought out psychological topics to write about. As a summa cum laude undergraduate at Columbia University, he had read Freud, Karen Horney, and Harry Stack Sullivan with interest and may have encountered Adorno's work there or during extensive later reading in psychoanalysis. Boroson knew works by Karl and William Menninger, Otto Fenichel, Melanie Klein, and Erik Erikson, and in 1964, he was studying several efforts in psychobiography. In his view, Freud's study of Dostoevsky, Erikson's *Young Man Luther*, and Arnold Rogow's recently published study of James Forrestal were all valid efforts. The Ginzburg archives contain copies of *The Authoritarian Personality* and Erikson's *Childhood and Society*.[53]

At least two extensive drafts of the "Goldwater: The Man and the Menace" piece survive. Both are typed, with handwritten corrections that appear to be in two different hands. One draft, which in its current form is the rougher and more fragmentary of the two, constructs a basic biography of Goldwater from a psychological point of view; it briefly mentions Freud, Daniel Levinson, Theodore Adorno, and other scholars. In this apparent first draft, Warren Boroson, with input from *Fact*'s research associate Rosemary Latimore, was fitfully developing the idea that Goldwater suffered from an authoritarian personality.[54]

The second draft of "The Man and the Menace" is the more coherent and polished of the two. It includes a more extensive discussion of personality theory and fascism, and bombastically describes Adorno's work and impact:

> I refer to a book that burst like a firebomb upon the academic community
> when it appeared in 1950, a book that in its intellectual repercussions has
> become the *Origin of Species* of the 20th century and that in the number
> of M.A. and Ph.D. theses it has inspired has even begun to rival *Moby Dick* –
> *The Authoritarian Personality.*

Much of this second draft is so broad that it comes off as caricature; it is
certainly not as lucid as the description of his intent that Boroson calmly
provided later. But it now quotes directly from Adorno and cites page
numbers conscientiously. His thoughts were coming together. Clearly
inspired by what Boroson sees as Adorno's effort to profile "potential
Fascists," he lists as typical attributes of the authoritarian personality
"ignorant," "confused," "sneaking admiration for Nazi Germany," and
"anal character traits."[55]

Freud had described the anal character as marked by orderliness,
parsimony, and obstinance. Freud's concept remained influential even
as psychoanalysts widened his individual focus to include considerations
of personality and culture. The concept of the anal-sadistic character still
commanded respectful discussion in leading textbooks of psychoanalytic
psychiatry in the 1950s. In the 1930s in Germany, Erich Fromm made use
of the idea of anal character in trying to understand vulnerability to
Fascism; once in America, he understood the sadomasochistic character
less in terms of anal eroticism and more in terms of authority issues.
Erikson, in his cautious psychosocial revisionism, continued to relate
body zones to personality development and maintained a certain allegiance to Freud while also moving the field forward. Erikson's work on
culture and oral and anal character inspired work by anthropologist
Margaret Mead, who was much favored in psychiatric journals of the
1940s and 1950s.[56]

According to Boroson's reading of Adorno, the potential fascist fears
his tyrannical father, identifies with his mother instead, and consequently
is forever uneasy about his masculinity. (These themes, as we have seen,
were also traced by Walter Langer in his profile of Hitler for the OSS.) He
"continually contends," Boroson summarizes, "against a deep-seated
desire to give up the never-ending struggle to prove himself a man" and
against a longing to yield passively, "like a homosexual, before all men."

The authoritarian personality, the second draft concludes, "can actually be summed up in just three words: *Barry Morris Goldwater.*"[57]

While much of the drafts are crude and provisional, they clearly locate Boroson and Ginzburg within postwar intellectuals' anguished effort to understand and grapple with the legacy of the Third Reich. The discussion was not limited to Adorno. John Hersey's *Hiroshima* (1946), Hannah Arendt's *Origins of Totalitarianism* (1951), and Norman Cousins's writing and lobbying against the atomic bomb in the 1940s and 1950s set many of the terms for this discussion. Erikson's *Childhood and Society* (1950), though more wide-ranging, contains a significant chapter on Hitler's appeal to German youth – and in 1963 had just appeared on college campuses in a wildly popular revised edition. Psychologically informed history, especially in the hands of someone as sophisticated as Erikson, seemed to Boroson and Ginzburg a promising tool in the armamentarium.

It would be easy to overstate the intellectual importance or even the lucidity of the drafts of "The Man and the Menace." But in comparison with the published version, the drafts do contain scattered passages that at least aim at moral sophistication. Boroson's hasty first draft offers this reflection:

> To understand all is not to pardon all, nor is to understand all to condemn all. Saints may do noble things because of their intensive guilt feelings; pacificists [*sic*] may ha[v]e ho[m]oerotic feelings toward others. ... [Goldwater] should better be judged on his viewpoints toward peace, toward dignity, toward the better development of human beings everywhere.

But as the paragraph continues, a more simplistic drift takes over and ultimately becomes all too evident: "on this score, the record seems to show how [*sic*] that his election may [v]ery well prove the single most greatest catastrophe in the history of civilization." The raw fear in evidence here was acknowledged later by Boroson, who recalled that he worried about Goldwater using nuclear weapons and said: "I thought he was suicidal." Ginzburg believed that "with the world today teetering on the brink of nuclear devastation," other issues dwindled into insignificance.[58]

As for ethical considerations, the first draft shows more sensitivity than the published profile. As Boroson and Ginzburg found their way into their topic, they tried to anticipate objections and address them. Here, complete with their idiosyncratic abbreviations and typographic errors, are their fragmentary early thoughts:

> Is it unethical to try to puse [use] psychology on a living person? publicly [*sic*]? In this case at hand, i [*sic*] think it is not only ethical but advisable. Barry Goldwater is attempting to guide the world to – any presid[ential] man who takes upon himself to guide the lives and destinies of other men should be willing to be studied in detail, and among his qualifications is his personality. It is quite as justifiable to [*sic*] for a politicalscientist [*sic*] to write about G's political views as it is for a psychologist to attempt to probe his personality dynamics. Irresponsible psychological [*sic*] profiles will [*sic*] could be one result, but irresponsibility is always possible. In a free society the reader will have to pick and choose.

Here Boroson and Ginzburg adopt the view, also entertained by others in later years, that by entering the political arena, a public figure loses some of his right to privacy. They emphasize, in the tradition of the Supreme Court's *Sullivan* decision, that debate in a free society is the best forum for ideas and opinions to be tested. In *Sullivan,* Justice Brennan had identified a "profound national commitment to the principle that debate on public issues should be uninhibited, robust, and wide-open." Probing for some resolution, the draft considers the argument that it is ethically sounder to wait until the subject's death before writing a profile. But finally it implies that by then, the entire world population may be dead too, presumably as a result of Goldwater's approach to the use of nuclear weapons.[59]

As they prepared the profile, Ginzburg and Boroson aimed for maximum publicity. Boroson sent a letter to Walter Reuther, onetime socialist and founder and president of the United Automobile Workers (UAW) labor union. Reuther never replied, but Boroson had done his homework. In 1958, Senator Goldwater had targeted Reuther at hearings of the Senate Rackets Committee (Senate Select Committee on Improper Activities in the Labor or Management Field). Questioned aggressively by Goldwater about union activities, Reuther defended himself capably. Even before the hearings the two had sparred: Goldwater charged Reuther with socialism and Reuther called Goldwater "mentally unbalanced." As Boroson knew, Reuther was likely to agree with most of the psychiatrists in the *Fact* survey. Goldwater, Reuther said in 1958, "needs a psychiatrist."[60]

Erik Erikson is not mentioned directly in "The Man and the Menace," but his presence was felt at *Fact*. Boroson said he read Erikson's *Young Man Luther* as he was preparing the draft, and his description of the book suggests that he used it as a model for his formulations. For example, Boroson understood Erikson as saying that Luther "had paranoid tendencies and that he was an anal personality." While this is not a sophisticated summary of Erikson's thinking, paranoia and anality are the traits that Boroson and Ginzburg emphasized in their profile of Goldwater. But there is more. As Boroson was preparing the profile, he phoned Erikson in Cambridge, and the two discussed Boroson's hypothesis that Goldwater's personality could be understood as authoritarian in Adorno's sense. According to Boroson, Erikson cautiously deemed his hypothesis "reasonable." Erikson, then a popular lecturer at Harvard and at the height of his fame, was likely no fan of Goldwater. Further, Ginzburg was widely seen on the left as a victim of censorship and may have been sympathetic. Boroson, an attentive student of psychoanalysis, had clearly done his homework and had much admiration for Erikson; the Columbia graduate may have come across as earnest and responsible.[61]

Boroson finished what he called his "research draft" and gave it to Ginzburg by late August 1964. By then, public perception of Goldwater as dangerous was growing. According to Gallup polls in August, voters thought the Democrats were "more likely to keep the United States out of World War III" – by a two-to-one margin. Ginzburg, with his keen sense of marketing and promotion, understood where things were headed. Almost none of Boroson's relatively sophisticated material – on Adorno, on Erikson, or on the ethics of comment from a distance – made its way into the published profile. Ginzburg kept some material on the authoritarian personality and defended the concept, leaving in place one brief reference from Adorno on the paranoid person's tendency to personalize events. But according to Boroson, Ginzburg rewrote his draft "substantially," placing heavier emphasis on Goldwater's paranoia and reducing the emphasis on Adorno's thinking. The emotional impact of Ginzburg's simplified version was greater than that of Boroson's: the published version took an even more alarmist approach, emphasizing nuclear war and downplaying any nuanced psychological thinking. Boroson was correct to regard his draft as more sophisticated than the version Ginzburg published; his claim is supported by the evidence of the drafts of the article.[62]

As Boroson revealed only after Ginzburg's death, he was so upset over Ginzburg's changes to the article that he abruptly resigned from *Fact* after the special issue appeared and demanded that Ginzburg remove his name from "The Man and the Menace." Ginzburg, he said, had not even shown him the final version. Disillusioned, Boroson continued to write on occasion for Ginzburg but ultimately concluded that he was fundamentally a marketer rather than a journalist. This is not entirely inconsistent with Ginzburg's own self-assessment that he was a serious and idealistic publisher intent on confuting society's hypocrisy – but also a "hustler."[63]

* * *

The published article's main points, hammered home flamboyantly but with some quotes and page citations for support, were clear. Goldwater was mentally unstable; he had childhood conflicts with his effeminate father; he was close to his mother; he had married a weak woman; he showed a streak of cruelty that raised the possibility of sadism and an anal personality; he was uncomfortable with his masculinity and his half-Jewishness. He was also paranoid and prone to attacking others, in several respects strongly resembling Adolf Hitler. In most particulars, these points all map onto Boroson's use of Adorno. Ginzburg made use of the many sources Boroson cited, but the guiding theory has been largely removed from the article. A portion of the opening paragraph captures Ginzburg's ominous yet flippant tone:

> In Goldwater's candidacy on a major party ticket, she [America] faces the
> possibility of electing a President whose grasp of international affairs

matches Harding's, whose personality traits are reminiscent of Forrestal's and McCarthy's, and who is backed by a well-organized, blindly ruthless, totalitarian, secretive, and powerful movement.

The tone of the published version is distinctly different from Boroson's typically more serious note of concern for the future. The final paragraph of the article sounds the Hitler note in the following way: "If it sounds like the death-fantasy of another paranoiac woven in Berchtesgaden and realized in a Berlin bunker not long ago, it is no surprise." If Ginzburg did not quite lead with the recognition of "humanity's capacity for evil," as many postwar liberals did, he at least thought he knew where evil was located and thought he saw how history might repeat itself in the United States.[64]

Ginzburg himself, though not a professional, had a long-standing interest in psychological issues. He had taken two psychology courses in college and, like Boroson, described much reading in the field. He clearly knew the language of psychoanalysis at least at a basic level (e.g., Freud's concept of the anal character), and he considered the *Fact* issue a venture in "applied psychoanalysis." The *Fact* cover letter of 1964 emphasized that "the mental stability of a Presidential candidate is of legitimate concern to everyone, especially in this nuclear age"; the magazine later sought to publish questions about the mental stability of Lyndon Johnson, George Wallace, and Republican candidate George Romney. In his research on Goldwater, Boroson had spoken with Erik Erikson, had sent a copy of his draft to psychologist Daniel Levinson, and had consulted a friend who was enrolled in a PhD program in psychology. As he reworked Boroson's draft, Ginzburg did not feel the need to consult a professional.[65]

In some ways Ginzburg's style was systematic and detailed. His daughter Lark recalled that her father liked to plan and organize; she told me that his office files were tidy and carefully numbered throughout, a point that I confirmed in the Ginzburg archives. Ginzburg's daughter Bonnie, a journalist herself, similarly recalls Ginzburg's files as "meticulously organized" and Ginzburg himself as "rigorously thorough as an editor and writer." Indeed, a later memo to his attorney shows that Ginzburg could pay scrupulous attention to detail in proofreading. Lark Ginzburg recalls: "He cared a great deal about getting things right. He had a dictionary, *Roget's Thesaurus,* and *The Elements of Style* by our dinner table for reference as his children learned to express themselves." Ginzburg would often say, "Let's look it up." But to others, Ginzburg could appear dramatic and impatient. In his memos to himself and to his staff, he habitually typed out his thoughts in capital letters or scrawled comments in a large, cursive script. Siebert, who worked for him later, remembers him "talking loudly and smartly about everything." Sitting at the typesetting machine entering ad copy, Siebert recalled, Ginzburg would "intone" his sentences aloud "as he thought of them" and explain his choices of language as he typed.

In 1964, under pressure of time, believing he was within his role as editor, Ginzburg edited his sources freely. In one instance, working over "Goldwater: The Man and the Menace," Ginzburg saw that Boroson had quoted from a *Time* magazine article. The original included a sentence saying that Goldwater had a poor record during his first year in a military academy but that at graduation he wore a medal as the school's outstanding cadet. Moving quickly, Ginzburg quoted only the first half of the sentence.[66]

* * *

The final product, termed "The Unconscious of a Conservative: A Special Issue on the Mind of Barry Goldwater," appeared in oversized paper-bound form and was designed in sleek type in black and white by Herb Lubalin. Freewheeling cartoons by Rick Schreiter appeared throughout and underlined the Cold War themes of impulsive aggression and world destruction. In many ways, these cartoons set the tone for the issue. In one of Schreiter's black-and-white cartoons, an officious-looking Goldwater is seen astride a phallic missile that is traveling through the air; in another, he is depicted as a cowboy with an evil smile on his face and a hydrogen bomb in his hand: the "fastest draw in the West," says the caption. Comic books and editorial cartoons had long served as a vehicle for the exploration of popular anxieties: here, about masculinity and world destruction. In 1962, the year of the Cuban Missile Crisis, Marvel Comics debuted *The Incredible Hulk* and *Spiderman,* both timid men who are transformed into hypermasculine superheroes by exposure to radiation.[67]

In the published issue, Ginzburg and Boroson's 19-page "Goldwater: The Man and the Menace" appeared first, under Ginzburg's name; its first page was presented alongside a full-page Schreiter illustration showing a close-up of a creepily smiling Goldwater. "What Psychiatrists Say about Goldwater" followed. It occupied the largest part of the September–October issue and showcased 40 pages of brief excerpts from the survey. Each comment was followed by the psychiatrist's name and address, except where Ginzburg substituted "anonymous" or "name withheld." The excerpts had been compiled by Ginzburg; a brief three-paragraph discussion of method preceded the excerpts over Boroson's byline, without any discussion of ethical questions. As he had in the article, Ginzburg ran a full-page Schreiter cartoon of Goldwater at the head of the section that excerpted survey responses. This time the inside of Goldwater's head was revealed, in the style of nineteenth-century phrenology diagrams of the human brain. Outwardly the would-be counterrevolutionary Goldwater sneered and stuck out his tongue, while the diagram showed the various sections of his head: "combativity," "destructiveness," "shortsightedness," or just "empty."[68]

The balance of the excerpts was hostile to Goldwater. One of the most dramatic comments, from a California psychiatrist, was placed early in the selection and ran as follows: "I believe Goldwater has the same pathological make-up as Hitler, Castro, Stalin and other known schizophrenic leaders." A New York psychiatrist said: "B.G. is in my opinion emotionally unstable, immature, volatile, unpredictable, hostile, and mentally unbalanced. He is totally unfit for public office and a menace to society." And another: "I consider Barry Goldwater unstable and dangerous." Many implied, and some said outright, that Goldwater was too dangerous to be president in an age of nuclear weapons.

It did not escape the respondents' attention that Goldwater (like Ginzburg) had Jewish ancestry. According to one psychiatrist, "Barry Goldwater's mental instability stems from the fact that his father was a Jew while his mother was a Protestant. . . . He cannot feel at home in either group." Another saw Goldwater as denying the Jewish part of his heritage and therefore complicit in causing Jewish suffering. The respondents who articulated these views could well have been familiar with Adorno et al., who investigated hostility toward minority groups (especially Jews) as well as inner conflict on the subject. The respondents may well have articulated these views spontaneously, but to some extent the excerpts also paralleled themes that Ginzburg and Boroson had highlighted in "The Man and the Menace." It is possible that Ginzburg chose them for that reason.

Hostile sexual implications were also evident in the responses. A small but vocal number of psychiatrists emphasized what they saw as Goldwater's discomfort with his own masculinity. Though the psychiatrists had not seen Boroson's article, here too they may well have drawn on a common stock of psychoanalytic assumptions derived from Adorno and others in the broader stream of clinical psychoanalysis itself. One who believed Goldwater would be militant and impulsive in office explained:

> To me Senator Goldwater appears an angry, frightened, intemperate man, whose speeches and public remarks have sadistic overtones. Descriptions of his early life that I have read indicate to me that his mother assumed the masculine role in his family background. My impression was that she was domineering and considerably lacking in her ability to provide affection and interest in her children. The picture, therefore, is of a domineering, emasculating mother and a somewhat withdrawn, passive, narcissistic father. It would appear that Barry had a stronger identification with his mother than with his father. This would provide a fertile background for sado-masochistic temperament, such as is seen in paranoid states.
>
> *[Name withheld], M.D. Reading, Pa.*

"The Man and the Menace" had made the case that Goldwater's father was a dandy and that his mother was masculine.[69]

The insinuation that Goldwater was uncomfortable with his manhood and identified with his mother carried a strong implication of possible homosexuality. Such implications had a special intensity at the time. Dagmar Herzog has argued that in the years after World War II, many psychoanalysts worldwide were converging on the belief that homosexuality was abnormal, but that American psychoanalysis was particularly homophobic. What Herzog calls the "uninterrogated assumptions" about homosexuality probably informed Ginzburg and Boroson's portrayal. In 1964, five years before the Stonewall Riots, homosexuality was still considered a mental disorder by the American Psychiatric Association; homosexual behavior was a crime under the laws of New York State. Even as Ginzburg and Boroson were compiling their issue, Mayor Robert Wagner was trying to improve New York's City's image for the 1964 World's Fair by entrapping and arresting gay New Yorkers. More than one historian has argued that the Cold War accelerated fears of public softness (including femininity) and promoted toughness as an alternative. Anything less was "soft and feminine and, as such, a real or potential threat to the security of the nation." Stabile notes that a particular kind of masculinity – involving what she sees as bullying and intolerance of disagreement, but in the service of protecting the country – informed the anticommunist movement during the Cold War. The image can be seen best in the "G-Man," the FBI's public face during this period. Though Ginzburg would likely have been repulsed by the hypermasculine G-Men, he seems to have shared a quasi-psychiatric view of homosexuality, at least in its repressed form, as problematic.[70]

Journalist and ethicist Meredith Levine has carefully quantified the use of insults in the special issue. She found that in "The Man and the Menace" there are 68 references to stated or implied mental illness and breakdown in general. Paranoia, emphasized in Ginzburg's revisions to Boroson, tops Levine's list of specific conditions at a hefty 27 references. The published version referred six to eight times each to delusional thinking, depression, suicidality, Jewish ethnicity, uneasiness about manhood, and similarity to Hitler. These numbers strikingly parallel those in "What Psychiatrists Say about Goldwater."[71]

Ginzburg did allow dissenting voices to appear in the sample. A few psychiatrists who did not know Goldwater said he seemed quite mature or otherwise mentally healthy; one who did know him personally said he was in no way "out of touch with reality." One pointed out that Lincoln had also been accused of mental illness, a point that might have been sobering if taken seriously. Another thought in political terms and predicted that Goldwater would moderate his extreme statements once in office, as politicians often do. And there were a number of protests, highlighted rather than suppressed by Ginzburg, that the whole venture was unethical:

> Your inquiry for a professional opinion regarding Senator Barry
> Goldwater's general mental instability is an insult to me. An inquiry of
> this type regarding any individual can only be based on ignorance of the
> field of psychiatry. No specialist could render such an opinion about
> anyone without personal examination.

Despite these minority voices, the cumulative impact of the issue is
powerful. The experience is one of immersion in a chaotic conversation,
of overhearing hundreds of opinionated experts having a vigorous conversation in which a common theme is mental illness, danger, and unfitness for office in the atomic age – and in which the anti-Goldwater side
wins out.[72]

It seems clear that the Cold War shaped the tone of fear and urgency in
the special issue. At the end of "Goldwater: The Man and the Menace," on
the last page of the issue, a cartoon mushroom cloud appears – giving
ominous if not very subtle meaning to the issue's final bold-type words,
"**the End.**" The cartoon is reminiscent of the last scene of Stanley Kubrik's
film *Doctor Strangelove*, released in early 1964. In that scene, the world is
destroyed in an orgy of nuclear warfare, in part due to the wild and paranoid
(and sexually twisted) beliefs of those with control of the missiles. The
presentation seemed to play both on Goldwater's unpopularity – a Gallup
poll in October showed his approval rating at only 29 percent – and on the
public's long-standing fears of nuclear war. According to polls, since the late
1950s, nuclear war had preoccupied as many as 60–75 percent of Americans;
the issue had special resonance less than two years after the Cuban Missile
Crisis. On that occasion, American ambassador Adlai Stevenson had called
missiles in Cuba an "aggressive threat to the peace," an intolerable introduction of "offensive nuclear weapons."[73]

* * *

Once the issue was complete, Ginzburg spent $80,000 or more on adver-
tisements for it. In a full-page ad that appeared in mid-September, he
promoted the issue and the survey with a provocative headline: "Is Barry
Goldwater psychologically fit to be President of the United States?" He
included a grim photograph of Goldwater. Ginzburg asked readers to
subscribe to *Fact* because of its flair and its independence:

> [*Fact*'s] sole obligation is to its readers, whom it assumes to be open-minded, intelligent adults weary of the blather that is American journalism today. ... [Subscribe] today and begin to enjoy an exciting new magazine which is dedicated to presenting the naked truth and letting all censors be damned.

Retailing at $1.25, the issue was heavily promoted in the *New York Times*, the *New York Herald-Tribune*, the *Philadelphia Inquirer*, the *Los Angeles Examiner*, and the *San Francisco Chronicle*.

On October 1, 1964, Ginzburg distributed more than 236,000 copies of his special issue for sale throughout the United States. The gauntlet had been thrown down.[74]

CHAPTER 3

"To Remove This Precedent"

Barry Goldwater Sues for Libel

A line must be drawn somewhere over which others cannot step in abusing people in this country and I hope that this case will provide the precedent for that.

Barry Goldwater, 1968[1]

The conservative movement, recent scholars have suggested, was more broad in composition and more complex in philosophy than historians once thought. Early students of the movement such as Richard Hofstadter and Daniel Bell depicted it as the work of paranoid reactionaries uncomfortable with the demands of modern life. Such depictions, along with media portrayals of conservative candidates, were resented for generations by conservative intellectuals. In fact, postwar conservativism was a complicated phenomenon. It grew not just in reaction to the New Deal and not just in the impoverished rural South, but also in prosperous middle-class suburbs in the West, where the defense industry was thriving and where antistatist views paradoxically also flourished.[2]

The figure of Barry Goldwater was central to the movement's early history and to its emergence into national prominence. Among Goldwater's many precocities was an early recognition that the law could be used actively by conservatives as well as liberals. In New York Times *v.* Sullivan *(1964), the Supreme Court had made libel suits much more difficult to win. But as Goldwater understood well in advance of his friend William F. Buckley, a libel suit could have value in protecting and consolidating his movement. He also hoped to set limits on the Warren Court's liberal activism, which was then at its peak. Ralph Ginzburg, he concluded, was a vulnerable target. As Norman Rosenberg argues, libel law often oscillates rather than moving steadily forward, reflecting power relationships and political conditions rather than timeless principles of progress.[3]*

It is not clear exactly when Barry Goldwater saw the *Fact* issue for the first time. Two weeks after the election, he said that he had not yet seen it; he asked a supporter for a copy. Theodore H. White's detailed narrative of the campaign, *The Making of the President 1964* (1965) did not even mention the magazine or its attack. Ironically, it was Goldwater's decision to bring a libel suit that brought publicity to the case and led the incident to be enshrined in the annals of journalism and conservative legend. The publicity in turn would pay political dividends. Thus the *Fact* episode fits what Corey Robin has called the core experience of conservativism: "a meditation on – and theoretical rendition of – the felt experience of having power, seeing it threatened, and trying to win it back."[4]

* * *

Twenty-seven million people voted for Barry Goldwater in 1964, a point his supporters would emphasize again and again in the coming years. A supporter signed her letter to Goldwater "One of the 27 million," and a commonly heard conservative slogan was soon "27 million Americans can't be wrong." In time, those who had worked for Goldwater would view the experience not only as formative but also as the dawn of a new era. Generations of conservatives, including future president Ronald Reagan, Chief Justice William Rehnquist, and conservative activist Phyllis Schlafly, would eventually devote themselves to public service "because of the influence of the senator." Goldwater's biographer has termed the primary campaign and the 1964 convention the "Woodstock of American Conservatism."[5]

He almost didn't run. After the assassination of John F. Kennedy, Goldwater initially feared that his supporters might be blamed. But he eventually said yes as a matter of principle. He would offer, he said, "a choice, not an echo."

Goldwater began his 1964 campaign with an inept appearance on *Meet the Press*. As William F. Buckley later ruefully observed, "in the television age everything uttered by a public figure became as of that moment public property." On the show Goldwater threatened to withdraw from the Nuclear Test Ban Treaty if it was advantageous for the United States to do so – and said he might reconsider diplomatic recognition of the

Soviet Union if it would win concessions from the Soviets. Even the *Washington Evening Star,* a prominent conservative paper, called Goldwater out for an "information gap" and an "inattention to detail and an impreciseness of utterance that could be troublesome."

According to Goldwater's biographer, supporters found his answers "candid and refreshing," but reporters found him "easy prey." Goldwater's impulsive comments regularly gave reporters a chance to run dramatic headlines, to such an extent that many felt "a little bit ashamed of picking on Barry." Yet Goldwater himself "became surly with reporters," and his provocative comments on nuclear weapons and Social Security continued to haunt him. His stand on race was so inflammatory that Dr. Martin Luther King Jr., when asked by *Playboy* which one person he would send to a desert island if he could, named Barry Goldwater.[6]

Goldwater tried to buff up his image. He hired an ad agency, but as the staff members who supervised his TV ads later admitted, they themselves lacked skill, polish, and even a basic familiarity with TV. Goldwater, conservatives often point out, rejected some proposed ads as racist. Instead he ran plodding 5–30-minute paid programs on radio and TV. Late in the campaign, Goldwater and Dwight Eisenhower took to the airways in a half-hour television special in which Eisenhower felt compelled to play down concerns about Goldwater's potential use of nuclear weapons. Ever alert to ratings, President Johnson gleefully told reporters that the Goldwater show had earned a Nielsen rating of only 8.6.[7]

Meanwhile Johnson had hired a sophisticated New York advertising agency, Doyle Dane Bernbach (DDB), to create a devastating media assault on Goldwater. The ad agency had many large Republican clients, but its management confessed to Johnson's staff that the agency was full of "ardent Democrats"; the prospect of a Goldwater victory was frightening. Doyle Dane Bernbach's "Daisy Girl" ad, which implied that Goldwater's election would lead to nuclear war, was only the most dramatic and famous of DDB's contributions. The agency also produced a TV spot that showed the eastern seaboard of the United States being sawed off and floating out to sea. This ad referred to an actual comment Goldwater had made during the campaign.[8]

Goldwater continued to sound his warnings about freedom, limited government, law and order, and the need to fight communism. In later years, these themes would inspire his followers. But by November 1964, many observers thought the campaign lacked a strategy and was merely keeping up a brave front in the face of futility. Indeed, Goldwater himself later acknowledged that he never truly thought he could win. "What remained to be settled," said reporter Theodore H. White, "was only how large, how broad, how deep would be Lyndon Johnson's sweep." Johnson was reelected by the largest popular vote ever recorded, 43 million to Goldwater's 27 million. Winning everywhere but Arizona and a handful of states in the deep South, Johnson amassed an electoral tally of 486 to Goldwater's 52.[9]

Many Democrats assumed that conservativism was finished. On the left, humor came easily. Columnist Art Buchwald agreed that the Democrats seemed poised to be the dominant party in America for a long time. Asked by *Playboy* whether he had ever thought the country was in danger from Goldwater, Buchwald said: "No, I don't think anything would have happened – except maybe by January 21 or 22, we'd all have been dead. But outside of that, I wasn't worried." Goldwater himself had a sense of humor about the loss. Back in Arizona, he told reporter David Broder that he and his wife were mostly relaxing. In a cherished anecdote, he said that "Peggy and I just [sit] on the hill, watching the sunsets, and occasionally humming to ourselves, 'Hail to the Chief.'"[10]

In reality, Goldwater was busy. He set up a basement office in his family's department store in Scottsdale, traveled, and gave many speeches for the party in Arizona. He did not wait long – only until mid-1965 – to announce that he would be a candidate for election to the Senate in 1968. Like many conservatives, he was proud that he had won for his movement the nomination of a major party and that conservativism could now be counted as part of the American mainstream. Where media issues were concerned at least, he was far from relaxed.

After the election, Goldwater unleashed a bitter tirade about the way he had been treated by the press – by which he clearly meant not the small-town papers that had backed him, but the liberal big-city press:

I'd never seen or heard in my life, such vitriolic – un-based [*sic*] attacks on one man as had been directed to me. Sometimes, they didn't spell it out. But "coward – uneducated – ungentlemanly – bigot" and all those things. I've never in my life seen such inflammatory language. .... I think these people should, frankly, hang their heads in shame. Because I think they've made the fourth estate a rather sad, sorry mess.

The sheer numbers were one issue. During the campaign, American newspapers had overwhelmingly favored Johnson: 445 papers had endorsed the Democrat, while only 368 had endorsed Goldwater. The daily circulation reflected in those endorsements stood at a combined 27.6 million for Johnson to only 9.7 million for Goldwater. Many newspapers had attacked him. However, his biographer says, *Fact*'s attack was the "most scurrilous."[11]

* * *

Once he had time available, Goldwater carefully examined the special issue of *Fact.* It is clear that once he saw it, he was upset. He later described its effect on him as "rather depressing" and emphasized that its cumulative impact was great. An individual hostile comment or two was one thing, he said, but reading page after page of vituperation weighed him down and made him feel as if he were carrying a burden of "several tons." In this way the *Fact* issue even made him doubt how the public viewed him:

> I still have the same feeling, that after having read this, and after having been defeated, which did not bother me a bit, when I walked down the street even in New York, people naturally recognized me and they smile[d]. I don't know whether they are smiling out of respect for me or friendliness or whether they are thinking there goes that queer or there goes that homosexual, or there goes that man who is afraid of masculinity.

Goldwater was testifying here about the relationship between himself and his public, a key dimension for any politician. The 1964 Republican nominee had been deprived of his Senate seat, his presidential prospects, and now his reputation. Non-introspective but wounded, Goldwater needed a way to fight back.[12]

* * *

While preparing for and recovering from minor surgery, Goldwater began systematically considering what could be done. At some point he consulted his friend William F. Buckley. Buckley, far from discouraged about Goldwater's recent loss, regarded the 1964 election as a "glorious disaster." Perspicacious as always, Buckley had already discerned the possibility that Goldwater could be viewed not as a failed candidate but as what Ronald Reagan would later call "a prophet in his own time." But, Buckley advised his friend, it would simply be "unprofitable" for Goldwater to bring a libel suit. This, he explained, was partly because the *Sullivan* decision had made libel suits so difficult to win and partly because the trial would take place in ultra-liberal New York City, the home of Goldwater's most intense critics and their "great and barbarous excesses." Ginzburg's home city, Buckley noted, had voted four to one against Goldwater.[13]

But Goldwater was undeterred. By mid-1965, he had hired Roger Robb, a prominent Washington, DC, attorney with experience in conservative causes, and had asked Robb to look into the merits of the case. Dean and Goldwater call Robb "a seasoned political observer"; in the 1950s, he had helped represent the government as special counsel in the security clearance hearing of Manhattan Project physicist J. Robert Oppenheimer. From his office in the Tower Building, a 14-story Art Deco building in Washington, DC, Robb replied to his client with a well-organized memo, carefully weighing the pros and cons of bringing suit. It was the work of a consummate professional.[14]

Goldwater had several questions for Robb. First, did they have a case? In 1965 this was not a straightforward question. *New York Times* v. *Sullivan* (1964) had only recently changed the libel landscape. As Ralph Ginzburg understood, *Sullivan* had dramatically narrowed the grounds on which public officials could bring libel suits, and those grounds still existed. The Court now allowed many kinds of false statements to be made about public officials, but it would not give protection to what *Sullivan* somewhat confusingly called "actual malice." The new standard included knowingly making false statements – what Justice Brennan called "the lie, knowingly and deliberately published about a public official" – but also, more importantly, the making of a statement with "reckless disregard of whether it was false or not." The actual malice standard could be met by lies, but recklessness also qualified.

Opinions about *Sullivan* varied, even on the conservative side. Buckley thought that Goldwater had been outrageously defamed, but he regarded *Sullivan* itself as moving "in the right direction" – that is, away from previous libel law. This alone set *Sullivan* apart from other Warren Court decisions that outraged conservatives, such as *Brown*, *Miranda* v. *Arizona*, and *Gideon* v. *Wainwright*.[15]

Goldwater did not provide an extended analysis of his views on whether *Sullivan* needed revision. During the trial, he did say that *Sullivan* "leaves open how much a man in public life can be libeled," which was not strictly true. On many occasions in his correspondence, he said he viewed himself as setting new precedent or as blocking the precedent set by Ginzburg and *Fact*. But his lawsuit did not aim to establish any new legal doctrine, merely to show that a suit could be won under *Sullivan*. While it is clear that Goldwater thought Ginzburg's actions should be challenged, he was probably rallying his supporters with this phrase. His conservative admirers, in discussing the legacy of *Goldwater* v. *Ginzburg*, also asserted that the case established "new precedent," but they specified that the precedent involved was that a public official "can prove 'actual malice.'" This operational rather than doctrinal sense is the same sense in which political scientist John Gruhl has claimed importance for the case: "This was one of the rare cases in which the plaintiff, despite having to show actual malice, was able to win the suit."[16]

Robb was well acquainted with the new standard, as was Goldwater. Robb reviewed the *Fact* issue carefully and concluded that the *Fact* allegations were "probably the most outrageous libel that I have ever seen." To Robb it was not a close call. He thought libel could be proved against *Fact* and perhaps against some of the psychiatrists whom Ginzburg quoted. Lewis Powell, a New York attorney whom Robb recruited to help on the case, agreed to help with the case from his Park Avenue office in midtown Manhattan.[17]

Was it feasible to proceed? From the determined press releases Goldwater issued, from the many letters from constituents he received and answered, and from the careful way he preserved his correspondence about the suit, it is evident that Goldwater believed there was value in bringing the suit. If he would not, who would? As a later supporter told him, the Supreme Court had made it nearly impossible for public figures to protect themselves from defamation. "You," however, "have the financial capacity and the public stature to press this case."[18]

Though he did not quite say so openly, Goldwater likely calculated that there was political advantage to be had in bringing the suit – even if he lost. Media attention in particular was there for the taking during a period when he was out of office. And indeed, the suit transformed an attack by an obscure self-financed publication into a national cause célèbre.

Examples of the suit's transforming effect may be found in letters Goldwater received from supporters during the course of the trial. Media accounts are prominently mentioned in these letters. One western supporter told Goldwater that he had never heard of the *Fact* scandal until Goldwater brought his libel suit; in 1964, that was true for many Americans. But in 1968, at the end of the district court trial, the same supporter stayed up until 5 AM waiting to hear the verdict on the radio – and writing Goldwater a warm letter of support. "You will of course be our next Senator," the writer assured him. Another correspondent confessed that he had once been a Democrat but then read a *Time* magazine article on *Goldwater* v. *Ginzburg*. Having done so, he said, "I would like to quote an old democrat [Harry Truman] – 'Give Im Hell'" [*sic*]. While Goldwater would speak of *Goldwater* v. *Ginzburg* as a battle against precedent, a public fight with an ultra-liberal New York journalist and perceived pornographer would not hurt his case with voters in Arizona or elsewhere.[19]

In character, Goldwater asked Robb for an estimate of the cost involved. The answer was not reassuring. Initially Robb estimated that a libel action would cost at least $25,000; this figure went up steadily as the case proceeded. Goldwater, who paid close attention to money, was taken aback by the figure. But he moved ahead with his assessment.

Robb coolly advised Goldwater that if he proceeded, he should be ready for the experience of seeing his family deposed and thereby "subjected to harassment." Goldwater was not fazed by this. In August 1965, he wrote to his family members, describing Ginzburg as a pornographer and making the case that the *Fact* issue was "a breach of medical ethics and political ethics and decency." No one, he said, should get away with this kind of attack. At that point Goldwater was giving fair warning to family members, including his wife, Peggy, whom Ginzburg had depicted as fragile and weepy; Goldwater wanted them to be ready. He had already instructed Robb to go ahead with the suit.[20]

* * *

In the context of the time, the charge of homosexuality was perhaps even more loaded than the charge of bigotry. The American Psychiatric Association (APA), operating under its psychoanalytically oriented diagnostic manual DSM-I (1948–52), viewed homosexuality as a psychiatric disorder. Stigma against gay and lesbian people remained great. Goldwater was clearly bothered by the insinuation in *Fact*'s "The Man and the Menace" and later confirmed that he understood it as a statement that he was "queer." (Boroson later said he did not intend what he wrote to be construed this way.) For Goldwater, the issue of homosexuality was not a passing anxiety. Since he read the *Fact* issue, he said, every time someone smiled or shook his hand, he had the nagging doubt about whether that person thought he was queer. By that point it had been at least three years, and he was shaking many hands as part of his Senate reelection bid.[21]

The issue of homosexuality was complicated politically for Goldwater, as it was for all politicians of the 1960s. Gay federal employees continued to be seen as national security risks, as they had been in the 1950s; traditional Protestant ministers preached against homosexuality; and national security and morality were two of Goldwater's signature themes. Thus when Lyndon Johnson's aide Walter Jenkins was arrested in a YMCA men's room in October 1964, Goldwater faced a dilemma. As a candidate already accused of racial bias, Goldwater could not afford to make grossly prejudiced statements himself. In his memoir, Goldwater proudly relates that when he learned of the Jenkins incident, he decided not to exploit it for political purposes, and his biographer supports his claim. Yet many important officials in the 1964 campaign did seize on the incident; it is not clear that he did anything to stop them. And he flirted with an insinuation himself. Johnson aides originally tried to convince newspapers to squelch the story, which Goldwater referred to as a cover-up of "rumors" in Washington, DC, in terms vague enough that they could be understood as referring to Jenkins. Vice-presidential candidate William Miller wanted to know if "this type of man" had compromised national security. More open was the scandal sheet *Lowdown*, which warned of "Washington's growing homosexual menace." Thus, as he did on other occasions, including on the issue of *Brown* v. *Board* and nuclear weapons, Goldwater stirred up public opinion, or allowed it to be stirred up, while maintaining a dignified-sounding public stance.[22]

* * *

The way Goldwater did his assessment – considering as fully as possible the risks and benefits before deciding to proceed – was in character for him. Goldwater felt strongly about the case, but his tactical decision to proceed does not appear to have been driven by emotion, even in the charged atmosphere created by the implication that he might be "queer." Goldwater's no-nonsense approach to the case was strikingly different from Ginzburg's hyperbolic style – and indeed different from his own inflammatory style on the stump in 1964. Goldwater kept his cool; he sought an opinion from a trusted professional, listened carefully, and heeded the advice he was given. By this point in his career, Goldwater had begun to adopt a "less shrill and more deliberate" tone in his public statements.

On September 2, 1965, Robb filed his complaint in the Southern District of New York, the usual jurisdiction when participants of diverse locations were involved. Goldwater, alleging actual malice under *Sullivan*, sought $2 million in damages. At his apartment in New York City, Ginzburg was served with formal notice.[23]

Not coincidentally, the suit was described in detail in Associated Press newspaper stories. Enthusiastic letters from supporters, often keyed to the appearance of a newspaper story, began to arrive at Goldwater's office as soon as the announcement appeared. Expressions of support arrived from a reader of the *San Angelo (TX) Standard-Times*, as they did from innumerable local readers of "Todays PAPER" [*sic*] throughout the country. A resident of a California apartment house wrote to report that she knew about Ginzburg, "a vile wicked, ungodly beast." He had once sent copies of *Eros* magazine to some of the "elderly ladies" in her building. Her own view was that he should be hanged, but as an alternative she complained to the postmaster general about *Eros*. This correspondent too had seen the story in the "papers." A supporter of the John Birch Society wrote to offer her opinion that Ginzburg was funded by communists. By 1966, Ginzburg's own report was that he was getting hate mail "saying 'Good for you, you kike Ginzburg!'"[24]

On September 9, just a few days after the announcement of the suit, Ginzburg wrote an unusual letter to William F. Buckley Jr. In it, he flattered Buckley as the wisest of Goldwater's advisers and expressed confidence about the outcome of the trial. But he also raised the specter of the "probing" public examination of Goldwater that would have to take place if the case went forward. It would be wise for Goldwater, he told Buckley, to dismiss the suit. Roger Robb's account of this moment is that Ginzburg panicked.

Robb and Goldwater had discussed the possibility of just such an offer well in advance. Buckley had his secretary acknowledge the letter but otherwise did not reply. Instead, he forwarded the telegram to Goldwater, who took no action on the offer. *Goldwater* v. *Ginzburg* moved ahead.[25]

* * *

As the case wound its way through the lengthy preparation process, Roger Robb outlined and developed his strategy. First came the due diligence. Having assessed the case as winnable and prepared Goldwater and his family for an ordeal, he now requested and received every scrap of paper that Ginzburg had created during the production of the *Fact* special issue. His mastery of detail would show in court. Second, he deposed both Goldwater and Ginzburg, probing vigorously for his antagonist's motives and exploring inconsistencies in his story in detail. Third, he deposed a handful of psychiatrists. This groundwork gave him a grasp of the factual and psychological territory on which the contest over malice would be fought. Robb was lucid and well organized, and his approach was penetrating. At one point he had his staff assemble a complete notebook of all the survey responses: on one page was the response as it appeared in Ginzburg's condensed and tweaked version, while on the facing page was the original unedited response on the facing page. Goldwater accepted Robb's assessments and had no complaints. He knew he could trust him.[26]

For his part, Ginzburg (with Boroson) believed that because Goldwater was a public figure they had wide leeway, and that the newly loosened libel law would cover them. But they would need a good attorney. Ginzburg chose Harris B. Steinberg. A short, balding graduate of City College and Harvard Law School, Steinberg was then in his mid-50s. He had much experience defending libel cases and was regarded as an expert in libel and other white collar criminal defense work. The *New York Times* later described him as tough, a "legend of the New York bar." During the trial, a Goldwater supporter wrote him with her nephew's impression that Steinberg seemed – that word again – "tough." Chief Justice Warren Burger, a moderate on the opposite side of many issues from the counselor, later damned Steinberg with faint praise, calling him "pre-eminent in his dedication and devotion to the administration of justice."[27]

Fact managing editor Warren Boroson was a more minor player in the drama, but he too now faced a potentially career-ending libel suit. He later recalled that Steinberg told him that unless his story and Ginzburg's matched, they would both lose. Boroson recalled being afraid that he would have to work the rest of his life to pay Barry Goldwater. His fear was real enough that he initially moved for separate trials. Robb, however, recognized that a joint trial would be more advantageous to Goldwater; the court denied Boroson's motion. As a result, both Ginzburg's attorney and Boroson's treated Ginzburg and Boroson as a single team during opening statements and during the trial. There are no known comments about this arrangement from Stanley Arkin, the attorney Boroson hired for the trial. But it may well have deprived Boroson of a useful defense. He never disclosed in court that he had quit *Fact* in disgust in 1964 after learning what Ginzburg – or, as he said later, Ginzburg's confidante David Bar-Ilan – had done to his article during revision. And while Arkin said of his client that he "did nothing with any dishonesty," he only mentioned, and perhaps felt he could not draw out the full legal implications of, Boroson's limited role as Ginzburg's employee – and his resulting inability to control what got published in the magazine.[28]

It was an unequal contest. The case pitted a major public figure who had the support of a large political constituency and a power base derived from his time as a US senator against the modest resources of a self-funded journalist and his former managing editor. The American Civil Liberties Union provided Ginzburg with moral support and an amicus curiae brief, but these resources would only go so far.

* * *

As the trial date approached, Goldwater stayed in touch with the American Medical Association. To Darrell Coover, the association's publicity director – and, remarkably, a former member of Goldwater's staff – he dictated in February: "I'm anxious to get it over with because these things are expensive but I am darned if I am going to let the precedence he [Ginzburg] established in politics and medicine stand if I can help it." The conservative press ran the story in admiring, partisan terms. During the trial, the chief of the *Chicago Tribune*'s Washington, DC, bureau was pleased to quote an Indianapolis newspaper editor's statement that there were two Americas in 1968, "the America of the east coast and the liberals, and the true America of the rest of the nation." *Goldwater v. Ginzburg* seemed to exemplify the contrast.

During the trial, Goldwater received many letters. From the *National Review*, Buckley's assistant wrote to tell Goldwater that his case was "immensely important." "I AM GLAD YOU ARE FIGHTING THE SLANDER CASE AGAINST THE GARBAGE SHEET," enthused one correspondent who used Western Union to make his point. Most of the letters were supportive, some complained about the Supreme Court, a few were seemingly unbalanced, and a few were critical. Not infrequently letters of support arrived on company letterhead. But there were thoughtful arrivals too. A Humphrey supporter wrote from New York City to commend Goldwater for his courage and dedication to principle, despite the fact that he disagreed with the senator politically. Most responded to media reports on the progress of the trial.[29]

For his part, Ginzburg was busy drafting a press release that announced victory in the case – a year and a half before the trial started. "Today's decision reaffirms the role of the press as the watchdog of

American society. We at FACT are proud of our contribution to that role and we hereby pledge to persevere in asking significant questions." Attorney Steinberg grew exasperated with what he called "drafting victory pronouncements when we have not the least idea whether we will win or lose." Steinberg had asked him to tone down an earlier version of the draft press release, which led Ginzburg to comment, "You're really making me work." Steinberg found the revised version to be "no better than the first"; Ginzburg's insistence on re-adding dramatic claims left him "more and more depressed."[30]

* * *

The trial was held in the Foley Square courthouse, a 1936 classical revival building in lower Manhattan that featured pillars and wide steps. To many, these distinctive features gave the awkward building a certain resemblance to the US Supreme Court in Washington, DC. Architecture critic Lewis Mumford, not a fan, called the Foley Square courthouse a "supreme example of pretentiousness, mediocrity, bad design and fake grandeur." The trial of alleged subversives Julius and Ethel Rosenberg had been held there in 1951, Alger Hiss was convicted of perjury there, and the House Committee on Un-American Activities met there on at least one occasion. The US Court of Appeals for the Second District of New York also sat in the building.

Goldwater v. *Ginzburg* would last for three weeks in May 1968. It would involve the calling of 17 witnesses, the review of depositions, and sparring over facts, principles, obscure details, and their contested interpretation. In all, the district court trial generated 2,300 pages of transcript, all faithfully typed by the court stenographer and then distributed to the parties. Goldwater would call it "the battle of Foley Square."[31]

* * *

In the years since Ginzburg published his special issue of *Fact*, the Vietnam War had escalated from a modest engagement to a major cause of American pride and of American deaths. In 1967, the March on the Pentagon had made clear how many Americans, including writers and artists, opposed the war; an estimated 35,000–50,000 took part. In 1968, more than 16,000 members of the American military died in the war, the highest count of any year in the war to date. Lyndon Johnson agonized over the war, knowing by then that it could not be won, yet also believing that appeasement of communism made withdrawal impossible. In the hypermasculine language of the day, Johnson could simply not be perceived as soft on communism: "If you let a bully come into your front yard one day," he said, "the next day he'll be up on your porch and the day after that he'll rape your wife in your own bed." In March, Johnson had withdrawn from the presidential race after a disappointing showing in the New Hampshire primary, barely beating antiwar candidate Eugene McCarthy. Robert F. Kennedy, Johnson's former attorney general and Ginzburg's old antagonist in the *Eros* case, had entered the presidential primaries and excited liberal hopes as he campaigned against the war. And in April, just one month before the *Fact* case came to trial, Martin Luther King had been assassinated in Memphis.[32]

On the Republican side, Richard Nixon, whose political career had seemed finished in 1964, was now the Republican presidential frontrunner. Goldwater was running unopposed in the primary to regain his Senate seat and had time to campaign for Nixon and in support of the war. The fight against communism was a prominent theme on the right, though Nixon tried to have it both ways: he pledged to negotiate with the Soviets, but at the same time his vice presidential candidate, Spiro Agnew, was making the inevitable charge of "soft on communism" – this time against Vice President Hubert Humphrey.[33]

In New York, the newspapers reported that Mayor John Lindsey was exhausted and was planning to take a vacation, a point that Goldwater noticed and could identify with. Times Square, not far from Ginzburg's offices, continued its descent into seediness. In midtown, Ginzburg had folded *Fact* but was keeping up a brave front and had started a new magazine, the aptly named *Avant Garde*. As we see in Chapter 5, in early 1968, Ginzburg boldly conducted a new poll of American psychiatrists for *Avant Garde* – this one about the mental health and fitness of Lyndon Johnson. In that same year, he also tried to stir up a controversy about George Wallace's mental health. But Johnson's withdrawal from the race deprived him of the publicity he sought, and the survey was never published.

Since 1963, Ginzburg had been busy fighting for his professional survival in the *Eros* case – gaining headlines but running up large legal bills in the process. In 1966, the Supreme Court had ruled against him in *Ginzburg* v. *United States*, the appeal of his 1963 obscenity conviction. The Court ruled that the mailing of materials in itself can constitute obscenity, even if the materials themselves were not particularly obscene. It thereby let Ginzburg's conviction stand. He was now notorious, and he devised ever more ingenious appeals. But Ginzburg's money could not last forever. Under the burden of defending *Eros* and *Fact* for years now, the First Amendment gadfly badly needed a win.[34]

* * *

Reporters jammed the courtroom and assembled outside it to cover entrances, exits, and statements. And indeed, mass media was part and parcel of the case. A media event in itself, *Goldwater* v. *Ginzburg* involved a publisher and had free speech issues at its core. During the trial, reporters sat in the front row. Stories in newspapers, in weekly newsmagazines, and on television were vital to both sides' ability to reach their followers and mobilize support. Letters from Goldwater's supporters were often occasioned by a media story. Even the judge had to deal with questions arising from the intense media coverage.[35]

On May 6, 1968, Robb opened with a concise, well organized, and lucid statement summarizing his argument that Ginzburg had published with reckless disregard for the truth. He developed a simple but powerful contrast between the image of Goldwater presented in *Fact* and the wholesome family man he knew, who had a record of serving his country in the military and in office. He described the case as a series of slurs on Goldwater, but he helpfully did so in accessible, patient, noninflammatory language, using specific examples to make his point, in order "to assist you," the jury, "in following the proof as it comes in." Even Steinberg described his opponent's opening statement as "very competent."[36]

Steinberg, on the other hand, opened his statement with a somewhat diffuse series of points, including an odd anecdote about his own wife. She had a favorite saying: "Don't tell me the other side [of any given case] because you will mix me up." Steinberg wanly said he hoped the jury would not take his wife's attitude, implicitly acknowledging that Robb had been persuasive. Steinberg eventually did land on the free speech mark, stressing that the point of the case was not whether Goldwater was a nice guy, "this simplistic issue that Mr. Robb so seductively hands you." The issue was whether Ginzburg had "a constitutional right" to publish the *Fact* issue in good faith. Steinberg mentioned several precedents for psychological profiling, such as studies of Leonardo da Vinci, James Forrestal, Gandhi, and Hitler; he also noted that the US government regularly commissions such profiles on living world leaders. He did try to establish an overarching vision that made *Fact* a valid effort: that at the time of publication, every American had been concerned about who has the power to make decisions about nuclear war. Steinberg ended up unwisely promising to prove a negative: "I am going to show you that there is nothing false in that magazine." "Virtually every word" that Ginzburg wrote in "The Man and the Menace," he asserted baldly, "was documented and quoted accurately from reputable sources." Further, Steinberg insisted, he would show that the psychiatrists included in the survey had been summarized accurately. Though at one point Goldwater's attorneys had anticipated the necessity of this argument, Steinberg's early pledges were invitations to trouble. The jury may find Ginzburg and Boroson "rude, brash, [and] tough," he said, but "you won't find them crooks, you won't find them deliberate liars, you won't find them character assassins." He contended that if the jury found that Ginzburg and Boroson did not lie and were not reckless, the jury's obligation would be to find them not guilty.[37]

In addition to seeming disorganized, Steinberg fumbled slightly in the trial's opening skirmishes. After denying any wish to impugn Goldwater's character, for example, he gently ridiculed Goldwater as oversensitive: "it is just too bad that a person as sensitive as he is" had placed himself in the rough-and-tumble of public life. Asking the jury to recall how terrifying the Cuban Missile Crisis had been, and how important the issue of nuclear war was, he made the grand claim that he could not imagine anything more useful or patriotic in 1964 than publishing the *Fact* issue. On May 6, Steinberg ineptly asked the judge to instruct a witness not to discuss the case with anyone, then rapidly withdrew his request. One can imagine

Judge Tyler's annoyance. The next day, Steinberg returned to his theme, beginning the day by noting Judge Tyler's failure to instruct the jury to refrain from talking to the press. At this the judge grew defensive, though he finally agreed. Tyler already had, at the start of the trial, told jury members of their duty not to speak with anyone about the case.[38]

As the trial proceeded, Judge Tyler was often irritable with Steinberg. In his cross-examination of Goldwater, Steinberg adopted a laborious "box score" strategy in which he read out loud each of Ginzburg's allegations and asked Goldwater to categorize them as true, false, or false but accurately quoted. This approach appeared to irritate Goldwater and drew sarcastic remarks from Roger Robb, which of course may have been part of the point. But it also meant that the defense case got bogged down in detail; Goldwater, meanwhile, had the luxury of appearing on the witness stand as the only authoritative witness on his mental state. The "false" tally seemed to grow higher and higher. At various points Steinberg appeared inadequately prepared, got lost in trivial points, read aloud material that had not yet been entered into evidence, and did not seem to know when to stop. He did not defer to the judge as much as did Goldwater's attorney, which may well have endeared him to Ginzburg. But he also vacillated, sometimes moving from challenging Tyler to abjectly agreeing with him. At the time, neither Steinberg nor Ginzburg knew that a brain tumor would kill Steinberg in 1969. It is unclear whether the tumor was affecting him in May 1968.[39]

* * *

As court protocol prescribes, Goldwater's witnesses were called first. In fact, all the witnesses were Goldwater's. It is revealing that no expert witness could be found to support Ginzburg – not even psychoanalyst Erik Erikson, who had at first thought the project on authoritarianism was reasonable. It is possible that even those who supported Adorno's notion of the authoritarian personality or of psychohistory felt that Ginzburg's methods were irresponsible.

As legal advocate for Goldwater, Robb had the burden of showing harm had occurred and had resulted from reckless disregard ("actual malice" in the Supreme Court's terminology). After making his brief opening state-ment, Robb shrewdly called Goldwater's wife, Peggy. The jury members had not yet heard much detail about Ginzburg or *Fact*, but they gained a vivid first impression of Goldwater, whom Peggy represented as an ordinary and devoted family man. She described his courtship of her and decried as "ridiculous" Ginzburg's allegation that Goldwater hated and feared her. Her husband's alleged nervous breakdown, she said, was simply a matter of tiredness, not of mental breakdown. And she patiently responded that she did not think any of the many other articles that had appeared over the years about him were defamatory – only the *Fact* special issue. Her husband was then called to testify, a process that would take all or part of seven days. Eventually the two Goldwater children would also take the stand and add their part to the glowing portrait of their father.[40]

Photos from around this time show that at 59, Goldwater typically wore a conservative suit and tie, large, distinctly unstylish horn-rimmed glasses, and a very serious expression. His receding grey hairline was brushed back to reveal a softly rounded widow's peak. On the stand himself, Goldwater was direct, but he took care to politely deny many of the accusations *Fact* had made against him. He presented himself as a man wronged – by Ginzburg, but empha-tically not by the world at large. Asked about Ginzburg's claims that like many paranoid people he often felt betrayed, Goldwater allowed Robb to walk him through anecdotes relayed by *Fact* about his dealings with President Eisenhower and others. He then calmly explained his feelings about each, which he portrayed as accepting rather than mistrustful. In his own demeanor, he maintained strict self-control, articulated cogent, high standards for himself and others, and even showed some self-deprecating humor. Asked about reports that he abused his staff, he admitted, "I am a perfectionist"; asked about the charge of moral cowardice, he referenced a line from the popular NBC television TV show *The Virginian* (1962–71) and joked, "When you call me that, smile." At one point during cross-examination he even thanked Steinberg for "being a gentleman." There was very little grandstanding to get in the way of his calmly reasoned argument.[41]

Goldwater did argue that he had been harmed, that the *Fact* issue had changed the way people view him, and that his major motive was to protect future politicians from abuse. He also raised the issue of medical ethics, asking directly "how a medical person can offer a diagnosis without seeing the patient." This ethics issue shows Goldwater's view that the *Fact* article and survey had a shaky ethical foundation and thus were elements in defamation. As Robb would stress to the jury, Ginzburg knew that the APA objected to the survey on ethical grounds, but Ginzburg went ahead anyway. In his memoir, Goldwater later stressed how the APA president and medical director had supported his view that the *Fact* survey was unethical. "It was obvious," he said years later, "that *Fact* was involved in a hatchet job."

On direct examination by Roger Robb, Goldwater stated plainly that he had never had a nervous breakdown, a charge he thought was particularly libelous. Except to ask for help for a troubled young man of his acquaintance, Goldwater said, he had never consulted a psychiatrist. Like his wife, he gave a straightforward account of a disputed episode in 1937 in which, he said, he had simply been overworked and grew tired. Here his wife's previous testimony clearly added credibility, as his personal physician's did later. Robb did not address *Fact*'s portrayal of Goldwater as an anal character and as sadistic – he focused on more commonsense issues and less on abstruse psychoanalytic concepts – but when Steinberg did so on cross-examination, Goldwater objected to the characterization as simply not based in fact. Asked on cross-examination about reports that in 1964 he had confessed to two past nervous breakdowns, Goldwater denied it. It may have been Robb's strategy to start with personal attacks, where collaborating witnesses and a personal testimony could establish Goldwater's humanity and credibility, before more difficult public issues were explored.[42]

* * *

It was the shadow of the Cold War that fell most strikingly over the exchanges in court, as it had over the 1964 campaign. During cross-examination by Steinberg, Goldwater was asked about, and defended, his view of the major Cold War controversies. Because Steinberg asked him at length about his past statements (under the guise of establishing whether Ginzburg's statements were true or false), Goldwater was able to reaffirm on the record many of his most cherished beliefs about the Soviets and how to contain them internationally and domestically. In court, he calmly agreed when Steinberg read his past statements that Senator Joseph McCarthy was a credit to the Republican Party and that Senator McCarthy's opponents were coddlers of communists. He agreed that he had been quoted accurately when he said his 1952 Senate opponent was a socialist. He affirmed his belief that the Korean War was a cowardly stalemate, that the war could have led to victory over China if it had not been for Truman, and that the United States should withdraw from the United Nations. Goldwater was even able to read a passage aloud in court from his 1962 book *Why Not Victory?*, in which he asserted that it was the atomic bomb and American air power that held Soviet aggression in check. Ginzburg, for his part, had to defend Lyndon Johnson by stressing that the Democratic candidate had repudiated the support of communists. He also was at pains to put down the communist newspaper *Worker*, which Roger Robb derisively called a "Communist mouthpiece." Ginzburg himself termed it that "little pipsqueak paper," referring both to the paper's small circulation and its negligible moral and political standing. Concerns about communism were not simply a public stance for court. Two years before, in the context of preparing for his deposition, Goldwater reflected that all of those who accused him of having a mental breakdown "have had rather various leanings toward communism from time to time, in fact, the whole pattern smacks of the techniques of the Russian police." Robb in turn was sure that Ginzburg had some link to communist organizations.[43]

The threat of nuclear destruction, intimately related to the Cold War, was the most emotional issue involved in *Goldwater* v. *Ginzburg*. Questioning his own witness, Robb shrewdly asked if Goldwater was trigger-happy with regard to the use of nuclear weapons. This was a delicate and advantageous way of phrasing the point. By summarizing the charges against Goldwater in the form of a caricature that included little or no specific factual content, Robb allowed Goldwater to frame his response creatively. His client said he had never advocated the use of nuclear weapons in Vietnam. This answer was not exactly *un*truthful, but it carefully navigated around the reality of his 1964 statement that "low-yield atomic weapons" could potentially have a role in the deforestation of Vietnam. Goldwater appeared to have the 1964 statement in mind as he answered, because without being asked he specifically emphasized that he had never suggested the use of large-tonnage weapons:

> ROBB: The last part of it [a psychiatrist's letter] says: "But in addition, he consciously wants to destroy the world with atomic bombs. He is a mass-murderer at heart and a suicide." I suppose those references might be phrased colloquially by saying the suggestion is you are trigger-happy for the atomic bomb. Let me ask you if that is true?
>
> GOLDWATER: No, it is not true. In fact, I have repeatedly in public statements advised against the use of atomic or nuclear weapons in Vietnam, and I have never at any time suggested that the weapons that these words refer to, the large megatonnage weapons, be used.

There was more, including a disclosure of the role of public relations in the nuclear issue. During cross-examination by Steinberg, Goldwater acknowledged that some of the campaign's "homey" publicity had been designed to counter the perception that he was a "madman" in connection with the potential use of nuclear weapons.[44]

Perhaps strategically, Robb's comparisons of Goldwater to Hitler only briefly touched on the explosive issue of Goldwater's alleged similarity to Hitler. But the exchange in direct examination was long enough to allow Goldwater a chance to calmly explain why he had planned to visit Berchtesgaden in Germany, a site associated with Hitler (he said it was to see and learn about an old friend who had accepted Herman Goering's surrender) and to flatly deny that he identified with Hitler and to "very, very vigorously" object to that allegation. Once again Robb's strategy of comparing *Fact*'s allegations to Goldwater's calm depiction of himself was effective – even if, as Ginzburg's attorney noted, it was somewhat off the point of Ginzburg's intentions and his constitutional rights. It was likely to be effective with the jury.

After Goldwater had established his wholesome image and his strong feelings, the Hitler issue clearly required delicate handling by Steinberg. When Steinberg suggested that it is difficult for associates of an authoritarian ruler to advise that he see a doctor, Goldwater shot back, "I am not a Hitler." When Steinberg probed for

Goldwater's opinion of Hitler's sanity, Goldwater demurred. When Steinberg, on cross-examination, explored the possibility that Hitler or a similarly disturbed leader might require evaluation, Goldwater was reasonableness itself. He agreed that in times of crisis, having psychological insight into a leader's fitness "would be desirable, if there was an indication that there was a need of it." But in such circumstances, he thought, both parties would likely agree to a personal examination by a professional. To Goldwater, that was not the important thing. What mattered, he said, was to fight back against unprofessional evaluations. This was the heart of his argument – not so much against the psychiatrists who had responded, but against Ginzburg the journalist:

> GOLDWATER: I do think it is a matter of paramount importance when an untrained man undertakes to write a paper on the psychological fitness of a man to be president without submitting this man to an examination or even talking to this man. I think that it is wrong. I think it is a very dangerous precedent, and that is why I am opposed to it.

Goldwater deftly turned the tables by agreeing to a reasonable point, then sharply differentiating what *Fact* did from what is reasonable. The rhetorical and substantive points in this exchange clearly went to Goldwater, and Steinberg could do little to budge the senator's stance of firm, concrete reasonableness.[45]

The debate over Hitler was relevant to the Cold War in part because so many Americans felt that in the 1930s the Western powers had failed to stand up to an expansionist, totalitarian leader. Direct or indirect Hitler comparisons were a staple of the right. Phyllis Schlafly characterized the leftist media, by which she meant the *New York Times* and "popular national magazines," as "goose-stepping" to prevent Goldwater's 1964 nomination, while the *National Review* argued that liberals had joined "Camp Appeasement."[46] In the final, stirring chapter of *Conscience of a Conservative*, Goldwater/Bozell had made the comparison between Hitler and Soviet totalitarianism explicit. The United States, they said, was in "clear and present danger" of being overwhelmed by despotic "alien forces" clearly reminiscent of the Third Reich:

This threat, moreover, is growing day by day. And it has now reached the point where American leaders, both political and intellectual, are searching desperately for means of "appeasing" or "accommodating" the Soviet Union as the price of national survival. The American people are being told that, however valuable their freedom may be, it is even more important to live. A craven fear of death is entering the American consciousness; so much so that many recently felt that honoring the chief despot [Khrushchev] himself was the price we had to pay to avoid nuclear destruction.

Here, in the conservative version, it is not Barry Goldwater but Nikita Khrushchev who plays the role of Hitler. Once again, in Goldwater/ Bozell's telling, the West is motivated by fear and is willing to make a deal to avoid world calamity. In the nuclear age, appeasement is far more dangerous than it was when Neville Chamberlain brokered his deal at Munich in the 1930s. But for Goldwater, in words that must have frightened many liberals, the alternative to appeasement is a willingness to fight and ultimately to win the Cold War: "We would rather die than lose our freedom."[47]

* * *

Goldwater's alleged paranoia had been a key feature of the *Fact* special issue. Questioned by Steinberg about his view that the press was against him, Goldwater once again was diplomatic. He tried to summarize the issue by saying that while there was a variety of views, "the majority of the press were not friendly to my candidacy." Here Steinberg was sharp and had the evidence readily at hand:

STEINBERG: Didn't you charge them [the press] with outright lies, utter dishonesty?

GOLDWATER: Yes, I think I did.

STEINBERG: And that is what you mean when you say they weren't friendly?

GOLDWATER: Yes.

Steinberg had exposed a contradiction in his argument, but Goldwater knew how to run damage control. Again he gained credibility by ultimately admitting the truth.

Certainly the black-and-white quality of the questioning created some odd moments, such as the one in which Robb asked Goldwater if he unconsciously wanted to destroy the world. Goldwater replied simply: "Totally inaccurate." The positive impression Goldwater conveyed had some limitations. His view of emotion, for example, was simple and straightforward. When Robb asked him if he had any shame or unease about working in a ladies' department store, or if this led him to any anxiety about his manhood, Goldwater said, "No, I was very, very proud of it." Asked if he hated his wife, he responded: "I don't know how you can hate someone that you love." These views were not the product of an urban mind steeped in psychoanalysis. Indeed, Goldwater said his method was simple: he had looked up "anal personality" in a dictionary and found nothing. All of these exchanges supported the picture of Goldwater as a simple, straightforward, genuine man. His bearing and his answers likely had appeal for the jury charged with weighing reckless disregard of the truth by the erratic Ginzburg.[48]

Finally, Robb went to an issue on which Goldwater could again present himself as well-meaning: the issue of race. During his direct examination by Robb, Goldwater repeated the case for his personal freedom from racism that he had made in the 1964 campaign and in *The Conscience of a Conservative* in 1960. Personally, he said, he favored school desegregation. Indeed, he said he had quietly desegregated his unit of the Air National Guard after two black fighter pilots brought segregation to his attention. He had also supported desegregation of the local high school and desegregated the restrooms at the local airport. And on the issue of *Brown* v. *Board*, which in *Conscience* he and Bozell had urged voters to resist as an abuse of power by the Supreme Court, Goldwater now backtracked. Under questioning from Steinberg on cross-examination, he admitted that on one occasion he had said the Supreme Court's decisions had been "jackassian" and therefore were not entitled to respect; but "I later retracted it and changed my position after consulting with lawyers as to what the role of the Supreme Court is in respect to the supreme law of the land." Similarly, he admitted that in *Conscience* he had implied that *Brown* v. *Board* was not truly the law of the land, but "I changed my position on that." (In later years, Buckley too softened his position on *Brown*.) Goldwater's responses to Steinberg were certainly awkward, and they contained no acknowledgment of political calculation or of any social damage that may have resulted from such anti-*Brown* comments. They did, however, establish Goldwater in 1968 as someone who could change his mind, who could acknowledge his mistakes, and who had respect for the court process in which he was now engaged.[49]

Overall Goldwater's testimony was compelling. The Goldwater who appeared in court (and who appears in his private correspondence with his attorney) bears no discernible resemblance to the impulsive, unstable warmonger Ginzburg portrayed in *Fact*. Quite the contrary: the overwhelming impression one gets of Goldwater from an immersion in the transcript is that of a well-organized and persistent, if somewhat unimaginative, practical man. Roger Robb had been superbly organized; with rare exceptions Goldwater restrained his temper and showed few if any signs of the impulsivity or irritability that had dogged him throughout the 1964 campaign. In his column for the *Washington Star* syndicate, Buckley commended Goldwater's presentation during the trial as "wholesome" and contrasted Goldwater's dedication to public service with what he saw as Ginzburg's "pandering to his readers' lubricous appetites."[50]

The media covered Goldwater's testimony in glowing detail, and even more letters poured in to Goldwater's office. Most though not all of Goldwater's correspondents supported him. The head of an eastern printing firm wrote, as did a political science professor from Pennsylvania, a mayor from a sizeable city in Illinois, the head of a rubber reclaiming company in the Midwest, and the head of a trust company in Los Angeles. It was psychiatrists, one correspondent said, who were well known to be "very insecure people." The deck was stacked against public officials, as the mayor reminded Goldwater: "the libelor must convince only one [juror] in order not to lose." The mayor said many fine citizens decline to serve in government for just this reason; he commended Goldwater for having the courage to go forward with the suit.[51]

* * *

Ginzburg was called to the stand on May 21. Several other witnesses, including Barry Goldwater Jr., Goldwater's primary care physician, and

Fact associate editor Warren Boroson, had preceded him. But Harris Steinberg had saved Ginzburg, and the substantial sparring he expected about *Fact*'s editorial methods, for last. Now for the first time, the jury would be able to observe the New York activist and provocateur. The springtime weather seemed to match Ginzburg's own buoyant presentation. Clean-shaven and balding, he sported dark-rimmed round glasses more stylish than Goldwater's, a dapper suit, a matching vest, and a lively striped tie. He grinned widely and appeared pleased with himself. Ginzburg was accompanied in court, though not on the stand, by his wife, Shoshanna, a smiling, confident-looking brunette. Though *Fact* had taken an almost prosecutorial-style approach to Goldwater, the structure of the trial made Ginzburg the defendant. He now had to overcome the positive, family-based image that Goldwater had established of himself.[52]

Harris Steinberg began direct examination of his witness by establishing the plain facts of Ginzburg's birth, education, military service, marital status, and successful publishing career. As he did so, Steinberg deftly turned a question about the name of Ginzburg's son Shepherd into an aside as to whether his son was sitting in court: "Is that the young man sitting right there?" It was.

Ginzburg explained that he had been appalled by Goldwater's acceptance speech in 1964. He said he was proud of *Fact*'s independence – it accepted no advertising – and he described it as following the muckraking tradition of H. L. Mencken, Jacob Riis, and William Lloyd Garrison. Ginzburg thereby linked his "completely independent" magazine with historic efforts to combat conventional morality, urban poverty, and slavery itself. In the aftermath of Goldwater's testimony, he defended both the survey and "The Man and the Menace" article, including its comparison of Goldwater to Adolf Hitler. Goldwater, he said, was both paranoid and a danger to society. His own motive in exposing Goldwater's mental problems was to "bring to the attention of the public what I thought I detected as an emotional instability in a man who would have the destiny of civilization, as we know it, under his control if he were elected President." If he doubted a national leader's sanity, he would "fulfill my obligations as a responsible journalist and get the facts."[53]

Ginzburg said that in putting together the *Fact* special issue he had used many reliable published sources on Goldwater's life, personality, and mental health. In the process, he said, he had followed standard editorial procedures to make his copy more effective. He had sought legal advice. Perhaps hoping to defuse the inevitable, Harris Steinberg took him through his methods. He had, Ginzburg said, used "anonymous" and "name withheld" interchangeably; he acknowledged that he had sometimes altered or conflated survey responses. The reason was primarily for space: "there was only so much material" that could be included.[54]

Ginzburg's self-regard began to show quickly. Asked by his own attorney to name the theme of his magazine *Eros*, he elaborated without prompting that "It was a beautiful magazine and really anyone who had seen it knows it was something of a work of art." Asked by Roger Robb if he showed obscene publications to his own children, Ginzburg gratuitously preached: "Contrary to what you and your ilk may believe, an ability to be intelligent and mature about sex is part of mental health." Only the dirty-minded would think otherwise. "You mean like the Supreme Court?" Robb interjected in his brisk fashion. Ginzburg shot back with a reminder that it was Goldwater who had called the Supreme Court jackasses, but elsewhere in his testimony he did admit the Supreme Court had found against *Eros* and that he had been sentenced to the federal penitentiary.[55]

As the trial proceeded, the judge often had to redirect the dramatic witness. Unlike Goldwater, who was in his element and had the advantages of due diligence, lucidity, and preparation, Ginzburg clearly struggled with the conventional setting of the Foley Square courthouse. Where Goldwater had presented himself as sincere and straightforward, one can sense Ginzburg looking for any opportunity to grandstand and explain too much. Instead, he was kept on a short leash. The dominant impression one gets from a close reading of the massive 2,300-page transcript is of Ginzburg as a dramatic and fragile improvisation artist, wriggling in the chair as Roger Robb steadily impugns his credibility. Robb had mastered the voluminous details of the case and at any point could be found taking Ginzburg firmly through specifics: exploring, confronting, pressing for definition and clarification, circling around suspected exaggerations. Sometimes Robb displayed a sardonic edge, but he stayed organized and focused in detail on his topic of the moment. It made for a long several days of testimony – even Goldwater's anthologizers Dean and Goldwater were moved to empathy for the jury, who had to listen to so much "deadly boring" discussion[56] – but on issue after issue Robb's technique proved effective:

> ROBB: I notice over here on the left-hand column – I should have said the right-hand column – you mentioned a number of individuals whom you identify as contributors to *Fact* magazine. Do you see that?
>
> GINZBURG: I do.
>
> ROBB: Were those people who actually wrote articles for you, or were they just people who answered questionnaires for you?
>
> GINZBURG: Both. . . .
>
> ROBB: Which were the ones who just answered questionnaires?
>
> GINZBURG: I would say the greater part by far.
>
> ROBB: You thought it was honest to refer to them as contributors?
>
> GINZBURG: I do.
>
> ROBB: What is your definition of a contributor?
>
> GINZBURG: Anyone who contributes anything by way of editorial material to a publication.
>
> ROBB: So you would identify all the psychiatrists who answered your questions as contributors?
>
> GINZBURG: Yes.[57]

No point was too small to pursue. Robb even pestered Ginzburg on his grades in college psychology. In other instances, more substantially, he tried to shed light on Ginzburg's editorial methods:

> ROBB: You just read those parts that you wanted to use, is that right?
>
> GINZBURG: The parts that were underscored for me by Mr. Boroson, for the most part.[58]

Robb's systematic approach, pushed to the point of exasperation, seemed to provoke or even disorganize Ginzburg. Remarkably in these circumstances, Ginzburg let Robb put words into his mouth. When Robb noted that Ginzburg had overlooked statements by Goldwater that showed pride in his Jewish heritage, Ginzburg defended himself by saying he did not have the full story at hand at the time and was under deadline. Robb was incredulous. "Are you now saying that you did not have time to get all the facts?" "Correct," replied Ginzburg. Thus Steinberg's opening boast that he could prove Ginzburg only used credible sources in good faith slowly crumbled.

> ROBB: ... I find on page 42 of that article the [Goldwater] quote that you used about the greatest enemy the Jew has, and so on, reads this way: "It is very difficult for me to understand the Jew" – and you have three dots, but in the article appear these words: "I happen to be half-Jew." Now, you omitted those words when you quoted from the article, didn't you?
>
> GINZBURG: Yes.
>
> ROBB: Why?
>
> GINZBURG: We had already established that he was half-Jewish. We didn't see the point of repeating it.
>
> ROBB: You don't think it changed the sense of the quotation?
>
> GINZBURG: No.

Robb took Ginzburg through a long series of survey responses from which Ginzburg had deleted indications of Democratic bias or concern about Ginzburg's methods and logic. Robb had Ginzburg read long passages he had deleted and defend their deletion. At one point Robb repeatedly rang variations on the phrases "aren't you," "didn't you," and "isn't that," without interruption by the judge and without objection from Steinberg. Ginzburg was reduced to replying, "I didn't say that."[59]

Often on the defensive, Ginzburg claimed that he was being "entirely apolitical" in putting together the special issue, a point that seemed to contradict much of the evidence that the jury had heard and that was hard to sustain under questioning. (Later in the trial, he admitted he had hoped to contribute to Goldwater's defeat.) He somewhat disingenuously distinguished between personality traits and mental illness, saying he had not meant to imply actual mental illness in Goldwater and thereby backtracking on what his special issue had claimed. More credibly, Ginzburg said that in publishing the issue he had performed a public service of which he remained proud; he said he had no regrets. But as the trial progressed, Ginzburg appeared to feel it was vital never to appear to change his mind or to admit an error. At times he appeared defensive, evasive, and self-contradictory. Even under friendly direct examination by Steinberg, Judge Tyler often had to interrupt Ginzburg's lengthy digressive answers and redirect him to the topic at hand: "Your lawyer asked you a very simple question." On one occasion he even required redirection from his own attorney. Ginzburg may have been seizing the bully pulpit – he knew that newspaper reporters were in the courtroom and free publicity was available, and he posed with his wife outside the courtroom – but in these ways he did not help his own case.[60]

* * *

Warren Boroson testified on May 20 and 21. At first glance his testimony appears to be an afterthought, but a closer look is warranted. It was Boroson who had consulted the psychological literature, read Adorno, put together "The Man and the Menace," and obtained Erik Erikson's behind-the-scenes blessing for the project. Quieter and less impressionistic than either Goldwater or Ginzburg, he calmly denied trying to defame Goldwater or ever knowingly saying anything false about him. But it was left to him to explain the way Adorno might illuminate Goldwater's personality and presumed discomfort with his masculinity. He, perhaps alone among the participants in the trial, could explain Freudian concepts and describe the research that supported them. More lucidly than anyone else, he could explain what Ginzburg and he had been thinking on the subject of Goldwater's alleged doubts about his masculinity.

When the facts of Boroson's career were established on direct examination by his attorney, it emerged that he had graduated summa cum laude and Phi Beta Kappa from Columbia, had read Freud and other psychoanalysts, and had taken a postgraduate course in the post-Freudians. He later worked at Ginzburg's magazine *Eros*. At Ginzburg's *Fact* he had written an article on the (then-new) Twenty-Fifth Amendment and the problem of removing a president from office. He recounted his responsibilities as a managing editor at *Fact*, noting that he suggested and researched articles but that the editor rather than the managing editor had final responsibility. He gave a detailed account of his sources and his view of the legitimacy of psychohistory; he said that in his view, psychiatrists could appropriately comment on people they had never met but whose behavior was well documented in the media and in print. But he gave little or no hint that he had left the magazine after the Goldwater issue was published.

Steinberg placed great emphasis on Adorno's *The Authoritarian Personality.* Boroson gave a summary of the book's findings and said the book was considered "a classic in its field"; he noted that the *New York Times Book Review* had listed it as one of the most important books published in the past decade. Boroson in turn saw an "extraordinary similarity" between the authoritarian personality type outlined by Adorno and Goldwater's own personality: his remote father had been hard to identify with and in prototypical style had therefore left Goldwater unsure about his masculinity. Goldwater consequently needed desperately to appear tough and could not afford to identify or sympathize with the weak.[61]

Under questioning from Robb, Boroson backed away from any implication that Goldwater was homosexual; he first said that Goldwater might fear that he was homosexual, but then took back even this characterization. It was possible, Boroson said, that Goldwater feared he was not masculine enough, or was a latent homosexual despite his marriage, or perhaps suffered from "repressed effeminacy." No psychologist had reviewed the written draft, he acknowledged. As noted in Chapter 2, Boroson had called eminent psychoanalyst and psychohistorian Erik Erikson, author of *Young Man Luther.* According to Boroson, Erikson had told him by phone that the hypothesis that Goldwater fit the authoritarian profile sounded reasonable. For Boroson, apparently supported by Erikson, fear of submission and weakness remained key parts of the syndrome he found in Goldwater.[62]

Roger Robb did not bother much with the concept of the authoritarian personality, "whatever that is." (Goldwater himself dismissed an excerpt from Adorno's book as simply impossible to understand.) With Boroson, Robb did his usual detailed job of cross-examination, noting the second thoughts implied by an Erikson follow-up letter and carefully working through Boroson's research draft. He especially noted discrepancies between dates given in Boroson's prior deposition and his current testimony. "Of course," Robb said, "you knew you were under oath when you made those answers?" Robb quoted a July 1964 letter from Boroson to United Auto Workers president and Goldwater enemy Walter Reuther; in that letter, Boroson had revealed that *Fact*'s profile "will say, basically," that doubts about his masculinity underlie Goldwater's belligerence and rigidity. Robb charged him with having already made up his mind about his conclusion before writing the profile. Boroson, like Ginzburg before him, grew evasive and defensive. When Robb established Boroson's changing answer on when exactly he had called Erikson, he said, "You didn't prepare for deposition, I take it?" Remarkably, Boroson replied: "That's right. I didn't prepare for my deposition."[63]

* * *

Closing arguments in *Goldwater* v. *Ginzburg* began on May 23, 1968. Here the pent-up emotions, contained for so long by the trial's obsessive focus on detail, finally were released.

Steinberg went first, reviewing the evidence in detail and then comparing the trial to the famous case of John Peter Zeneger, a free speech hero, and to the Scopes Monkey Trial. He told the jurors that they were faced with the chance to make constitutional history. "You know what this trial is. It is a book burning." For Steinberg, the case once again had nothing to do with whether Goldwater was a nice man. It had to do with "whether he can come in here and bull his way through to a judgment, clearing his records so he can run in Arizona." Instead, Steinberg suggested, Goldwater should stand before the voters and let them decide. He was confident, he said, that the jury would, in prayer and in earnestness, separate the real issues from the "phony ones" and acquit the defendants.[64]

Robb, in pain from a foot injury, began in a low-key and ironic way. He apologized to the jury if the proceedings had been complicated and detailed, and therefore "slightly lacking in excitement." But, he knew, they understood that the detail was necessary. Robb then reviewed the issues at stake, gave an extensive account of Ginzburg's culpability, and showed how his actions fit the Supreme Court's definition of actual malice. Ginzburg, Robb claimed, had admitted as much in his testimony when he said the truth of the psychiatrists' responses did not concern him. Ginzburg had had plenty of time to have the issue reviewed by qualified psychiatrists but had not done so, a point that he thought in itself suggested recklessness. In a prolonged and bitter conclusion, Robb said that Ralph Ginzburg and Warren Boroson had intended to be derogatory all along. The *Fact* editors, he said, had produced just what they intended, "a poison pen job ... conceived in malice and fraud and carried out that way," a "witches' brew of slander, libel, defamation."[65]

It was not at all clear to observers which way the verdict would go. In a report on the trial, *Time* cataloged Ralph Ginzburg's many improprieties but emphasized that the burden of proof was on Goldwater. According to *Time*, the many attorneys observing the proceedings could not see how Goldwater could possibly win. Even if he did, they speculated, the Court of Appeals might rule against the senator. Goldwater had read the *Time* article. But he remained his usual unruffled self; he believed that he and his attorneys had presented his case effectively. While he was in New York, he wrote to a supporter that his case offered the best chance anyone would have to prove malice under existing law. Ginzburg may well have been anxious, but in view of the consensus noted by *Time*, he too had fair reason to be hopeful about his prospects.[66]

The jury's deliberations began on Friday morning, May 24, 1968, and extended late into the night. Little is known about their deliberations. But as instructed by Judge Tyler, the standard they applied was preponderance of the evidence. At 1 AM on Saturday, May 25, the jury returned with their verdict. As Judge Tyler asked the foreman to read the verdict, the courtroom was nearly empty.

The unanimous judgment was for Goldwater. The jury awarded him a total of $75,000 in punitive damages from Ginzburg and *Fact* and compensatory damages of just $1. The low compensatory damages hinted to some that Goldwater had not been harmed significantly; the total award, far less than the $2 million he had sought, was only about enough to cover his legal fees. But after years of diligent work, Goldwater and the ever-organized Roger Robb had proven malice under *Sullivan*. On the matter of principle, Goldwater was vindicated.[67]

* * *

"WHO'S LOONEY NOW?" asked a delighted Goldwater supporter, one among many who wrote him or sent him telegrams of congratulation after the district court victory. "TOO BAD IT WASN'T $75,000,000," exclaimed another. Goldwater received so many letters congratulating him that he developed a form letter that he used for replies; he often added a one-sentence personal comment to the standard reply. Even as they congratulated him, many correspondents wished Goldwater well in the upcoming 1968 Senate election. They seemed to assume that he would win reelection easily, as in fact he did.[68]

Goldwater himself was delighted by the decision in *Goldwater v. Ginzburg*. An Associated Press wire photo shows him outside the Foley Square courthouse, grinning in his restrained way; his suit, tie, and awkward oversized glasses are firmly in place. The photo ran above a caption that says in large type, "VINDICATED, GOLDWATER SAYS." In private, he wrote one of the warmest letters he ever sent in the case, a missive of gratitude to Roger Robb: "May I salute you on this bright Monday morning first as a man of great courage, dedication and determination and, secondly, as a decidedly fine lawyer. ... It was a great experience, Roger, and I will never forget it." Years later, Goldwater said to Robb that they had set Ginzburg "back a bit," something that he said he would continue to feel proud of.[69]

A limit had been set on *New York Times* v. *Sullivan*. Goldwater had shown that a public figure could win a libel suit in the aftermath of that revolutionary decision. In his view, he was standing up for his own reputation and trying to prevent future attacks on public figures, including liberals, not specifically trying to advance his own electoral prospects in Arizona in 1968. In the process, Goldwater had also defended the conservative movement, restated and defended his beliefs about the Cold War and communism, and used libel law as a political weapon against a vulnerable opponent. Well in advance of the conservative legal movement that flowered in the 1970s and 1980s, Goldwater understood how to make the law work for him.[70]

For Ginzburg and his attorney, the question was entirely different. For them, there was nothing inherently political about encouraging the public to discuss the risk of nuclear war and world annihilation. Instead, Ginzburg felt a moral obligation to speak out when he felt a leader's mental instability threatened the world's survival. In the district court trial, he believed, an injustice had been done. It was for this reason that he and his wife stood on the steps of the courthouse and vowed to take *Goldwater* v. *Ginzburg* to the Supreme Court. Though he had been defeated, a chance for more headlines and a hope for a reversal of the judgment awaited. On the courthouse steps at Foley Square, he appears in his element, confident, almost buoyant.[71]

Of the major participants, it was Warren Boroson – no longer in Ginzburg's employment, but bound to him as codefendant against his own wishes – whose fate was perhaps the most unsettling. Boroson, also concerned about Goldwater's mental health, had done serious research into the best current thinking on how to prevent a recurrence of fascism; he had contacted the leading practitioner of psychohistory for an opinion; he had not been involved in altering the survey responses as Ginzburg had. Once he saw what Ginzburg (or David Bar-Ilan) had done to his article, he resigned and then kept quiet about it. Though his draft of "The Man and the Menace" was simplistic, it was at least an effort to explain a complex psychological idea to the general public; any recklessness, if present, was less pronounced.

As *Time*'s camera clicked and Ralph Ginzburg smiled, the next step was about to begin.

CHAPTER 4

Ginzburg, Goldwater, and the Supreme Court

I hope they do appeal and I hope the Supreme Court will uphold the conviction. It will be a real milestone in American jurisprudence and one long overdue.

Barry Goldwater to Roger Robb, May 1968[1]

In 1964, on the 10th anniversary of Brown v. Board, Newsweek *magazine reported on the polarizing effect produced by US Supreme Court decisions under Chief Justice Earl Warren. The Warren Court, which had brought profound changes in American life, commanded headlines and inspired fierce debate. "Friends call it progressive, foes call it arrogant – or worse." For his part, Goldwater had privately told President Eisenhower that he thought Warren had been "leaning toward Socialistic ideas for some time." In 1968, in the full glare of the media,* Goldwater v. Ginzburg *had exemplified that division of opinion and done something to alter the balance between free speech and protection of public figures.[2]*

In June 1968, as the Vietnam War escalated and the American left entered its annus horribilis, *Chief Justice Earl Warren told President Johnson that he planned to retire soon. Politics, as it turned out, would complicate the 77-year-old's decision.[3] Congress fought over Warren's replacement as Ralph Ginzburg and Barry Goldwater eagerly anticipated the Court's next decisions in libel law. Both men knew that these decisions – perhaps including a review of* Goldwater v. Ginzburg *itself – would determine how the broad principles articulated in* New York Times v. Sullivan *(1964) would take shape in practice.*

Ralph Ginzburg and Barry Goldwater were both eager to have their case heard before the Supreme Court. While each man hoped to be vindicated, each had special hopes as well: Ginzburg argued that bad law would out itself, and he cited Ulysses S. Grant's notion that "the best way to get rid of a bad law is to enforce it vigorously."[4] Public opinion and the media, then, would act as a check on the government. Ginzburg probably believed that *Fact* was within the protection of *Sullivan*, but he may have hoped to induce the Court to define new protections for journalists in libel law. Goldwater, for his part, hoped to establish more clearly than had been done before the limits of the *Sullivan* decision in a permissive era. His attorney Roger Robb, believing *Fact* was a gross libel, thought it was a public service to proceed. Each side had an interest in publicity for its cause, and each saw value in ensuring that its case got a hearing at the highest level.

The hearing each hoped to obtain would happen outside the courtroom door as well, in the glare of TV spotlights and in the columns of the booming national press. On the left, President Johnson was so aware of the impact of mass media that he asked a federal commission then investigating urban riots to look into the effect of the media.[5] On the right, William F. Buckley had been hosting his public affairs television show *Firing Line* on PBS since 1966, but Buckley's audience was dwarfed by the readership of the *Los Angeles Times*, which had been undergoing a transformation under publisher Otis Chandler and served an audience of up to 1 million by 1960. Daily newspapers and weekly newsmagazines, then reaching the apogee of their circulation and influence, provided Goldwater and Ginzburg a magnificent microphone for their debate. Mail continued to pour into Goldwater's office whenever media stories about the case appeared, and Ginzburg had the number of the Associated Press handy whenever he needed to issue a press release.[6] Whether he won or lost in court, a litigant knew dramatic headlines could yield increased book sales, magazine subscriptions, and mass support, not to mention influential allies in the system, and votes.

Goldwater's files bulge with letters that originated in a supporter's exposure to a media story about the trial. "I just finished reading the article in *Time* magazine concerning your Libel suit," said one. "May I just say that I think you are the bravest man I've ever heard of in all my life." "Enclosed [is] an Editorial from my hometown [paper]," wrote another, who seemed to find a sense of connection to Goldwater in the process of clipping and sending the piece. "I thought [it] would be of interest to you ... this article expresses our sentiments, too, along with millions of other people." Goldwater's typical way of handling such letters was to dictate a reply thanking the supporter, reinforcing the principle he thought was at stake in the trial, and often to foster an even greater sense of connection: "It is gratifying to know that people share the beliefs I fought for, and I appreciate your support." Thus media stories on the trial provided a platform for an indispensable sense of shared belief and connection between this public figure and his public.[7]

The conservative press had rejoiced over the district court ruling in *Goldwater* v. *Ginzburg*. William F. Buckley Jr., in a 1968 *National Review* column, presented the district court victory as a triumph for the "wholesome" Goldwater over the irresolute "pornographer" Ginzburg, and as a victory for all those interested in public service. He suggested that in future, the loser in libel suits should have to pay the legal costs of the winner. In the wake of the district court victory, Tennessee's *Greenville Sun* had commended Goldwater for his "determination and patience." The paper saw the win as "a blow in behalf of reasonable limits on those who gamble that candidates for public office have no protection against defamation of character." Echoing the point Goldwater had so often made himself about wanting to protect future public figures, the *Sun* declared that all "those who seek public office, and all Americans, are in his debt" for fighting Ginzburg in court.[8]

Oddly, Ginzburg offered to settle the case after the district court decision went against him. Goldwater told Robb that he considered it for exactly "eleven and a half minutes" and then concluded that there was a principle at stake. Thus, as early as 1968, before the case even went to the appellate level, he was certain about what he wanted: "I want this to go to the Supreme Court so that we can give that august body a chance to draw a line." In August 1969, the US Court of Appeals obliged by upholding the judgment of the district court. By late 1969, Ginzburg had filed a petition for a writ of certiorari, hoping to induce the Court to review his case; in turn, attorney John Wilson had filed a brief on behalf of Goldwater. In character, in his private correspondence with Goldwater, Wilson described Ginzburg's petition as "a lying, cheating document."[9]

As Ginzburg and Goldwater waited for the Court's answer, the Vietnam War continued to rage. The North Vietnamese renewed the Tet Offensive in 1969, and many American soldiers lost their lives in that year trying to take Hamburger Hill, a spot of little strategic value. The number of American servicemen killed in the war would total 11,780 for the year, down from a bloody peak of 16,899 a year earlier. On television, journalists brought the war into American livings rooms. But it was the counterculture variety show *Laugh-In* that earned the largest viewership of the year; during the presidential election, Richard Nixon had appeared on the show and delivered its recurring punch line in his typically awkward way: "Sock It to Me." Meanwhile, the popularity of the westerns *Gunsmoke* and *Bonanza* testified to the enduring divisions in American culture and society; Goldwater's favorite western, *The Virginian*, was still running even as *Laugh-In* made fun of conventional society. In March 1969, the cover of Ginzburg's *Avant Garde* magazine tweaked a traditional painting of American Revolutionary soldiers marching with flute, drum, and flag. In Ginzburg's multiracial version, a white man, a white woman, and an African American man are dressed in garb suggestive of Vietnam.[10]

* * *

The *Fact* appeal had first gone to the US Court of Appeals for the Second District of New York. (The appeals court, coincidentally, sat in the same grandiose Foley Square courthouse where the district trial for the case had taken place.) In 1969, the appeals court sided with Goldwater, finding that the district judge had acted appropriately in reaching the libel judgment against Ginzburg. It was now up to the Supreme Court.

Politics and mortality had taken their toll on each side's legal team. In April 1969, Richard Nixon appointed Roger Robb, Goldwater's attorney in the district court contest, to the US Court of Appeals for the District of Columbia Circuit. It was a traditional launching pad for the Supreme Court. To replace Robb, Goldwater chose John J. Wilson, known as a "combative and outspoken" trial attorney and a staunch conservative Republican. Ginzburg's attorney, Harris Steinberg, had died suddenly in June 1969 of brain cancer. Thus the embattled publisher too was represented by a new set of attorneys.[11]

Ginzburg may have hoped that in the rapidly changing climate of the late 1960s the Court would further extend what was permissible in free speech law. His chances were unclear, but there was much good publicity at stake, and he took advantage of every opportunity to publicize his cause. By now he was a veteran of Supreme Court appeals. In the *Eros* case, the district court in Philadelphia had convicted him on obscenity charges; Ginzburg felt that an injustice had been done, and there is some evidence to support his view.[12] When the appeals court upheld the *Eros* verdict, Ginzburg learned that taking a case to the highest level could have its advantages. *Freedom on Trial* (1966), Bob Reitman's adoring mass-market paperback, appeared just after Ginzburg went to the Supreme Court – and portrayed him as a hero.

The Supreme Court has a well-defined process by which persons can seek to have a case reviewed by the Court: one has to file a petition asking the Court for a writ of certiorari. (The word *certiorari* comes from the Latin for "to be informed.") If this writ was granted, as it was in the *Eros* case, Ginzburg could have his say at the highest level. Reporters would notice, and he would have at least a chance to become even better known as a free-speech champion or even a martyr to the cause.

But if a writ is granted, dangerous shifts in the terrain can also emerge unexpectedly. In the *Eros* trial, for example, the district court had focused only on whether *Eros* and Ginzburg's other publications were obscene, but in its plea before the Supreme Court, the Justice Department decided to argue on different grounds altogether. The content of Ginzburg's publications might have some medical or other value, it now acknowledged. But the salacious *way* Ginzburg advertised the materials in 1962 had violated the federal statute against mailing obscene material – even if the contents of the publications were not especially offensive in themselves. This was a creative change. "If Mr. Ginzburg had distributed and sold and advertised these books solely to ... physicians ... we, of course, would not be here this morning."[13] An angry-looking Justice William Brennan had delivered the Court's decision: the Court agreed with the government in the *Eros* matter.[14] Ginzburg must have winced at the five-to-four margin. In ruling *Eros* obscene, Brennan had been joined not only by Justices Clark and White but also by Chief Justice Earl Warren. The Court found that Ginzburg had "deliberately represented" the materials as "erotically arousing" and exploited their sales potential using only their "prurient appeal," regardless of their actual content. It was an almost trivial approach, focusing as it did on the risks involved in how admittedly harmless material could be advertised. But it lost Ginzburg the protection of the First Amendment.[15]

The close call in the 1966 *Eros* case was widely protested on the left. In character, Justices William Douglas and Hugo Black had dissented, as they had in *Roth*. Justice Black had reiterated his long-held view that all speech is protected by the First Amendment and that the *Roth* test is unworkable. He had found that the Court had violated Ginzburg's due process by shifting to a standard of pandering rather than a standard of inherent obscenity in the mailed material itself. (Thus *Playboy*, which in *its* advertisements mainly emphasized a lifestyle for men, was on safer ground than the innocuous *Eros*.) Justice Douglas incredulously listed the many experts who had testified to the Ginzburg material's redeeming social value and agreed with Black that the First Amendment protects the expression of "all ideas." Justice Harlan, who had worried in *Roth* about the dangers of federal censorship, had also dissented. He too was alarmed about the Court's novel reasoning, which he thought shifted criteria away from the material itself and onto the defendant's attitude and motives. "This seems to me a mere euphemism for allowing punishment of a person who mails otherwise constitutionally protected material." To Harlan, the *Eros* decision had been "an astonishing piece of judicial improvisation" that threatened to move established First Amendment thinking distinctly backward.[16]

* * *

As he filed his petition for a writ of certiorari in the *Fact* case in 1969, Ginzburg had some reason to hope that the Court might accept the case for review and might reconsider First Amendment law.[17] For one thing, at the time Ginzburg filed his petition, there were continued indications of a liberal trend on First Amendment issues that came before the Court. The Court had begun to consider the more subtle ramifications of *Sullivan* and had begun to clarify some disputed points. In *Curtis Publishing* v. *Butts* and *Associated Press* v. *Walker*, both in 1967, the Court had reaffirmed the importance of public figure status to the question of whether the actual malice standard would be used. In *Butts*, the Court found that the same narrow standard of actual malice in libel cases applied to public figures as it did to public officials. (In this case, the figure was a football coach rather than a politician.) Some experts believed that the Court's language about the importance of "uninhibited" debate in *Sullivan* implied that protection might soon be extended to speech in the areas of government policy, privacy, and other general matters of public interest. There was a slow, lurching movement in this direction. In *Time Inc.* v. *Hill* (1967), the Court rebuffed a citizen's action for invasion of privacy and defined greater protection for the press. If a private citizen's story was newsworthy, the Court ruled, a media outlet had the freedom to publish. Though *Hill* was not technically a libel case, for a time some judges in lower courts read it to mean that *Sullivan*'s narrow actual malice doctrine now applied not just to statements about public figures but also to statements on any public issue.[18]

In 1969, the Court still had its First Amendment absolutists. Ginzburg admired them extravagantly. In *Hill* and *Curtis Publishing Co.* v. *Butts*, as he had been in Ginzburg's own *Eros* case and in *Sullivan* itself, Hugo Black was in fine form. In concurring with *Sullivan*, Black questioned the "actual malice" test, calling it "an elusive, abstract concept, hard to prove and hard to disprove." Instead he asserted "an absolute immunity for criticism of the way public officials do their public duty."[19] Justice Douglas could be relied on to join Justice Black on any case where free speech was involved. There was one possible complication: Ginzburg had once paid Justice Douglas $300 to write an article for *Avant Garde*, a point that some thought should disqualify Douglas in the *Fact* case.[20] So, while there were two justices likely to vote to hear Ginzburg's writ, it was a wobbly two. Ginzburg needed four.

One strong possibility was Thurgood Marshall. To the joy of liberals, the former legal director of the NAACP had joined the Court in 1967. Presumably he would be sympathetic; he had recently pushed First Amendment law forward in *Stanley* v. *Georgia* (April 1969). There Marshall wrote the Court's opinion in a case involving possession of obscene material. Marshall was eloquent. No one dissented when he found that the Constitution allows individuals to possess such material in their own homes:

> Whatever may be the justifications for other statutes regulating obscenity, we do not think they reach into the privacy of one's own home. If the First Amendment means anything, it means that a State has no business telling a man, sitting alone in his own house, what books he may read or what films he may watch. Our whole constitutional heritage rebels at the thought of giving government the power to control men's minds.

This was encouraging. If Ginzburg could count on Thurgood Marshall, Black, Douglas, and the great liberal leader Earl Warren – all likely to be sympathetic to some degree – his petition for certiorari would be assured.

Douglas, in the actual event, did not recuse himself, so he was available to vote on the writ. But by the time the case came to a vote, Ginzburg no longer had Justice Warren. Warren had tendered his resignation in June 1968, hoping to give Lyndon Johnson a strategic opening to nominate a Democrat before he left office. But many key Senate Republicans had declined to consider any Supreme Court nomination at all before the fall election. To complicate matters, there was a scandal when Johnson attempted a complex reshuffling of the Court. He had earlier nominated his close friend Abe Fortas to replace the ultra-liberal Arthur Goldberg (who would likely have been a pro-Ginzburg vote if he were still on the Court). Now Johnson nominated Associate Justice Fortas to replace Warren; the move backfired when Fortas was forced to resign amidst a scandal. Of critical importance for Ginzburg's case, that not only left a liberal associate justice's seat vacant; it also gave the incoming Republican president the right to name a chief justice. Richard Nixon took office in January 1969 and chose Warren Burger to be chief justice. With Justice Black about to turn 83 and a moderate Republican now on the Court in Earl Warren's place, the liberal window was closing.[21]

* * *

Petitions for writs of certiorari were typically considered at the Court's weekly Friday conference. In a paneled conference room next to the chief justice's office, the justices met to decide the fate of pending cases.

By tradition, the chief justice spoke first on each case and was followed by each justice in order of seniority.

From the vast number of petitions for certiorari it receives, the Court typically grants only a handful. And merely granting a writ is not the same as concluding that the petitioner is right on the merits of the case. Goldwater's new attorney, John Wilson, told him that the motivations of the justices in accepting or declining a case are always mysterious. Considerations of timing may come into play. Does the Court want to reopen a major constitutional question just then? Has a previous Court decision had barely enough time to become established as a precedent, or is it long overdue for review? For those justices who do wish to revisit a precedent or make new law, can a case command a majority in the desired direction, or will accepting it lead to an ill-timed and embarrassing loss?[22]

On this Friday in 1969, for unclear reasons but perhaps because he had so recently joined the Court, Burger declined to participate in the decision about Ginzburg's petition. Hugo Black, the senior associate justice at 83, likely ran the conference in Burger's absence. Black probably sensed that he was in the minority but circulated an opinion for review. Justice Douglas joined Black in what proved to be a dissent. No other justice voted to hear the case. On January 26, 1970, the Court announced its decision to deny certiorari in *Ginzburg* v. *Goldwater*. *Sullivan* would not be extended or reconsidered, at least not in the matter of Ralph Ginzburg. The district court judgment would stand.

Thurgood Marshall's vote must have been a particular disappointment to Ginzburg, given his investment in the advancement of civil rights for African Americans. Justice Marshall, however, did not share Black and Douglas's absolutism on the First Amendment, and he was not necessarily looking to overturn recently established precedent. (In *Stanley* v. *Georgia*, despite his powerful rhetoric, he had left room for existing obscenity law of the kind under which Ginzburg had been convicted in the *Eros* matter.) Because even Justice Black thought Ginzburg's conviction under the *Sullivan* standard was done fairly, it is likely that the five justices in the majority also had difficulty finding any technical or procedural grounds for overturning Ginzburg's conviction. There is no reason to think the five who voted against Ginzburg had any wish to revisit *Sullivan*.

If there was any consolation for Ginzburg, it was that his hero Hugo Black made the unusual decision to publish a searing dissent in the case. Black gave a ringing endorsement of Ginzburg's First Amendment rights, seeing him as the most egregious illustration of what was wrong with libel law in 1970:

> I cannot subscribe to the result the Court reaches today because I firmly believe that the First Amendment guarantees to each person in this country the unconditional right to print what he pleases about public affairs. ... This case perhaps more than any I have seen in this area convinces me that [*Sullivan*'s] constitutional rule is wholly inadequate to assure the "uninhibited, robust, and wide-open" public debate which the majority in that case thought it was guaranteeing.

Black further noted that Goldwater was the nominee of his party for president of the United States and thus potentially the holder of "almost unbounded power for good or evil." For this reason, he said, the public has an "unqualified" right to have the press scrutinize candidates. Any benefit from libel suits like Goldwater's are outweighed by the risks of not allowing misleading information to appear.

Looking closely at the issue of harm, Black was not persuaded that Goldwater had suffered any. He singled out Ginzburg as the victim of a retaliatory and punitive judgment based on his speaking out:

> Another reason for the particular offensiveness of this case is that the damages awarded Senator Goldwater were, except for $1.00, wholly punitive. Senator Goldwater neither pleaded nor proved any special damages, and the jury's verdict of $1.00 nominal compensatory damages establishes that he suffered little if any actual harm. In spite of this, Ginzburg and his magazine are being punished to the extent of being forced to pay Senator Goldwater $75,000 punitive damages. It is bad enough when the First Amendment is violated to compensate a person who has actually suffered a provable injury as a result of libelous statements; it is incomprehensible that a person who has suffered no provable harm can recover libel damages imposed solely to punish a defendant who has exercised his First Amendment rights.
>
> I would grant certiorari and reverse the Court of Appeals summarily.[23]

Ginzburg, as he had so often before, issued a statement to reporters. "This is a black day," he said, "for the Constitution." He had lost on *Eros* in 1966 and already thought he was the victim of a witch hunt; he probably faced prison soon. Now he had lost definitively on *Fact*.[24]

* * *

If Barry Goldwater was jubilant at the outcome of the case, there is no evidence of it in his papers. Once again serving in the Senate, he had other business to attend to. His file on the case for 1970 contains mostly dry attorneys' exchanges about money. In 1968, he had been effusive to Roger Robb. But I could find no letter of thanks from Goldwater to John Wilson.

The victory passed into conservative legend. William F. Buckley continued to follow Ginzburg's career, and eventually John Dean and Barry Goldwater Jr. (2008) would describe the case in glowing terms and include extensive excerpts from Goldwater's testimony in *Pure Goldwater*, an anthology of the senator's writings. According to the *New York Times* account of the Supreme Court's vote, *Goldwater v. Ginzburg* was only the second time the Supreme Court had upheld a libel verdict in the post-*Sullivan* era. Technically the Court allowed Ginzburg's libel conviction to stand rather than upholding it (that could only happen if the Court granted Ginzburg's certiorari petition). But the point is important nonetheless. Only once before – in 1967's *Curtis Publishing Co.* v. *Butts* – had the Court applied the new *Sullivan* standard to a case involving a libel action by a public figure. *Butts* and *Goldwater* v. *Ginzburg* had solidified the *Sullivan* doctrine on the issue of public figures. Goldwater had not established new law, but he demonstrated conclusively what was needed to prove actual malice.[25]

Goldwater and Robb continued to follow news of Ginzburg long after the *Fact* case was resolved. "As far as I am concerned," Goldwater wrote his old friend and ally in 1972, "if they put Ginzburg in jail and throw away the key I couldn't care less. I personally think the guy is a little off his nut."[26]

* * *

It is likely that Ginzburg's editorial manipulations in *Fact* would still meet the standard of actual malice if tested in court today. *Sullivan*'s revolutionary doctrine on the libel of public figures, though it has been more fully developed in the years since 1964, remains firmly in place.[27]

Did Ginzburg ultimately contribute to the formal evolution of First Amendment law? Given that Goldwater won, the answer is no. What Ginzburg contributed to the law and to the social permissiveness of the 1960s was his gift for provocation. It was an ironic legacy. In fact, he was easy prey for a senator, for a gifted attorney, and for reporters who could easily portray him as irresponsible at best and as a pornographer at worst. Representative of an advanced urban lifestyle during a period of rapid social change, his best and only hope was the support of liberal intellectuals, writers, and artists. In 1970, after the Court's decision, Ginzburg posed for a publicity shot holding a gigantic stage check for $75,000. The check was made out to Barry Goldwater.[28]

In a further irony – and there were many in the case of Ralph Ginzburg – his most lasting memorial would not be in the form of the publishing success or the advance in First Amendment doctrine he sought. Ginzburg would be best remembered in an ethics rule of the American Psychiatric Association. That rule would be devoted to ensuring that psychiatrists could never respond to a survey like Ginzburg's again.

PART II

PROFESSIONALIZATION AND THE RISE OF THE GOLDWATER RULE

CHAPTER 5

"To Protect Public Figures"

The APA and the Goldwater Rule

Every psychiatrist should be aware of his position as a representative of the profession to the general public and help portray the profession in its proper perspective as a thoughtful, dignified, difficult discipline always motivated to help human beings in distress and never to do harm. ... It seems superfluous to add that under no circumstances should a "diagnosis" be given unless an adequate examination has been made and proper written authorization has been granted by the patient.

"Guidelines for Psychiatrists: Problems in Confidentiality," draft statement prepared for consideration by the APA Board of Trustees, December 1969[1]

While Barry Goldwater was preparing his libel suit against Ralph Ginzburg and Fact *magazine, the nation's largest organization of psychiatrists was following Ginzburg's career with alarm. The American Psychiatric Association (APA), which had been in existence and powerful for 120 years, was in the process of reshaping itself to meet the demands of a more complicated and specialized world. The APA was appalled by the special issue of* Fact *in 1964 and objected to its publication. Ginzburg ignored the APA's letter. In 1973, the APA's board of trustees formally adopted what is now section 7.3 of its code of ethics, informally known as the Goldwater Rule. It could as easily have been called the Ginzburg Rule, after the publisher who had been such a thorn in the organization's side. The text of the Goldwater Rule, altered slightly in 1975 and much argued over in the following decades, generated anxieties and controversies all its own.*

The American Psychiatric Association (APA), founded in 1844, began as an association of mental hospital administrators. By the years after World War II, it had become what it is today: a big tent of general psychiatrists, subspecialty practitioners, residents and fellows, educators, administrators, advocates for the mentally ill, and psychological and biological researchers. At the APA's annual meeting there is something for all the members of this enormous and powerful organization. New scientific discoveries are presented, educational courses are given, controversial topics are explored, and prominent speakers are listened to attentively and argued with. At its business meeting, held in the few days before or after the annual meeting, the APA's board of trustees takes up and decides on major issues of policy.[2]

The tumultuous years from 1964 to 1973 were years of triumph and disappointment for the board. In that decade, the APA saw Medicare, Medicaid, and the Great Society blossom under Lyndon Johnson, then falter. Mental health care funding mushroomed under Lyndon Johnson and then was substantially cut back during the Nixon administration. With the emergence of new treatments, new attitudes toward patients' rights, and more modern views of homosexuality, psychiatry itself was transformed. Psychoanalysis, once the dominant model of treatment and psychiatric understanding, gave way to an increasing emphasis on biological psychiatry. The public perception of psychiatry, once glowing, entered rocky terrain. For example, Hollywood's age of enchantment with psychiatry and psychoanalysis peaked in the mid-1960s. Thereafter film began to preoccupy itself increasingly with images of psychiatrists as repressive, as "pseudoscientists," or even as mentally ill themselves. The new, more skeptical era would be represented memorably by the Oscar-winning film *One Flew over the Cuckoo's Nest* (1975), in which the psychiatric system is depicted as a tool of social control rather than a means of human liberation. Cases of psychiatrists having sex with their patients, commonplace in the movies, began to appear as real-life problems for the APA ethics committee and as stories in the news media. *The Myth of Mental Illness*, a bestselling book by Syracuse University psychiatrist Thomas Szasz, influenced many readers and concerned the APA greatly. Szasz offered an accessibly written but bitter attack on psychiatric coercion and what he saw as the irrationality of the very concept of mental illness.[3]

The conservative movement that Barry Goldwater had led in 1964 was no longer what Richard Hofstadter had once predicted it would be, a permanent minority isolated even within the Republican Party. Instead, the conservative movement had ever more success in convincing Americans of its anti–big government views, in gaining control of the Republican Party, and in achieving positions of power. On the defensive, the APA would have to counter adverse publicity more often as the United States tumbled from Vietnam to Watergate, endured the inflation and moral crises of the 1970s, and then entered a new era of drastic cutbacks in the social programs it cherished.[4]

* * *

By the early 1960s, the APA was going through a period of introspection and self-criticism. Officials at the APA believed the organization needed to be modernized; they also recognized that the organization had too nebulous an approach to ethics. In the 1940s, the APA had acknowledged that it had at best an ill-defined process for ethics hearings. In a typical year during the 1950s, the APA received an average of only three or four ethics complaints. Presumably this small number reflected underreporting, to be expected in an age that was deferential toward authority and in which the accountability of organizations to their clients had not yet been well defined. The field of bioethics, only beginning, did not yet formally exist. At the time, the APA relied informally on the unmodified ethics code of the American Medical Association (AMA). This arrangement may have been adequate in the relatively small world of medicine before World War II, but by the early 1960s, the APA recognized that it needed something more specific. The APA started formulating "guidelines for psychiatrists," aimed at providing its members with help in coping with the distinctive problems of the specialty. Guidelines would henceforth be more specific, more formalized, and more enforceable.[5]

The APA's push toward a specialty model again took its cue from the world of medicine. In the postwar era, hospitals and academic medical centers played an increasingly dominant role, and the AMA's big tent was no longer an adequate home for the country's newly minted specialists. The general practitioner and his tradition of house calls (it was generally him, except in pediatrics and psychiatry) became an endangered species.

The new, highly trained specialists were proud of their identities. Pediatrics had long had its own professional organization; within internal medicine, neurology led the way by forming its subspecialty society in 1948. Cardiology followed in 1949. As early as 1944, in its official history of psychiatry – "The history of American psychiatry *is* the history of the American Psychiatric Association" – the APA devoted an entire chapter to the new identity of the psychiatrist.[6]

Within psychiatry, *sub*specialty organizations were also proliferating. In the 1950s, child psychiatry established itself, first with the founding of the American Academy of Child Psychiatry and then with the status the field gained as a subspecialty area for board certification. By the end of the 1960s, as the courts increasingly sought expert testimony, forensic psychiatrists had formed an association, the American Academy of Psychiatry and the Law. And in 1970, residency directors in psychiatry created a group of their own devoted to educational and administrative issues. After a quiescent period across most professions in the 1950s, the rise of medical ethics in the 1960s placed medicine well ahead of the legal profession and other professions in formulating ethics codes.[7]

The years between 1965 and 1985 were a boom time for the professionalization of ethics, as formal ethics codes were published and organizations dedicated to the study of professional ethics proliferated: the Center for the Study of Ethics in the Professions was founded in 1976, the International Society of Ethicists in 1985. Businessmen, corporations, and engineers among others wrote or rewrote ethics codes. In the aftermath of the Watergate scandal of 1972–4, which had involved so many lawyers, the legal profession tried to remedy its public image. The American Bar Association began to require courses in legal ethics in 1979 and published its *Model Rules of Professional Conduct* in 1982.[8]

In the 1970s, Gallup polls, by no means limited to the standing of political candidates, showed that despite the social changes in the role of doctors, Americans viewed the health professions as among the most ethical of the professions. The health professions were followed by teachers, clergy, and police – and only then by business executives, lawyers, and journalists. In 1976, even as *Washington Post* reporters Woodward and Bernstein were making investigative reporting seem glamorous and important, only 33 percent of the American public rated the ethics and honesty of journalists as high or very high.[9]

* * *

In the early 1960s, the APA appointed a series of task forces to review, and if necessary to reform, its organizational structure – and, a year after the assassination of John F. Kennedy, to consider the organization's relationship to the wider society and to the Johnson administration. The task forces gave much thought to their work. They then met at a special session of the APA Council, then the most powerful administrative body within the APA. (The board of trustees did not yet exist in its current form.) The session was held at Airlie House, a plush neo-Georgian conference center in northern Virginia known for providing comfortable seclusion. There, government agencies and nonprofit organizations could find the space to think. Martin Luther King had done some of the planning for the 1963 March on Washington there. The APA Council and its invited guests, including past presidents, engaged Airlie House for the weekend of September 11–13, 1964. Thus, just as Ralph Ginzburg was preparing to release his special issue of *Fact*, the APA's leadership was giving thought to how to modernize and reenergize its organization. A new, more formal approach to ethics would be imagined at the meeting and would eventually come to fruition in the early 1970s.

Under the leadership of APA president Daniel Blain, the Council considered and adopted a set of principles for reform of the organization. Known within the APA as the Airlie House propositions, these principles provided a vision for reform. Implementing the reform itself would prove a slow and deliberate process; it would take almost a decade but would prove lasting. Among the Airlie House–inspired changes were the replacement of the APA Council with a board of trustees, the formal adoption of the AMA's ethics code as the basis of the APA's own ethics rules (1968), and the development of a formal, written ethics document to guide APA members specifically. Framed as a series of annotation to the AMA ethics code, the *Principles of Medical Ethics with Annotations Especially Applicable to Psychiatry* was adopted by the APA board of trustees in 1973. The document contained what is now section 7.3, the discussion of the ethics of comment on public figures informally known as the Goldwater Rule.[10]

By the time of the Airlie House proceedings, the role of the psychiatric expert was beginning to be questioned in many quarters. In the 1950s, academic books like Stanton and Schwartz's *The Mental Hospital* had assumed the value of psychiatry while exploring with a well-informed eye the sociology and psychology of institutional and staff roles. Influential but hard-to-please literary critic Alfred Kazin, in essays published in the 1950s and early 1960s, referred to Freud as a hero and a conquistador as well as a major force in contemporary American life. By 1960, however, psychiatrist Robert Coles had published a very public critique of what he saw as his field's heartless specialization. By then, psychiatrist Thomas Szasz had published his first major attack on psychiatry; he would soon appear in testimony before the US Senate. Szasz thought psychotherapy was helpful as a form of self-exploration, but he sought to undermine the literal-minded acceptance of psychiatric diagnostic categories. For years he would cause the APA leadership what it called "much anguish." Thus the Airlie House conference could not afford to look exclusively inward. It had important business to attend to in the world around it.[11]

At Airlie House, the APA Council approached its work in a well-organized way, bringing together its past and current leaders for discussion and hiring a sociologist to consult. What emerged was a vision of psychiatry's predicament as combination of technical problems, legislative desiderata (and need for liaison with government agencies), and difficulties with public image. The world needed to be educated about psychiatry. For example, the conferences covered technical matters that required interfacing with the government: the FDA had recently withdrawn but then reapproved the antidepressant Parnate, and the APA reported to its leadership on its role in obtaining the reapproval.[12] On broader matters, the Council approved expenditures for an APA committee working on issues of poverty and discussed the best response, if any, to a perplexing array of other social problems.[13]

The APA's political dilemma was not spelled out but was implicit in the Airlie House minutes on the legislative scene for 1964. At the time, politics were in upheaval, with Lyndon Johnson proposing a civil rights bill and striving to carry on the legacy of the Kennedy administration, but with many general physicians remaining staunch Republicans and many Southerners appalled at what Johnson (a Southerner himself) had done. At Airlie House, medical director Walter E. Barton recommended that the APA send a letter of commendation to US Senator Sam Ervin Jr. Ervin had worked to advance the rights of psychiatric patients, and the APA was appreciative. On the other hand, Ervin, a Democrat from North Carolina, had not only opposed *Brown* v. *Board* in 1954 but with Barry Goldwater had staunchly opposed the Civil Rights Act of 1964. The bill had only just passed Congress and been signed that year: "I do not feel," Ervin had written to a constituent earlier that year, "that I can in good conscience support this legislation." The APA, though its members voted Democratic, had long felt that it was unwise to get involved in partisan politics, even when major issues of race and social justice were at stake. Ervin's case illustrates why. The terrain was simply too tricky to navigate; friends of psychiatry might be on either side of the aisle or might be at odds with even more powerful officeholders. In the 1950s, when African American member Charles Prudhomme asked the APA to write an amicus brief in *Brown* v. *Board of Education*, the APA had advised him to "remain aloof from such a political issue."[14]

Occasionally the APA's well-organized, typed minutes of 1964 managed to sound an anxious or annoyed note, but generally they involved discussion of professional issues or barriers that stood in the way of psychiatric progress. As far as I can determine, the APA only touched on the issue of nuclear war that had so dominated national discussions during the Cuban Missile Crisis just two years before. The Airlie House minutes do note, but without elaboration, that the Council discussed the importance of the APA's role "in the prevention of war." Exactly what this meant was unclear. At the moment when Goldwater's public statements on nuclear weapons were raising anxieties, just as Ginzburg was printing an image of a mushroom cloud in *Fact*, and just as *Doctor Strangelove* was playing on movie screens, it appears that the APA held to a relatively narrow view of the boundaries of its own role and of the functioning of its members.[15]

As it probed its own identity, the APA recognized the need to develop "a document of guidelines for psychiatrists concerning values, ethics, and the maintenance of public image." The idea for a formal written guide, said the task force at Airlie House, was not that the new guideline would replace the AMA's code of ethics, a general document which at that point was already formally "part of our Association's policy." Instead, the new document, if developed, would "supplement" the AMA code in a way that might be more meaningful to psychiatric specialists.[16] It would take almost a decade to develop, but in time this guideline would become the *Principles of Medical Ethics with Annotations Especially Applicable to Psychiatry*. From the beginning the *Principles* was intimately related to the APA's effort to protect the image of psychiatry – or what Barton's daughter summarized as her father's effort to help psychiatrists "look better and *be* better."[17]

* * *

From two sources in 1964 – letters from its members but also "radio programs" – APA headquarters began to get word about Ralph Ginzburg's survey. Medical director Walter Barton had already learned that the AMA mailing list had been used to contact psychiatrists. What he learned now concerned him deeply.[18]

A Chicago-trained psychiatrist with a friendly and efficient style, Barton had grown up in Elmhurst, Illinois, and had extensive experience as an administrator in the Massachusetts state hospital system. During the war, as a young psychiatrist, he had been inspired by the leadership style of William Menninger. For Barton, APA president Menninger was to be admired for launching new conferences and new publications, for creating the position of APA medical director, and perhaps especially for revitalizing APA committees, including the organization's executive committee. "It was his belief," said Barton of his mentor, "that committees must meet if they are going to make significant things happen." Barton himself served as APA president for a year, then in 1963 was appointed as medical director – usually a longer-lasting and more powerful position than president. In his more than a decade in the role, Barton put his Menninger-inspired administrative philosophy into action. He worked to develop the capacities of his staff members, reasoning that a secure leader had no need to claim credit. Instead, he "plants ideas as though they were seeds, nurtures them, but lets others enjoy the harvest and claim the produce grown as though entirely the result of their own effort." Barton soon gained a reputation as a skillful administrator on the national scene.

In a conventional studio portrait taken in the mid-1960s by prominent photographer Louis Bachrach, Walter Barton is warm-looking yet contained. Sporting a mustache and horn-rimmed glasses, he is dressed professionally in a suit and tie. A more personal glimpse is provided by Barton's daughter Gail, a psychiatrist herself and later a coauthor with him. She recalls her father as an inspiring and charismatic leader as well as a consensus builder. "He was creative, neither humdrum nor rigid." She saw Barton as an effective conceptualizer who was "very careful to hear all points of view, discuss what was just said, and create a plan for action." In meetings, Barton carried a stack of index cards with him and noted issues he wanted to follow up on, and by the next day, he had typically done so. When he began to delve into a topic, those around him often ended up eager to follow him: "Suddenly it would be a whole new ballgame." Respected by patients and APA staff, at times consulted personally by members of Congress, Barton was in his late 50s and brand new in the position of medical director when the *Fact* issue came across his desk.[19]

In August 1964, from Washington, DC, in the midst of preparing for the Airlie House conference, Barton took his first step. Barton wrote to Ginzburg and strenuously objected to the survey and its methods. For Barton, it was a cardinal principle that giving a psychiatric opinion without an interview was grossly inappropriate. It was clear to him that Ginzburg had violated this principle:

Many members of the Association have, with justifiable indignation, called our attention to a questionnaire you have sent them asking whether they "think Barry Goldwater psychologically fit to serve as President of the United States."

A physician renders an opinion on the psychological fitness or mental condition of anyone in the traditional (and confidential) doctor–patient relationship in which findings are based upon a thorough clinical examination.

Being aware of this, should you decide to publish the results of a purported "survey" of psychiatric opinion on the question you have posed, this Association will take all possible measures to disavow its validity.

When I asked Gail Barton about why her father felt so strongly, she replied: "He didn't want people to be casually throwing diagnoses around. He thought it was very unprofessional, and he said 'I wouldn't want people to do that to me.'" Barton, who attended Christian services regularly, saw the Golden Rule as his guideline.[20]

Ginzburg did not reply to Barton and did not include his letter in the *Fact* issue. Instead, on the second day of the Airlie House conference (September 12), Barton and other APA officials opened their copies of the *New York Times* to find Ginzburg's full-page advertisement for the upcoming issue of *Fact* about Goldwater. Ginzburg appealed to the reader to buy this "exciting new magazine which is dedicated to presenting the naked truth and letting all censors be damned."[21] At Airlie House the next day, Walter Barton gave the APA Council a crisp summary of the situation. There was a discussion. One member of the Council suggested a letter to the *New York Times*, showing both where the APA got its news and where it believed its statements would have the most influence. But the *Fact* issue, though heavily advertised, had not yet appeared. Others noted that there had already been "a certain amount of publicity in New York papers" about the APA's objection to the survey. Was it really wise to adopt "the tactic of disavowing an advertisement"? Why not prepare material now "and have it ready to go as quickly as possible after the article is published"? Barton agreed that it was best to wait.[22]

Once the special issue of *Fact* was published, the APA was ready. Barton had likely worked effectively behind the scenes. In October, APA president Daniel Blain released a press release condemning the survey's inappropriate mix of politics and psychiatric opinion. "To the great embarrassment of our association some psychiatrists unwittingly replied to the question *in their capacity as psychiatrists.*" In 1964, the APA Council passed what it termed a "consensus statement" that was "DISAPPROVING" of "APA MEMBERS ATTEMPTING TO DIAGNOSE INDIVIDUAL PUBLIC FIGURES WHO [*sic*] THEY HAVE NOT EXAMINED CLINICALLY."[23]

At an APA Council meeting in the fall, Barton presented a short overview of media coverage of the incident. The Associated Press and United Press International, he noted with apparent satisfaction, had not carried any news about the incident at all. The *New York Times* and the *New York Post* had published only short items. But *Time* and *Newsweek*, with their "nationwide circulation," had said more. In fact, *Time* noticed that the APA hadn't explained "why so many psychiatrists confused the analytical couch with the political stump."[24] The damage that the APA feared from nationwide publicity, and the difficulty it had in understanding its members' thinking, was evident.

* * *

As the 1960s proceeded, it became increasingly clear how much the APA had to lose from future incidents like the *Fact* survey. Blain said that the *Fact* episode was an embarrassment to the APA, but the risks went beyond this. Patients might wonder what credibility psychiatry had if psychiatrists diagnosed people without meeting them, or if they allowed politics to influence their professional judgment.[25] Public figures might take note of mental health–based attacks on them as the APA asked them to vote on mental health care funding and other issues.[26] Barry Goldwater, at least, was pleased to have the support of the AMA and the APA as he framed his libel suit against Ginzburg. After winning reelection in 1968, he was back in the Senate representing Arizona.

The APA, and the AMA with it, now had much at stake when they traveled to Washington, DC, to make the case for funding. In the 1950s and 1960s, the federal government had made a massive investment in medical research; the National Institutes of Health underwent an "astounding expansion." At medical schools, doctors took on new clinical roles; after Medicare and Medicaid, teaching hospitals boomed financially. In 1965, President Johnson signed legislation to create the Medicare and Medicaid programs. Medicare and Medicaid would transform the medical landscape as well as medical education, not only expanding the accessibility of medical services but also creating a vast new stream of income for physicians and medical centers. These changes followed the already significant rise in the availability of private health insurance; demand for medical services was high even before Medicare and Medicaid made it skyrocket.[27]

The APA too was growing. More than 500 people attended the APA's fall meetings on "The Future of the Mental Hospital" in 1964. In that same year, the APA noted with approval the United Auto Workers (UAW) labor union's success in obtaining insurance coverage for its members' psychiatric conditions: it expected 1.5 million people to gain new coverage.[28] By 1969, APA membership stood at 17,000.[29] Minutes from 1968 show that the agendas for the organization's committees, task forces, and coordinating councils were proliferating so uncontrollably that there was not enough time to have a thorough discussion of "all of the actions recommended or taken," even if weekends were mobilized.[30]

In these years, Walter Barton was everywhere: gathering information, reaching out to other professional organizations, summarizing issues for the APA leadership, gathering committee recommendations, reporting back to the Council with the results, and offering judicious advice throughout.

* * *

By early 1968, while the Vietnam War raged on and consumed increasingly more of President Johnson's time, Barry Goldwater and publisher Ralph Ginzburg were working on the pretrial preparation phase of *Goldwater* v. *Ginzburg*. The APA was preoccupied with its own matters, including evaluating the track record of the community mental health centers, which many hoped would destigmatize psychiatric conditions and offer a workable alternative to the state hospitals.[31]

Then, in January 1968, to everyone's surprise, Ginzburg suddenly stepped into the spotlight again. His new magazine *Avant Garde* had, he announced, conducted a survey of psychiatrists. This time he was seeking expert opinion on President Lyndon Johnson. Was Johnson mentally stable? Was he fit to be president? Just as in the *Fact* episode, Ginzburg implied that the answer might be no. As *Avant Garde* explained to psychiatrists in a flattering cover letter, they alone had the expertise to answer these questions – at a time when the president's seemingly bizarre and dangerous decisions threatened to continue the Vietnam War.[32]

Two of the letter's recipients grew concerned and quickly forwarded a copy to the White House, where Johnson's staff took notice almost immediately.[33] Johnson's key assistants on the matter were Fred Panzer, the White House polling expert, and Marvin Watson, chief of staff to the president. They collected material on Ginzburg's history, including his conviction for what they viewed as "pornography," and rapidly assessed the survey as "an attempt to discredit the president." (Panzer pointedly noted the polling data on the voting habits of physicians, who were "overwhelmingly" Republican – "except," as he noted in a telling distinction, "for psychiatrists.")[34] If Ginzburg, with the *Fact* libel suit still being litigated, had boldness on his side, Johnson's men had the gift of assessing a situation rapidly for its political implications.

The prospect of losing support among a group that ordinarily voted Democratic was concerning. It did not escape Panzer that one of the pro-Johnson letters in hand from a psychiatrist was "very quotable." Would it be good to respond? Perhaps feed the information to a columnist whom Johnson could count on for support? Panzer's question went directly to the president.

That evening, Johnson personally dictated a comment: "Yes, but it might just advertise it." His plan was simple: "Ask Harry."[35] Johnson's terse reply, dictated while a war and a presidential election season were going poorly, demonstrates how important the issue of psychiatrists' views was to him. The president's thought process is deliberate: he weighs the pros and cons of issuing a public statement denouncing Ginzburg, calibrates his response carefully, and opts for further consultation. The moment shows something of what Martin Luther King Jr. meant when he called Johnson "an extremely keen political man."[36] At that point the White House did not respond publicly.

"Ask Harry" refers to Harry McPherson, an attorney and political veteran who had served as an aide to Johnson in the Senate. In 1968, Mr. McPherson was serving as special counsel to the president.[37] McPherson wasted no time in replying that "to give this information to a columnist would merely advertise the poll." To McPherson, *Avant Garde*'s small circulation and its "unstable reputation among the intellectual community" were significant. Both had political and tactical implications.

At Harry's advice, the Johnson staff decided to "wait until they [*Avant Garde*] publish their story and see if it is picked up by any reputable wire service, magazine, or newspaper. At that time, we could let these comments be released to a columnist or newspaper."[38]

To top off his already savvy advice, Harry McPherson suggested a further consultation, this one with Philip Lee, MD, who was then serving as assistant secretary for health and scientific affairs in the Department of Health, Education, and Welfare (HEW). Ask Lee to find out, McPherson suggested, "what the American Psychiatrist [*sic*] Association is going to say about this poll." A handwritten note appended to the memo of February 2, likely written by Jones, says simply: "GET THIS DONE." The staff then reported, as if Dr. Lee had either offered an opinion himself or was reporting back on the opinion of the APA: "Phil Lee told all it would be highest ethical impropriety to participate."[39]

By February 16, when Ginzburg announced that he was planning to stage an event in front of the White House, Johnson aides knew definitively which way the wind was blowing. "Correspondence indicates it's been denounced by the American Psychiatric Association, American Psychoanalytic Association and the chairman of the AMA Council on Mental Health – among others." At this point the White House had even more letters in hand from psychiatrists who had denounced the survey, in case such political ammunition was needed.[40]

Interestingly, the *Avant Garde* cover letter also made its way to the files of Barry Goldwater, who exchanged letters with his attorneys about Ginzburg's latest effort. It was Darrell Coover, public relations director of the American Medical Association, who helpfully sent Goldwater a copy in 1968. When he saw the letter and the announcement of a survey about Lyndon Johnson's mental health, attorney Robb sent Goldwater a sardonic letter: "This project should put the President on our team. Maybe he would like to join us, amicus curiae."[41] Not long afterward, Goldwater was still expressing his satisfaction with the American Psychiatric Association and the way it had spoken out in the *Fact* episode against "those members of the profession who did not act in a proper ethical way."[42]

Thus it appears that something like a de facto working alliance existed between major political figures and organized medicine and psychiatry. If needed, the president and indeed any major candidate knew he could turn to the APA and the AMA for an opinion and quite possibly for support in the media. With an ethics opinion from the organization in hand, a public figure knew he could attack his political opponent as unethical.

* * *

The APA must have groaned when it read of Ginzburg's *Avant Garde* survey. It was yet another Ginzburg fire to put out. Medical director Walter Barton kept the executive committee informed. According to Barton, when the survey appeared in the mailboxes of 14,000 psychiatrists in January, 100 angry APA members protested to the APA leadership. On January 19, Henry W. Brosin, then APA president, urgently wired the presidents of the APA's district (state) branches:

> URGE YOU TO DO ANYTHING YOU CAN TO HELP ENSURE THAT NO APA MEMBER REPLIES TO QUESTIONNAIRE ON PSYCHOLOGICAL FITNESS OF PRESIDENT MAILED TO PSYCHIATRISTS THIS WEEK BY AVANT-GARDE MAGAZINE IN NEW YORK CITY. THIS QUESTIONNAIRE EMANATES FROM SAME SOURCE AS FACT MAGAZINE'S 1964 QUESTIONNAIRE ABOUT MR. GOLDWATER. IMPLICATIONS ARE MANIFEST.

Those manifest implications presumably were the potential for further damage to the public image of psychiatry. In his cover letter to psychiatrists, Ginzburg had already quoted several APA members in a manner that Barton considered "out-of-context."[43]

This time the APA was prepared. In the minutes of the APA executive committee for February, the issue got a separate heading and its own moniker: "*Avant Garde*'s Malicious Mischief." The APA's official newspaper, *Psychiatric News*, ran an editorial in that same month entitled "More Mischief Afoot." The brief editorial, appearing over the initials "R.L.R.," reminded members that "an unbecoming number" of them had responded to an almost identical survey four years earlier. R.L.R.–Robert

L. Robinson, the APA's public relations officer – assumed that the member responses to the *Fact* survey of 1964 had represented "impulsive armchair diagnoses" rather than principled replies or carefully thought out comments. He did not appear to consider that members might reach conclusions different from the APA's. Instead, he chided members about the "chilling effect" their comments had had in the 1964 election. This time, he was sure, "the profession will have less cause for embarrassment." The AMA, whose ethics code was still the model for the APA's, ran a similar story in its in-house publication, *AMA News*, on February 5. These articles, and the not very subtle reminders they contained, reached the large APA and AMA memberships in the United States and worldwide.[44]

There was more. On February 24, the APA's executive committee took up the issue. It had "a desire to publicize the APA's disapproval" of psychiatric opinions given without interview and consent. But it also wanted to impress strongly on APA members that "such irresponsible conduct [responding to the survey] will not be tolerated by the Association." After some discussion, the executive committee voted to have the APA secretary, psychiatrist Robert Garber, make written inquiries of the APA members who had responded. On a motion proposed by a past APA president and seconded by a future one,

THE EXECUTIVE COMMITTEE INSTRUCTED THE SECRETARY TO WRITE EACH MEMBER WHOSE NAME IS REPORTED BY RALPH GINZBERG [*sic*] AS RESPONDING TO THE <u>AVANT-GARDE</u> SURVEY OF PSYCHIATRISTS' OPINIONS ABOUT PRESIDENT JOHNSON'S PSYCHOLOGICAL COMPETENCE, ASKING THEM WHAT THEY WROTE (WITH COPIES OF THE LETTERS, IF AVAILABLE) AND THE BASES OF THESE STATEMENTS. THE SECRETARY SHALL SEND THE RESPONSES TO THE ETHICS COMMITTEE FOR ITS CONSIDERATION AND ACTION.[45]

Like the February 1968 editorial by public relations director Robinson, the minutes of the executive committee show no inkling of the possibility that some APA members might have responded to the survey out of conscience – or that they had the right to disagree with their professional organization, even in the midst of the bitter and divisive war over which Johnson was then presiding. The investigatory tone, the plan to automatically send all the received information to the ethics committee for review, and the ominous prospect of unnamed action suggest that by 1968, the APA had confidently bureaucratized its ethics processes and knew what it thought. It is not clear, however, that the APA processes were respectful of members or of the diversity of their opinions in a national crisis. It was important to impress on members, said the executive committee, that "irresponsible conduct will not be tolerated by the Association."

In the aftermath of the February executive committee meeting, three APA members were singled out for special scrutiny. All had been quoted by Ginzburg in the press release that announced the *Avant Garde* survey.[46] All received letters from the APA secretary on behalf of the executive committee, quoting their alleged comments to Ginzburg and asking for confirmation that the member had been quoted accurately. If the Ginzburg quote was inaccurate, the executive committee would appreciate "a copy of the full text of your reply," along with any comments the member had made in support of his reply.[47] This request was slightly toned down from the wording proposed in the executive committee meeting.

One of the three APA members singled out had referred to Johnson's view of communism as paranoid and suggested that the president did not grasp the cost and the futility of the Vietnam War. A second member had allegedly termed Johnson sadistic and blamed him for the deaths of American soldiers in Vietnam. This second statement echoed the reasoning about personality type and danger to society that had motivated Ginzburg and Boroson in 1964, Erich Fromm in the 1930s and 1940s, and Theodor Adorno in *The Authoritarian Personality* in 1950. A third APA member had drawn a parallel between Johnson's public behavior and that of Rudolf Hess, Adolf Hitler, and others. In Johnson he detected omnipotence, "a disregard for truth, an intolerance of opposition, a callousness toward human life," and other dangerous traits characteristic of narcissistic leaders. The response was dramatic, but its author claimed much relevant experience evaluating totalitarian dictators.[48] The APA's impatience with its antiwar members was striking.

As it turned out, the White House never had to use its 1968 dossier on Ralph Ginzburg. On February 27, CBS television anchor Walter Cronkite aired a special report on the war in Vietnam and concluded that "we are mired in stalemate." A negotiated withdrawal, he said, would be the only option left. Lyndon Johnson was watching from the White House and recognized what had just happened. If he no longer had Walter Cronkite, the country's most trusted journalist, he no longer had the country.[49] In March, after doing poorly in the New Hampshire primary, Johnson withdrew from the presidential race and in one stroke rendered Ginzburg's latest survey irrelevant. Ginzburg never published it and instead moved on to preparing for his *Fact* trial.[50] From the APA's point of view, however, the incident had already caused damage. The risk it represented had to be vigorously contained.

* * *

As the 1960s ended, many younger APA members began to feel that the organization's leadership was too conservative. The shootings at Kent State University in 1970 and the spread of the Vietnam War into Cambodia angered many psychiatrists. Younger members especially were watching the Walter Barton-led APA leadership, and many reacted with disgust to its stolidity in the face of social change. "It appalled me, and others, that the organization's leaders would not comment on, or even listen to its members about Cambodia and Kent State," recalled psychiatrist Lawrence Hartmann.[51] These same members of the APA leadership, many of them World War II veterans, had mobilized to fight Ginzburg's attack on Barry Goldwater in 1964; they were in earnest in their defense of ethical standards as they saw them. But to some, the APA now gave the appearance of clamping down on dissent during the Vietnam War.

Psychiatrist John Talbott recalled that in 1970, he and another young faculty member tried to shut down an APA event in 1970 to protest the shootings at Kent State University. Talbott thought that Lawrence Kolb, APA president in 1968–9, was "secretly pleased."[52] In the early 1970s, Hartmann and others founded the Committee for Concerned Psychiatrists, which had some success in getting more liberal and "social-psychiatrically thoughtful" psychiatrists into APA leadership positions. In a relatively short time, this younger generation within the APA would play a key role in policy changes. In the meantime, gay protestors had demonstrated at APA meetings, including in 1970, and in 1972, psychiatrist John Freyer donned a mask and tuxedo and spoke at an APA panel on the experience of being a closeted gay psychiatrist. In December 1973, the APA board of trustees voted to remove homosexuality from DSM-2.[53] At the May 1973 meeting in Honolulu, the board of trustees commended its flagship *American Journal of Psychiatry* for naming a woman to its board. As yet the APA board of trustees had only one female member, but change was clearly on the way.[54]

* * *

Regardless of who was elected president, the APA had to sit at the federal negotiating table and make the case for mental health care legislation and funding. This consideration was significant in an age of federal largesse – in 1967, the National Institute of Mental Health (NIMH) had a budget of more than $1 billion – and of federal changeability. In the decades after World War II, large amounts of money were already flowing from the NIMH to psychiatry for research and education. The flow would increase even further during the Johnson administration. In the February 24, 1968, meeting in which it approved the investigation of members who had responded to the *Avant Garde* survey, the APA executive committee also noted the receipt of a grant from the NIMH and of a request to review the Johnson administration's plan for a reorganization of drug abuse programs at the HEW.

Lyndon Johnson, an advocate for health care initiatives because of his own family's history of cardiovascular disease and cancer, had wasted no time in getting started in 1964. He created the Commission on Heart Disease, Cancer, and Strokes and developed a proposal to build a set of federally funded hospitals, but quickly abandoned the idea after the AMA called it socialized medicine. Changing course, Johnson then put his full support behind Medicare instead. The measure, which had the public behind it, would fund hospital insurance for the elderly, fund insurance to pay doctors' bills, and create new state-based health coverage for the indigent (Medicaid). In 1965, Johnson brought the considerable force of his personality and political acumen to convince the AMA to support the measure.[55]

* * *

While Lyndon Johnson made his case for Medicare and the war, Ralph Ginzburg was using up the last of his appeals in the *Eros* case. He had become something of a cause célèbre. The Committee for a Free Press, a group of distinguished writers and other celebrities, placed an ad in the *New York Times* in February 1972 to support him. The list of signers, many of whom had publicly supported Ginzburg since at least 1966, was extensive. It included playwright Arthur Miller, novelist James Jones, comic Dick Gregory, journalists I. F. Stone and Nat Hentoff, *Playboy*'s Hugh Hefner, attorney Marvin Belli, and at least two law professors, not to mention the legal director of the American Civil Liberties Union. Arthur Miller perhaps put it most eloquently when he described Ginzburg's *Eros* conviction as absurd. By the standards of 1972, almost 20 years after *Playboy*'s debut and in the year the movie *Deep Throat* was released, it was.

> After all the legal, moral, and psychological arguments are done, the fact remains that a man is going to prison for publishing and advertising stuff a few years ago that today would hardly raise an eyebrow in your dentist's office. This is the folly, the menace of all censorship – it lays down rules for all time which are ludicrous a short time later. If it is right that Ralph Ginzburg should go to jail, then in all justice the same court that sentenced him should proceed at once to close down ninety percent of the movies now playing.

Even after reviewing Ginzburg's flaws, journalist Merle Miller concluded that Ginzburg was sincere, that he believed "every sentimental word" of what he said. "Here and now a great injustice has been done, and nobody seems to care very much."

In February 1972, Ginzburg was handcuffed and taken into custody at the federal district court in Lewisburg, Pennsylvania, then was transferred to the Allenwood Penitentiary. In character, he described the court's holding cell as "claustrophobifacient" (a near-neologism of Ginzburg's, the word meant "tending to produce claustrophobia"). In prison, his hair was cut and the stylish mustache he had grown was shaven off. Ginzburg was fitted with standard-issue prison clothing. Two hundred miles from the city, he missed his wife terribly and worried about his young children. Of a sentence of three years, he would serve a total of eight months, with probation to follow.

On the day of his release from prison, Ginzburg's wife and daughter drove him to the Allenwood prison gate, where reporters and TV cameras were assembled. There, with a serious demeanor and with his large drooping mustache back in place, he accused the Supreme Court of "high crimes and treason, namely, of mocking the Constitution, trammeling Freedom of the Press, and playing fast and loose with one man's liberty – mine." He promised to continue his fight with a new appeal. If the APA noticed, I have not been able to find evidence of it in the organization's archives.[56]

* * *

The image of psychiatry was an increasing problem for the APA. For one thing, the "Szasz point of view," the APA believed, was still spreading: the organization's president would see to it that *Psychiatric Annals* responded to the attack on psychiatry.[57] But media stories about sexual misconduct by psychiatrists were also growing more common. Speaking bluntly, Walter Barton, then nearing the end of his years as medical director, explained to the chair of the APA ethics committee that the APA *had* to have a strong public statement on record on ethical issues. That way negative publicity could be more easily countered:

> Our work is simplified when we can respond to adverse newspaper publicity by quoting to a reporter that we already have a strong statement on a psychiatrist's behavior when sexual indiscretions occur. When we are silent and have no position, we continue to convey the impression to the public at large that we are really not concerned with anything other than our own welfare.[58]

The APA's public statements were understood explicitly as protecting the public image of psychiatry, as a kind of shield against unfavorable publicity. In 1973, the APA considered that greater attention to "position statements" and the hiring of "a large Washington law firm" would be essential as it contemplated the likelihood of future class-action lawsuits. At the same time, appropriately publicizing ethics violations "via the media" remained a mainstay of the APA's approach and was felt to increase public safety.[59]

During this period, the APA was also refining its approach to Congress. Melvin Sabshin, a psychiatrist who was dubious about psycho-analysis, succeeded Barton as medical director in 1974 and made it a priority to press for what he called "sophisticated involvement with governmental agencies." Lobbying, previously seen as "crass and undignified," would become an increasing priority for the APA. Sabshin, deeply concerned about the public's negative perception of psychiatry, believed that "the best way to influence the government was to increase the scientific image of the field." Science, not ideology, would be the watchword of the APA, and image would be crucial. Developing this broad and politically sensitive approach to government and to media, in 1975, the APA renamed its joint commission on legislation, which would henceforth be called the Joint Commission on Government Relations. It was a suave choice appropriate to a more sophisticated age.[60]

* * *

As he noted in his memoirs, Richard Nixon won the 1972 election by dimensions that he called "gratifying." Quoting the cables of congratula-tions that he received and reviewing their tone carefully for any critical implications, Nixon tried to feel pleased. "No presidential candidate had ever won so many states." But there were some details he felt compelled to acknowledge. His more than 47 million votes represented, he said with grim precision, 60.7 percent of the popular vote. The figure was reported so precisely because it rankled slightly: in the contest for highest percen-tage of the popular vote ever received, he had placed second. Lyndon Johnson, defeating Barry Goldwater in 1964, had achieved 61.1 percent.[61]

In the Nixon years, the APA had significant problems to monitor and to respond to. The consensus that had favored funding for mental health research in the 1960s was falling apart. In the Johnson administration,

Wilbur Cohen served one of the shortest tenures in department history, claiming more success for community mental health centers than was warranted. Elliot Richardson, a liberal Republican, went on to serve as defense secretary and then as attorney general; Caspar Weinberger, a conservative, was aggressive in pushing for federal budget cuts in health care programs. In January 1973, the administration proposed budget cuts of $6.5 billion for the coming year. The APA medical director, Walter Barton, his daughter recalls, was "not a happy camper" during this period; one of his prized possessions was a pen that President Kennedy had used to sign the 1963 Community Mental Health Centers Act. For his part, Nixon knew the cuts endangered many jobs and government contracts, and said he was proud of recognizing that fact. But, he thought, the cuts were a bold move for that very reason; "I was prepared to take that heat." In his memoirs, he recalled, in character, that even the *New York Times* thought he was serious about making the cuts. He was proud of that. But Congress, more favorably disposed toward NIMH funding and community mental health centers, allowed the mental health centers to continue.[62]

* * *

In the years between the *Fact* debacle and the adoption of the Rule in 1973, the APA worried over its new ethics standards – drafting language, trying out and rejecting formulations, experimenting with the right tone. But the project the APA first envisioned at Airlie House was moving forward. In 1969, a draft was presented to the board of trustees that tried to establish perspective on the many new situations in which psychiatrists were being asked to comment. These included not only the profiling of candidates and presidents, but occasions when the media asked about social problems, such as "problems of youth, racism, education, and others." Forensic psychiatrists were speaking to the media about their cases. In general, in a time of rapid social change, psychiatrists were "very much on the spot" when asked to comment. To refuse altogether might be an abrogation of responsibility: "After all, who is supposed to be expert in these matters?" Yet to be too hasty was even worse: "Every psychiatrist should be aware of his position as a representative of the profession to the general public and help portray the profession in its proper perspective as a thoughtful, dignified, difficult discipline always motivated to help human beings in distress and never to do harm." When the statement is compared with previous iterations of the APA's position on media statements, the word "difficult" stands out.[63]

In preparation for its 1973 annual meeting in Honolulu, Hawaii, the APA Assembly and Executive Committee gave one last revision to the new ethics rules, then ratified them. The board of trustees held extra sessions in advance so that it could devote itself exclusively to policy matters at the meeting. The new ethics rules were paramount. On May 10, 1973, they finally came to a vote before the board of trustees.

At the Sheraton-Waikiki, then a new hotel, more than 7,000 psychiatrists and attendees had dealt with a full schedule of educational presentations, certification sessions, sessions on new research, scientific sessions, films, lunches, and receptions for army and air force psychiatrists, not to mention allied meetings of psychoanalysts, forensic psychiatrists, and psychiatry residency training directors.[64] The hotel's stunning view of the beach may have helped compensate for any meeting fatigue.

The vote itself took place on a Thursday, during a 7:45 AM meeting. The incoming board of trustees, composed of 13 APA members from across the country who were assuming new responsibilities or continuing their service, was there. Board members included Robert Garber, who had sent the letter of inquiry to the three APA members quoted in Ralph Ginzburg's 1968 *Avant Garde* press release, and several past APA presidents who served on an *ex officio* (nonvoting) basis. These included Daniel Blain, architect of the Airlie House reforms that were now coming to fruition, and APA veteran Walter Barton, now in his 60s. Psychiatrist Melvin Sabshin, a Chicago psychiatrist who was soon to succeed Barton as medical director, was also on the board. The experience and the caution of this group, and its opposition to what it believed Ralph Ginzburg represented, were evident.[65]

Assembled in the Honolulu-Kahuka Room at the hotel, the board dealt with a long agenda of nominations and committee business: it considered a resolution of support for Vietnam veterans, and it approved a resolution supporting the extension of the Community Mental Health Centers Act. The revised "Ethical Guidelines" were then presented for consideration. The item was described as routine in the minutes of the meeting. But the consensus on the Goldwater Rule, though strong, was not quite unanimous. Psychiatrist Alan Stone, a new member of the board, voted against the Rule. A future APA president, Stone argued that the proposed rule went against psychiatrists' right to free speech, or at least the right to be foolish. In his words, one cannot "legislate against stupidity." As Stone recalled later: "The circumstances around adoption of the rule suggested to me that the rule was best understood as serving the profession's public image and relationship to the medical community rather than reflecting a professional responsibility to our patients."[66]

The APA published the *Principles*, its new ethics guidelines, in September 1973.[67]

* * *

What, exactly, was the APA's new rule about comment on public figures? The text of the Goldwater Rule approved by the board emphasized, in the male-oriented language of the day, the ethical difficulties that arise when psychiatrists comment in the media:

> On occasion psychiatrists are asked for an opinion about an individual who is in the light of public attention, or who has disclosed information about himself through public media. It is unethical for a psychiatrist to offer a diagnosis unless he has conducted an examination and has been granted proper authorization for such a statement.[68]

To many, the APA appeared to be articulating a general principle here – that it is *never* ethical to diagnose unless there has been an interview and consent. Seen from this angle, the Goldwater Rule was apparently a general statement about the centrality of a personal interview and consent. Yet seen from a slightly different angle, the Rule's wording, with its oddly contingent frame (*when* approached by the media ...) seemed to assume the centrality of a narrow zone in which this resounding general principle would come into play. Was the Rule applicable only in media settings, or had the media setting suggested a broader, more general rule? The text did not say.[69]

At the time of the Rule's adoption, the APA ethics committee had developed a filing system to handle the expected complaints, a procedure for handling them, and a classification scheme to facilitate access to the committee's rulings.[70] But the organization's archives show that it wrestled with innumerable problems in the aftermath of the ethics code's adoption.

A flood of questions and requests for opinions began as soon as the summer months of 1973. In June, the APA's flagship journal, the *American Journal of Psychiatry*, wanted an opinion from the ethics committee on the ethics of publishing a psychological profile that had been presented in court as part of a high-profile criminal case. The subject, who appears to have been Sirhan Sirhan, the convicted assassin of Robert Kennedy, had undergone psychological testing as part of his court proceedings. His attorney gave consent for publication, but the subject himself had not done so. In the new climate, the *Journal* felt obligated to ask about the ethics of publication. Was it ethical? The ethics committee reviewed the matter and found that "there are no questions involving breach of ethics, confidentiality, or unlawfulness in the publication of the article."[71]

The APA's distinct branches, the ethics committee told the board in December 1973, were in confusion over ethics matters. Methods of handling ethics complaints varied wildly, with only about half of district branches having ethics committees and 4 of 24 branches surveyed reporting no mechanism for handling ethics complaints at all. When ethics complaints were brought to the district branches – a rare occurrence – "there was often confusion as to how to proceed and sometimes fear of legal entanglement. Furthermore, there was confusion over what constituted a problem of ethics and what was a problem of business competition or professional clinical judgment."[72]

Individual APA members soon began to write to the ethics committee to express their uncertainty about what was appropriate in light of the new rules. Over the next few years, these questions expanded into a flood. Was it acceptable for a forensic psychiatrist to testify in court if the person being evaluated refused to be interviewed? Could an administrator in an insurance company make a diagnosis based solely on a review of records? What about writing a profile for a police department that was trying to catch a serial killer? And – perhaps the most central question of all – was it ethical for a government psychiatrist to comment on the mental stability and leader-ship style of a world leader, as the CIA had done for decades?

* * *

The APA ethics committee has the responsibility for answering members' questions. Its preferred method is to publish questions and answers on topics of concern as *Opinions of the Ethics Committee on the Principles of Medical Ethics with Annotations Especially Applicable to Psychiatry.* Covering the whole range of possible ethical dilemmas, but including the Goldwater Rule, the *Opinions* includes a disclaimer that the committee's opinions are not the same as board of trustee–approved publications. But the ethics committee's judgments carry weight and are the closest thing we have to the APA's interpretation of its own rule.[73]

Can a forensic psychiatrist testify in court based solely on a review of records? Yes, said the ethics committee, even if the defendant did not grant consent. What about other settings? Could a psychiatric consul-tant to a religious organization give opinions on annulments without interviewing the parties involved? "Yes. ... To ask [consultants] to per-form a personal examination in each case would be impractical and prevent such agencies from benefiting from psychiatric consultation." Could a psychiatrist working for an insurance company decide if a patient's death was a suicide even though the patient could not be interviewed? He could. Were curbside consultations acceptable? Yes, with qualifications. These had to do with acknowledging the limitations of one's knowledge and the nature of one's role. Could a psychiatrist who supervised another mental health professional diagnose a patient who is under the care of that other professional? Yes, again with qualifications.

Was psychological profiling for a government agency acceptable? This issue was complex. Initially, the APA's opinions unfolded in a nuanced way as the organization grappled with the implications of the new rule. In 1973, because of the numerous issues and uncertainties here, the board of trustees asked the ethics committee and a special task force on psy-chohistory to look into the problems and difficulties that now existed under the new rule.

The easiest of the task force's challenges involved psychohistory. Much in vogue at the time, the psychoanalytically inspired analysis of deceased figures in historical context was celebrated with awards and much public acclaim. Now this field, in light of the Goldwater Rule, had suddenly become problematic. Was the kind of psychohistory Erik Erikson practiced ethically acceptable now? It was unlikely that the task force would reject this form of profiling, given its centrality to the psychoanalytic tradition and its contribution to a positive view of psychiatry. For example, in the same year that the task force completed its report, psychiatrist John Mack, a member of the task force himself, published a sophisticated psychobiography that would go on to win the Pulitzer Prize: *A Prince of Our Disorder: The Life of T.E. Lawrence.* And psychiatrist Robert Coles, a former teaching assistant of Erikson's and friend of Mack's, had recently published perhaps the most probing reflection on psychohistory ever written. The task force report acknowledged that Erikson's work was widely regarded as masterful rather than as unethical. Other than the possibility that a deceased subject's living relatives might be offended, the task force ended up finding little problem with psychohistory.[74]

Among the more pressing issues was a "need for guidelines" on whether government psychiatrists may profile living figures. As Walter Barton drily noted to his colleagues, "Profiles have been prepared on national figures for many years." In fact, the issue of profiling living figures for government agencies and for law enforcement would resurface for years in the APA ethics literature. At first the APA ethics committee was flexible, doubting the usefulness of profiles but reporting to the board in late 1973 that "despite the strong prohibition" in the Goldwater Rule, "we believe some exceptions could be made." These potential exceptions included psychohistory but also the profiling of unknown or "hypothetical" perpetrators for law enforcement. As for government agencies, the ethics committee's provisional thought in 1973 was that the ban on profiling in the United States should apply equally to "citizens of other countries" – though its language indicated mainly concern about the improper use of profiling and the committee did not indicate just what an improper use might be. The plaintive note suggesting that profiling of foreign citizens should be bound by the same rules as domestic profiling was repeated in an ethics committee report of late 1974. But it rarely if ever appeared again in the APA ethics literature and specifically would not appear in the task force's 1976 report. The 1976 report mentioned the risk of leaks to the media but did not mention the inherent risks of profiling for the government, including the obvious point that a profile is typically a contribution to national security or even a war effort. It either did not occur to the task force or was not emphasized that there might be a risk of physical harm or death to an enemy subject when profiled by a psychiatrist for a government agency. The task force concluded that there was no substantial ethics difficulty involved in the profiling of foreign leaders.

The confusing wording of section 7.3 meant that questions continued to arise. Perhaps the ethics committee's frankest and most systematic answer about the Rule came in response to a 1983 question. By now, 10 years had passed since the adoption of section 7.3. The APA's members, it was evident, remained unclear on its meaning and applicability:

Question: A psychiatrist testifies for the state in a criminal case about the competency of the defendant. The psychiatrist based the testimony on medical records and did not examine the defendant nor have the defendant's approval to render an opinion. Was this ethical?

Answer: Yes. . . . Confusion has arisen by taking the second sentence above [of section 7.3] and not connecting it to the first sentence as was intended. It is common for forensic experts to offer opinions as was done according to the question. Further, it would be too great an extension of the Goldwater Rule to say that a person, by being a defendant in court, has entered into "the light of public attention." This annotation was developed to protect public figures from psychiatric speculation that harms the reputation of the profession of psychiatry and of the unsuspecting public figure.

This opinion makes clear that in the ethics committee's view, no general rule banning psychiatric comment from a distance ever existed. The Rule's media frame defined the limits of its interpretation and applicability. And the committee was open about the intention of the Rule, which was "to protect public figures" and to protect the public reputation of psychiatry – not to get in the way of routine psychiatric work for the courts, for the government, or for other institutions.[75]

* * *

Once the code was in place, ethics complaints showed a "marked increase." Formal complaints to the APA now affected 1 member per 100 in the organization. Though the vast majority involved improper conduct of other sorts, between 1950 and 1980, there were eight complaints involving what was then section 10 (not section 7), the portion of the code designed to promote and protect the welfare of the community. Barton and Barton's study of the distribution of complaints shows that the majority of the section 10 complaints were made in the 1970s rather than in the earlier decades. One of the three examples given by the Bartons involves a book "written about a prominent person which brought discredit upon the profession." The discredit involved was described in the Bartons' contained language as going beyond what was "prudent" in psychohistory. Little information is available on to what extent the APA has enforced the rule since 1973. But in this case, the APA held a hearing, found that the complaint was justified, and reprimanded the member. According to Alan Stone, who served as APA president in 1979–80, in the early years, some members were sanctioned or warned in connection with the Goldwater Rule; this is consistent with the Bartons' statistical study. According to Stone, however, issues of due process led the APA to abandon the effort at sanction.[76]

What remained consistent over time is the APA's interest in issuing high-profile reminders about the Rule and its importance. This is partly because when an ethics problem arises publicly, the APA's tools for fighting back are limited; the organization does not discuss ethics complaints against its members in identifiable ways. After a period of figuring out how *Psychiatric News* should describe ethics violations, the APA appears to have decided that vigorous public statements – ironically, conducted as a kind of media campaign – were its best tool for fighting back against public misperception.[77] Notably, the APA's public affirmation of the principle satisfied Barry Goldwater in the *Fact* matter, even before the rule was formally adopted. In 1974, the ethics committee recommended a policy of publishing groups of ethics complaints with attention to the privacy of APA members. The APA itself would increasingly feel compelled to review the *Principles of Medical Ethics* to make sure that any potential APA recommendation did not conflict with the new rules.[78]

In the 1970s and 1980s, textbooks in psychiatric ethics began to include discussion of the newly enshrined principle and its origins in the *Fact* case. Now, authors adopted a dismissive tone toward the *Fact* survey, as if the principle has been self-evident and uncontroversial from the beginning. One ethics textbook mentioned the *Fact* survey twice, describing it first as "obviously biased" and later as a "heinous" example of psychiatrists' "misuse of their professional reputations." Even as it argued against "the illusion of omnipotence," which it saw as "an occupational hazard of the profession," the textbook opined confidently that the surveyed psychiatrists' motives were politically motivated rather than based in evidence. There was little or no consideration of the possibility that socially worthwhile motives had led psychiatrists to respond to the 1964 survey, and no discussion of the fact that Ginzburg had altered the psychiatrists' responses. This vein of concrete thinking would become common in discussions of the *Fact* survey after the adoption of the Rule in 1973. Ultimately it would harden into a cliché.[79]

* * *

As the APA's new ethics rules gained a foothold, American newspapers were in a complex position. In the 1960s, the media had played an important role in advancing a critical understanding of psychiatry. For example, its stories helped reveal "the inadequacies of the mental hospital system."[80] But in the aftermath of the *Fact* debacle, there was little evidence of introspection on the part of journalists and editors, or publishers. Ethics in journalism, viewed skeptically by the public, developed and professionalized slowly in comparison with developments in medical and legal ethics. As Meredith Levine notes, journalism never developed the equivalent of a Goldwater Rule.[81]

Journalists in the 1970s and 1980s were coping with continued humiliations. In 1970, Nixon had proposed legislation that exempted newspapers from antitrust laws, but this modest business advantage was offset by the general tone of Nixon's political strategy, which was to systematically "discredit the 'liberal news media.'" Reporters believed that the Nixon administration was "less sensitive to First Amendment rights than any since that of John Adams." Newspapers found themselves in court to fight Nixon in the Pentagon Papers case and the Watergate affair. At the same time, ironically, they were more and more dependent on the news leaks that Nixon was trying to clamp down on.[82]

Between the time of the APA board's vote on the Goldwater Rule in May and its first publication in September 1973, former White House aide Alex Butterfield revealed to Senator Sam Ervin's staff that there was a secret taping system in the Nixon White House. The news, disclosed to the public the next day, had a "stunning" impact on the media. "Nixon Bugged Own Offices," screamed the *New York Daily News*. Under investigation by both a special prosecutor and by Ervin's Watergate Committee, the APA's least favorite president in years debated whether to destroy the tapes that would eventually implicate him.[83]

The Watergate hearings were covered live by the networks beginning in May 1973 and seemed to make television news even more relevant. The highest audience to date for any presidential speech, 110 million viewers, watched Nixon resign on television in 1974. Yet jobs in newspaper journalism at least were increasingly insecure. Major afternoon papers in one big city after another were closing or switching to morning publication: "Death in the afternoon became a catchphrase of newsrooms and circulation conventions." *Washington Post* reporters Bob Woodward and Carl Bernstein had hardly had time to make investigative journalism glamorous again when a wave of superficial reporting crested and then broke on the disillusioned country's shores. After only a year of publication, the slickly packaged, colorful, and carefully market-tested *USA Today* (1982–) saw its circulation climb to 1 million. By the mid-eighties, as Ronald Reagan proclaimed "morning in America," *USA Today* had the third largest circulation in the country – higher than the *New York Times*, the

Post, or the formerly conservative papers *Los Angeles Times* and *Chicago Tribune.*[84]

* * *

In the years since 1973, the APA's rule on psychiatrists and the media has itself been through several vicissitudes of interpretation and revision, as American society continues to wrestle with the way it views psychiatry, politics, and safety. As noted earlier, in 1975, the APA board of trustees changed the wording of the rule, replacing "it is unethical for a psychiatrist to offer a diagnosis unless ... " with "it is unethical for a psychiatrist to offer a professional opinion unless ... " It thereby widened the applicability of the rule considerably. The Rule itself not only was not immutable, but views on it within the APA were not always unanimous. In late 1974, the ethics committee took a conservative stance on diagnosis from a distance, but one member offered a "minority opinion," which was simply "not acceptable to the other members." Henry Grunebaum observed that if psychiatrists can contribute to the understanding of deceased leaders, they surely can contribute to understanding living leaders too. Grunebaum offered the simple solution that in the absence of a personal examination, "great care" should be taken with comment and that defamation should be avoided.[85]

With the American Psychological Association's guidelines more flexible than the APA's, psychologists had more leeway to explore. An occasional APA official, especially in the early years after adoption, did take a flexible view of the Rule's mandate. Jeremy Lazarus, who served as chair of the APA ethics committee, took it for granted that the Goldwater Rule could not be taken literally. For Lazarus, the Rule was valuable but needed to be integrated with other ethical principles; "rigid overscrupulosity" was a significant risk, and there might be circumstances in which public safety considerations outweighed harm to the person profiled. But in general, the tone of official APA communications between 1973 and 2008 grew increasingly rigid and even literal-minded. It was an incongruous stance for sophisticated professionals who otherwise pride themselves on their ability to think independently.[86]

When media stories appeared about President Bill Clinton's character in the late 1990s, for example, a column by APA president Herbert Sacks was heavy-handed: "Psychobabble reported by the media undermines psychiatry as science." From the tone of these statements, of which there were many, the moral rightness of the Rule appeared self-evident; no hint of the complexity or larger context of the issue was offered. Neither was any hint that APA members had ever disagreed or had any reasonable basis to do so. After shootings at Virginia Tech University in 2007, the APA's *Psychiatric News* quoted Sacks and asserted: "These *Principles* are 'standards of conduct that define the essentials of honorable behavior for the physician.' Within these *Principles* can be found clear direction on the ethical requirements for communicating with the media." Thus was the long history of uncertainty and ambiguity about the Rule and its meaning obscured.[87]

* * *

In the early 2000s, there was evidence of some possible loosening of the APA's public position. In 2008, the ethics committee received this inquiry from psychiatrist Jerrold Post about leadership studies:

Question: Does the ethical prohibition embodied in Section 7, Paragraph 3 of the Annotations apply to psychologically informed leadership studies based on careful research that do not specify a clinical diagnosis and are designed to enhance public and governmental understanding?

Answer: The psychological profiling of historical figures designed to enhance public and governmental understanding of these individuals does not conflict with the ethical principles outlined in Section 7, Paragraph 3, as long as the psychological profiling does not include a clinical diagnosis and is the product of scholarly research that has been subject to peer review and academic scrutiny, and is based on relevant standards of scholarship.

This answer did not offer a clear definition of "historic figures" and excluded diagnosis as unethical. It allowed for the first time, though, the possibility that the APA could allow comment on a living public figure that a psychiatrist had not interviewed and from whom he or she had not obtained consent.[88]

At about this same time, the APA made a rare, though still only implicit, public acknowledgment that internal disagreement over the Goldwater Rule has recurred: it appointed a special task force to review the ethics annotations. Some task force members argued that the Rule needed to be loosened, and press stories followed. Though the wording of section 7.3 was not changed, the task force, in conjunction with the APA ethics committee, did eventually issue a guide to what it called "ethics in practice." This 2015 report included what appeared to be a somewhat a more liberal view of how the Rule might be interpreted. On the topic of public figures it seemed to embody a new spirit of toleration: it raised the possibility that under the right circumstances offering a diagnosis could be ethical: "In some circumstances, such as academic scholarship about figures of historical importance, exploration of psychiatric issues (e.g., diagnostic conclusions) may be reasonable provided that it has a sufficient evidence base and is subject to peer review and academic scrutiny based on relevant standards of scholarship."

By 2015, then, there were some signs of possible change in the attitude of the APA and its ethics committee on the Rule. On the one hand, *Psychiatric News* continued to issue firm public reminders about section 7.3 and periodically reasserted its view that comment on public figures was meeting a pathological need of any APA member who did it. Any psychiatrists who "cavalierly" diagnose a public figure in the media, it said in 2014, had the goal of meeting "their own needs for self-aggrandizement and attention." And in a later interview with me, APA ethics committee chair Rebecca Brendel said that there had, in her view, "never been a 'loosening' of the rule." Instead, Brendel prefers to use the word "specification." But the thoughtfulness of the 2015 *Guide to Ethics in Practice* and the possibility of an evolution in ethics committee opinions on the Rule gave some observers of the APA grounds for hope.[89]

CHAPTER 6

The CIA and the White House

Adventures in Assessment

The preparation of this profile [of Daniel Ellsberg] was specifically approved by then Director Helms in late July of 1971. The actual compiling of the profile was done by the CIA's medical services staff and, in particular, its chief psychiatrist [Bernard Malloy]. Testimony has indicated that a meeting was held on August 12, 1971, in which both Howard Hunt and Gordon Liddy participated. They told the CIA psychiatrist that Ellsberg had been undergoing psychiatric analysis. Hunt and Liddy discussed with him their desire to "try Ellsberg in public," [and] render him "the object of pity as a broken man." . . . The psychiatrist has testified recently that he was extremely concerned about Hunt's presence and remarks. He so reported this to his CIA superiors.[1]

Senator Howard Baker, individual contribution to the
Senate Watergate Report, 1974

The American Psychiatric Association's (APA) comfort with government profiling was seldom expressed in dramatic headlines. But the organization carefully interpreted the Goldwater Rule in such a way as to allow the Central Intelligence Agency (CIA) to continue to create psychological profiles of foreign leaders, as the Office of Strategic Services (OSS) had done for Adolf Hitler during World War II. Critics have documented the many problems of government profiling, but even they have concluded that there will likely be "a continued demand" for psychological profiles over time, as presidents must often assess "an inscrutable adversary in the heat of crisis" and tend to turn to profiling for help.[2]

In the late 1960s, psychiatrist Jerrold Post founded the CIA's Center for the Analysis of Personality and Political Behavior. For more than 20 years, Post directed an interdisciplinary team that regularly created thoughtful at-a-distance

*profiles for the use of CIA staff members, diplomats, and the president. It was,
he said later, a "great comfort" to know that the APA viewed his work for the
Agency as ethical. But when Post moved from the CIA to a university setting,
he realized that the protections of the APA's Goldwater Rule were less clear. In
1990, during the developing crisis in the Persian Gulf, Post accepted an
invitation from two committees in the House of Representatives and testified about
a psychological profile he had created of Iraq's Saddam Hussein. Several congressmen expressed their gratitude. Afterward, Post learned that the APA had received
complaints from members, some of whom saw his public testimony as a violation of
the Rule. In a spirited defense of the ethics of his life's work – the best-informed and
most thoughtful rationale for profiling yet published – Post developed the doctrine of
a "duty to warn."[3]*

*As a recently declassified CIA internal report makes clear, Post and other CIA
psychiatrists faced their own ethical dilemma in 1971. In that year, as the Vietnam
War raged, the Nixon administration asked Agency psychiatrists to create a profile
of an American citizen – a request that probably violated the CIA's charter and
raised a host of ethical issues for the Agency.*

Richard Nixon was outraged. While working for the RAND Corporation,
a former Pentagon aide named Daniel Ellsberg had leaked much of the
contents of the Pentagon Papers, a collection of revealing government
documents on the Vietnam War, to the *New York Times* and the *Washington
Post.* Ellsberg had become concerned about the conduct of the war and
believed that public exposure of the government's actions and misstate-
ments would serve as a valuable correction to government policy. The
Nixon administration had tried but failed to get a court to order prior
restraint of the Papers' publication. The Federal Bureau of Investigation
(FBI) was investigating the leaks, but Nixon was impatient. To Nixon and
his aides, Ellsberg was a clear national security risk. Noting that "we were
heading into an election year," Nixon said that Ellsberg's antiwar views
"had to be discredited." The president directed his staff to "find out
everything we could about his background, his motives, and his co-
conspirators, if they existed."[4]

For this task, the White House needed its own political operatives,
and so the "Plumbers" – a group of White House staff members dedicated to investigating and plugging information "leaks" – were born.

Working in Room 16 of the Executive Office Building "under the over-all aegis" of Nixon's chief domestic adviser, John Ehrlichman, the Plumbers consisted of four men. They were David Young (like Ellsberg himself, a former aide to Henry Kissinger); Egil "Bud" Krogh; G. Gordon Liddy, a former FBI agent; and Howard Hunt, a former agent with the CIA.[5]

The CIA's exploration of domestic profiling began in earnest in July 1971, just "a few days after the publication of the Pentagon Papers began in the *New York Times*." Ehrlichman called the CIA's deputy direc-tor and told him that Howard Hunt had just been appointed to the White House staff. Would the Agency cooperate with him? The CIA asked few questions at the time; Hunt was working hard and creatively on the "Pentagon Papers problem," and the CIA was in the habit of accommo-dating presidents. The Plumbers hoped to gather material that would help in understanding Ellsberg's personality but that would also advance the court case against him (Ellsberg was then facing charges of espio-nage, stealing government property, and conspiracy). Almost immedi-ately, Hunt suggested that David Young approach the CIA and ask for a psychological profile of Ellsberg. In a meeting on the project, Hunt referred to "trying Ellsberg in public" and said he aimed to discredit him. According to the CIA's own internal documentation, the Nixon White House believed "an example must be made of Ellsberg to forestall future leaks."[6]

For years, as Hunt and David Young were well aware, psychiatrists on the CIA staff had produced intriguing psychological profiles of world leaders; they knew the psychiatric staff could put together profiles as needed.[7] But this request was different. Ellsberg was an American citizen. That meant creating a profile of him would risk falling outside the Agency's domestic mandate and could well be illegal.[8] Nonetheless, the Plumbers made the request and gave the CIA information they thought would be useful for the politically charged profile.

What happened next can be traced in detail, thanks to several con-gressional investigations, the work of a presidential commission, and a remarkable secret internal report put together by the CIA's inspector general and only released to the public as a result of a lawsuit in 2016. The CIA's "Watergate History" was drafted in 1973–4 and made available to the Rockefeller Commission in 1975. Broadly congruent with multiple other sources, the report provides many details about the Ellsberg profile that have never been known before, including names and detailed actions of some of the participants – and also new information on how the CIA itself viewed the actions and ethics of its psychiatric staff during the episode.[9]

As the report shows, then-CIA director Richard Helms had significant reservations about the White House request for a profile. He took the time to call David Young of the White House personally and to express his concerns. Young told him the request "had the highest White House level support," including from John Ehrlichman and Henry Kissinger. Young argued that the National Security Act of 1947 actually *required* the Agency to protect intelligence sources and methods against leaks. Hearing this, Helms deferred to Young, "reluctantly." Thus the Ellsberg profile went forward, arguably because the CIA accepted the view that it fell within the domain of national security.[10]

When the CIA's profiling staff members were assigned the work, they too were concerned about the White House's request. According to the House of Representatives' investigation, the team had initial concerns about the limitations, risks, and possible illegality of the profile:

> The CIA psychiatric personnel involved, including medical doctors, expressed varying degrees of concern over the propriety of the project in view of the limited information on Ellsberg at hand, and the question of whether it was CIA-mission oriented since the subject was a U.S. national. Also there was concern that the product could be misinterpreted as coming from a doctor–patient relationship, which, of course, would not be the case.[11]

The CIA's internal report shows that Dr. John Tietjen, director of the Agency's Office of Medical Services (OMS), "accepted the requirement to prepare the study" while also emphasizing the limited information available on Ellsberg. Dr. Tietjen in turn delegated the work to the (unnamed) chief of the psychiatric staff, who is identified elsewhere as Dr. Bernard Malloy.[12] At this point Malloy involved both a deputy chief and Dr. Jerrold Post, who at that time was a psychiatrist on the CIA staff. According to the CIA report,

Dr. Post was reluctant to undertake such a study and cited his reservations about the propriety of conducting such an assessment of a U.S. citizen. [Redacted] indicated he shared these reservations and concerns, but cited approval by the Director [Helms] and his [redacted] understanding that the White House was concerned about the security problems caused by Ellsberg's revelations and hoped, by an understanding of his psychology and motivations, to be able more effectively to deal with this type of threat to national security.[13]

Post then "was asked" to prepare the profile using publicly available sources, and he did so. But when medical services director Tietjen and at least one other person then reviewed the profile, they told Post that changes would be "needed."

The CIA's internal report says it was likely that at this point material was added to Post's initial profile from FBI files on Ellsberg and from State Department documents. The CIA report left unclear who added this material, but it was probably not Post: his name conspicuously drops out of the report at this point. A 1976 *New York Times* article identifies Malloy as the author of the expanded profile, as does Malloy's own sworn affidavit and testimony before a House subcommittee that investigated the incident.[14] The final result was "cleared" by several high-ranking CIA officials: John Coffey, the deputy director for support; Henry Osborn, the Agency's director of security; and ultimately Director Helms himself. With the approval of these officials, the Ellsberg profile was delivered to David Young of the White House staff on August 11, 1971.[15]

* * *

Pulled together from a variety of unsatisfactory sources under pressure from the White House, the profile that the CIA delivered – the first of two, as it turned out – was a cursory, halfhearted effort. In a follow-up meeting on August 12, Young, Hunt, and Liddy eagerly inquired about the kind of material the CIA would need to do an in-depth profile of the kind usually done on foreign leaders; plenty of additional information was available, Hunt assured the CIA. This material included "the fact that Ellsberg had been under psychiatric analysis, [and] that his former wife could be interviewed, and was willing to testify." Referring to the *Fact* episode (see Chapters 2–4), Hunt asked if the CIA could assemble data of the kind that "psychiatrists found out about Barry Goldwater in 1964." Hunt helpfully provided the name of Ellsberg's former psychiatrist and psychoanalyst, Dr. Lewis Fielding of Beverly Hills, whom Ellsberg had seen between 1968 and 1970. David Young once again pulled rank. The request for the Ellsberg profile, he reminded chief psychiatrist Malloy, came from John Ehrlichman and from national security adviser Henry Kissinger (Young's former boss). Nixon himself "had been informed of this study" and it "had the highest priority."[16] In a memo written the day before, Young and Krogh had given Ehrlichman a status report and recorded in writing how disappointed they were with the initial profile's superficiality. The plan, they said in the August 11 memo, was to "meet tomorrow with the head psychiatrist, [redacted], to impress upon him the detail and depth that we expect." Young also followed up with a phone call to the CIA's security director to express his dissatisfaction.[17]

The August 11 memo to Ehrlichman, so scathing and so disappointed about the initial Ellsberg profile the White House staffers had received that day, made a firm case that more adequate information was needed for use in a better profile. But in their memo, Young and Krogh went further. In a proposal meant for Ehrlichman's eyes rather than the CIA's, they said: "In this connection, we would recommend that a covert operation be undertaken to examine all of the medical files still held by Ellsberg's psychoanalyst covering the two-year period in which he was undergoing analysis." Here was more information with a vengeance. Proposing an illegal burglary that would violate a citizen's confidentiality and expose his mental health records in order to discredit him, the White House staff did not appear to have qualms about the project. John Ehrlichman initialed the approval line on the memo "with the initial 'E' and a note that said, 'if done under your assurance that it is not traceable.'"[18]

Most of the participants' memoirs acknowledge that one of the motives for the burglary of Dr. Lewis Fielding's office – which took place in 1971 – was to gather more information for the CIA psychological profile of Daniel Ellsberg. Egil Krogh, it is true, suggests that the Plumbers' dissatisfaction with the profile led the Plumbers to turn *away* from the profiling project and undertake a burglary instead, in the spirit of what he mordantly calls a "self-help attitude." If taken seriously, this comment might suggest that the CIA staff's reservations about creating the profile in the first place had some braking effect on the White House, at least as far as profiling specifically was concerned. Much firsthand evidence suggests otherwise, however. John Ehrlichman, to whom Krogh reported and who approved the project of seeking Ellsberg's psychiatric files, said the burglary's purpose was the enhancement, not the abandonment, of the CIA psychological profile. Ehrlichman said that the plan was that Hunt and Liddy would go to California, find out what Dr. Fielding knew, and then "feed that information to the CIA's profilers." Liddy too said that the burglary was driven by a wish to get further information for use in a revised profile.[19]

While the burglary moved forward, the CIA continued to delay on producing the revised and expanded profile that David Young of the White House was still expecting. CIA administrators were uneasy. When he received additional information about Ellsberg from Young, OMS director John Tietjen expressed concern "over the ethical and political considerations involved." Tietjen consulted John Coffey, the CIA deputy director for support. Tietjen and a colleague whose name is redacted (apparently a physician, because the CIA report calls them "the Doctors") explained to Coffey in detail about their continued reservations about the profile. They and Coffey openly discussed the pressure they were getting from the White House, and the physicians believed they had Coffey's sympathetic support. Young and the Plumbers put even more pressure on the CIA, and Coffey's support proved transient. Could the profile, the Plumbers wondered, include information about "Ellsberg's sexual proclivities"? Was there any information "which could be used to defame or manipulate" him? And could the White House have the profile within a week? Coffey unhelpfully advised the staff to "continue working on the paper."[20]

In early November, the second (expanded) profile was complete. By now John Tietjen, ambivalent and in a difficult position, had rethought the ethics question. He implied to Coffey that it no longer concerned him. He explained the change in a cover note that accompanied the finished profile: "We have re-thought our concerns and they can be subsumed under one major concern; i.e., entering into matters beyond the Agency's purview." Yet he was not willing to say no. Since the White House had requested it, the "OMS stands ready to deliver this material to Mr. David Young at the Executive Office Building whenever agreeable." Tietjen was ready, perhaps, but was not able to authorize the delivery to the White House. Presumably because he was raising concerns about the profile's legality, he suggested strongly that Director Helms review the profile. In his note sending the profile to Helms, Coffey of the Support Division summarized the physicians' concerns as follows: "Their worries did not at this time involve professional ethics or credibility. Instead, they are concerned lest the Agency's involvement in the development of this information [the profile] should become known." Coffey said the CIA physicians would prefer it if Young "could be reminded that the Agency's connection with this matter must never surface."[21] The CIA internal report objected to this characterization of the main concerns of John Tietjen and his Office of Medical Services. Nonetheless, the language Coffey used ended up featured in a portion of the Senate Watergate Report, where it left the inaccurate impression that the CIA staff members who developed the profile had never had concerns about professional ethics.[22]

Helms was aware of the chief psychiatrist's objections but approved the second Ellsberg profile anyway. This one was delivered to the White House on November 12, 1971. In a special note to David Young, Helms described a spirit of cooperation: "I have seen the two papers which [name redacted] prepared for you. ... We are, of course, glad to be of assistance."[23]

* * *

Was the request for the profile ethical? The memoirs of Nixon and Kissinger are notably silent on the issue, and much of the CIA report emphasizes the national security justification for the request. But the White House's motives in asking for a profile were transparently political. The Plumbers were open about their wish to damage an American citizen's reputation, what Egil Krogh called their effort "to discredit Ellsberg." As Krogh later acknowledged in a memoir, in the Plumbers' work he had failed to differentiate between "matters of national security and matters that were primarily political." Indeed, Krogh called his memoir an "apology"; he dedicated it to "those who deserved better." The CIA's reservations about the profiling were evident. The agency's own carefully worded summary is as follows: "The Agency cooperated, though reluctantly, in producing psychological profiles on Daniel Ellsberg." Director Richard Helms, in testimony before the Watergate Committee, did not quite apologize, but said he had "genuine regrets about being pressured" into providing the profiles. "I'm not proud of that one."[24]

Did the CIA's employees act ethically? The Ellsberg matter, everyone in the CIA recognized, presented "peculiar problems" for all. There was the obvious difficulty of saying no to the Nixon White House; there was the technical question of whether the profiling staff had enough information at hand to create a profile; there was the issue of psychiatric ethics raised by John Tietjen; and there was the issue of legality and the Agency's charter raised by psychiatrist Jerrold Post early in the process. Generally the CIA played down ethics concerns in its report, but even the CIA saw fit to commend "the performance of the lower and middle level echelons during this trying period." The Agency's report found that these employees, especially John Tietjen, "acted properly and promptly in bringing to the attention of the upper levels their fears and concerns" that creating the profile meant exceeding the Agency's charter. Caught between their ethical and legal obligations on the one hand and the demands of the White House and the upper ranks of their agency on the other, CIA psychiatric staff members faced a dilemma. Whatever their qualms, Tietjen and Malloy finally elected to deliver the profile to Helms and thereby to the White House. Post, though he raised concerns, wrote an initial profile that his superiors were able to revise for use by the Plumbers.[25]

Then there is the question of harm to Daniel Ellsberg. In 1973, Ellsberg described as particular outrages the activities of the Plumbers, the CIA, and "domestic law-breaking" by the Nixon administration. When Egil Krogh of the Plumbers saw fit to apologize and acknowledge his wrongdoing, Ellsberg said publicly that Krogh's action meant a great deal to him; he was large enough in spirit to write an introduction to Krogh's memoir. Krogh was referring to the burglary, but from these sources, it seems likely that Ellsberg felt there had been a breach of trust by the CIA and that had needed to be repaired. The breach could well have involved the profile.[26]

Separating the harm from the creation of the Ellsberg profile from that of the closely associated burglary is a difficult and finally unrewarding task. Both were initiated by the White House and facilitated, if reluctantly, by an intelligence agency. Both involved lawbreaking and gross disrespect for the rights of an American citizen. It is notable that when the House Judiciary Committee approved articles of impeachment against President Nixon in 1974, it specifically mentioned the Plumbers and their misuse of Ellsberg. Article 2 listed the following charge against Nixon:

> He has, acting personally and through his subordinates and agents, in violation or disregard of the constitutional rights of citizens, authorized and permitted to be maintained a secret investigative unit within the office of the President, financed in part with money derived from campaign contributions, which unlawfully utilized the resources of the Central Intelligence Agency, engaged covert and unlawful activities, and attempted to prejudice the constitutional right of an accused to a fair trial.

Finally, given the numerous lines of evidence that exist – the specifics of the impeachment article, the results of several congressional investigations, the recollections of Ehrlichman and Liddy, and the Agency's own ambivalent internal investigation – it is reasonable to conclude that the CIA's willingness to create a profile of Ellsberg had a ripple effect. The Agency's willingness to engage in domestic psychological profiling not only facilitated the Ellsberg break-in by providing the Plumbers with a motive, but in the process made a contribution to the greatest constitutional crisis in our nation's history.[27]

* * *

The 1973 disclosure of the Ellsberg burglary was a media sensation. As a front-page story in the *New York Times* reported, all charges against Ellsberg were dismissed. Reporters filled the courtroom as the judge disclosed that the CIA had become involved in the Ellsberg prosecution at the request of the Nixon White House. On the same day, on a tape recording made by the Oval Office recording system, Nixon can be heard saying of Ellsberg: "The sonofabitching thief is made a national hero . . . and the *New York Times* gets a Pulitzer Prize for stealing documents. . . . What in the name of God have we come to?" As the wider Watergate scandal developed further, Nixon began to make crude attacks on what he called the most "outrageous, vicious, distorted reporting" he had ever seen.

Nixon, it eventually turned out, had specifically directed the CIA to interfere in the Watergate investigation. He had long denied being part of a cover-up, but his mishandling of the crisis and the eventual release of a transcript of a 1972 White House tape led what little support he had left to collapse. Conservatives had long mistrusted Nixon; Barry Goldwater now regarded him as a liar. In August 1974, following the new disclosure and the passage of articles of impeachment by the Judiciary Committee, Goldwater and two other senators went to the Oval Office and conveyed to the president the bleak situation in the Senate. Nixon resigned the next day.[28]

The CIA's reputation went into precipitous decline in 1974–5 when the *New York Times*, again in a front-page story, reported on allegations of domestic spying by the Agency. Over the next year, a presidential commission and two congressional committees looked into the Agency's functioning and history of covert operations. The resulting revelations were damaging. The public learned that the CIA had been extensively involved in domestic espionage and warrantless surveillance, had spied on Vietnam War dissenters, and had conducted covert operations against a democratically elected government in Chile. Lyndon Johnson was so interested in finding out whether there were foreign influences on American antiwar protestors that CIA director Helms formed Operation CHAOS, a domestic counterintelligence program about which Johnson frequently inquired. The CIA had funded research centers and cultivated "clandestine relationships" with members of the American and Canadian intellectual and university communities and funded experiments with LSD and other mind-altering substances.[29] The Agency was later sued by victims. A set of CIA-funded experiments at McGill University, for which no patient consent was obtained, was conducted by former APA president Ewen Cameron of McGill University. Intelligence officials expressed few if any legal or ethical concerns about their programs, but they did worry about public exposure. When the CIA's secret program of opening Americans' mail was finally discontinued in 1973, it was because the Agency feared headlines – what the Church Committee called "political risk" and what CIA documents termed "flap potential."[30]

Leftists were appalled, and the public image of the CIA was permanently tarnished by the revelations. In his personal copy of the committee's final report, writer Gore Vidal marked and underlined many passages related to the CIA's domestic surveillance programs and to its secret use of reporters and academic authors. Many in the Agency considered the release of Agency documents to the Senate an act of betrayal, and many on the right were outraged. What outraged them was not the CIA's covert actions, which they supported as necessary for national security, but the committee's decision to release the information. Barry Goldwater served on the Senate Intelligence Committee during the 1970s. In committee hearings, he had few questions for the CIA director and instead publicly emphasized the problem of "sensational headlines": "At the present time it is virtually impossible to get a kind word about the CIA and this country's intelligence community published in an Eastern newspaper." What, he wondered in a column, were the backgrounds and motives of those who spread rumors about the CIA in such conspiracy-like fashion?[31]

Intelligence rules were reformed, but the revelations kept coming. In 1977, journalist Carl Bernstein published an article in *Rolling Stone* that detailed the CIA's close relationship with the media. Extending the revelations of the Church Committee that had concerned Vidal, Bernstein documented that for more than 20 years, the Agency had made use of journalists on a paid and volunteer basis. A handful of columnists with views favorable to the CIA, including at the *New York Times*, were considered "known assets": these columnists could be counted on to cooperate with the Agency. Newspaper and TV reporters and stringers were debriefed after their travels, served as sources, and were paid in cash for travel expenses, retainers, and "specific services performed." Editors, publishers, and executives cooperated. Arthur Sulzberger of the *New York Times* approved these arrangements, provided cover roles for CIA agents, and signed a nondisclosure agreement with the Agency himself. The Agency's closest working relationships, Bernstein concluded, were with the *New York Times* and CBS, but *Time* and *Newsweek* were also involved.[32]

These revelations, and a ready flow of conveniently timed leaks, gave substance to former CIA director Frank Wisner's boast that he could play the media like a "mighty Worlitzer." In fact, media sources had long worried about the risk of exposure, arrest, or even assassination if their use by the CIA became known. Future president George H. W. Bush, then the CIA director, banned the practice of using media in this way. The public image of the Agency had fallen a long way since 1963, when Bill Cosby and Robert Culp starred in NBC's top-20 television hit *I Spy*, about an interracial pair of secret agents.[33]

* * *

The APA was aware of the Ellsberg disclosures. In 1973, the APA's omnipresent medical director Walter Barton, soon to retire, conveyed a request from the board of trustees: Would the ethics committee look into ethical issues involved in psychiatric profiling? "This question," the committee explained, "was stimulated by the public discussion of the Daniel Ellsberg case where it was alleged that a psychiatrist had drawn a psychiatric profile from various information that was available to him." On that occasion, however, the ethics committee conducted only a general discussion of profiling, since notably "the ethical case was not brought to us for discussion."[34]

It is not at all clear what this strikingly passive phrase in the ethics committee's report to the board of trustees implies. But it apparently does not mean that the APA failed to look into the Ellsberg profile. It simply may have done so at a different time or in a venue separate from that of the ethics committee. According to a report by the *New York Times*, at some point psychiatrist and APA member Robert Jay Lifton requested that the APA censure the author of the Ellsberg profile, psychiatrist Bernard Malloy of the CIA. The APA, for reasons I have been unable to determine, declined to do so.[35]

* * *

During the 1970s, the US government had its hands full in the Middle East. Where once the shah of Iran had seemed a reliable ally with a firm base of support in his own country, by the late 1970s, protests began to flourish and his public support shrank. The shah, once forceful in style, became "depressed, dispirited, and uncertain." Many Iranians, the CIA reported with concern, thought the shah was "losing his grip." Meanwhile, the CIA's profile of Ayatollah Khomeini helped American "officials to think anew about their adversaries" and allies as the world changed.[36]

Jimmy Carter, then president, hoped to achieve what few had been able to thus far: a peace agreement in the Middle East. In 1978, as he prepared for a Camp David summit, President Jimmy Carter asked the CIA to prepare psychological profiles of Menachem Begin of Israel and Anwar el-Sadat of Egypt. Carter had invited these historic antagonists to Camp David, where he hoped they would sit down together and negotiate. At first, it was not clear that they would do so much as meet face to face.[37]

The Camp David profiles were crafted by Jerrold Post and his team. It is possible that Post's history of raising concerns about the Ellsberg profile in 1971 had heightened his status within the Agency after the Watergate revelations. In any case, he now enjoyed President Carter's full confidence. During a vacation in the Grand Tetons before the summit, Carter recalled, he studied the profiles with extraordinary care. The president enjoyed the "breathtaking" view of the mountains and the time to be with his family during the vacation:

> But at its close my thoughts were not on the cutthroat trout, the delicious food, or the beauties of nature. It was late at night, and I was very tired. I was studying a thick volume, written especially for me, about two men – Menachem Begin and Anwar el-Sadat. In a few days, on September 5, I would welcome them to Camp David. ... An intensely personal effort would be required of us. I had to understand these men![38]

The president, struggling politically at the time, hoped that Middle East peace could become a signature achievement of his administration.

Agency profilers said Begin had a provocative style and a "preoccupation with legal precision." He would want specifics. Sadat, in sharp contrast, had an "abhorrence of details," a preoccupation with the "big picture," and a capacity for surprise.[39] Post's team, grasping the profound differences in the two leaders' personalities, planned for the possibility that Carter would have to hold separate discussions with the two men. That is exactly what happened. But a prolonged and intensive negotiating effort by Carter eventually led to a combined meeting, a compromise, and a peace agreement. In his memoir, Carter said the profiles paid "rich dividends," and he repeated his praise over time. Contemporaneous CIA documentation supports Carter's public account. In a report to CIA staff just after the summit, the Agency's deputy director said that Carter had described the briefing papers and profiles as "superb." According to Director Stansfield Turner, the success at Camp David led to increased demand for psychological profiles within the Agency.[40]

Carter, as far as I can determine, has not directly commented on any risks that may have been associated with the Camp David psychological profiles. But the diplomatic effort that the profiles supported clearly had its risks – and perhaps its unintended consequences. History staff member of the CIA Matthew Penney, for example, sees the accords in a complex matrix. Penney acknowledges that the Palestine Liberation Organization (PLO) was not happy with the accords; the organization denounced them as "an Egyptian surrender and called for punishing any who supported the Accords. The Muslim Brotherhood, likewise, considered them a betrayal." As Penney notes, in retrospect it is possible to see certain things that were not clear to participants at the time, including any foreknowledge that "animosity toward Sadat from the most fervent elements in Egypt" would lead to the leader's 1981 assassination.

Carter handles Sadat's assassination very circumspectly in both of his memoirs, but it is clear that he felt devastated by the news. The president ultimately evoked a religious understanding, asserting that Sadat "had given his life for the Middle East peace that he and Begin and I had consummated." Profiling's greatest achievement was thus inseparable from the historic – and risky – process that it supported.[41]

* * *

The final year of the Carter administration, described by the president as "the most difficult period of my life," saw the taking of American diplomats as hostages in Iran and the associated rise of intense media coverage. In 1979, ABC television ran a special report on the crisis whose title reflected the paralysis that seemed to be affecting the entire nation: "America Held Hostage." A complicated CIA covert operation to rescue the hostages failed. The crisis occupied 20 percent of American news time, led to the creation of a nightly ABC show called *Nightline*, and helped Ronald Reagan defeat Carter in the fall. The administration changed, as did national priorities. But profiling continued.

William Casey, newly confirmed as CIA director, had the great luxury of focusing on other issues; the hostages had been released on Ronald Reagan's inauguration day. Among his priorities were undoing the limitations Congress had placed on the Agency's covert activities. Almost as soon as he was sworn in, Casey was given a secret intelligence estimate called "Libya: Aims and Vulnerabilities," prepared by the CIA and the National Foreign Intelligence Board. The report predicted that Libyan leader Muammar Quaddafi's aggression would be an increasing concern for the United States. Quaddafi had bought weapons from the Soviets and faced only disorganized opposition at home. A psychological profile included in the report addressed Quaddafi's childhood, his sensitivity to slights, his religious "fanaticism," and his "indiscriminate support of rebel causes throughout the world."

In December 1981, the *Los Angeles Times* reported favorably on the existence of the CIA profile. Noting that such profiles are rarely released to the public, the authors said that this one indicated that Quaddafi was "more dangerous than ever." Quaddafi, it said, had recently sent troops into Chad and may have tried to assassinate President Reagan. He was so irrational that it was hard to predict how he would react to adverse publicity. The CIA had no public comment, but it pointedly kept a copy of the *Los Angeles Times* piece in its files, suggesting that it was leaked in order to build support for an anti-Quaddafi policy. The article was full of glowing praise for psychological profiling and its beneficial influence on the thinking of American leaders and on American foreign policy. The CIA and the State Department did indeed develop a plan for covert operations against Quaddafi. These operations eventually included the provision of assistance to Quaddafi's enemy in Chad, even though some in Congress had questions about the rival's human rights record.

Casey enjoyed a close relationship with President Reagan; he had been his campaign manager in 1980. Under Casey, the CIA began to adapt its profiles to President Reagan's style, which was visual rather than textual. At Camp David and at the White House, the CIA showed the president video profiles of foreign leaders, including Quaddafi. The president "was impressed," a point that Casey's staff made sure to convey to CIA staff. When Reagan later sent aircraft carriers to the Libyan coast, he expressed special fascination with a CIA report that Quaddafi had once donned women's makeup and shoes. "Quaddafi," said Reagan, "can look in Nancy's closet anytime." The 1986 American attacks on Libya resulted in deaths on both sides of the conflict.

As the Quaddafi example shows, psychological profiling was intertwined with the covert aims of the CIA in undermining a foreign leader – and was part of the portfolio of information given to a president for purposes of planning a military operation against that leader. Nothing in the APA's Goldwater Rule prevented it.[42]

* * *

Decades of CIA profiling have generated surprisingly little discussion of ethics. By far the most interesting and substantial discussion yet published on the Goldwater Rule – including the ethics of profiling for the CIA – belongs to Jerrold Post. His article "Ethical Considerations in the Profiling of Public Figures" (2002) remains central to any discussion of the topic. Based on his extensive reading of APA history and its statements on the Goldwater Rule, Post had been reasonably sure that his work profiling foreign leaders for the CIA would not cause ethics problems. He admired Walter Langer's work on Hitler and saw himself as working in that tradition, contributing to the defeat of dangerous tyrants. But when Post left the Agency in 1986 to become a professor at George Washington University, he realized that the Rule would very likely constrain his future work in profiling. It was only when Post *stopped* contributing to military and presidential efforts that the Goldwater Rule became relevant.

In "Ethical Considerations," Post reviewed the history of the Goldwater Rule in greater depth than had ever been done before, documented internal debates within the APA over its formulation and interpretation, and raised fundamental questions about whether profiling could so easily be dismissed as unethical. For him, the core dilemma of the Rule was that it conflicts with another core ethical principle. The APA's annotated *Principles of Medical Ethics*, Post thought, encouraged a member both to educate society about mental illness *and* to withhold comment when a leader is mentally ill and dangerous: "In weighing whether and how to respond, psychiatrists will find themselves caught between the Scylla of public service and public education and the Charybdis of the ethical prohibitions that are spelled out in section 7." For Post, section 7.3 was "a masterpiece of internal contradiction" that has "regularly concerned, confused, confounded, and constrained me." But, he thought, his dilemma was relevant to psychiatrists who may also wish to speak out in the service of public education.[43]

Post's appreciation of this dilemma arose from painful personal experience. Post had created a personality profile of Iraqi leader Saddam Hussein for the CIA. At George Washington, he then created a public profile that was similar to the CIA version. In August 1990, CIA intelligence analysts were trying to predict for President George H. W. Bush whether Hussein would cross the border into Kuwait. As it happened, Hussein invaded Kuwait one day after the CIA predicted he would not. Post was invited to present a profile of Hussein before the House Armed Services Committee – and did so. The resulting newspaper headlines led to a phone call from an APA committee chair who told him that there had been an ethics complaint about his public testimony. Post, enraged at first, explained his view that when ethical principles conflict, one must decide how to balance or reconcile the two. His own solution was that speaking publicly about a leader is justified when a leader is dangerous and when "policy decisions are being made based on errant perceptions that could lead to significant loss of life." In this case, he thought, he had a "duty to warn." Post says he consulted with the APA ethics committee, which cleared him.[44]

At a panel I chaired at the 2015 APA annual meeting, Jerrold Post participated by videotape in a discussion of the Rule. He recounted the problem of conflict of principles, narrated his disagreement with the APA, and gave his justification for his life's work. It was clear to me from comments at the panel how much APA members and leaders valued him – and how grateful they were that he had not left the organization over the Goldwater Rule when he easily could have. It was Post who submitted the 2008 inquiry to the ethics committee that led to the interpretation about diagnosing historical figures, one of the significant if small steps toward flexibility that the APA ethics committee took in the early 2000s. He took the committee's response as ethical validation for his form of psychologically informed leadership studies.[45]

Post's contribution has been to place public service and public education back into the ethical equation – and thus to construct a complex ethical system in which a true moral dilemma must be faced. Post did not claim that profiling was free of risk or that it would lead in a simple way to the formation of better policies. But he gave evidence that his profile of Saddam Hussein was gratefully received by lawmakers and other influential public figures. By his lights, if psychological misunderstanding could lead to loss of life, a well-informed psychological profile aimed at changing government policy would be justified: "It would have been unethical," he told the APA, "to have withheld this assessment."

Withholding a profile, as Post recognized, is a form of silence that itself can have consequences. Post told the APA ethics committee that he had often held back opinions on other public figures because of the Rule, "not contributing to public discourse at times when I felt I might usefully do so." If one takes Post's argument seriously, as Yale psychiatrist Bandy Lee would later do, silence about the psychology of dangerous leaders can amount to allowing a disaster to happen – and to impoverishing the public conversation while the crisis unfolds.[46]

Despite Post's efforts, psychological profiling continued to strike many as a dubious undertaking at best. Thomas Omestad, in a still influential article that appeared in *Foreign Policy*, summarized the many cases in which the CIA is known to have profiled foreign leaders over the decades. He interviewed Post and many American officials, including former national security adviser Brent Scowcroft and former secretary of state George Schulz. These officials identified a number of problems. Omestad focused on the strategic and policy implications of profiling. But most of the former Republican administration officials he spoke with expressed concerns about the usefulness of psychological profiling as well. Criticisms included its inaccuracy, its lack of foundation in a personal interview, and perhaps most of all its tendency to ignore broader policy contexts and reduce foreign policy issues to matters of the psychology of one leader. Yet even Omestad ended up concluding that profiling would always be with us. The most urgent recommendation he made was to improve, not to eliminate, psychological profiling.[47]

CHAPTER 7

Furor

The Debate over Donald Trump

Possibly the oddest experience in my career as a psychiatrist has been to find that the only people not allowed to speak about an issue are those who know the most about it. ...

... [I]t would be accurate to state that, while we [coauthors] respect the rule, we deem it subordinate to the single most important principle that guides our professional conduct: that we hold our responsibility to human life and well-being as paramount.

Bandy Lee, in *The Dangerous Case of Donald Trump*[1]

On January 20, 2017, real estate developer Donald Trump was inaugurated as president of the United States. At age 70, the first billionaire to become president, he had never held elected office before. The day, Trump said in his address at the Capitol, "will be remembered as the day the people became rulers of the country again." Trump promised to make America proud and great again. Said a conservative writer: "He could not possibly deliver quickly on such promises." There were protests throughout Washington, DC, some leading to violence against the police, and there were counterdemonstrations by Bikers for Trump. Within a year, Trump had managed some successes. By then, however, his approval ratings stood at only 40 percent. State and local governments were defying his policies, business leaders had resigned from his presidential advisory boards, and he was under investigation for possible collusion with the Russians during the 2016 election. Some were openly discussing his removal from office, "either through the impeachment process or on grounds of psychological inability." Trump's "strange mélange" of virtues and weaknesses, said that same conservative writer, "is unique in U.S. presidents."[2]

THE DEBATE OVER DONALD TRUMP

In 1987, *Newsweek* magazine published a cover story on a brash young New York real estate developer, whom it called the "symbol of an era." The cover shows Donald Trump in business regalia, gazing confidently and perhaps a bit dismissively at the reader. His hands are on his hips, his long red tie is in place, and he appears ready for even more publicity. The *Newsweek* reporter joined the billionaire in his $2 million helicopter for a flight to Atlantic City. The helicopter hovered over the World Trade Center's twin towers, but Trump barely noticed the view. "A reporter is present, and it's showtime." The article portrayed Trump as a dynamic and successful businessman who was dedicated to money and success, to conspicuous consumption, and to media exposure. "Trump can hardly walk the streets of his native New York without being hounded by autograph seekers, most of whom seem starstruck." Comfortable with bragging about his wealth, the article said, Trump was a brilliant promoter who constantly "feeds the hype machine."[3]

Trump's first high-profile real estate project was the rehabilitation of what is now the Grand Hyatt Hotel on 42nd Street in midtown Manhattan, just a half mile from the tower on 40th Street where journalist Ralph Ginzburg launched his fusillades against Barry Goldwater and racism in the early 1960s. Trump convinced New York to give him a tax break to renovate the hotel, and the deal was widely regarded as a key to bringing the declining block back to affluence. Trump's methods, according to sources interviewed for the article, included not only bravado but also intimidation. He himself commented on his philosophy of business: "If people screw me, I screw back in spades."[4]

Trump's signature approach was in evidence when the federal government accused Trump and his father, Fred, of housing discrimination in the 1970s. The accusations involved discrimination against African American tenants. For advice, Trump turned to staunch and controversial anticommunist attorney Roy Cohn. Cohn had served as counsel to Wisconsin senator Joseph McCarthy; his strategy has been described as "never surrender, counterattack at once, and claim victory no matter what really happened." The biggest reason for criticism of McCarthy, Cohn thought, was not McCarthy's behavior but the public's acceptance of the way McCarthy was portrayed in the liberal media. Jews, whom he thought dominated the media, seemed to have a special sensitivity because of their persecution by Hitler; they were often, he found, unreasonable in their opposition to McCarthy.[5]

By the 1970s, having narrowly beat many legal charges over the years, Cohn was using "ruthlessness, ferocious loyalty and, some say, elastic ethics" to make a comeback. (Trying to preserve his looks, the middle-aged Cohn developed a fondness for custom-made tanning lotions, which, *Newsweek* reported, had "cured his skin to a light tobacco hue.") His advice to Trump was to countersue the Justice Department, a move that helped Trump to win a settlement and to claim victory. Cohn later helped Trump fight the city to win a tax abatement for Trump Tower. In 1979, Trump commented happily to *Newsweek*: "If you need someone to get vicious toward an opponent, you get Roy. . . . People will drop a suit just by getting a letter with Roy's name at the bottom."

Where would Trump's upward trajectory end? *Newsweek* was not sure. The year before, *Forbes* magazine had listed Trump as the 50th wealthiest man in America. At the time of the *Newsweek* story, Trump had just taken out full-page ads in the *New York Times, Washington Post,* and *Boston Globe* to showcase his comments on American foreign policy. And he had just scheduled a speech in New Hampshire. "I'm not running for president," he said, "but if I did . . . I'd win."[6]

* * *

The media itself, over which many observers thought Trump showed impressive mastery, was changing. By the time Trump and his wife Ivana played out their divorce war in the New York media market, the Federal Communications Commission (FCC) had relaxed its rules. Now corporate ownership of TV stations was less tightly regulated. Beginning in 1985, a frenzy of mergers and acquisitions (sometimes hostile) affected the three major television networks, as network profits declined and cash-rich corporations moved in for leveraged buyouts.[7] New cable networks like Home Box Office (HBO) and the Turner Broadcasting System (TBS) were causing new problems for the networks: they could specialize and innovate, introducing ideas like

24-hour news. In January 1991, an extraordinary 1 billion people watched CNN's coverage of its breaking news, the American military's Operation Desert Storm in Iraq. Correspondents from CNN broadcast live from a hotel room in Baghdad during the American air attack on the city, and the public watched with fascination. It was the beginning of a new era for CNN's founder and cable entrepreneur Ted Turner. Turner was named man of the year by *Time* in 1991.[8]

The networks responded as best they could to the new developments. The rise of the Internet led to a new medium that was international in scope and paradoxically TV-compatible. After 1995, digital technology would bring not only Internet service but also improved television quality into living rooms, and eventually onto portable devices as well. A new culture of "24/7" electronic access and reduced downtime was notable to many observers. As of 2003–5, the broadcast networks were producing their latest craze, reality shows like *Survivor* on CBS and Donald Trump's *The Apprentice* on NBC. Reality shows were cheap to produce and could make use of product placement as needed, thereby generating additional revenue. But in 2004, when a television network announced a profit of more than $1 billion – the highest number ever recorded by a network to that point – the announcement came not from a broadcast network, but from HBO.[9]

The cable and Internet boom fractured the traditional broadcast medium. Soon viewers could "live in completely different news environments" in which political partisanship reigned. Democrats could faithfully watch CNN, Republicans could tune into Fox News, and for better or worse neither had to leave their comfort zones.[10]

* * *

On June 16, 2015, Trump and his wife Melania descended the oversize escalator in their opulent tower at Fifth Avenue and 56th Street in New York City. Begun in the 1970s and completed in 1983, the gold-plated Trump Tower was built in the glare of publicity. Trump had very public fights with tenants, workers, and others in the city in the early 1980s. He had paradoxically gained much negative publicity as a result. Trump believed that negative attention had its value for him: it showed the public an image of what his biographer calls "a formidable, if ruthless and not entirely ethical, operator."[11]

In his 2015 announcement speech at the tower, Trump denounced many Mexican immigrants as "rapists," a hostile and unsubstantiated claim that would be a harbinger of themes to come in the campaign. Observers on the left found his treatment of African American supporters, African American journalists, and race relations in general appalling.[12] As the election neared, Trump reemphasized his campaign promise to reform immigration, build a wall and make Mexico pay for it, and in the process fight back against the "out of touch media elites." His audiences roared back, "Build the wall! Build the wall!" In October, it emerged, he had once bragged on tape that as a celebrity he could do whatever he wanted with women: "I just start kissing them. It's like a magnet. Just kiss. I don't even wait. And when you're a star, they let you do it. You can do anything. ... Grab 'em by the pussy. You can do anything."[13]

Widely viewed as a joke at first, Trump's campaign succeeded despite the odds, rising to prominence through a crowded field of primary antagonists. Trump thereby came to the attention of liberals who were repulsed by what they saw as his crudeness, his hostility to immigrants and to women, and his authoritarianism. On CNN, Watergate journalist Carl Bernstein termed Trump authoritarian and a "neo-Fascist." In academic circles, UCLA education professor Douglas Kellner drew on the work of the Frankfurt School to argue that Trump's rise represented a form of "authoritarian populism." Trump, claimed Kellner, relied on destructiveness and "media spectacle" – a combination of politics and performance – for his success. Bernstein had declined to compare Trump to Hitler, but Kellner did so, citing Erich Fromm's analysis of Hitler, of narcissism, and of "malignant aggression" in *The Anatomy of Human Destructiveness* (1973). For Kellner, Trump was a threat to democracy and to world peace.[14]

Conservatives were divided. Phyllis Schlafly, active in the movement since Goldwater, launched her argument for Trump by saying that he offered what Goldwater had, "a choice, not an echo" in a society that had lost its way. But in January 2016, during primary season, *National Review* published a hostile editorial and a section of essays by conservatives called

"Against Trump." To *National Review,* Trump's primary opponent Ted Cruz was the true conservative; the magazine portrayed Trump as "a philosophically unmoored political opportunist" who would betray conservativism and instead bring the country "free-floating populism with strong-man overtones." The Cato Institute once argued that American politics consists not simply of a left/right division, but of a liberal wing on one side and a shifting coalition of groups – libertarian, conservative, and populist – on the other. Trump's populism caused a shift in the balance of the political forces and interests on the right.[15]

By election day, the polls showed that Hilary Clinton was overwhelmingly likely to win. Clinton had an elaborate victory party ready, a fact that some Republicans found quite arrogant. As the evening advanced, however, a different story emerged in the media. Confident liberals who had gone to bed early awoke to an unpleasant surprise. Though Clinton had won the popular vote, Donald Trump was the victor. The New York billionaire took the previously Democratic states of Michigan, Wisconsin, Ohio, Pennsylvania, and Florida – and won the election by the relatively modest margin of 306 electoral votes to Hilary Clinton's 232. Clinton won the popular vote, won the votes of women by a large margin, and did well in central cities and big city suburbs. Trump scored increasingly large margins in small cities, rural cities, and remote rural areas, respectively.[16]

In this highly complex situation, the candidate himself tweeted that the victory was "a landslide." He said his margin would have been even bigger if millions of Clinton supporters had not voted illegally. It was neither the first time nor the last that observers found Trump's claims to be unsupported by evidence. Meanwhile the American Psychiatric Association, hoping to advance the interests of patients, sent Trump an urgent message pledging "to work in partnership with the Trump administration and Congress."[17]

* * *

As Trump took office, he promised that "America will start winning again, winning like never before." Breitbart News, the right-wing media outlet that had adoringly covered Trump's election, called it "the most astounding election in American history" and prepared for "the Trump revolution." On the left, there were a thousand variations on the question that Clinton later posed in her memoir, *What Happened*. She put it as a statement, but as a question it needed urgently to be answered by her followers. What had been wrong with the polls and their confident predictions of a Clinton victory? Who were the Americans who had voted for Trump in that wide swath of red territory in the South, the West, and especially the once-blue Midwest? Hundreds of thousands of women across the country planned and executed a protest to be held in January 2017, on the day after Trump's inauguration. Involving approximately 4 million people across the country, and not just women, the Women's March represented 1.3 percent of the American population. It was probably the largest single-day demonstration in American history Looking on, one conservative commentator later called it an "orgy of raging exhibitionism."[18]

In office for only a week, Trump proposed a temporary ban on immigration from several Muslim-majority countries, igniting more outrage and more nationwide protests. He nominated a conservative Supreme Court justice to replace conservative Antonin Scalia, much to the delight of traditional conservatives and much to the dismay of Senate Democrats. What many saw as his volatile temperament and his inexperience in government led to delays in appointments and to rapid staff turnover. Ethics questions became a problem as early as February, when national security adviser Michael Flynn resigned. Starting with Flynn, evidence began to emerge to suggest that some Trump associates may have reached out to Russian operatives during the campaign and then lied to Congress or to federal agents about it.

In May 2017, attorney and former FBI director Robert Mueller, a longtime Republican, was appointed to look into the charges of Russian interference in the campaign. Media-averse and systematic in his approach, Mueller had a more limited mandate than previous special prosecutors such as those in the Watergate affair. Mueller moved systematically, seemingly getting closer and closer to Trump. He eventually secured 33 indictments against, and numerous guilty pleas from, people close to the president. These included not only Flynn but also Trump's campaign adviser George Papadopoulos, his business associate Paul Manafort, his former attorney Michael Cohen, and others. By late 2017, for those who had watched Watergate unfold in the press, there was an uncanny feeling of déjà vu. It was all complicated by Trump's habit of disparaging the investigators and the liberal media.

* * *

Many psychiatrists in 2016 were appalled by the rise of Donald Trump and were shocked when he actually won. Was he ill? What would happen now that he had access to the nuclear launch codes? Given the Goldwater Rule, it was unclear whether staying silent was an ethical obligation or, now, an ethical betrayal. Some began to speak out.[19]

Three weeks after the election, Harvard psychiatrist Judith Lewis Herman, along with two colleagues, wrote a letter to President Obama, who was then in office. Herman, an expert on trauma and domestic violence, expressed "grave concern" about President-Elect Trump's mental stability and recommended that he undergo a full medical and neuropsychiatric evaluation. She never heard back and considered the exercise "fruitless." In one sense, it was. But on the day of the Women's March in January, feminist activist Gloria Steinem read Herman's letter to the crowd and expressed her own concern about Trump's mental health. As a result, Herman's letter received wide publicity.[20]

Other mental health professionals spoke out as well. In February 2017, a letter to the *New York Times* signed by Lance Dodes and 34 additional mental health professionals expressed concern about Trump's lack of empathy and distortion of reality, suggesting that he was not safe to serve as president. In March, Herman and Columbia University psychiatrist Robert Jay Lifton wrote to the *New York Times*. Herman and Lifton emphasized their view that Trump had paranoia and noted his "repeated failure to distinguish between reality and fantasy." Representatives in Congress should "take the necessary steps to protect us from this danger-ous president." Meanwhile psychologist John Gartner and others orga-nized a group called Duty to Warn, which embodied the principle of preventing harm that Jerrold Post had proposed in his 2002 article "Ethical Considerations." According to Gartner, Duty to Warn's petition drive attracted 41,000 signatures by April 2017.[21]

By that point Bandy Lee, a forensic psychiatrist at Yale who has done much work on violence, had also grown alarmed. Trained in medical anthropology as well as psychiatry, Lee brought a global perspective to the issue. Lee's ethnographic work in Tanzania had shown her that some governments can keep their countries peaceful even during an epidemic of violence around them. For years Lee had also co-taught a course on immigration legal services at Yale Law School, teaching and assisting law students who served in Yale's renowned Immigration Clinic. Political refugees from around the world sought out the clinic's help. The asylum seekers, Lee told me in an e-mail,

> had often come to this country after witnessing their family members murdered before their eyes, and then being imprisoned, tortured, and gang raped – all for taking or being suspected of taking a political position that is different from the government's. Hence my concern was not Democrat or Republican, but whether a government affirms life or promotes violence and death. The destructive governments I became acquainted with had leaders with psychological features that included an inability to tolerate dissent and seemed to translate into rhetoric or policies that promoted widespread violence. Having seen this in multiple settings, and through the multiple accounts in the asylum clinic, I was well aware that "It could happen here."[22]

Lee became convinced that under Donald Trump, it *was* happening here. Like Herman, she had circulated a letter of concern to her colleagues but got little response. Reaching out to Herman, to Lifton, and to her mentor James Gilligan, Lee began planning a conference that would explore the ethical rationale for public comment on a president's mental health in a situation of danger. The question Lee decided to debate publicly was this: What if psychiatric symptoms in a person who holds power imply "danger not just to one person or a few, but the whole nation and the world?"[23] Herman, Lifton, and Lee, along with Leonard Glass, would form a constellation of allies in the effort to articulate a rationale for commenting on Donald Trump.

* * *

In person, Judith Herman is a mild-mannered, serious, and confident psychiatrist. In her 70s, she welcomed me in an earnest way, making sure

I did not have a cat allergy before we began. (The cat was nowhere to be found during our conversation.) I asked Herman about a framed etching that hung near her desk, and she identified it as an original Rembrandt self-portrait that her parents had brought back from Europe. As I learned, and as I knew already from occasional teaching with her, Herman's serious demeanor and soft voice frequently yield to moments of humor; she does not hesitate to express her opinions forthrightly.[24] I could easily imagine her as the antiwar and antinuclear activist she was in the 1970s and 1980s. Herman told me that she has been inspired by Robert Jay Lifton's work; she regularly attended Lifton's conference on psychohistory, held annually for decades in Wellfleet, Massachusetts. As the Rembrandt etching hinted, Judith Herman's mother was also implicitly in the room with us. Helen Block Lewis, a psychologist, was called before Joseph McCarthy's Permanent Subcommittee on Investigations in 1953. Citing the Fifth Amendment, she declined to answer if she was now or had ever been a member of the Communist Party. As a result, she was blacklisted and could not obtain an academic position.

When I asked Herman if her work on Donald Trump relates to her work on trauma, she exclaimed, "Oh, of course!" "My work on trauma comes out of understanding the dynamics of exploitation and of oppression," she said. "When you see a would-be dictator who is both mentally unstable and totally unprincipled – except in matters of racism – then you want to warn the public that this is not the sort of person you would want having access to the nuclear codes." She told me that she has no regrets about speaking out.

* * *

On March 15, 2017, before the Yale conference took place, the APA ethics committee issued an opinion that shocked the Herman-Lifton-Lee group and many APA members. Going into far more detail than any opinion on the Rule in the past, the opinion led with a clear statement that when a psychiatrist is concerned about public safety, it is not just diagnosis but *any* psychiatric comment that is unethical:

Question: May a psychiatrist give an opinion about an individual in the public eye when the psychiatrist, in good faith, believes that the individual poses a threat to the country or national security?

Answer: Section 7.3 of *The Principles of Medical Ethics with Annotations Especially Applicable to Psychiatry* (sometimes called "The Goldwater Rule") explicitly states that psychiatrists may share expertise about psychiatric issues in general but that it is unethical for a psychiatrist to offer a professional opinion about an individual based on publicly available information without conducting an examination. Making a diagnosis, for example, would be rendering a professional opinion. However, a diagnosis is not required for an opinion to be professional. Instead, when a psychiatrist renders an opinion about the affect, behavior, speech, or other presentation of an individual that draws on the skills, training, expertise, and/or knowledge inherent in the practice of psychiatry, the opinion is a professional one.[25]

Accounts differ on to what extent the APA sought out the opinion of its members before issuing this statement.[26] Judith Herman told me she was upset that the APA had not consulted its members adequately on this and other statements, but a later letter from the APA board of trustees insisted that the APA had done so. The opinion seemed, to me at least, to reverse the gradual liberalizing trend that had been detectable in recent APA statements on the Rule.[27] Many took the opinion to be a broadening of the scope of the Rule; Lee called this the Rule's "radical expansion," and to some, it was nothing less than a "gag order." Herman and Lee saw the APA's reaffirmation as "questionable" because it required psychiatry's usual norms of concern for health and public safety to be suspended when the issue is a president's health and its impact on the nation. A rule originally designed to protect the profession from scandal, they argued, "might itself become a source of scandal" when an organization acquiesces to political pressure.[28]

In the aftermath of the opinion, psychoanalyst Leonard Glass of the Boston Psychoanalytic Society and Institute, like Judith Herman a Distinguished Life Fellow of the APA, contacted the APA leadership and urged it to "rescind" the opinion. The APA asked psychiatrist Rebecca Brendel, a consultant to the ethics committee, to consult with Glass, who turned out to be a former supervisor of hers.[29] The conversation was respectful but did not result in an agreement; the APA did not alter the Rule. In April 2017, Glass resigned from the APA in protest, believing that he was in an untenable position. "I told the APA I wouldn't practice under a cloud of ethical suspicion," he related to me in an interview afterward. Glass resigned both his membership and his Distinguished Life Fellowship. In his resignation letter, he told APA president Maria Oquendo that if the APA had simply advised its members to use caution when commenting on public figures, "I would take that as prudent advice and not object."

> But to establish that it is an ethical violation to comment on matters in the public sphere [while] identifying oneself by one's profession is entirely excessive, intrusive, unnecessary, and insulting. The membership of APA are presumably fully trained and competent psychiatrists. To ordain a gag rule out of concern that they will misspeak or damage the profession of psychiatry because they lack the judgment to speak with appropriate restraint is offensive and stifling.

Glass's concern about the infantilizing effect of the Rule and its inappropriate use of "a cloud of ethical doubt" against members was echoed in at least one other member's experience. Later in 2017, California psychiatrist Judith Vida was the subject of an ethics investigation by her APA district branch because she had signed the February letter to the *New York Times* about Trump. Under the circumstances – precisely the circumstances Leonard Glass had hoped to avoid – Vida negotiated a resignation from the APA and ended up profoundly disillusioned.[30]

A close look at the March 2017 opinion shows a familiar twin stance in the APA's public statement. As had happened in many clarifying statements over the years, the APA's seeming firm stand on the principle of no comment without interview is quickly qualified by a list of exceptions to the seemingly general principle: it sought both to publicly uphold a dramatic general principle and to explain exceptions as if they were routine. For example, after emphasizing that a patient must be interviewed and give consent, the opinion acknowledged that often there is an acceptable substitute for a patient's consent. In this way, the opinion at least was explicit about the fact that exceptions exist, a point that the organization had not typically emphasized in the past. Now it said:

When a psychiatrist comments about the behavior, symptoms, diagnosis, etc., of a public figure without consent, the psychiatrist violates the fundamental principle that psychiatric evaluation occurs with consent or other authorization. The relationship between a psychiatrist and a patient is one of mutual consent. In some circumstances, such as forensic evaluations, psychiatrists may evaluate individuals based on other legal authorization such as a court order. Psychiatrists are ethically prohibited from evaluating individuals without permission or other authorization (such as a court order).[31]

The committee also noted that profiles commissioned by government agencies are acceptable. The committee then gave a lengthy and defensive list of objections that critics might make to its opinion – and the reasons that all of those objections were wrong. In the end, almost half of the 2017 opinion was taken up with objections to the objections. At the time, I myself found it hard to see the opinion as respectful of APA members who felt the safety of the country was at stake.

* * *

The Yale conference now had to proceed under conditions very different from those under which it was planned. Paradoxically, the ethics committee's reaffirmation of the Rule meant that opinions expressed at the conference would receive increased attention. Some participants worried that President Trump might retaliate if they spoke out about him.[32] But the conference moved forward. The late 2017 conference, and the book that followed, provided an urgently articulated case for psychiatric action in the name of national safety. The distinguished reputations of many of the participants assured that their thinking would have a major impact. The book, entitled *The Dangerous Case of Donald Trump*, quickly became a bestseller.[33]

In both the conference and the book, Lee took the lead by arguing against silence. "Possibly the oddest experience in my career as a psychiatrist," she said, "has been to find that the only people not allowed to speak about an issue are those who know the most about it." Lee criticized the Goldwater Rule for lacking any limits, and she made the case for stepping in during a national emergency rather than remaining a bystander.[34]

Herman and Lee took seriously an objection they frequently heard from colleagues. If psychiatrists got involved in politics, wouldn't harm result? After all, Soviet psychiatrists had "collaborated with the secret police to diagnose dissidents as mentally ill and confine them to prisons that fronted as hospitals." Seeking additional examples, however, Herman and Lee reflected on a widely reported incident in which it was revealed that the leadership of the American Psychological Association revised its ethics guidelines in such a way as to allow the organization's members potential leeway to participate in secret interrogation and torture in government settings. The moral reflection Herman and Lee derived from that incident was more complex than the usual argument that mixing psychiatry and politics is hazardous:

> It seemed clear that the government officials responsible for abusive treatment of prisoners went to some lengths to find medical and mental health professionals who would publicly condone their practices. We reasoned that if professional endorsement serves as important cover for human rights abuses, then professional condemnation must also carry weight.

The American Psychiatric Association, they noted, had taken a strong stand against participation in torture, and psychiatry and society had emerged better for it. "When there is pressure from power," Herman and Lee reflected, "is exactly when one must abide by the norms and rules of our ethics." (The APA would shortly make a similar point in support of the Rule: that it is exactly when there is political pressure that one should stand by a long-established ethics rule.[35])

Taking a favorable view of the Goldwater Rule under ordinary circumstances, Herman and Lee nonetheless argued that in some circumstances, the principle of protecting public figures must be balanced against other rules and principles. If a person "who holds the power of life and death over us all shows signs of clear, dangerous mental impairment," staying silent is a violation of public trust. Thus, in an emergency a physician may break the Goldwater Rule. "We believe that such an emergency now exists."[36]

Further foundation in moral reflection was provided by Lifton, who had spent much of his career in psychiatry studying situations in which doctors' moral integrity was compromised. Lifton's book *The Nazi Doctors: Medical Killing and the Psychology of Genocide* (1986) had required him to conduct in-depth interviews with Nazi physicians and concentration camp survivors and to try to draw conclusions. The resulting painful moral reflections led him to the notion of "malignant normality," a situation where the usual norms of society are gradually suspended and abnormal behavior comes to seem normal. In Lifton's view, the collaboration of physicians in the extermination of Jews was the proto-type for professional participation in genocide, or for "adaptation to evil." The support of a large professional organization, he asserted in his foreword to *The Dangerous Case*, is highly effective in sustaining malig-nant normality.[37]

Like Lee, Lifton thought professional expertise can become overly technical and thus be oblivious to the social and moral context in which it operates. As an alternative, Lifton advanced the concept of the "witnes-sing professional." This larger concept of professional ethics includes consideration of "who we work with, and how our work either affirms or questions the directions of the larger society." Lifton's proposal bears a family resemblance to the moral test advanced by Herman and Lee: "We would argue that the key question is whether mental health profes-sionals are engaging in political *collusion* with state abuses of power or acting in *resistance* to them."[38]

* * *

At the Yale conference there was a vigorous dissenter from the "duty to warn" position. Charles Dike, a member of the APA ethics committee and a forensic psychiatrist at Yale, was invited to speak first. Dike argued in favor of the Goldwater Rule as conceived by the APA – and against an overly broad notion of duty to society. Dike recounted the 1964 *Fact* episode, defended the APA's response, and strongly critiqued the notion that a psychiatrist has a larger duty to warn. "Our duty is to help the patients get better," he asserted. "When they get better, society is safer. We do not owe society a primary duty." This position corresponded closely with the March 2017 opinion by the APA ethics committee. "I am here," he said, "to support the position of the APA." Current ethics committee chair Rebecca Brendel and then-president Anita Everett of the APA told me that Dike brought back to the ethics committee a summary of the various opinions expressed at the Yale conference. The committee discussed and considered those opinions in some depth. "We were interested in what they were saying," Brendel told me. But consistent with its philosophy of prioritizing discussion within the APA membership, the committee elected not to debate the matter in the media.[39]

Meanwhile, public and media reaction to the conference and the book was dramatic. *Newsweek* ran excerpts from the book, emphasizing not the ethical reasoning behind the issue but attention-getting quotes about Trump's personality and dangerousness. Some websites and blogs on the left featured Lee sympathetically, but there was also much skepticism. "Dr. Lee's claims come across as partisan meanness," said a *National Review* column, "and they undermine the integrity of the medical profession." Psychiatrist Steven Moffic politely suggested that diagnosis from a distance is "inadequate, unreliable, and invalid" and underlined the risks to public figures. Repeating the argument about psychiatry in the Soviet Union, Moffic asserted that a public diagnosis "lends itself to political propaganda." At a special panel on the issue at the APA annual meeting in May 2017, two former APA presidents weighed in. Paul Appelbaum agreed that diagnosis from a distance is inadequate and thoughtfully emphasized the harmful impact it could have on the public; Paul Summergrad doubted that psychiatrists could have much impact on public opinion at all. Psychiatrist Jerome Kroll, reviewing Lee's book, saw it as helpful but nonetheless elaborated at length on his wish that the book had been more philosophical and scholarly. In his review of the book, former APA president Alan Stone, who had voted against the Rule in 1973, similarly noted that most of the book's chapters were brief and had no scholarly ambitions. Several, he thought, "read like the op-ed columns they originally were." The APA did not mention Lee by name, but in a press release later in the year specifically clarified that the "duty to warn" concept can apply only within the physician–patient relationship.[40]

Elsewhere, skepticism yielded to frank and sometimes personal criticism. In the APA's *Psychiatric News*, psychiatrist Jeffrey Lieberman of Columbia University said he himself objected to Trump's behavior and to his policies. But he thought Lee's book was "political partisanship, disguised as patriotism" and that publishing it was "unprofessional, unethical, and irresponsible." For Lieberman, *The Dangerous Case* was "not a serious, scholarly, civic-minded work, but simply tawdry, indulgent, fatuous, tabloid psychiatry." In a letter to a prestigious medical journal, he repeated his criticism, calling Lee's morality "misguided and dangerous." Lieberman also took to Twitter, charging Lee with inaccuracy and repeating that she was misguided. The former APA president even tweeted an ad hominem comment about Lee's academic credentials, which he found sorely lacking. Lee had been described by another commentator as eminent. "What Eminent Psychiatrist Has Been an Asst Professor for 20 Years," he tweeted. Lee and "her band of so-called #mental health experts" were so "out to lunch" that rational debate, in his view, was impossible.

For Lieberman, the best way a psychiatrist could deal with an ill president was not by speaking out publicly – or even by initiating the president's removal from office under the Twenty-Fifth Amendment. It was, he said, to "assist in the process" under the Twenty-Fifth Amendment "as needed." As he later told me, this assistance would be an appropriate part of a psychiatrist's professional role: helping in the process of "applying the constitutional mechanisms for abridging the President's authority or removal from office" if needed. Lieberman felt strongly, he said, that the risks of psychiatrists "using their professional credentials for political purposes" were substantial. For him, these included collusion with tyrannical regimes. Psychiatrists, he noted, had colluded with the Nazi eugenics movement and in the misuse of the mental health care system in the Soviet Union.[41]

Lieberman told me that there are several means by which concerns about a president's competence and performance in office can be addressed: "elections, impeachment, and the Twenty-Fifth Amendment. A fourth means is the annual medical exam that POTUS undergoes." Psychiatrists, he pointed out, "could readily be involved" in that exam. For

Lieberman, roles and professional boundaries are clear. While physicians have a role to play "in the adjudication process of constitutionally defined procedures," it is the government's responsibility to initiate the process; it is not the role of professionals. The inaction of members of the administration and Congress is not a justification for medical professionals to insert themselves into constitutionally defined mechanisms."[42]

* * *

On January 3, 2018, a firestorm broke out when Lee disclosed that she had met with 12 members of Congress in late 2017 to discuss Trump's mental health. "He's going to unravel," the article quoted her as saying, "and we are seeing the signs." Along with others in the National Coalition of Concerned Mental Health Experts, she took note of the growing nuclear tensions with North Korea; in a letter in early January, she and the group urged Congress and those around Trump to take "urgent steps to restrain his behavior."

What Lee and the coalition meant by that was not clear. The reaction was swift. On January 8, conservative talk show host Rush Limbaugh first questioned Lee's academic qualifications, then attacked her personally and politically. He announced incorrectly that Lee lacked a degree in psychiatry and questioned whether it was Trump or Lee who was insane. Limbaugh gave listeners his impressionistic version of the Goldwater Rule and its history, chastising Lee as the latest of those who use "the same page of the playbook any time there's a Republican president." "Folks," he concluded, "you want to talk about dangerous, these people are deluded." Then, on January 9, the APA itself issued a strong calling for "an end to psychiatrists providing professional opinions in the media about public figures whom they have not examined." The statement flatly declared that "[a]rmchair psychiatry or the use of psychiatry as a political tool" is "unacceptable and unethical." The APA had not named Lee specifically, but, according to Lee, many right-wing outlets quickly concluded that she was the subject of the APA's statement.[43]

It did not help Lee's case when, a few days later, the *Atlantic* reported Lee as telling the congressmen that in some urgent circumstances Trump could be forced to undergo an emergency psychiatric evaluation. If no other psychiatrist came forward, the article cited her as saying, she might have to. The article's headline represented Lee as telling Congress that "Trump Could Be Involuntarily Committed." When a reporter told him of Lee's comment, Lieberman said, "You've got to be kidding. That's preposterous."[44] By this point Lee was receiving what she called a "barrage" of death threats.

Lee herself told me she felt strongly about the *Atlantic* article, which she said had abbreviated and sensationalized her comments and been insensitive to the nuances of what she said. It represented her as drawing conclusions that she had not herself reached. She emphasized that she had not approached government officials; instead, they had approached her for a consultation. When several members of the White House staff called her in November 2017 out of concern for Trump's mental state, for example, she had referred them to an emergency room. Then several congressmen had called her seeking a consultation; the December meeting, she highlighted, took place at their request and in her view was consistent with the APA's ethics directive to consult with government when needed (section 7.1 of the APA's *Principles*). She said that she met with the congressmen (she was sometimes accompanied by psychiatrist James Gilligan), explained the usual commitment criteria in psychiatry, and "emphasized that he [Trump] met the criteria for dangerousness." The congressmen, she said, were all concerned about Trump's dangerousness. She did not recommend any next steps – and she did not act to detain Trump. "I didn't say 'We have to detain the president.'" Lee said she specifically declined "several" invitations to work with groups of attorneys who offered to obtain a court order mandating a psychiatric evaluation for Trump. That, she thought, might lead to more violence. Instead, when the congressmen told her there was little they could do, she decided to refocus her efforts on public education. While media accounts portrayed her as "preparing to detain the President immediately," in Lee's view, her role was "clearly educational" in nature.[45]

The delicacy of Lee's position was apparent to me when I interviewed her. Are there some circumstances, I asked Lee, when detaining a president might be necessary? "Yes," she said, emphasizing that a psychiatrist has a responsibility to society and clarifying that she sees education of the public as the main intervention she had in mind. She also underscored the need for caution. She said that detaining a president would not be a good idea in any immediate sense and said she "probably will never" get to that point herself. Indeed, in her public statements in the aftermath of the *Atlantic* controversy, Lee seemed to back away from any implication that Trump could be detained. Instead, she returned to questioning his judgment. The concern about Trump's judgment, she told me, was the point of the letter she signed (along with 150 others in the National Coalition of Concerned Mental Health Experts) asserting that Supreme Court nominee Brett Kavanaugh also appeared unbalanced and needed an evaluation.[46]

In the aftermath of the APA's January statement, and as the controversy raged, Lee, Herman, and Lifton wrote an open letter to the APA. The result was the only documented personal exchange between the organization and its most prominent dissenters. The authors said they believed the Goldwater Rule was wise to adhere to in ordinary circumstances, but that the humanitarian aims of medicine also must be considered. The "original" version of the Rule, they asserted, had prohibited only diagnosis; they asked the APA to "reconsider and rescind its recent [March 2017] ill-considered expansion of the 'Goldwater Rule'" to include any comment on public figures. They defended their own public statements about Donald Trump this way: "When a man who has the authority to initiate a nuclear strike shows signs of mental instability, we believe that our profession fails in our ethical duty if we remain silent." The authors said they sought further dialogue on the issue with the APA.

On March 23, the authors received a reply from the full 19-member APA board of trustees. The board thanked them for their letter and said that the APA encourages debate about the Rule; it said the ethics committee had discussed the issue with members and that a vigorous discussion had occurred within the APA about the Rule. But the board then took sharp issue with Lee, Herman, and Lifton's claims that the Rule had originally prohibited only diagnosis and that the Rule's scope had been expanded in March 2017. These claims, the board said flatly, were just wrong. Section 7.3, it said, had always prohibited professional opinion, not just diagnosis. It also asserted that section 7.3 had not changed since its adoption in 1973.[47] The board asked the authors to cease mischaracterizing the March 2017 opinion. Flexing ethics rules to allow for a political intervention, it contended, is never right and invariably leads to harm. The letter took a dim view of the notion of duty to warn and said that psychiatry does not have the responsibility for deciding if a public figure is fit to serve. For those reasons, the board said, the Rule will continue to be APA policy.[48]

The Lee group was not surprised at the response. Lifton told me that he and his colleagues eventually "came to expect" rigidity from the APA. "They've been quote closed on this issue – quite closed." Lifton now shifted mainly to a consulting role within the group, but a subgroup of those who had contributed to *The Dangerous Case of Donald Trump* worked out a detailed proposal for the Rule's revision. The plan was to send the proposal to the APA and also to release it publicly. Asserting that the Rule undermined psychiatrists' efforts to "protect the public's well-being," the subgroup defended the social responsibility involved in speaking out and outlined a seven-point proposal for revision. The letter was signed by 22 of the *Dangerous Case* coauthors and released publicly; the consensus of the group was that Lifton and Herman, both Distinguished Life Fellows of the APA, would also send the letter under their names to Anita Everett, then the president of the APA. In so doing, Lifton and Herman told the APA, they saw themselves as "citizen professionals" who were advocating for the "welfare of the community." Their letter went unanswered.[49]

* * *

I was curious to ask the APA about its views on section 7.3 and about the controversy with the Lee group. The organization, knowing I was skeptical about the current Rule, not only allowed me free access to its archives but also made two high-ranking organization officials available for detailed interviews while I was writing this book.

Saul Levin, the APA's medical director, is a skillful spokesman for the organization. South African by origin, he trained in California and at Harvard and has held many influential positions in American and international psychiatry and medicine. (He was recently made a fellow of the Royal College of Physicians of Edinburgh.) At the start of our phone interview, Levin thanked me effusively for being a long-standing APA member and asked how he could help. When I inquired about the APA's view of the Rule, he gave me a lucid overview of the organization's viewpoint on the issue.

The Goldwater Rule emerged as an issue, he said, when a number of people grew concerned about Donald Trump. During the 2016 campaign and after the election, there was "clearly a lot of angst," but eventually "it became clear that the Goldwater Rule had stood the test of time." Levin explained that the APA concluded that standing by the Rule was a matter of "protecting the art and science of psychiatry – that we don't do armchair psychiatry." It was true, he acknowledged, that "a very small group" of APA members wanted to speak in the media about President Trump's mental health. To Levin and to the APA, however, it became clear that the vast majority of members were behind the Rule. By this point, he told me in July 2019, "fewer and fewer members are calling. I can count on two hands the people who are trying to change the Rule, most of them through books and television."

Could the Goldwater Rule be altered? Levin emphasized that changing the Rule would only add to the already existing burden of stigma on mental health issues. How would that increase stigma, I asked. Without the Rule, he replied,

> anyone can give anyone a diagnosis. As we know from history, mentally ill people were burned at the stake as witches because someone publicly called them such. The point is that it's important not to demonize people with mental illness. Suppose you had a personality disorder and the press said you were a danger. How would you feel?

I felt a bit uncomfortable, but I saw Levin's point. Attacking a person's mental health, he said, is "essentially trivializing" – as opposed to assuring that "a comprehensive in-person mental health evaluation and analysis is carried out effectively."

Rebecca Brendel, head of the APA ethics committee, is a psychiatrist at Massachusetts General Hospital. A forensic psychiatrist and ethicist who also trained in law, Brendel told me that "I've never been prouder to be a member" of the APA. The reason, she said, is precisely the APA's strong and effective effort in advocacy: advocacy for the ability of patients to access care and against the adverse effects of "policies that are contrary to the mental health interests" of Americans. "There's very little disagreement, I would argue, that the policies of this administration have the potential to be divisive," whether on discrimination, on Title 10, the rollback of environmental protections, on the move away from universal health care coverage, or on the separation of children from their parents at the border. Consequently, the APA has actively spoken out against misguided policies of the Trump administration, bringing lawsuits and issuing vigorous policy statements in opposition. But it is important to speak out in an appropriate way, she contended, not through ad hominem attacks on a person's mental health.

In Brendel's view, Bandy Lee and her associates err in just this way. For Brendel, it is misleading to suggest that the key issue is whether to speak out or to stay silent, as Lee's framing of the issue suggests. "*Nobody* is arguing that psychiatrists should not be speaking out." Instead, the APA's disagreement with the Lee group is over what constitutes a professionally responsible way to act. "There's a view that the only way to make a change is through an open and professionally irresponsible critique of the President's mental health." But diagnosis in the media gets us nowhere, she said, and magnifies the role of one individual in a complex political process. Thus to focus only on the Goldwater Rule is "myopic." Instead, she emphasized the myriad professional ways that psychiatrists can speak out and act when political and policy issues concern or outrage them.

I shared with Brendel my impression that both sides in the debate over the Goldwater Rule are acting in good faith and are morally sincere. What would be wrong, I asked, in adopting a pluralistic approach to the ethics of comment on the mental health of public figures? She agreed that both the APA and its critics are "seriously, morally concerned." For her, that was not the issue. "The Rule is about making a claim for which you don't have evidence or permission. The entire profession of medicine is based on a fundamental respect for persons and their dignity." For Brendel, the indignity of being subjected to public diagnosis is the core problem.

Rebecca Brendel was confident and articulate. As we spoke, though, I couldn't help recalling the moment when she had reached out, on behalf of the APA ethics committee, to her former supervisor Leonard

Glass when he raised objections to the Rule. He had, I knew, resigned from the APA after the conversation with her. Could I ask her something personal? Brendel said yes. I observed that a confrontation with her mentor, who disagreed with her so profoundly and then felt obliged to leave the organization on principle, had all the elements of a tragedy. What were her feelings? Brendel explained that she's spent her life debating and thinking about ethical questions. She's always tried, she stated, to look at all the ethically acceptable alternatives, not simply to decide what's right and wrong. She has "great respect and affection for Len." The conversation was a warm, cordial, and collegial exchange. But "I did not hold the belief that one can do a diagnosis in the media."

If she had any regrets about the conversation with Glass, Brendel told me, it was that she had hoped they would be able to think together about the Goldwater Rule in a larger context. She reflected in a comment I heard as wistful: "What I still don't understand is the core or kernel of what has led [people] to such ferocious opposition." As she said more formally in a follow-up discussion, "Why is it that this small subset of psychiatrists are adamant that the best and perhaps the only way to influence public safety is through the media without following the methods of the profession?" Section 7.3, she said, has never prevented "conscientious and concerned ethical psychiatrists from performing competent and well-informed work for the betterment of society in accordance with the values and methods of the psychiatric profession."[50]

* * *

The question of the APA's openness, and its responsiveness to its critics, remained on my mind after my interviews with Judith Herman and Robert Jay Lifton. Herman had told me that Anita Everett, APA president at the time, did not respond to their letter of June 2018, and others in their group echoed the perception that the APA had been unresponsive to their concerns. Everett, in a letter to me, seemed to understand that the APA's internal processes can be mysterious to the public and even to its own members. The APA, she emphasized, is a "membership organization." (Brendel also used this term.) This means that "members participate, but we do not invite media to our meetings." Often, she acknowledged, "the depth and breadth of our deliberation is not known or obvious to individuals who do not participate in the process." I had long been unclear myself on just how my organization operated.

The APA, Everett explained, collected information on its members' views through publications, through meetings, and through "organizational governance." This forbidding term referred to the activities of district (state and local) branches, APA committees, councils, and the APA Assembly, a large body of APA members elected from each of the 74 district branches and state psychiatric associations that comprise the 38,700-member APA. I thought I recognized the process from my study of the Goldwater Rule's history. A typical starting point is for the APA administration to ask a committee, task force, or council to study an issue and suggest possible approaches. The various groups to which the issue is assigned may issue a report or a position paper. Then, if further action is indicated, the APA Assembly will discuss and vote on the matter. Finally, the board of trustees may vote on whether to adopt any policy change the Assembly has recommended.

In the case of the Goldwater Rule, Everett and Brendel said the APA has created a number of such opportunities for members to participate in discussions of the Rule. The APA gives the floor to any member who requests discussion of the Rule at a meeting of the ethics committee; it offers an open forum for debate on the Rule at each APA annual meeting; it sends representatives to participate in district branch discussions on the Rule; and it sent an ethics committee member (Charles Dike) to participate in the 2017 Duty to Warn conference. As I can attest from my own experience in organizing a panel in 2015, Everett is correct in asserting that the APA often has sessions at its annual meeting that are devoted to debates over the Rule and that are "attended by APA leadership." In 2018, the APA Assembly considered an action paper that formally recommended that the Goldwater Rule be reconsidered. After what Everett calls "a robust debate," the measure "was overwhelmingly defeated." This may be the basis for her belief, which Saul Levin shares, that "most of our members are in favor of keeping the rule as it is."

In response to the open letter from Lee, Herman, and Lifton in 2018, Anita Everett told me that the APA board "carefully considered" all of the information and views it had gathered on the Rule from members, from the ethics committee, and from media statements by the Lee group. "APA responded with a lengthy and detailed letter addressing the points raised." When she received Lifton and Herman's follow-up letter, she and the APA executive committee, of which she was a member, "concluded that the letter did not identify any new issues or points for discussion to add to the Board's prior response."[51]

* * *

As 2018 came to a close and the new year began, liberals had reason to feel more hopeful than at any time in the Trump administration. The Democrats had regained control of the House in the midterm elections. In the new balance of power, investigation, more effective negotiation, and even impeachment might now be within reach. Trump's immigration policies had been moderated after a battle in the courts, and his standoff with nuclear power North Korea had so far been resolved without war. A profusion of Democrats, including several women and persons of color, announced that they were running for president: if all else failed, there was 2020.[52]

On the right, many remained conflicted about Trump, finding in him a mix of the appalling and the politically useful. Trump, after all, had attacked William Kristol, a conservative icon, and dismissed the *National Review* itself as a "dead paper"; his populism could be divisive in a party of libertarians and traditionalists. In 2018, *National Review* columnist Dan McLaughlin analyzed the first year of the administration. Giving Trump demerits for his racial insensitivity, his tweets, and his sex scandals, McLaughlin did note his success with Supreme Court nominations, tax cuts, efforts at regulatory relief, support of the national defense, and immigration policy. McLaughlin also singled out for praise Trump's controversial decisions to move the American embassy to Jerusalem and to withdraw from the Paris climate accords. But there were limits. Too many of his fellow conservatives, McLaughlin contended, had tried to "defend Trump as a positive good rather than a necessary evil." In this way, he said, some on the right have "cheapened the currency of their principles for all time." A certain discomfort with Trump was even evident in a putatively hagiographic biography by former newspaper baron Conrad Black. The book blithely compared Trump to America itself, citing his optimism, his confidence, and his disregard of convention. According to Black, Trump saved the Republican Party from paleoconservatism. Yet even Black had to acknowledge that Trump's methods often seemed like political hucksterism.[53]

Trump, adopting the by-now traditional conservative disdain for the liberal press, took it to new heights. He referred more than once to the press as "the enemy of the people." The habit alternately earned praise and disgust from commentators at the *National Review*. Some thought the press richly deserved Trump's vilification, but others heard distinct echoes of the terror during the French Revolution and under Soviet communism and were moved to defend a free press as essential to democracy. In 2018, Trump taunted television reporters, saying that they depended on him for ratings and that if he didn't win reelection, "they're all out of business." On that point at least, Trump was not far off base. During the 2016 election, CBS executive Les Moonves said that Trump-related drama "may not be good for America, but it's damn good for CBS . . . the money's rolling in and this is fun." One observer said the "Trump bump," representing increased digital subscriptions in 2016, was "saving newspapers," especially the *New York Times* and *Washington Post*.[54]

* * *

The issue of libel law, seemingly settled with the consensus around the Supreme Court's *New York Times* v. *Sullivan* (1964) case, remerged during the early years of the Trump administration. Trump promised twice that he would make it easier to sue the media for defamation. His statements, though ominous-sounding, were vague and did not seriously engage any of the specifics of reigning libel doctrine; scholars and the American Civil Liberties Union alike were skeptical about the feasibility of his proposals. It was not clear how a president could change a Supreme Court decision, and Trump never followed up in any practical way on the proposal. When Neil Gorsuch, Trump's first Supreme Court nominee, was questioned by anxious congresspeople, he specifically denied having any plans to change *Sullivan*. But as usual, Trump was able to make headlines with his dramatic announcement, and the overall tenor of his remarks seemed to suggest that he viewed libel law, as Barry Goldwater had, as a potential weapon with which to attack the liberal media.

Conservatives in other branches of government followed up and developed the reform agenda for libel law into a politically useful theme. In 2019, the longest-serving justice on the Supreme Court, conservative Clarence Thomas, denounced *Sullivan* as inconsistent with his legal philosophy of originalism. Thomas's mentor, conservative justice Antonin Scalia, had often made the same point. Others, in the tradition of Goldwater, pursued libel actions against liberals. In March 2019, Republican congressman Devin Nunes filed a $250 million lawsuit against Twitter, arguing that the service had allowed its users to demean him for political purposes. Fox News gave Nunes's lawsuit sustained attention, and President Trump retweeted a story about the suit, implying his support. Once again legal experts were skeptical about the validity of the case. Fox host Sean Hannity was even driven to explain to his viewers the stringent standard involved in *Sullivan*'s "actual malice" doctrine.[55]

* * *

Trump continued to attack individuals in the media who criticized him, often singling out reporters and commentators by name. He frequently watched four to eight hours of cable television news daily and did not hesitate to tweet attacks on liberal hosts such as Mika Brzezinski and Joe Scarborough of MSNBC. When NBC's long-standing TV comedy *Saturday Night Live* persisted in showcasing Alec Baldwin's satirical imitation of Trump, the president called NBC "Fake News" and tweeted: "How do the Networks get away with these total Republican hit jobs without retribution?" What kind of retribution he meant, and who was to undertake it, Trump left unclear. Baldwin wondered if he was being targeted and if he and his family were safe, a question that led to much ridicule of him as a "baby" in the conservative blogosphere.[56]

One could not help but wonder if Trump was following Roy Cohn's advice to counterpunch hard and declare victory, or even that he was, like

Joseph McCarthy, hoping to keep the press off balance with new accusations and new headlines. Trump may have been channeling his mentor when he called female journalists and Democrats "sick" and attacked the Mueller investigation itself as a McCarthy-style investigation: "A TOTAL WITCH HUNT."[57]

On February 15, 2019, when Congress rebuffed Trump's request for funding for the wall along the border with Mexico, Trump declared a national emergency. "I want to get it done faster, that's all," he said. Public interest groups and attorneys general from multiple states thought the announcement was driven by expedience rather than by a bona fide emergency and announced lawsuits;[58] both the House and Senate soon voted to end the declaration, which only led to a Trump veto. Trump's proposal was defended by Fox News but skewered by comedians on late night TV, in a pattern reminiscent of the 2017 controversy over Trump's immigration policy and of the media treatment of Barry Goldwater in 1964. Even in the Republican Party, many critics saw the declaration as an unconstitutional power grab. A former Bush administration official saw it as evidence of mental illness, proof that Trump was "not well."[59]

* * *

To its critics' dismay, in 2018 the APA remained mostly silent about the Goldwater Rule. In January, the group tweeted that "a proper psychiatric evaluation requires more than a review of television appearances, tweets, and public comments." But the overall lack of public response to the opposition was frustrating for the Lee group. Judith Herman told me, "They've refused to engage with us"; psychiatrist Leonard Glass said "they've stonewalled us." The APA board of trustees' response to Herman, Lifton, and Lee requires that this claim be qualified; the board did respond to them, though it left no room open for alteration of the Rule.[60]

It was not that the organization was indifferent to developments in government or in public policy. With its membership at 37,896 and climbing, the scale of APA lobbying and of interacting with the federal government was vast. In 2017, the APA reported, 6 percent of its total expenses, or $3 million, went to funding for advocacy. The organization continued to respond to negative portrayals of psychiatry, viewing this role as one of its primary missions. A 2019 issue of *Psychiatric News* reported on an accusation in a *New York Times* article, which had claimed that little of practical value had resulted from the billions of dollars the government had poured into biological research in psychiatry. The newspaper's editor's response, featured in the *Psychiatric News* article, was to criticize the *Times* and urge psychiatrists to "push back when necessary to defend the profession and patients."

More than most APA presidents, psychiatrist Althea Stewart emphasized the broad social context in which psychiatry operates. Social determinants of health, she was proud to say in *Psychiatric News* on the 175th anniversary of the organization's founding, were now receiving renewed emphasis in psychiatry; groups previously excluded from attention were gaining a voice in psychiatry. While Stewart did not directly suggest political action, in 2019, she placed the APA's social and political shortcomings in the spotlight even as she celebrated the organization's history and mission. In the 1950s, she noted, the APA told a prominent African American member not to get involved in advocating for *Brown* v. *Board of Education* "and remain aloof from such a political issue." An "Ethics Corner" column in *Psychiatric News* in 2018 advised members how they could be politically active while still protecting the safety of the consulting room and their therapeutic role.

Between 2017 and 2019, the APA board of trustees announced its opposition to the Trump administration's policy of separating children from their parents at the border; approved position statements on the prevention of violence, on police interactions with persons with mental illness, and on domestic violence against women; advocated for reform of the way prisons treat psychiatrically ill inmates; opposed cuts in Medicare psychiatric drug benefits; and joined a lawsuit against the Trump administration, objecting to Trump's plan to expand the use of drastically limited health plans under the Affordable Care Act. The APA defended the rights of LGBT citizens and reaffirmed an earlier position paper deploring the "Use of Stigma as a Political Tactic."[61] While it said little further about the Rule, the APA perhaps more than ever before was taking a stand in the wider world of politics and society.

* * *

In early 2019, a constitutional crisis loomed in the United States. In February, former acting FBI director Andrew McCabe revealed that at one point he and another high-ranking Justice Department official had discussed the possibility of invoking the Twenty-Fifth Amendment, due to their concerns about the president they served. Trump's long-time personal attorney Michael Cohen, testifying before a House investigatory committee, alleged that Trump had lied about Russia and made an illegal payoff to porn star Stormy Daniels while president. The country and the media endured a seemingly interminable wait for special counsel Robert Mueller's report, which was expected to detail the findings of his two-year investigation. The question of obstruction of justice was on the minds of many Americans.

There were dilemmas for all involved. If House Democrats decided to impeach President Trump, as some wished to, the Republicans controlled the Senate, where a trial would have to take place if Trump was to be forced out of office. The prospects for that outcome appeared dim, and at first Speaker Nancy Pelosi publicly said impeachment would be unwise. Meanwhile the country's divided opinions had not softened. On CBS-TV, late-night comedian James Corden joked that the most effective way to get Trump to leave the White House was to leave a trail of French fries for him. On the right, political analyst Boris Epshteyn suggested that Trump's image belonged on Mount Rushmore.[62]

In March, Mueller delivered his report. Democrats were stunned by Mueller's conclusion that Trump had not engaged in collusion and that no conclusion could be reached on the issue of obstruction of justice. President Trump declared the report an "exoneration," suggested an investigation into the investigation, and did not hesitate to say that some of his opponents had done "treasonous things." In what many called a "victory lap," Trump highlighted at rallies how many of his goals he had met during his first two years and implied that he was ready to run for reelection in 2020. Yale psychiatrist Bandy Lee, asked about the Mueller report, emphasized that its focus was legality and that as a result its findings did not change the need to evaluate Trump's fitness for office. In May, she and her coauthors underscored what they saw as the report's evidence of Trump's "mendacity" and incapacity to hold office.

The House of Representatives developed concerns that moved beyond the Muller report when the media disclosed that in July 2019, President Trump had asked the president of Ukraine to investigate former vice president Joe Biden – a strong contender to face Trump in the 2020 president election. Trump allegedly made the request as part of an arrangement to trade the restoration of American aid to that country for an investigation. By late 2019, an impeachment inquiry was under way in the House, and Lee announced that Jerrold Post and several other psychiatrists would be available to testify.[63]

Whatever one's politics, the furor over Donald Trump represented the greatest constitutional crisis the country had seen since the Watergate scandal. In the media, Fox News and CNN appeared locked into almost completely separate worlds of discourse on the issue. As for the place of psychiatry in the national crisis, firm opinions remained arrayed in opposition to each other within the psychiatric community and outside it. The issue of diagnosing from a distance remained unresolved and, for the immediate future at least, seemed unresolvable.

CONCLUSION

On History, Ethics, and Pluralism

The attempt to understand the past . . . is not an arcane academic activity. It is part of a society's struggles over policy and belief and present action. It is part of the effort to enable individuals to resist power, to make independent judgments, to evaluate for themselves the claims and counterclaims about the past that form the core of much public discourse.

Alan Brinkley (1994)[1]

This book opened with a series of questions, all revolving around the psychiatrist's relation to society. The American Psychiatric Association's (APA) Goldwater Rule does not touch on all of these questions, but our historical exploration of psychiatric comment on public figures has provided the beginning of an account of the ethics of that complex relationship.

In this chapter, I offer some historical reflections that grow from the evidence I have assembled in this book. But I also step out of the historical frame and draw some conclusions of my own about the ethics of psychiatric comment on public figures. Accepting that all psychiatric comment on public figures has risks, I differentiate my stand from the American Psychiatric Association's by focusing on the location of those risks, which I believe are diffuse and inherent to all psychiatric comment on public figures – and not unique to media comments by individual psychiatrists. I therefore argue for greater pluralism in the psychiatric conversation about public figures – and also for its corollary, greater respect for the autonomy of psychiatrists in decision-making on this complicated issue. I hope that readers and psychiatrist will each draw their own ethical conclusions from a review of the historical material I have explored.

In my view, when ethics principles conflict in complex ways and when profes-sionals of good faith disagree (as they clearly do in the case of the Goldwater Rule[2]), the deciding factor should not be the dictate of an organization, but respect for the conscience and professional judgment of the individual psychiatrist. I present a working model of this more liberal way of thinking and discuss its advantages, its limitations, and its own significant risks. I also differentiate its usefulness on the issue of public figures from its inappropriateness in situations such as direct participation in torture or the exploitation of psychiatric patients. But in the case of the Goldwater Rule, respect for conscience, deeply rooted in philosophical principle and in the American tradition, ultimately offers a sounder foundation for an ethics of psychiatric comment on public figures than we have had since the adoption of the Rule in 1973.

HISTORICAL REFLECTIONS

THE NATURAL HISTORY OF NOVEL LEGAL DOCTRINES. The evidence I have presented in this book about *Fact* magazine and *Goldwater* v. *Ginzburg* suggests several conclusions about America in the 1960s and after. In many ways, this book is a study of what happens when a progressive Supreme Court decision changes long-established norms and standards. *New York Times* v. *Sullivan* (1964) loosened libel law dramatically and thus gave free speech a new prominence. As Justice Brennan declared for the majority, the case was best seen "against the background of a profound national commitment to the principle that debate on public issues should be uninhibited, robust, and wide-open." Without the traditional tools that public figures had available for use in retaliating against their critics (seditious libel and the presumption that a libel charge was true until proven otherwise), public figures after *Sullivan* had to tolerate a much higher level of public criticism, even when that criticism was factually inaccurate. After *Sullivan*, a public figure could win a libel suit only if he proved negligence or the deliberate publication of falsehood. It was an entirely new concept in libel law, and it fit with the Warren Court's bold style and progressive direction on other issues in the 1950s and 1960s.[3]

If *Sullivan* protected crusading journalists in the civil rights era from legal retaliation by Southern officeholders, it also let journalists push the boundaries of what was permissible in their claims about public figures. Without *Sullivan*, I believe Ralph Ginzburg would never have launched his special issue of *Fact* about Barry Goldwater so confidently.

Yet progressive Supreme Court decisions can often bring a backlash. As legal historian Michael Klarman (2004) has shown in his study of *Brown* v. *Board*, liberal decisions may have unexpected consequences that are at odds with what proponents hoped – and that may well inspire countermovements. Barry Goldwater's vigorous (though peaceful) early stand against *Brown* is one example, as are the later calls by Donald Trump, Antonin Scalia, and Clarence Thomas for modification of the doctrine established in *Sullivan*. As of this writing, it remains unclear how likely such changes are, but the recent rightward movement of the Supreme Court certainly raises the possibility that *Sullivan* will be revisited at some point.

In this overall context, Goldwater's libel suit and the APA's incorporation of section 7.3 into its formal code of professional ethics appear in a new light, as more or less conservative efforts to probe the limits of the new American permissiveness about speech in the 1960s. After 1964, in the limited areas they could control – libel law and psychiatric ethics – Goldwater and the APA showed that the leeway the Court created in *Sullivan* could be limited in court and in the voluntary professional sphere. Public figures' ability to recover damages for malicious falsehoods was established as a practical matter by *Goldwater* v. *Ginzburg*; in the realm of civil society, the APA's Goldwater Rule showed that a professional organization could set its own limits on what its members did in the new era of free speech. In the decade after *Sullivan*, it became clear that in legal theory and in professional practice, the freedoms promised by the decision were not limitless. It is possible for organizations to push policies so far that their own members feel they have been muzzled for no good purpose. Sometimes there can be a backlash to the backlash. This phenomenon, I believe, is illustrated in part by the Bandy Lee group's defense of psychiatric assessment from a distance. In the words of Robert Jay Lifton, in some circumstances, "our professions can become overly technicized"; then ethical guidelines can feel like an undue burden rather than an appropriate means of safeguarding the profession's integrity.[4]

THE LEGACY OF *GOLDWATER* V. *GINZBURG*. My examination of the genesis of Ralph Ginzburg's *Fact* issue and of Barry Goldwater's libel suit against *Fact* suggests several new conclusions about that notorious episode. First, Ginzburg was not the mere "pornographer" and ethics violator that many cursory or moralistic accounts suggest he was. Ginzburg was, as he himself acknowledged, a flamboyant promoter, even a "hustler," but one with a serious purpose. At a time when the Supreme Court was allowing free speech greater reign, Ginzburg hoped for even more: first the normalization of healthy sex and the destigmatizing of writing about sex (*Eros*), then the further liberalization of libel law (*Fact*). He was a First Amendment crusader (though an imperfect one) and a student of history, art, and literature (though not a deep one). He was not the panderer to debased public taste in sexual matters that his conservative detractors alleged he was. And as the dissenting opinions of Hugo Black and William O. Douglas in the *Fact* case showed, Ginzburg's case was legally far from outlandish. He persuaded the two most liberal members of the Court that his journalism was protected by the First Amendment he loved and counted on. If Ginzburg's editorial methods left a misleading impression with his readers and conveyed an overly simplistic view of Goldwater, it was not unreasonable of him to work in the public sphere to advance the progressive values he cared about. The tragic thing about Ginzburg (and I do not believe that is too strong a word) is that his methods sometimes undermined his own lofty goals.

Second, a review of Barry Goldwater's letters and files on the libel case shows that his private persona was at odds with the flamboyant stance he took in public during the presidential election of 1964. In his testimony and his many letters to his attorney, family, and supporters during the trial process, Goldwater does not present as the raving paranoiac or unstable nuclear madman of the kind Ginzburg and Boroson feared he was – and portrayed him as in *Fact*. Instead, Goldwater emerges privately as a rational, conventional man not prone to introspection but determinedly responding to a felt personal slight. Against the advice of his friends he advanced a libel suit in order to obtain justice, to fight "a breach of medical ethics and political ethics and decency." He also made the most of the political opportunity he saw. For Barry Goldwater, Ginzburg the convicted "pornographer" offered an easy target.

Goldwater, far ahead of the rest of the conservative movement and far more perspicaciously than his friend William F. Buckley, grasped the value of bringing lawsuits when he felt unfairly treated by the liberal media. The more systematic legal activism of the conservative movement in the 1980s and 1990s was in part his legacy.[5] The personal satisfaction and the legal victory heartened him. As he hoped, it also gave some protection to future public figures who wished to enter politics and not to have to fear malicious attack. It gave his movement publicity and increased its morale. The many future conservative politicians who worked for Goldwater or were inspired by him have every reason to be grateful to him for *Goldwater* v. *Ginzburg*.

In the professional domain, the APA in 1973 secured its own form of retaliation against Ginzburg, who had long been a thorn in its side. In one way, the Goldwater Rule may be seen as an important and valuable control on irresponsible psychiatric comment. It also was an attempt to clarify the fuzzy boundary between psychiatry and politics, what *Time* called the difficulty some APA members had when they confused "the analytical couch with the political stump." Yet several features of the rule it put into place suggest that the organization went too far. It framed the *Fact* episode as evidence of a simple breach of psychiatric ethics and reacted accordingly. The APA did not emphasize that Ginzburg had changed and combined many of the psychiatrists' survey responses, a point that had emerged clearly in open court in 1968 and that could at least have complicated the issue of psychiatric ethics involved in the emerging Rule of 1973. More substantially, it did not acknowledge that in the media domain there can be any conflict between competing ethical principles (for example, respect for public figures vs. public safety or public education). Yet the existence of diverging opinion that we have traced within the APA over the decades is testimony to the fact that reasonable people can and do disagree on the potential for conflict of principles. The Rule that the APA actually passed in 1973 is marred by its mysterious phrasing, by its seeming absolutism, by its paradoxical and exclusive focus on media settings, and consequently by an unacknowledged double standard in which individual psychiatrists are liable to ethical sanction while government profilers may do their work unchecked. The Rule's insensitivity to the moral seriousness of many APA members and to the possibility of conflicting principles has needlessly made some of the most distinguished psychiatrists in America into ethical violators – and in some cases has led to their exit from the organization.

CONTINUITIES IN PSYCHIATRIC COMMENT OVER TIME. The work of American psychoanalysts on Adolf Hitler, of Ralph Ginzburg on Barry Goldwater, and of the Bandy Lee group on Donald Trump took place in very different historical circumstances. But to my eye, the periodically recurring surges of comment on an allegedly dangerous and mentally ill leader suggest the persistence of strikingly similar forms of reasoning over time. In each of these cases, its adherents believe that psychiatric or psychological understanding had something meaningful to contribute to the conduct of political affairs and foreign policy. The safety of the nation or the world is often felt to be at stake. The historical and ethical core of this reasoning is found in Fromm and Adorno's formulation of the authoritarian personality, with its roots in psychoanalysts' effort to understand Nazism and to prevent its recurrence in new forms. As Horkheimer and Flowerman said in their preface to Adorno's book, "an aroused conscience is not enough if does not stimulate a systematic search for an answer."[6] The Ellsberg case, in which Nixon's men sought to use profiling to discredit a citizen they perceived as a dangerous enemy of the state, reflects these motivations through a glass, darkly.

Except in the case of Hitler, morally concerned psychiatric comment on public figures seems regularly to call forth a condemning response rooted in concerns about professionalism. The close association of these responses with organized psychiatry is notable (though in the Ellsberg case it was individual psychiatrists in the CIA and elsewhere who took their concerns to people in power). It may be, as James Gilligan argues, that concerns about professionalism owe an intellectual debt to sociologist Max Weber's 1918 essay "Science as a Vocation," which makes the case for the social scientist as a detached professional observer of society.[7] But if so, the point is true only in a very limited sense. Professionalism can itself be a way of standing up in a crisis. As the APA emphasized to me, policy advocacy is legitimate and important, *especially* in times when misguided policies are put in place by a presidential administration. The APA, as we have seen, has formally objected to separations at the border, believing that such separations are likely to cause trauma for generations. It is not political action at all but rather the misuse of the professional psychiatric evaluation that is of grave concern to the APA: it is important not to mix *professional* comment with politics, the analytic couch with the political stump. It is in this sense that the APA and its supporters are advocates for professionalism.[8]

Significantly, the morally engaged psychiatric evaluators (advocates of the role of witnessing professional) and the defenders of professional, in-person evaluation share rhetoric that derives from the philosophy of "never again." In fundamental ways, both are post-Holocaust movements of moral concern.

IMAGE AS MOTIVE. A recurring theme that runs through the evidence presented is the importance of the media setting, and the related fact of participants' near-universal interest in educating, and protecting their standing with, the public. Each antagonist has attended to its image in the media, what the APA called "the scientific image of the field," in an era when psychiatry was under attack from many quarters. This motive implicates the media as the central and most influential site for the contests over ethics that I have chronicled. Langer's and Erikson's work for the Office of Strategic Services was initially done in secret, for good reason. But one cannot imagine *Fact, Goldwater* v. *Ginzburg,* or the Goldwater Rule existing without a media environment to facilitate them. The media setting, often seen as a harmful or corrupting influence, made the debates examined in this book possible and necessary, whether participants were motivated to speak to the public about leaders or to avoid public embarrassments for the profession.

I myself see the media domain not primarily as a site of information degradation or of chronic ethical compromise but as a national microphone: a loud and imperfect facilitator of debate.[9] The microphone is vulnerable to odd feedback loops, to domination by the loudest and the least thoughtful speakers (including those who aim to stigmatize others), and to moments of ear-splitting static. But even the high-minded critics of public figures depend on its use to make their points. And well-informed, responsible views can also exist there and can compete in the intellectually diverse media marketplace. We have seen Erik Erikson, in *Psychiatry*, take skeptical public note of the ways in which Hitler tried to appeal to his followers using the media of the time (autobiography and speeches). But in tandem with psychoanalyst Ernst Kris and others, Erikson hoped the United States could find ways to alter Hitler's relationship with his followers by using democratic (media-based, educational, nonauthoritarian) interventions. Kris's suggestion was the use of a kind of matter-of-fact realism about newsworthy events to undermine the Fuhrer's heroic image on German radio.[10] Similarly, in the Ellsberg case, the patient reporting of the *New York Times* and the *Washington Post* went far to counter Richard Nixon's efforts to damage an enemy's public reputation by digging up dirt that could be leaked to the media. Here too the conduct of a war was at stake, in this case Vietnam; media was both a weapon and a counter-weapon on the home front.[11]

James Madison, in suggesting a design for the Constitution, saw much value in setting opposing forces against each other to the benefit of the country. The media was very much on Madison's mind as part of this equation. Some of the biggest ethics problems in the functioning of our democracy have resulted not from concerned experts speaking to the press, but from government overcontrol of information, as examples from the secrecy around the atomic bomb to the rise of the Cold War classification system demonstrate.[12] Correction can happen only if the public and the relevant government agencies have needed information. Regarding the press, Madison's comment remains apropos:

> A popular Government, without popular information, or the means of acquiring it, is but a Prologue to a Farce or a Tragedy; or, perhaps both. Knowledge will forever govern ignorance: And a people who mean to be their own Governors, must arm themselves with the power which knowledges gives.

Madison's emphasis on the value of information in a democracy is certainly consistent with section 7.2 of the APA's *Principles of Medical Ethics with Annotations Especially Applicable to Psychiatry*, which emphasizes the importance of psychiatrists sharing their expertise with the public on mental health issues in general. I also think it provides a rationale for the thoughtful, responsible public discussion of the psychiatric issues of public figures.[13]

ETHICAL REFLECTIONS: PROBLEMS OF THE CURRENT GOLDWATER RULE

At present, morally serious APA members are not able to participate in the media domain in a Madisonian spirit. To clear the ground for reasonable psychiatrists to participate, several problems of the current Rule will need to be addressed. In my view, ethical guidelines must be clear; differential ethical standards, if they exist, must be openly acknowledged; and perhaps most central of all, the hazards of ethical absolutism must be understood, including the impact of rigid ethical rules on members of a professional community who are acting in good faith on an issue where reasonable people may disagree with each other.

UNCLEAR LANGUAGE. The first difficulty of the Goldwater Rule has to do with unclear language. At first, many who read the text of the Rule believe the APA is banning *all* psychiatric comment without interview and consent.[14] This is a position that the APA has never endorsed and that it never intended. A careful reading of the text and of the APA ethics committee opinions that elucidate it confirms that the APA intended only to ban individual psychiatrists from commenting in media settings on the mental health of public figures. An ethics committee opinion called this comment undertaken "cavalierly." The organization has never seen the Rule as covering the profiling of foreign leaders by government agencies, the evaluation for the courts of defendants who decline to be interviewed, or the diagnosis by insurance company administrators of patients they have never met. In many of these settings, of course, no interview or consent from the subject is obtained. In one of its franker moments, the APA ethics committee noted that the purpose of the Rule is not to ban all comment without interview or consent, but "to protect public figures" from groundless psychiatric speculation. Unclear language has led many members to write the APA ethics committee asking what is ethically acceptable and what is not, under this surprisingly confusing central principle of ethics.

The Goldwater Rule's unclear language obscures an important difference in the way the APA views the ethics of comment in various settings. As the Goldwater Rule is currently formulated, it involves an implicit double standard – implicit because not stated clearly in the text itself. It takes work to adjust one's eyes to the odd way the APA ethics committee has explained the text of section 7.3: "Confusion has arisen by taking the second sentence above and not connecting it to the first sentence as was intended." Traditionally, APA statements have not emphasized the restricted application of this supposedly general principle of ethics.[15] Yet it is hard for me to imagine a rule that is specific to media statements and does not apply to government, court, or insurance company psychiatrists functioning as a truly core principle of psychiatric ethics.

RISKS OF HAVING TWO STANDARDS. Without frankness about the acceptability of profiling for the government, the Goldwater Rule has the potential to be perceived as involving a double standard. The public, naïvely believing that psychiatric comment is never acceptable in the absence of interview and consent, may be confused to learn that psychiatric comment without interview and consent is perfectly acceptable to the APA if permission is given by a court or by the US government.

The APA's recent language for this anomaly, which is more explicit than past statements, speaks of a principle that has certain "exceptions." The first exception, it says, involves situations in which there is a (domestic) "court authorization for the examination" or "opinion without examination," issued with parameters for confidentiality; this appears to cover the routine practice of forensic psychiatry. The second exception involves national security situations in which "proper authority" is given to a psychiatrist, presumably by a government agency and again with confidentiality parameters. This second exception covers profiling for the CIA and other agencies.

If the Goldwater Rule requires such "exceptions" that cover entire areas of usual psychiatric practice, why it is framed as a central principle of ethics?[16] And if an exception may be made for forensic psychiatry, for profiling in the CIA, and for diagnosis in insurance company decisions about coverage, why may not an exception be made for the responsible, morally sincere concerns of an individual psychiatrist who is concerned about the impact of a president's mental health on national safety? Barry Goldwater's experience shows that there are risks to such comment. But as the Ellsberg case and the close alliance between CIA profiling and the actions of the US military demonstrates, there are also risks inherent in comment by government psychiatrists who have not conducted an interview and have not obtained the subject's consent.

RISKS OF AN ABSOLUTIST RULE. At the 2017 Duty to Warn conference at Yale, psychiatrists Bandy Lee, Judith Herman, Robert Jay Lifton, and others presented their evaluation and ethics recommendations in a calm manner that was supported by a philosophically coherent stance. The Lee group invited public debate and invited a member of the APA ethics committee to participate in their discussion. When Lifton, Herman, and Lee wrote to the APA to express their concern about the Goldwater Rule, they politely proposed a dialogue. As we have seen, they were met with a rigid response from the APA board of trustees. The APA ethics committee had already sought, and would continue to seek, opinions from its members; the APA relied especially on its formally elected Assembly as a guide to the opinion of APA members on the Rule. But in its letter to Lifton, Herman, and Lee, the board of trustees presented what I read as a unidimensional view of the issue and actually demanded that the authors (two of whom were APA members) stop misrepresenting the Goldwater Rule, a demand that is hard for me to reconcile with a stance of respectful disagreement and of openness to dialogue. Indeed, follow-up letters to the APA from Herman and Lifton went unanswered. Three current or former APA members who are critical of the Rule – Herman, Lifton, and Leonard Glass – told me that they feel the organization has been unresponsive to their concerns.

While these interactions can be understood in different ways, to me they are significant mainly because they are predictable sequelae of adopting an absolutist rule. I refer here to the Rule's position that it is *never* ethically acceptable for an individual psychiatrist to comment on the mental health of a public figure under any circumstances (not to the widely shared belief that there are, in addition, many alternative ways of improving public safety or actively fighting a misguided leader's policies). In my view, denying the possibility of conflict between ethics principles closes off discussion rather than opening discussion up. When a rule leads with the statement that media comment by psychiatrists is unethical, when it implies (unclearly) that psychiatric comment may well be unethical under any circumstances, and when it omits mention of the acceptability of psychiatric comment on public figures in a variety of institutional settings, it invites misunderstanding and self-righteousness to flourish. The current Rule, I can only conclude, is supported by a strongly and sincerely held view of ethics but is, in practice, insensitive to the autonomy and the conscience of individual APA members.

COERCIVE PATERNALISM AND ITS PROBLEMS. What perspective can we bring to this dilemma? As it happens, over the same decades in which the APA was moving toward the adoption of its ethics code and then defending it, philosophers and legal scholars have been exploring many of the questions at stake in the debate over psychiatric comment on public figures. Sarah Conly (2013) has made what is probably the strongest possible case for the kind of position adopted by the APA. In political and legal philosophy, it is termed "coercive paternalism."

Coercive paternalism argues that it is unwise to give individuals a choice in situations where they will be better off if no choice is allowed. Citing data from behavioral economics, Conly argues that in many cases, individual choice actually *undermines* an individual's own goals, and that it is therefore often wisest for government to prevent individuals from acting on their preferences. She aptly quotes George Eliot: "The mistakes we male and female mortals make when we have our own way might fairly raise some wonder why we are so fond of it." The version of coercive paternalism Conly advocates for aims to maximize individual welfare, including its subjective aspects. With human welfare as its goal, it justifies "making people do what is good for them." (Dr. Brendel of the APA ethics committee said she disagreed with my view of the Goldwater Rule as paternalistic, "unless you would consider any ethical position paternalistic.")

Conly acknowledges that paternalism often raises anxiety among its critics. Common critiques of paternalism, she notes, include its perfectionism and its tendency to overreach (that is, paternalism's "errors of scope," such as interfering with freedom of thought and speech). Perfectionism in this context may be defined as valuing more highly what the lawmaker sees as an "objective" good over what the affected people themselves think is good for them. As she notes: "Being forced to attend a church in which you do not and don't want to believe, as Locke pointed out in his *Letter on Toleration*, does not make a person into a believer." These comments capture, I believe, much of the dilemma currently faced by those APA members who disagree with the Goldwater Rule.[17]

In reviewing problems of coercive paternalism in the law, British legal philosopher H. L. A. Hart notes some issues that are even more concerning than failure to value the subjective belief of the governed. Hart notes the problem of how law enforcement affects "those who may never offend against the law, but are coerced into obedience by the threat of punishment." Here, he argues, the threat of punishment "is itself the infliction of a special form of suffering." The recent spate of resignations from the APA over the Rule appears to confirm this concern. Philosopher Joel Feinberg emphasizes the risk that paternalism will reduce autonomy when there are "illiberal uses of the criminal law-making power." Over-criminalization thus raises the problem of what Feinberg and others in this complex tradition call "moral limits of the criminal law."[18] In the case of the Rule, where principles conflict and reasonable psychiatrists differ, I believe it is a mistake to treat media comment on public figures as a central ethical violation, as coercive paternalism does.

As Martha Nussbaum demonstrates in her book *The Fragility of Goodness* (1986/2001), at least some philosophers and writers since fifth-century Athens have sought to minimize the problem of conflicting goods by trying to "simplify the structure of one's value-commitments." This exercise in one-dimensional vision, with all of its unforeseen consequences, has often provided material for tragedy. Nussbaum reads Sophocles' play *Antigone* in just this way, as a case study in coercive paternalism gone wrong. She shows how a king's exclusive emphasis on civic good leads him to deny the possibility that his enemies deserve respect. In the case of Antigone, it is the respect of an appropriate burial for her brother, an enemy of the state in wartime and also a relative of the king. In his insistence on the existence of one value alone, Creon, the king, cannot acknowledge the possibility of conflict between moral principles or see the value of pluralism. His refusal to consider other points of view is bound up with an impoverishment in his own "moral imagination," says Nussbaum, an impoverishment that leads him to attack those who recognize the possibility of moral conflict or who adhere to views other than his own. As a model of leadership, Creon is considerably harsher than the APA (he sentences Antigone to death), but the play illustrates in dramatic terms the potential for a clash between sincere moral viewpoints as well as the risks of intolerance. In philosophical terms, what is at stake here is whether it is possible to acknowledge the existence of a "plurality" of values and "the possibility of conflict among them."[19]

ETHICAL REFLECTIONS: ALTERNATIVES

AN ALTERNATIVE MODEL: RESPECT FOR AUTONOMY AND PLURALISM. The APA is not alone in believing that some ethical principles should be absolute. When I interviewed 1988 presidential candidate Michael Dukakis about the Goldwater Rule, he expressed a firm belief that the Rule has served psychiatry well. As it happens, comment on the mental health of public figures is a topic close to his own experience. In 1988, President Ronald Reagan was asked about rumors that Dukakis had received psychiatric treatment. Reagan replied: "I'm not going to pick on an invalid." Dukakis has devoted much of his post-1988 career to fighting stigma. He told me that the Rule is needed for the protection of public figures, but also "for the sake of the profession" itself. In other words, the credibility of psychiatry is placed at risk in thoughtless comments and may lead to adverse sequelae for those who need help from the psychiatric profession. This argument has also been capably advanced by forensic

psychiatrist and former APA president Paul Appelbaum. The fact that a thoughtful public figure and a former APA president reached similar conclusions, and on similar grounds, is striking.[20]

I agree that there is potential for harm in psychiatric comment from a distance – particularly from "cavalier" comments, but likely from any form of comment that is not based on an interview and consent from the subject. Nonetheless, at some point is it necessary to ask whether there are alternatives to coercive paternalism, whether noncoercive alternatives are credible ethically, and if so, how such alternatives might work. With many in psychiatry advocating for the Rule and many seeing public safety as a valid reason to override it, we must consider whether these arguments are advanced in good faith – on both sides. I believe they are. If one accepts this argument, then a central ethics problem emerges: When we form our profession's ethics rules, can we find a way to respect those who disagree with us? If so, what are the limits of that respect?

Here I believe the work of philosopher John Rawls on justice and pluralism can help. In 1976, Rawls published *Political Liberalism*, a book that has proven influential in liberal political and ethical theory ever since. Rawls's point of view, along with related work by philosophers Jacques Maritain and Martha Nussbaum herself, asks that we find a way to grapple with the existence of diverse points of view in a society where people hold strong and sincere beliefs. Rawls and the tradition to which he belongs can be helpful in establishing perspective on the situation represented by the Goldwater Rule – and in considering alternatives based on respect for the diversity of opinion within the APA and within psychiatry.

JACQUES MARITAIN: TOLERANCE. Jacques Maritain (1882–1973) was born in Paris into a liberal Protestant family; at age 25, he converted to Catholicism. His long career as a philosopher and teacher included positions at the Catholic Institute of Paris, the University of Chicago, the University of Notre Dame, and Princeton University. Maritain was heavily involved in the formulation of the United Nations' Universal Declaration of Human Rights in 1946.

In his short essay "Truth and Human Fellowship" (1961), Maritain takes note of a particularly American problem. Men and women, he observes, "coming from a great diversity of national stocks and religious or philosophical creeds," have to "live together." Given so much diversity, how is living together possible? Maritain finds both moral absolutism and reactive relativism to be unsatisfactory answers. Early in the essay, he discusses "the error of the absolutists who would like to impose truth by coercion." Moral absolutists, he says in a striking formulation, think that "error has no rights of its own and should be banished from the mind," just as "man when he is in error has no rights of his own and should be banished from human fellowship." Relativists, meanwhile, often react to religious wars by trying to "get rid of any zeal for truth." Maritain's vision of toleration includes room for humans to probe and seek for their own path to truth, while remaining engaged in respectful conversation with others who disagree.

Maritain's preoccupations can be gauged by two of the essay's headings: "Can Philosophers Cooperate?" and "Mutual Understanding between Men of Different Religious Faiths." The questions could easily apply to adherents and opponents of the Goldwater Rule. Seeing humans as weak but predisposed to seek power, Maritain finds much value in the effort that he calls the "*mutual grasp* which various philosophical systems can have of each other." This is clearly an effort at mutuality designed to prevent authoritarianism. A fellowship, or a species of cooperation, "real though imperfect" in Maritain's terms, can arise from this effort at mutual understanding. It is a fellowship based on respect for the other, not on relinquishing one's own beliefs:

> [T]hese [diverse] outlooks are irreducibly heterogeneous; these worlds of thought never exactly meet. Until the day of eternity comes, their dimensions can have no common measure . . . if, instead of being men, we were patterns of Pure Ideas, our nature would be to devour each other in order to absorb into our own thought whatever other such worlds might hold of truth.
>
> But it happens that we are men, each containing within himself the ontological mystery of personality and freedom: and it is in this very mystery of freedom and personality that genuine tolerance or fellowship takes root.

Tolerance and fellowship are founded, Maritain says, on intellectual justice, the effort to understand the thought of others sincerely and fairly rather than to enforce a single uniform belief.[21]

JOHN RAWLS: "REASONABLE PLURALISM." Rawls is best known for his book *A Theory of Justice* (1971/1999). There Rawls derives his political principles from the idea that in theory, each member of society should have to decide on the rules for getting along together without knowing in advance what his or her eventual place in the society will be. As Nussbaum notes, the result of this thought experiment is that members of society are "forced to choose principles that are fair to all, since any one of them might be anybody." Thus impartiality and respect have prominent roles in Rawls's thought. Liberty of conscience in particular, Rawls asserts, is so important that reasonable people in his scheme will be very likely to value it. Like Maritain, then, Rawls seeks a nonauthoritarian basis for mutual coexistence and cooperation.

But as Nussbaum notes, it is in his later work, especially *Political Liberalism* (1993/2005) and in his essay "The Idea of Public Reason Revisited" (1997) that Rawls grapples most directly with the issue of fairness in a diverse society. In these late works, Rawls identifies ambiguities in his earlier work and asks the difficult question of how people of different beliefs can get along together politically. For Rawls, the key arena is the political sphere in a democratic society, where diverse people hold different core moral beliefs, or what he calls "comprehensive doctrines." These doctrines are not limited to religious beliefs; they may include the bedrock beliefs of atheists, religious minorities, and others. The problem is complex, but Rawls describes it clearly in "The Idea of Public Reason Revisited": "a basic feature of democracy is the fact of reasonable pluralism – the fact that a plurality of conflicting reasonable comprehensive doctrines, religious, philosophical, and moral, is the normal result of its culture of free institutions." In Burton Dreben's paraphrase of the problem, "reasonable and rational people will inevitably differ on fundamental doctrines."[22]

According to Rawls, only oppressive state power can maintain a "continuing shared understanding on one comprehensive religious, philosophical, or moral doctrine."[23] But reasonable people need not use their power in this way; neither is it morally workable to base a political arrangement on the enforcement of just one point of view. What citizens in a democracy must do instead is find a way to honor the reasonable competing opinions in their society without suppressing them and without oppressing the minority that advocates for them.

Here, in contrast to the "comprehensive doctrines" themselves (such as religious systems), Rawls introduces what he calls a "political conception of justice." Political conceptions are the necessarily complex approaches that we develop in order to live together in a morally diverse world. A political conception is not in itself a moral doctrine but a guideline by which a diverse society can function in the face of conflicting moral beliefs among its members. Rawls advocates for fairness as an approach to the problem of pluralism: he sees its advantages as including its acceptability to competing groups, its reasonableness and rationality, and its association with social stability over time. (Perhaps for these reasons, he specifically excludes unreasonable and irrational comprehensive doctrines from his notion of reasonable pluralism.) With fairness as a foundation, Rawls hopes to encourage the development of an "overlapping consensus" in which citizens of varied but reasonable core beliefs can come to some form of working political agreement. This is the kind of agreement that has not happened consistently within the APA.[24]

Without respect for different reasonable comprehensive beliefs, Rawls believes, societies break down into oppressive majorities and oppressed minorities whose status is endangered by the majority. In these circumstances, the majority defines and suppresses "heresy" in order to preserve the shared belief of the majority. In this constantly re-equilibrating situation, an essential point, for Rawls, is whether a well-ordered society can generate enough shared continuity and purpose – whether it can sustain "a plurality of reasonable comprehensive doctrines" that can accept a working political conception – to achieve stability over time. The challenge here is the diversity of viewpoints in society. In our terms, when an organization imposes a single point of view on a diverse membership, the integrity and continuity of the professional organization are at stake. I conclude that the APA, though with the best of intentions, has entered the situation Rawls describes.[25]

MARTHA NUSSBAUM: FREEDOM OF CONSCIENCE. Martha Nussbaum, to whose work I am much indebted in this chapter, sharpens the issue further in her book *Liberty of Conscience* (2008). Rawls had said that "the free exercise of free human reason under conditions of liberty" leads to a fair political conception of justice.[26] Maritain had implied, though did not explicitly discuss, the role of liberty of conscience. Nussbaum, in a chapter called "Living Together: The Roots of Respect," develops the argument into a full defense of liberty of conscience in the American context. While her focus is religious liberty, the arguments Nussbaum makes have distinct relevance to the Goldwater Rule.

Discussing the recurring dilemmas over religious liberty that have been part of American life – and that have come before the Supreme Court – Nussbaum documents both the shared understanding of fairness underlying the tradition of religious liberty in this tradition and the "periodic attacks" that have been made on it. She identifies a tradition, begun by Roger Williams in Connecticut by the 1640s, that includes two distinctive components. First, she argues that American thinkers have repeatedly placed emphasis on the need for "a mutually respectful civil peace among people who differ in conscientious commitment." Here she clearly is taking up the problem of reasonable pluralism framed by Rawls. She also quotes Maritain on "real and genuine tolerance," which comes only with conviction both of one's own truth and of the right of others to theirs. Nussbaum, who regards Maritain's word *tolerance* as too weak, prefers *respect*, a term that is more familiar to psychiatrists.

The second feature of this American tradition of fairness, Nussbaum argues, is a personal, "highly emotional" sense of the "preciousness and vulnerability of each individual person's conscience." This sense of preciousness, of what Nussbaum calls "inner and intimate searching," shows conscience as "a living thing that must be respected by institutions."[27] As psychiatrist Claire Pouncey has plaintively remarked, "The APA seems to not trust its members or recognize us as moral agents who are the arbiters of our own integrity. I wish the APA would trust me."[28]

A PRACTICAL EXAMPLE OF PLURALISM. What might this kind of trust look like in practice? The American Psychoanalytic Association's

(APsaA) response to *Fact* magazine during the campaign of 1964 is an example of a thoughtful and liberal approach that respected the diversity of views among its members. It illustrates one possible application of the approach of Maritain, Rawls, and Nussbaum to the issue of psychiatric comment on public figures.[29]

APsaA, headed at the time by psychiatrist Heinz Kohut, was a small organization, but it was not naïve about publicity. Like the American Psychiatric Association, APsaA had a public relations office: the psychoanalytic group's Committee on Public Information was headed by a psychiatrist, Burness Moore, MD. Moore was in close contact with Kohut throughout the episode and drafted APsaA response based on a detailed conceptual outline by Kohut. APsaA sent its statement to three major newspapers, three newsmagazines, and two wire services: the *New York Times*, the *New York Herald Tribune*, the *New York Post*, *Time*, *Newsweek*, *U.S. News and World Report*, the Associated Press, and United Press International.[30] The process it used and the statement it published reveal a restrained approach that expressed concern about the survey but also demonstrated respect for its own members.

In July 1964, when individual psychiatrists began to receive Ralph Ginzburg's survey, several members of APsaA leadership argued for making a public statement condemning *Fact*'s approach. Kohut and Burness Moore conferred and decided to wait rather than take precipitous action. Their main reason was that in July, it was still unclear whether *Fact* might listen to the many negative comments its survey elicited and "desist from its plan."[31] Instead, Kohut and Moore each wrote personal letters to *Fact* emphasizing their concern. "You are asking psychiatrists to give their expert opinion about a candidate," Kohut wrote to *Fact* managing editor Warren Boroson, "without access to verifiable, relevant facts, in response to biased questions, and in an atmosphere of partisanship." Kohut stressed that under these conditions, isolated psychological insights could not possibly be valid – and in any case, few public figures "could ever have been elected" if the criteria for high office were full mental stability. Kohut elected to write as an individual psychiatrist and at that point did not presume to speak for APsaA.[32]

It was a lost cause. In September, Kohut learned that Ginzburg had run a full-page advertisement for the *Fact* special issue in the *New York Times*. After "some hesitation and a good deal of reflection," he told the executive committee, "I have come to the view (though without enthusiasm), that we should consider preparing a statement." The draft statement, intended for use only after APsaA had seen the actual issue, would aim for a "small, educated group" rather than a mass audience; Kohut told the executive committee that he needed to "avoid 'defensiveness' throughout the whole statement." He thought a priority was to "make a positive statement expressing, generously, our understanding that some psychiatrists might wish, out of a sense of social responsibility, to share their specialized knowledge with the general public." Yet the statement also should include "a thoughtful, measured, and moderate discussion" of the difficulty of making a "scientifically valid contribution in this field." Kohut included detailed specifications on the issue of scientific validity. He ended by saying that he thought it would be unwise for APsaA to defend itself against "an uninformed, ill-meaning crowd," and he was not entirely sure APsaA should say anything at all. But if "we can contribute something to rationality on a reasonably high level of thought, we might have added a useful trifle to the maintenance of civilization." In this dry and witty memo, Kohut kept his own contribution in perspective and grasped, as a first principle, that his organization's members had a sense of social responsibility that was to be respected.[33]

As drafting and redrafting proceeded, public relations director Burness Moore was in touch with the American Psychiatric Association. Moore reported his impression that the APA "is quite exercised about the matter. They believe that there is considerable organized political pressure and money behind the *Fact* report."[34] (The APA's suspicion on this point, as far as I can determine, was unfounded; Ginzburg worked with his own staff and used his own money for the publication.) Some consideration was given to whether APsaA should participate in a joint statement with the psychiatric organization, but APsaA ultimately decided to issue its own press release. The statement, issued on October 5, 1964, said that APsaA "views with concern" the use that *Fact* had made of the psychiatrists' responses.

It is understandable that some members of the professions dealing with mental illness might wish – out of a sense of social responsibility – to share their knowledge with the public in order to make a contribution to one of the most important activities in a democracy: the choice of a leader. However, professional judgments regarding the mental stability of any person have to be based on carefully evaluated psychological data which must be secured through a detailed review of the life history and a thorough clinical examination. Such information is most reliable when obtained in a therapeutic relationship in which there is the expectation of confidentiality and the wish to be relieved from emotional suffering as a motivation for self-revelation. These conditions do not exist in a political campaign.

The APsaA statement acknowledged that psychiatrists and psychoanalysts have as much trouble as anyone in being objective during political campaigns. The judgment about suitability for office was best made by the public on the basis of information "open to the scrutiny of all" and not by specialists based on a candidate's emotional conflicts. In a campaign, misusing the private views of psychiatrists "serves no constructive purpose" and may be damaging to psychiatry and psychoanalysis.[35]

The psychoanalytic organization's statement was notable for what it did *not* say. Trying to hold its members' diverse points of view, the APsaA issued a warning rather than a prohibition. Though APsaA agreed with the APA about the unscientific nature of *Fact*'s methods and the difficulty of evaluating personality from a distance, it did not use the word "unethical." And it did not blame its own membership. In their current form, the APsaA guidelines on the issue of comment on public figures advise "extreme caution" about diagnosis from a distance but do not prohibit the practice, ultimately leaving the decision up to individual members.[36]

LIMITS OF AUTONOMY AND PLURALISM. A pluralistic approach, with its greater respect for conscience, itself has limitations and problems. The Rule, relaxed from its current coercive paternalism into a guideline that acknowledges the potential for ethical principles to conflict, would have to rely on individual psychiatrists to make their own decisions about the ethics of comment. But as APA ethics committee chair Rebecca Brendel argued in her interview with me, professional discipline is what allows psychiatry to be a self-regulated profession. While individual conscience may be a sound guide at times, it can also lead psychiatrists into poor choices and the kind of regret George Eliot decried. One has to be responsible for the consequences of one's choices. Without coercive paternalism, we will have to live with greater diversity of ethics decisions, all made by imperfect individuals.

My own argument is that an urgent, credible, and evidence-based concern for the safety of the country may reasonably override our usual respect for public figures' dignity and privacy. (This is the kind of balancing test that Justice Black so heartily disliked in all matters involving the First Amendment.) Like Post, Lifton, Herman, and Lee, I believe that in an emergency, comment on a public figure's mental health should be considered ethical. Both the responsibility for the ethical reasoning and the definition of an emergency would be in the domain of the individual psychiatrist and his conscience. For me, a relaxed Rule would make psychiatric comment available when an individual psychiatrist concludes that such comment is not only relevant but urgently necessary in the name of public safety, whether (for example) in the fight against fascism, an unjust war, nuclear annihilation, or genocide.[37]

In contrast, I would not invoke such respect for the individual psychiatrist and her conscience in situations where it seems to me that reasonable people cannot reasonably disagree. Such situations include the issue of exploiting patients financially or sexually or of participating in torture.[38] On these issues, it is important for the APA to use coercive paternalism to protect public safety; it would be (literally) unconscionable to allow a psychiatrist choice here. But on the Goldwater Rule, where basic principles conflict in a substantial way, where the harm is modest, and where thoughtful psychiatrists can disagree, I would let a psychiatrist make her own choice, weighing the risks and benefits of responsible comment on a public figure's mental health against the potential benefits and risks of that comment to society. I would not differentiate ethically between comment undertaken for a government agency on the one hand and comment by an individual psychiatrist on the other. A psychiatrist's comment on public figures should be undertaken only after much deliberation and only if, in her view, the safety of a nation or a people makes it imperative.

The ethical task of the public-minded psychiatrist will grow more difficult, not easier, if the absolutism of the current Goldwater Rule is modified. But the potential for conflict among principles and the need for ethical reasoning under imperfect conditions are simply too complicated to be covered by a simple Rule. That leaves us with what Steven Cooper in another context calls a "melancholic errand."[39] In considering the ethics of diagnosis from a distance without the Rule, none of the available choices may be easy, clear, or free of risk. Asking the individual psychiatrist to choose, and then living with the imperfect result, as opposed to insisting on the need to overcontrol, is a sad but morally necessary task. I think of Winston Churchill, who said that democracy is the worst possible system except for all the alternatives. All things considered, I would replace the current Goldwater Rule with something like the American Psychoanalytic Association's advice to its members on comment on the mental health of public figures: proceed only with "extreme caution."

CONCLUSION. There are likely to be as many opinions on the ethics of psychiatric comment on public figures as there are readings of the history I have presented in this book. My own conclusion is that in the absence of interview and consent, psychiatrists should comment on the mental health of public figures only sparingly and only in situations that involve urgent safety issues for society. Given the clear risks of government profiling and the tendency for profiles to be leaked, I see little basis for an a priori ethical differentiation between comment in the media and comment undertaken for a government agency. While the harms from any psychiatric comment undertaken without interview and without the consent of the subject are very real – as evidenced by Barry Goldwater's sworn testimony and by the case of Daniel Ellsberg and the CIA – I hope we can find room in our ethical reasoning to acknowledge not only the risks, but also the moral dignity, of responsible psychiatric comment on public figures.

As a longtime and a current APA member, I admire much that the organization does. I have long been grateful for its deep commitment to professional education, its commitment to fighting for those with mental and emotional issues, and its advocacy for resources to protect those who have long been discriminated against. During the Trump administration, the APA has not hesitated to bring lawsuits when necessary (for example, to fight proposed changes in the Affordable Care Act) and has used its considerable power to advocate against the separation of children from their parents at the border. I am proud of my professional organization on these issues, and I plan to remain a member. But on the issue of the Goldwater Rule, the APA and I have come to different conclusions.

In my view, organized psychiatry needs to value the right of psychiatrists to reach different conclusions on the ethics of commenting on public figures. We must somehow find a way to balance respect for public figures with the need to address public safety in a responsible way. Clearly this is a complex ethical task and should not be done in a cavalier fashion.

Whatever opinion the reader adopts for herself, I hope that in the course of our professional discussions, the diversity of our opinions on the Goldwater Rule can be transformed into a strength. I have in mind what philosopher John Rawls described and argued for: a way of agreeing on the rules for living together in a society where people hold very different, but still reasonable, beliefs. We do not need to give up our own beliefs in order to respect our colleagues' points of view and to respect their form of social conscience, on whichever side of this issue it resides. Pluralism, while far from perfect, seems to me our best hope. We will need each other if we are going to move ahead.

The Goldwater Rule in 1973 and Today

On occasion psychiatrists are asked for an opinion about an individual who is in the light of public attention, or who has disclosed information about himself through public media. It is unethical for a psychiatrist to offer a diagnosis unless he has conducted an examination and has been granted proper authorization for such a statement.

From section 10 of The Principles of Medical Ethics with Annotations Especially Applicable to Psychiatry *(1973)*

On occasion psychiatrists are asked for an opinion about an individual who is in the light of public attention or who has disclosed information about himself/herself through public media. In such circumstances, a psychiatrist may share with the public his or her expertise about psychiatric issues in general. However, it is unethical for a psychiatrist to offer a professional opinion unless he or she has conducted an examination and has been granted proper authorization for such a statement.

Section 7.3 of The Principles of Medical Ethics with Annotations Especially Applicable to Psychiatry *(2013)*[1]

Boston psychoanalyst Walter Langer helped many Jewish analysts escape from Vienna and then wrote a psychological profile of Adolf Hitler for the Office of Strategic Services (OSS). (Photo courtesy of the Boston Psychoanalytic Society and Institute)

Child psychoanalyst Erik Erikson recognized the threat Hitler posed early on. Erikson wrote a cultural take on Hitler's appeal to his young followers that was later incorporated into his best-selling book *Childhood and Society*. (Photo courtesy of the estate of Clemens Kalischer)

Adolf Hitler, circa 1938. Erik Erikson noted that "Hitler's performances are … always a mixture of shrewd, planned, directed elements and of unplanned, impulsive, emotional ones. Goebbels lets him loose as a trainer does a tamed beast" (Erik H. Erikson, "Comments on Hitler's Speech of September 30, 1942," in Erikson [1987], p. 351). (Photo courtesy of Alamy.com)

Hitler addresses the German Reichstag, 1938. (Photo courtesy of the National Archives and Records Administration)

Fact magazine publisher Ralph Ginzburg and his wife, Shoshana, on the steps of the Foley Square courthouse in New York City during the *Goldwater* v. *Ginzburg* trial. His motive in publishing the special issue, said Ginzburg, was "to bring public attention to the emotional instability of a man who would have the destiny of civilization under his control." (Photo courtesy of AgeFotostock)

Goldwater rides a phallic missile in a Rick Schreiter illustration for *Fact*. (Photo courtesy of the American Heritage Collection, University of Wyoming/Estate of Ralph Ginzburg)

Barry Goldwater, 1968. In a letter to his family, Goldwater described Ginzburg as a pornographer and said the *Fact* issue on his fitness for the presidency was "a breach of medical ethics and political ethics and decency." (Photo courtesy of AP Images)

An idealized portrait of Justice Hugo Black of the US Supreme Court, Ginzburg's best hope in the libel case. (Photo courtesy of Office of the Curator, Supreme Court of the United States)

Walter E. Barton, medical director of the American Psychiatric Association, mid-1960s. To Ginzburg he wrote: "Should you decide to publish the results of a purported 'survey' of psychiatric opinion on the question you have posed, the Association will take all possible measures to disavow its validity." (Photo by Louis Fabian Bachrach Jr., in collection of the American Psychiatric Association; in public domain)

President Richard Nixon and his chief domestic policy adviser, John Ehrlichman, 1971. After the leak of the Pentagon Papers by antiwar activist Daniel Ellsberg in 1971, Nixon concluded that Ellsberg's views "had to be discredited." Ehrlichman's "Plumbers" – Egil Krogh, David Young, G. Gordon Liddy, and Howard Hunt – convinced the CIA to create a psychological profile of Ellsberg that could be used to discredit him in public. The Plumbers kept Ehrlichman advised on their progress, and Nixon was briefed on the plan. (Photo courtesy of the National Archives and Records Administration/Nixon Library)

Psychiatrist and trauma expert Judith Lewis Herman of Harvard. (Photo courtesy of Judith Herman)

Forensic psychiatrist Bandy X. Lee of Yale. Herman and Lee grew concerned about President Donald Trump's mental health and the risk they believe it poses to the country. Only "in an emergency," they argue, "should a physician breach the Goldwater rule. We believe that such an emergency now exists." (Photo courtesy of Bandy X. Lee)

The American Psychiatric Association (APA) issued ethics opinions, presidential columns, and institutional tweets conveying that no APA member should violate its Goldwater Rule (section 7.3 of *Principles of Medical Ethics with Annotations Especially Applicable to Psychiatry*). Here, a tweet repeats the firm view of former APA president Maria Oquendo. (Image used with permission of the American Psychiatric Association)

President Donald Trump. (Photo courtesy of Alamy.com)

Notes

INTRODUCTION: AN ETHICAL DILEMMA

1. American Psychiatric Association (2013), p. 9.
2. "Not for squares," "obliteration": endpaper and back cover, *Fact* 1:5.
3. Dukakis interview: Martin-Joy, Vijapura, and Carey (2014). Panel: Martin-Joy et al. (2015); Levine (2017); Appelbaum (2017).
4. Martin-Joy (2017a) and (2017b).
5. Libel law: Stone (2011); Liptak (2019); Borchers (2016).
6. Sheed: quoted in Whitfield (1988), p. 35.
7. Ahead of his time: "To the Right, March," 1968; Teles (2008). Burden of proof, "presumed to be false": Hall and Urofsky (2011, pp. 40–41; quote on p. 40); Lewis (1991, pp. 156, 165). Before *Sullivan*, libel standards were set by state laws, which could vary considerably (Hall and Urofsky 2011, p. 37).
8. Martin-Joy (2017b); Post (2002).
9. Lewis (1991), p. 36.
10. On immigrants and minorities, see Lee (2017), pp. 137–138, 142, 163, 291–292.
11. AMA endorsed: Stone (2017).
12. Schulman (2001), p. 45; Heidenry (1997); Perlstein (2001), p. 438.
13. On psychology and biography, see Elms (1994) and Mayer (2010f).

1 PSYCHOANALYSIS, MEDIA, AND POLITICS FROM THE RISE OF HITLER TO THE 1950S

1. Quoted in Langer (1972), p. 10.
2. Langer (1972), p. 3.
3. My account derives from Overy (1999) and from the Hossbach memorandum (Hossbach 1937), which prosecutors presented at the Nuremberg Trial as evidence of Hitler's aggressive intentions in Europe; William Shirer's popular *Rise and Fall of the Third Reich* emphasizes its importance (Shirer 1960, pp. 418–422), as does Overy. Historian A. J. P. Taylor later famously questioned its provenance and influence, leading Hugh Trevor-Roper to reassert its centrality (Overy 1999).
4. Kershaw (2000), pp. 65–83; quote is on p. 71.

5. Vienna's churches: Kershaw (2000), p. 81. "Heil Hitler," "monotonous": Walter C. Langer to Sanford Gifford, June 29, 1975, BPSI archives, box 2.

6. Walter C. Langer to Sanford Gifford, June 29, 1975, BPSI archives.

7. Langer: William C. Langer to Sanford Gifford, June 29, 1975, BPSI archives. Kohut: Strozier (2001), pp. 58–59. "Rupture": quoted by Danto (2012), p. 215.

8. APsaA helped: Danto (2012), pp. 214–218. No room in New York: Langer to Sanford Gifford, June 29, 1975, BPSI archives, box 2, pp. 5–6. Langer and affidavits: Walter C. Langer to William Langer, August 22, 1974; Walter C. Langer to Dr. Sanford Gifford, June 29, 1975; both in BPSI archives, box 2; Waggoner (1981).

9. Danto (2012), pp. 214–216.

10. Langer (1972). "Exceptional opportunity": quoted in Müller (2016), pp. 148–149. Half: Müller (2016), p. 150.

11. Lay analyst: Langer to Gifford, November 11, 1975, p. 9, BPSI archives. Langer and Gifford (1978) quote vast stretches of Langer's letters to Gifford dated June 29, 1975, and November 11, 1975, but provide almost no scholarly comment.

12. Langer (1972), esp. pp. 10–14. "No such study": Langer (1972), p. 10. "Well suited": Mandler (2016), p. 102. Murray's draft: Murray (1943); Carey (2005); Hoffman (1992), pp. 268–269. Langer donated his personal copy of his 1943 OSS report, complete with handwritten corrections by Langer, to Harvard's Houghton Library (Langer 1943). Much later, Langer (1972) published the profile under his own name, not acknowledging Kris, Murray, or Lewis on the title page, as he had in the 1943 report. Published as *The Mind of Adolf Hitler*, it received wide public attention. I have quoted from the 1972 version, which differs only slightly from the 1943 version.

13. Quotes from Langer: Langer (1972), pp. 16–17. Nuremberg: Langer to Gifford, June 29, 1975, BPSI archives.

14. Femininity and homosexuality are issues that contemporary psychoanalysis sees very differently (Herzog 2017).

15. Langer (1972) on Hitler: self-image as immortal, pp. 29–39; early development, pp. 145–146, 149–151, 163–168, 193–196, 201–202; autopsy, p. 227; sexual tastes and niece, pp. 168, 171–172; alleged femininity, pp. 163–175. Predictions: Murray (1943), pp. 13, 31; Langer (1972), pp. 210–212. Need for propaganda: Murray (1943), p. 33. "Too late," "too much to expect": Langer (1972), pp. 22–23. Review of Langer, "adventurous": Lifton (1972). Wilhelm Reich, writing in German, had published an early exploration of Nazism and mass culture, *The Mass Psychology of Fascism* (Reich 1933/ 1946); Langer owned a copy of the 1946 edition (Walter C. Langer personal library, BPSI). Elizabeth Lunbeck (2018) gives a well-informed account of how many psychoanalytic thinkers in the 1930s sought to participate via theory in the fight against Fascism.

16. Erikson biographical information: Friedman (1999). "First to take . . . seriously": Lifton interview.

17. Erikson (1950/1963); Roazen (1975/1992), pp. 510–515; "Erikson's rise" quote is on p. 515.

18. Hoffman (1992), pp. 266–267. Erikson (1942) on Hitler: "uniqueness," p. 475; symbols and encirclement, pp. 476, 483; "the tune," pp. 476, 483; Germany as mother, p. 477; Hitler as older brother, p. 480; Germany as adolescent, pp. 486, 490, 493; "how this can be accomplished," p. 492. Erikson (1950/1963, p. 327) recalled that he was asked to help prepare the government for the arrival of the first Nazi prisoners. In memos written for the Committee on National Morale during the war, Erikson extended his metaphor for Nazi Germany as a kind of adolescent whom Hitler had given permission to run wild; in this way he continued to develop a culturally sensitive approach to the immediate psychiatric questions posed by the war (Erikson 1987, pp. 341–374).

19. Remains unknown: Hoffman (1992). "Completing Our Mobilization": "Editorial Notes" (1942), p. 263. Important to differentiate: Mandler (2016), pp. 102–108. Donovan's lobbying: Turner (2005), pp. 17–34.

20. "The Legend of Hitler's Childhood": Erikson (1950/1963), pp. 326–358. Came to idolize: Friedman (1999), pp. 240–241. Lessons of Hitler: Erikson (1950/1963), pp. 326–327, 358. "Black miracle": Erikson (1950/1963), p. 326.

21. Langer's ethical situation, "He must have had the sense": Lifton (1972); APsaA Committee on Morale and its "first tasks": Müller (2016), p. 149.

22. Grew faster: Herman (1995), pp. 19–21. Alienated: Langer and Gifford (1978).

23. Herman (1995), pp. 128–129. "Old-boy networks": quoted in Herman (1995), p. 127. Barton: "Walter Barton: A Job Well Done" (1974); Barton (1967).

24. Gary R. Edgerton, "Not Going According to Plan: Remodeling the Tube in a Time of Crisis – 1940–1947," in Edgerton (2007), pp. 63–71.

25. Gary R. Edgerton, "Not Going According to Plan," in Edgerton (2007), pp. 73–75; Sarnoff quote is on p. 77.

26. Growth of early TV by region and nationally: Kathryn H. Fuller-Seeley, "Learning to Live with Television: Technology, Gender, and America's Early TV Audiences," in Edgerton (2007), pp. 103–107, including especially table 3.1, p. 103.

27. Gary R. Edgerton, "The Halcyon Years: Beyond Anyone's Wildest Dream – 1955–1963," in Edgerton (2007), pp. 246–247.

28. Davies (2006), p. 51; Brinkley (1998).

29. Vaudeo Days, "Here Comes Television: Remaking American Life – 1948–1954," in Edgerton (2007), p. 125. "Phenomenal": Davies (2006), p. 112.

30. At first: Davies (2006), pp. 49–51, 130. Made it hard to reach: Thorn (1987), p. 65. Moved to the suburbs: Jackson (1985). Newspaper circulation: Pew Research Center (2018). Cf. American population: US Census Bureau (2002), figure 1–1, p. 11.

31. Thorn (1987), pp. 27–28, 97.

32. Production costs: Thorn (1987), p. 69; Davies (2006), pp. 111–113. Suburban newspapers, decline in per-household circulation: Davies (2006), pp. 113–114, 136; *Editor and Publisher* is quoted on p. 114. Higher incomes: Thorn (1987), pp. 69, 100–101. Offset printing: Davies (2006), pp. 80–81. Corporate cultures; Thorn (1987), p. 165; cf. Hamilton (2016); Davies (2006), pp. 80–81, 111–114, 136. Fixed costs and eccentric local cultures: cf. Hamilton (2016).

33. Perspective and context: Bradlee (1995), p. 294. Schoolboy writers: Wilson (1944), pp. 117–119. "Blasé sanctimoniousness": Aldridge (1966), pp. 171–172. Circulation of weekly newsmagazines: John and Silberstein-Loeb (2015), p. 164. Minow: quoted in Rothman (2016). Professionalization: Davies (2006), pp. 23, 135.

34. *Time* cover: "Psychiatrist Will Menninger." Popularity of psychiatry: Lazarus (2000), p. 547; quote is from Don R. Lipsitt, "Psych and Soma: Struggles to Close the Gap," in Menninger and Nemiah (2000), p. 161.

35. Growth of Menninger, "direct and straightforward": *Memorial for William C. Menninger* (1967), esp. p. 25. Menninger as role model: Barton (1967); quote is on p. 18. Was it ethical?: Lazarus (2000), pp. 546–548. "I hope": Thomas J. Heldt to William C. Menninger, April 1, 1949, quoted in Lazarus (2000), p. 548. Lazarus says this correspondence was about allowing *Time* to name Menninger its Man of the Year. In the actual event, that honor went to Winston Churchill.

36. Boyer (1985/1994) quotes both Berryman (p. 252) and Mumford (p. 284).

37. See Danto (2012) on Marxist analysts, Hoover's quotes (p. 213), and APsaA's response (p. 219). Friedman (1999, pp. 399, 555) documents that Erikson was later himself the target of an FBI investigation.

38. Erikson (1950/1996); quotes are on pp. 278–279, 280; Friedman (1999), p. 248.

39. Danto (2012), p. 219; Erikson (1996), p. 282. Friedman (1999, pp. 245–252) speculates that because Erikson kept his research position at the university, he must have signed a later version of the oath; according to Friedman, the consensus of liberal activists at the time was that it was best to sign the relatively harmless oaths and choose more substantial battles instead.

Loyalty oaths – which required an employee to certify that he or she was not a communist (also known as a test oath or special loyalty oath) – should be differentiated from the more common and more widely accepted oaths of allegiance (Israel 1966). Oaths of allegiance, similar to the oath of office undertaken by the president of the United States, were often routinely required of teachers by state governments. In time, the California Supreme Court ruled the California loyalty oaths unconstitutional on technical grounds in an interrelated group of decisions (*Tolman* v. *Underhill*, 1952; Stickgold 2010). Some professional organizations voted to express approval of the court's action. The American Psychiatric Association (APA), according to Danto (p. 219), was not one of them. Though at least one University of California psychiatrist had been affected, the APA's Executive Committee considered the matter and decided to "take no action in this regard."

40. "Appalling record": Goldberg (1995), pp. 59–60, 92–93; quote is on p. 93; cf. Dean and Goldwater (2008), p. 170. "Now is the time": quoted in Goldberg (1995), p. 95. Labor unions: Goldwater (1960), pp. 44–57. Reuther: Perlstein (2001), pp. 30–32.

41. Salesman: Goldberg (1995), pp. 96, 98–99; quote is on p. 100. "Most patient," "hot stuff": Goldwater (1988), pp. 125, 126. "Aw shucks": Richard Rovere, quoted in Mann (2011), p. 23.

42. Credibility: Goldberg (1995), p. 106. "Maximum exposure," attention: Davies (2006), pp. 41–42. "Coddle": quoted in Goldberg (1995), p. 106. "Applause," "industrial cities":

Goldberg (1995), pp. 105–106; quotes are on p. 106. "Kept the wheel turning": quoted in Davies (2006), p. 41. Reporters repeated: Hulten (1958), p. 15. Army–McCarthy hearings: Nixon (1978), p. 147. Interpretative pieces, press–government relations: Davies (2006), pp. 42–48. House Committee on Un-American Activities (HCUA) hearings on communist infiltration and subversion in the United States also had a dysfunctional relationship to the media, even before McCarthy. The committee realized it could gain headlines by questioning Hollywood writers, directors, and actors about alleged subversion in the entertainment industry (Navasky 1980, pp. vii, xiv; Miller 1987, pp. 403–412). In the Red Scare too there was a regional pattern that mimicked the unequal spread of television across the country. Many of those investigated or kept under surveillance were Jewish and European, or if native-born, had grown up in New York City (J. Robert Oppenheimer, Arthur Miller); the urban demographic was more liberal. The congressional investigators, on the other hand, tended to be Midwesterners or Southerners and more conservative (e.g., McCarthy of Wisconsin, Kenneth Wherry of Nebraska, Edward E. Cox of Georgia, and R. Carroll Reese of Tennessee) (Johnson 2004; Danto 2012).

43. Barely mentioned socialism: Adorno et al. (1950), pp. 186–207. Horkheimer: Adorno et al. (1950), p. v. Most influential: mentioned by Warren Boroson in GG transcript, p. 1695. Taken up: Hofstadter (1954/1979), pp. 43–44. "Pathology of normalcy": Fromm (1955), p. 11. Stalinism: Fromm (1955), p. 247. Atomic bomb: Fromm (1955), p. 4. *The Sane Society* profoundly influenced essayist and soon-to-be novelist Walker Percy, who reviewed the book in "The Coming Crisis in Psychiatry" (1957), reprinted in Percy (1991), pp. 251–262.

44. "Psychopathic personality": Conklin (1950). "Smear": Whitmer (2018). "Instability": de Toledano (2005).

45. Cannell (2017), esp. pp. 97–108, 115–116, 196, 231, 246. "Appreciate," "publicize": pp. 97, 106.

46. Nash (1976); Buckley (2008), pp. 11, 13. Smant (2002) documents that Frank S. Meyer was also a major force in unifying the various conservative strands of thought.

47. Tiny world: Bridges and Coyne (2007), p. 28. Like the *Nation*: Edwards (2018). Uneasy coalition: Phillips-Fein (2009). Offices: Bridges and Coyne (2007), pp. 39, 62. First issue, "yelling Stop": *National Review* publisher's statement (1955), quoted in Bridges and Coyne (2007), p. 5. As strong as its rhetoric: Phillips-Fein (2009).

48. Bridges and Coyne (2007), pp. 43, 74–75; Buckley (2008), pp. 67–70.

49. Buckley pushed him: Buckley (2008), p. 81. Ghostwriting: Buckley (2008), p. 54; Phillips-Fein (2009), pp. 127–128. "Conservative political action": Phillips-Fein (2009), pp. 127–128. Sales of *Conscience*: Mann (2011), p. 19.

50. "Perhaps not . . . our man": Smant (2002), pp. 143–145. More moderate Republicans: see, e.g., Brinkley (1998), pp. 444–445, on Henry Luce. Sympathetic to libertarianism, religious: Shermer (2008), p. 678; Hess (1999), pp. 181, 169. Only real choice: Smant (2002), p. 145. "Would not bend": Buckley (2008), pp. 149, 191–192. Goldwater's changing position on *Brown* v. *Board*: Goldwater (1960); excerpt from testimony in *Goldwater* v. *Ginzburg* (1968), in Dean and Goldwater (2008), p. 172.

51. "Rubbed the noses": "Khrushchev in Budapest" (1959). Buckley on Khrushchev: Upton (2011). Nixon: Barbas (2017), pp. 171–190. Any meaningful difference: Schlesinger (1960) acknowledges the claim and works hard to refute it.

52. "Total destruction": Goldwater (1960), pp. 118–122. Kennedy on potential 1964 race against Goldwater: Goldberg (1995), p. 178.

2 RALPH GINZBURG: PROVOCATEUR

1. GG transcript, p. 1346.

2. "Uncontested": Brinkley (1998), p. xi.

3. "The Decision": The term appears in Walker Percy, "Stoicism in the South" (1956), reprinted in Percy (1991), p. 84. Concerned: e.g., Goldwater (1960), pp. 31–37.

4. Histories of obscenity law: Barbas (2017), pp. 185–186. "Major force": quoted in Heller (2006).

5. "Most celebrated": cover of Reitman (1966). "Refinement of definitions": *Time*, May 31, 1968, p. 41. "1,189," special issue: cover of *Fact*, volume 1, issue 5, September–October 1964. As far as I am aware, other than the brief use by Mayer (2009b), no previous scholar has drawn on the Ralph Ginzburg papers in describing the *Fact* episode.

6. Despite sometimes slipshod methods: *Fact* managing editor Warren Boroson told me Ginzburg was "a clever, talented guy" who could be generous with his staff – on one occasion he paid for the college education of an employee – but that he also "oversimplified things." According to Boroson, on at least two occasions not related to Goldwater, Ginzburg suggested that the magazine exaggerate or change statistics in the interest of making a better story. Boroson and Rosemary Latimore overruled him (Warren Boroson interview).

7. Reitman (1966), pp. 28–29, 216, 194; Miller (1972); Alumni Association of the City College of New York (2007).

8. Cook (2007), esp. pp. 15–21; Bell quote is on p. 15.

9. City College of New York: GG transcript, pp. 1831–1833; Alumni Association of the City College of New York (2007). "Brashly outspoken": Hentoff (1966), p. 287. "Windy": Miller (1972). Ginzburg's daughter Lark says that Ginzburg himself created this nickname, "honoring his self-image as a sassy clarinet player" (Lark Ginzburg, e-mail to the author, March 11, 2019). "Loudmouthed": Heidenry (1997), p. 78. "Promoter and hustler": Hentoff (1966), p. 308.

10. First wife: Reitman (1966), p. 30. Psychoanalysis: Miller (1972). Worked nights: Alumni Association of the City College of New York (2007). Public information office: Reitman (1966), p. 30. Sources disagree on whether he was discharged in 1951 or 1953.

11. GG transcript, pp. 1833–1835; Reitman (1966), pp. 30–31; Miller (1972).

12. "Attention-grabbing": Heller (2006). "Direct selling": Seibert, n.d. "Damned good one": quoted in Reitman (1966), pp. 31–32. *Unhurried View*: GG transcript, pp. 1835–1837; Heidenry (1997), p. 78.

13. Ralph Ginzburg, memos and letters on George Wallace, September 1968, in Ginzburg Papers, box 33, folder 33.

14. Cuneo (1966); Hamilton (2011).

15. Redden (2017); Heidenry (1997), p. 78.

16. Reik: Jay (1973/1996), p. 90; Ginzburg (1958), pp. 8–10, 17; Kazin, "The Language of Pundits," in Kazin (1962). Freud had written *The Problem of Lay Analysis* in response to Reik's professional dilemma in Vienna in the 1920s.

17. Ginzburg (1958), quotes on pp. 20, 83.

18. *Lady Chatterley's Lover*: Jordan (1997); Kaplan (2009). "O life": Kazin (2011), p. 214.

19. Sexual revolution: Isserman and Kazin (2000), pp. 147–154. "A force at the margins": Brinkley (1998), p. ix.

20. Serett and the *Handbook*: Reitman (1966), esp. pp. 62–63; Frank (2018).

21. Quoted in Reitman (1966), pp. 196, 198.

22. Quoted in *Ginzburg v. United States*, p. 11.

23. On *Eros*: throughout, Corliss (2006), including "stunningly designed," "set off," and "higher IQ." My examples of articles in *Eros* are all from volume 1, issues 3 and 4. French postcards: *Eros* 1:3, pp. 72–79. "Black and White in Color" (*Eros* 1:4, pp. 72–80). Honest antidote: Hentoff (1966), p. 290.

24. *Playboy*'s Monroe: "What Makes Marilyn?" (1953). Ginzburg's Monroe: "MM 6/21/62: Photographs by Bert Stern," *Eros* 1:3, pp. 2–19.

25. One observer: Alfred Kazin, "Lady Chatterley in America," in Kazin (1962). Granahan: Miller (1972). *Eros* circulation and charges: Reitman (1966), pp. 70–71. Knight circulation: Davies (2006), p. 119. $3 million: Heidenry (1997), pp. 79–80.

26. Miller (1972); Reitman (1966), pp. 69–73.

27. Criminal rather than civil charges: Heidenry (1997), p. 80. Optimistic: Reitman (1966), p. 433. Body: *United States v. Ginzburg* (1963). Bail and sentence: Miller (1972). Support: Heidenry (1997), p. 82.

28. Ginzburg (1962/1988), p. 9 and promotional blurb on back cover.

29. Ginzburg (1962/1988); quotes on pp. 5–6.

30. GG transcript, p. 1831; 1964 photo, in Ginzburg family collection.

31. "Important, timely": Boroson (2008). Philosophy of *Fact*: "Publisher of *Eros* Plans New Journal" (1964).

32. Staff: *Fact*, 1:5. Office wager, liked the best: Warren Boroson interview. Voted against: "Win or Lose, Barry Going to Alps for Rest," newspaper unidentified, June 20, 1964, clipping in BG Papers, 52:11.

33. Kennedy, "people will start": quoted in Goldberg (1995), p. 178. Defoliation and fascism: Goldberg (1995), pp. 191, 201, 192. Boroson: GG transcript, p. 1699.

34. McNamara (1969), p. 13. "Frighteningly real": GG transcript, p. 30. "In our new age": Shirer (1960), p. xiii. Shaking fists at reporters: Brinkley (1998), p. 253.

35. Ginzburg was alarmed: GG transcript, pp. 1840–1842. Acceptance speech, "extremism": Goldwater (1964); Goldberg (1995), pp. 205–206. Goldwater's adviser Karl Hess, who wrote the speech, notes the similarity to some sentences of Cicero's: "I must remind you, lords, senators, that extreme patriotism in the defense of freedom is no crime. And let me respectfully remind you that pusillanimity in the pursuit of

justice is not virtue in a Roman" (Hess 1999, pp. 167, 173). "Sensation-seeking," reporters: Brinkley (1998), p. 254.

36. *Chicago Defender*: quoted in Delmont (2016). Eisenhower: GG transcript, p. 650. Nixon: Goldberg (1995), pp. 205–208; Nixon quote is on p. 206. Goldwater's staff: GG transcript, p. 640. Robinson: GG transcript, p. 1894.

37. Johnson was not unhappy: Mann (2011), pp. 48–51. Pat Brown: Goldberg (1995), p. 207. "Secret armies": Mailer (1964). Believed Goldwater could win: Mailer (1964), p. 41. In New York, Ralph Ginzburg heard the speech much the same way, as advocating "an overuse of power" (GG transcript, p. 1840). The FBI has files on both Ginzburg and Mailer. Ginzburg's file focuses on the *Eros* case, but it mentions *Fact* briefly (author's Freedom of Information Act/FOIPA request # 1424924–000 on Ralph Ginzburg; file received circa December 15, 2018). The contents of Mailer's file are detailed in Brown, Lipton, and Morisy (2018), pp. 263–270.

38. Scene at *Fact* offices: GG transcript, pp. 1842, 1645–1646; Boroson (2008). Boroson recalled that what scared him most was Goldwater's "brinkmanship" (Warren Boroson interview). On the genesis of the *Fact* special issue, see Boroson (n.d.). Mayer's series of *Psychology Today* articles documents the case vividly and in detail; he relies mainly on publicly available sources, but he did interview Boroson and review his draft.

39. "Well being," "public attention": GG transcript, pp. 1344, 1846. Divided up: GG transcript, p. 1843.

40. GG transcript, pp. 1701–1702, 1847–1848.

41. Boroson (1964c), p. 24; GG transcript, pp. 1701, 1848, 2054, 2060. Cover letter and survey: Warren Boroson to "Dear Doctor," n.d. [July 1964], in Ginzburg papers, box 2, folder 7.

42. GG transcript, p. 1858.

43. Frank: Kelly (2005). Concerned Ginzburg: GG transcript, pp. 1851–1853, 1860; cf. also p. 1479.

44. GG transcript, pp. 1364, 1855, 2023, 2029, 2051–2052, 2007.

45. GG transcript, pp. 1452, 1457, 1471, 1481, 1855.

46. GG transcript, pp. 1461–1462.

47. Saw changes as fair: GG transcript, pp. 2049, 2027. "Made the point stronger": GG transcript, p. 1486; cf. pp. 2023, 2044. True to the spirit: GG transcript, p. 1481.

48. Medical director objected: GG transcript, p. 22. Barton and Blain: quoted in Levin (n. d.). Decided not to print it: GG transcript, p. 1989.

49. GG transcript, p. 1366.

50. In common law, as distinct from libel law, malice does refer to intent and can therefore be relevant for the portion of a trial focusing on punitive damages (Samantha Barbas, personal communication).

51. *Sullivan* generally: Lewis (1991); Barbas (2017), pp. 142–151. *Sullivan* as a civil rights case: Hall and Urofsky (2011). Before *Sullivan*: Thomas I. Emerson, "Freedom of the Press under the Burger Court," in Blasi (1983), p. 3. Libel law in Commonwealth countries: Williams (2000); Hurley (2009); UK Ministry of Justice (2013). ACLU:

Barbas (2017), p. 146. Quotes from the decision and concurring opinions: Barbas (2017), pp. 148–150.

52. GG transcript: articles and books, pp. 1377, 1873, 1417, 2056; underlined, e.g., p. 1373; revised, pp. 1898–1893.

53. Boroson and Adorno: GG transcript, pp. 1693–1697; Warren Boroson interview. Widely shared: Greif (2015). Fromm: Friedman (2013), pp. 50–54. Tried to understand: Adorno et al. (1950), p. v; Jay (1973/1996). Authoritarian syndrome: Adorno et al. (1950), pp. 759–762. "The basic conclusion": GG transcript, p. 1694. Boroson background and views on psychobiography: GG transcript, pp. 1646–1649, 1705–1708. Erikson: GG transcript, pp. 1728–1731. In the Ginzburg papers, both volumes of *The Authoritarian Personality* are in box 15; *Childhood and Society*, marked with index cards at the start of the chapters on Hitler and Gorky, is in box 18.

54. Two drafts: Ginzburg papers, box 1, folders 19 and 20; GG transcript, p. 1700; Boroson (1964a) and (1964b). Boroson reviewed the more polished of the two drafts and confirmed to me that the draft was his; he said he had not seen the draft in 50 years. He identified his own handwriting and said that the second hand, or "flowery handwriting," belonged to Rosemary Latimore. Latimore, he said, was independent-minded and would have made her own comments rather than simply following Ginzburg's instruction. At some point, according to Boroson, the whole piece was rewritten by David Bar-Ilan, an Israeli pianist and confidante of Ginzburg (Boroson interview).

55. "I refer to a book," traits: Boroson (1964b), pp. 666, 777. Quotes directly: GG transcript, p. 888.

56. Freud (1908); Benedek (1952), pp. 71–74. Fromm: Jay (1973/1996), p. 99. Erikson and Mead: Erikson (1950/1963), pp. 247–254; Kluckhohn (1944), pp. 599–600.

57. GG transcript, p. 777; Boroson (1964b), p. 888.

58. "Greatest catastrophe": Boroson (1964a), no page number. "I thought he was": Boroson (2008). "Teetering": GG transcript, p. 1846.

59. "Is it ethical": Boroson (1964a), p. 666; I have omitted several illegible corrections made on this passage. Entire population may be dead: Boroson (1964a), p. 566.

60. Sent to Reuther: GG transcript, pp. 1698–1699; Warren Boroson to Walter Reuther, July 16, 1964, in Ginzburg Papers, box 1, folder 19. Called Goldwater unbalanced: Goldberg (1995), pp. 121–123.

61. Boroson read *Young Man Luther*: GG transcript, pp. 1706–1707. "Reasonable": GG transcript, pp. 1697, 1700, 1713–1714. Erikson later wrote to *Fact* with second thoughts, advising that the hypothesis of the authoritarian personality would need to be qualified by further consideration of "time, place, and circumstance" before being applied to Goldwater (GG transcript, pp. 1726–1731); I have been unable to locate this letter in the Erik Erikson papers at Harvard University. For Erikson's own comments on Luther's anality, see Erikson (1958), pp. 79, 244–250.

62. "Research draft": GG transcript, p. 1714. Polls: Mann (2011), p. 98. Ginzburg kept: GG transcript, p. 1435; Ginzburg (1964), p. 20. Ginzburg rewrote: GG transcript, in pp. 1171–1248; Boroson (2008). Boroson (n.d.) later said David Ben-Ilan had done a rewrite of the article for Ginzburg. Mayer (2009f) also evaluates the Boroson draft,

takes note of Boroson's respect for Adorno, and observes how much the draft was changed for the published version. Mayer's overall judgment is that Boroson's draft "represented one reasonable attempt to understand Senator Goldwater" using "a reputable psychological theory of the time, a theory which, in updated versions, continues to inform the field."

63. Boroson (2008); Boroson (n.d.).

64. Main points: Ginzburg (1964); GG transcript, pp. 1369–1373; cf. Robb's opening statement in GG transcript, pp. 6–7. "In Goldwater's candidacy": Ginzburg (1964), p. 3. "If it sounds like": Ginzburg (1964), p. 22. "Capacity for evil": Brinkley (1988), p. 105.

65. Ginzburg's interest in psychology: GG transcript, p. 1357. Knowledge of the anal character concept: GG transcript, p. 1866; cf. Freud (1908). "Applied psychoanalysis": GG transcript, p. 1912. Johnson: see Chapter 5. Wallace: see note 13 of this chapter. Romney: Boroson (1967). "Mental stability": Warren Boroson of *Fact* to "Dear Doctor," n.d. [July 1964], in Ginzburg Papers, box 2, folder 7. Levinson: Warren Boroson to Daniel J. Levinson, August 27, 1964, in Ginzburg Papers, box 1, folder 19.

66. Liked to plan, "Let's look it up": Lark Ginzburg Kuhta interview. "Meticulously organized": Bonnie Ginzburg Erbé-Leckar interview. Later memo: Ralph Ginzburg to Harris B. Steinberg, May 30, 1966, in Ginzburg Papers, box 1, folder 1. "Intone": Siebert (n.d.). First half of the sentence: GG transcript, p. 21. "Public attention": GG transcript, p. 1894.

67. Schreiter: "The Unconscious of a Conservative" (1964), general and pp. 38, 47. For discussion of a cartoon that arguably made Goldwater look like Hitler, see p. 39 and GG transcript, pp. 845, 1928. Marvel and Cold War: Nicholson (2011), pp. 247–248.

68. "Goldwater: The Man and the Menace": Ginzburg (1964). "What Psychiatrists Say about Goldwater": "The Unconscious of a Conservative" (1964), pp. 24–64.

69. Ginzburg's excerpts from psychiatrists' responses: "same pathological make-up," p. 26; "B.G," p. 31; "I consider," p. 42; too dangerous, pp. 28, 30; "cannot feel at home," p. 31; "denying," p. 48. Adorno et al. investigated: e.g., pp. 322–323, 758. "To me," dandy: "Unconscious of a Conservative" (1964), pp. 39, 4–6.

70. Herzog (2017), p. 63; Carter (2004). Masculinity and anticommunism: Stabile (2018), p. 71.

71. Levine (2017).

72. "The Unconscious of a Conservative" (1964), pp. 31, 52, 34, 60.

73. "The End": "The Unconscious of a Conservative" (1964), p. 64. Polls: Mann (2011), pp. 9–14, 100. Cuban Missile Crisis: Stevenson (1962).

74. $80,000: GG transcript, p. 1228. "Sole obligation": "Is Barry Goldwater Psychologically Fit?" (1964). Heavily promoted: GG transcript, pp. 1322, 1328–1330. Distributed: GG transcript, p. 1333. The *New York Times* reported the issue's final sales figures at 160,000 copies; see Jamieson (1984), p. 203.

3 "TO REMOVE THIS PRECEDENT": BARRY GOLDWATER SUES FOR LIBEL

1. Goldwater to Miles C. Whitener, MD, September 9, 1968, in BG Papers, 52:16. Very few scholars have made substantial use of the Goldwater papers or the district trial transcript in presenting the *Fact* episode; exceptions are the relatively limited material presented

by Dean and Goldwater (2008), by Mayer (2009–10), and by Martin-Joy (2017a) and (2017b).

2. Alan Brinkley, "The Problem of American Conservativism" (1994), in Brinkley (1998), pp. 277–297; Nash (1976); Phillips-Fein (2009).

3. Rosenberg (1986).

4. Still had not seen: Goldwater to Mrs. M. C. White, November 23, 1964, in BG Papers, 52:11. Did not mention: White (1965). "Meditation on": Robin (2011/2018), p. 4.

5. "One of the 27 million": supporter to Goldwater, May 8, 1968, in BG Papers, 52:15; Goldberg (1995), p. 236. "Because of": Dean and Goldwater (2008), p. xi. Woodstock: Goldberg (1995), pp. 181–209.

6. Goldberg (1995) on 1964 campaign: initially feared, p. 179; "choice, not an echo," p. 181; *Meet the Press* and *Washington Evening Star*, p. 183; "easy prey," p. 185; "ashamed" (Ben Bradlee of *Newsweek*), p. 224; "surly" and provocative comments, pp. 183, 185. "In the television age": Buckley (2008), p. 56. Provocative comments: see also White (1965), pp. 303, 328. King: *Playboy Interviews*, p. 378.

7. Lacked skill: Jamieson (1984), p. 173. Plodding: Mann (2011), pp. 32, 94–95; Hess (1999), pp. 172–173. Took to the airways, Johnson: Jamieson (1984), pp. 206–207; White (1965), p. 330.

8. Jamieson (1984), pp. 198–203, 172–173 (a still from the East Coast ad may be found on p. 187); Mann (2011), especially p. 45.

9. Warnings: Jamieson (1984), p. 211. In later years: Dean and Goldwater (2008), p. xiii. Many observers: White (1965), pp. 216, 340. Never truly thought: Dean and Goldwater (2008), p. 136. What remained: White (1965), pp. 378, 380; quote is on p. 378. Winning everywhere: Schulman (2001), p. 113.

10. Buchwald: *Playboy Interviews* (1967), pp. 188–189. "Peggy and I": quoted in Goldberg (1995), p. 241.

11. Did not wait long: Goldberg (1995), pp. 241–242. Proud: Smant (2002), p. 148. "I'd never seen": quoted in Dean and Goldwater (2008), p. 143. "Scurrilous": Goldberg (2008), p. 223. For an example of a pro-Goldwater editorial, see the clipping "Fact … Or Falsehood?", newspaper unidentified, September 20, 1964, in BG Papers, 52:11.

12. "Depressing," "I still have the same feeling": Dean and Goldwater (2008), p. 154. "The masculinity slur," *Time* reported, "especially worried him, and still does." See "Fact, Fiction, Doubt & Barry" (1968). On the lawsuit, see Boroson (2008), Boroson (n.d.), and the Mayer articles.

13. Recovering: Goldwater to Roger Robb, August 9, 1965, in BG Papers, 52:11. Buckley: Edwards (2018). Reagan: Goldberg (1995), pp. 237, 302. "Unprofitable": Buckley (1968); Goldberg (1995), p. 390. Stabile (2018, p. 21) notes: "With its cultural and intellectual elites, interracial social venues, and more liberal attitudes toward gender and sexualities, New York City loomed large in the anti-communist imagination as an incubator for subversive ideas, organized dissent, and, ultimately, revolution."

14. Dean and Goldwater (2008), p. 145; "Judge Roger Robb" (1985); Robb confidential memo, n.d. [July 22, 1965], in BG Papers, 52:11.

15. Brennan: "lie," quoted in Hall and Urofsky (2011), p. 186; "knowledge that it was," quoted in Lewis (1991), p. 147. "Right direction": Buckley (1968). Set apart: Smant (2002), p. 42.

16. "Leaves open": Goldwater, quoted in Dean and Goldwater (2008), p. 175. Admirers: Dean and Goldwater (2008), p. 176. "Rare cases": Gruhl (1980), p. 510.

17. As was Goldwater: e.g., A. Wallace Brewster to Goldwater, May 8, 1968, in BG Papers, 52:15. Not a close call: Robb, confidential memorandum, n.d. [July 22, 1965], in BG Papers, 52:11. Agreed: Powell to Robb, July 29, 1965, in BG Papers, 52:11.

18. R. Wallace Brewster to Goldwater, May 8, 1968, in BG Papers, 52:15.

19. "Our next Senator": supporter to Goldwater, May 25, 1968, in BG Papers, 52:15. "'Give Im Hell'": supporter to Goldwater, May 14, 1968, in BG Papers, 52:15.

20. Cost, "subjected to harassment": Roger Robb, confidential memorandum, n.d. [July 22, 1965], in BG Papers, 52:11. "Breach of medical ethics": Goldwater to family, August 11, 1965, in BG Papers, 52:11.

21. Stigma: John O. Beahrs, "The Cultural Impact of Psychiatry: The Question of Regressive Effects," in Menninger and Nemiah (2000), p. 327; Herzog (2017), pp. 56–86. Boroson told me: "I was genuinely surprised that anyone would read what I wrote and conclude that I was saying Goldwater was a homosexual" (Boroson interview). Nagging doubt: GG transcript, pp. 457–460, 462–470.

22. Proudly relates: Goldberg (1995), pp. 230–231. *Lowdown*: Johnson (2004), pp. 197–198, 260. Later in his career Goldwater supported gay rights, to the consternation of his fellow conservatives.

23. "Less shrill": Goldberg (1995), p. 241. Was served: Roger Robb to Goldwater, September 3, 1965, in BG Papers, 52:11.

24. Letters from supporters to Goldwater, all in BG Papers, 52:11: "Todays PAPER," September 2, 1965, and September 3, 1965; resident of California apartment house, September 12, 1965; funded by communists, September 3, 1965. "Kike": Hentoff (1966), p. 301. The letters I cite in this chapter and the next – and the profusion of similar letters preserved in Goldwater's papers – are evidence against Peter Filene's argument that in contrast to elites, ordinary Americans in the Cold War era were not especially concerned with communism. See his "'Cold War Culture' Doesn't Say It All."

25. Unusual letter: Ginzburg to William F. Buckley, September 9, 1965, BG Papers, 52:11; a copy is also in Ginzburg's papers, along with a curt response by Buckley's assistant (box 1, folder 1). Ginzburg sent a similar telefax to Goldwater, n.d., probably also September 1965, in BG Papers, 52:11. Robb's account: Robb to Goldwater, September 13, 1965, in BG Papers, 52:11. Had discussed: Robb to Goldwater, July 29, 1965, in BG Papers, 52:11.

26. Robb to Goldwater, December 19, 1965, in BG Papers, 52:11.

27. Ginzburg believed: Boroson (2008). Steinberg biographical information, faint praise: Truell (1998), "Harris B. Steinberg Dies at 57" (1969). "Tough": supporter to Goldwater, May 15, 1968, in BG Papers, 52:15. As Truell notes, Boroson's attorney Stanley Arkin began his career as an associate of Steinberg's.

0

28. Court denied: Peter Corbett to Goldwater, July 28, 1967, in BG Papers, 52:13. Later recalled, no known comments: Boroson (2008). Treated as a single team: GG transcript, pp. 32, 47–51. Never disclosed, Bar-Ilan: Boroson (2008); Warren Boroson interview; Boroson, (n.d.); cf. GG transcript, pp. 1662, 1664. Boroson told me Bar-Ilan did not want his name to be used on the article. "Did nothing with any dishonesty": Arkin, in GG transcript, p. 51. Much later, Boroson claimed that most of the time during the trial, "Goldwater lied, we lied" (Boroson 2008). When I asked him about this claim, he told me he meant that he and Ginzburg left out the fact that Bar-Ilan had rewritten "The Man and the Menace" and the fact that Boroson had resigned from *Fact*, but "we didn't tell any blatant falsehoods" (Warren Boroson interview).

29. "I'm anxious": Goldwater to former staff member Coover, February 13, 1968, BG Papers, 52:15. "America of the east coast": Walter Trohan, *Chicago Tribune*, May 8, 1968, photostatic copy in BG Papers, 52:15. "Immensely important": A. Lawrence Chickering to Goldwater, May 15, 1968, in BG Papers, 52:15. "I AM GLAD," Humphrey supporter: supporters to Goldwater, both May 10, 1968, in BG Papers, 52:15. Goldwater to Miles Whitener, MD, May 9, 1968, BG Papers 52:16.

30. Ralph Ginzburg to Harris B. Steinberg, October 30, 1966; Harris B. Steinberg to Ralph Ginzburg, November 1, 1966; both in Ginzburg papers, box 1, folder 1.

31. Foley Square courthouse: Gray (2006). "Battle": Goldwater to Louis H. Powell, May 27, 1968, in BG Papers, 52:15.

32. March on the Pentagon: Mettler (2017). 16,000 died: National Archives (2008). "Bully": Kearns (1976/1977), p. 270. 1968 in general: Dallek (1998), pp. 519–600; Issermann and Kazin (2000), pp. 221–240.

33. Goldberg (1995), p. 251; Nixon (1978), p. 320.

34. Could identify with: GG transcript, pp. 637–638. Withdrew: GG transcript, pp. 1913–1914. Let Ginzburg's conviction stand: Reitman (1966). Where possible, I cite the easily accessible excerpts provided in Dean and Goldwater (2008) rather than the unpublished trial transcript itself.

35. GG transcript, pp. 2168, 3, 90–91.

36. GG transcript, pp. 4–26, 28.

37. GG transcript, pp. 27, 29, 52, 33, 30, 36–37, 45. Had anticipated: Robb to Lewis Powell, November 29, 1965, in BG Papers, 52:11.

38. GG transcript, pp. 42, 44–45, 29–30, 39, 88, 90–92, 3.

39. GG transcript: "box score" strategy, pp. 537–539; inadequately prepared, p. 350; trivial points, pp. 441, 537–556; read aloud, p. 430; did not seem to know, p. 332; vacillated, p. 584.

40. "Ridiculous," tiredness: GG transcript, pp. 61, 55, 74–75.

41. Goldwater's attire and glasses: see photo section. GG transcript: calmly explained, pp. 270–277; "perfectionist," p. 288; "smile," p. 266; "gentleman," p. 853. *The Virginian*, which aired on Wednesday evenings from 7:30 PM to 9:00 PM, was a great success for NBC in 1962–1963; see Gary R. Edgerton, "Not Going According to Plan," in Edgerton (2007), p. 252.

42. GG transcript: harmed, p. 317; view him, p. 468; protect, p. 530; "offer a diagnosis," p. 868; Ginzburg knew, p. 22; never had a nervous breakdown, p. 357; never consulted,

p. 296; added credibility, pp. 642, 950–1048; anal character allegation not based in fact, 589–590, 637; denied it, p. 348. "It was obvious": Goldwater (1988), p. 205. Overworked: Dean and Goldwater (2008), pp. 149–150. The perplexed Goldwater looked up the anal personality in a dictionary, but, he reported, "I couldn't find it." See "Fact, Fiction, Doubt & Barry" (1968).

43. Goldwater, in GG transcript: McCarthy, pp. 727–728; socialist and Korean War, pp. 724–725; withdraw from United Nations, p. 731; atomic bomb, p. 813. Ginzburg in GG transcript: on Lyndon Johnson and "pipsqueak paper," p. 2006. "Russian police": Goldwater to Roger Robb, May 31, 1966, in BG Papers, 52:12. Link to communist organizations: Robb to Goldwater, July 13, 1966, in BG Papers, 52:12.

44. "Low-yield atomic weapons": quoted in Goldberg (1995), p. 191. "The last part of it": Dean and Goldwater (2008), p. 155; comma added. Acknowledged: GG transcript, p. 350.

45. GG transcript: "vigorously," pp. 296–299; "not a Hitler," p. 649; demurred, pp. 803–805; "would be desirable," p. 807; "I do think," p. 807 (also in Dean and Goldwater [2008], p. 174).

46. Schlafly: quoted in Perlstein (2001), p. 362. "Camp Appeasement": Smant (2002), p. 76.

47. "This threat," "would rather die": Goldwater (1960), pp. 88, 91–92, 118–123.

48. Dean and Goldwater (2008): "Didn't you charge them," p. 172; "totally inaccurate," p. 156; "proud of it," p. 151; "hate someone you love," p. 153. Looked up "anal personality": Waxman (2017). An early *National Review* article, "They'll Never Get Me on That Couch," spoofed the great social handicaps faced by Hollywood conservatives who had not undergone psychoanalysis. See Bridges and Coyne (2007), p. 41.

49. Goldwater denies racism: GG transcript, pp. 498–499. *Brown*: Goldwater (1960), p. 36. "Changed my position": Dean and Goldwater (2008), p. 172. Buckley: Bridges and Coyne (2007), p. 81.

50. Buckley (1968).

51. Supporters to Goldwater, May 8, 13, 24, and 29, 1968, and May 29 and 14, 1968, in BG Papers, 52:15. "Very insecure people": supporter to Mrs. Goldwater, May 8, 1968, in BG papers, 52:15.

52. See photo in "Ginzburg Loses Again" (1968).

53. GG transcript: "sitting right there," p. 1832; no advertising, muckraking tradition, pp. 1844–1845; defended survey and article, pp. 1850, 1899; "emotional instability": p. 1894; "fulfill my obligations," pp. 1914–1915. These arguments are strikingly similar to those made by Bandy Lee and her group in 2017 with regard to Donald Trump; see Chapter 7 and Lee (2017).

54. GG transcript: legal advice, p. 1851; interchangeably, p. 1852; "only so much," pp. 1856–1861, 2023.

55. GG transcript: "work of art," p. 1837; "you and your ilk," p. 1915; "you mean like the Supreme Court?", p. 1917; did admit, p. 1837.

56. Dean and Goldwater (2008), pp. 173–174.
57. GG transcript, pp. 1341–1342.
58. GG transcript: grades, p. 1359; "You just read those parts," p. 1366.
59. GG transcript: "did not have time," "half-Jew," pp. 1363–1364; Democratic bias, pp. 2029–2032; methods and logic, pp. 2019–2027; variations, "I didn't say that," p. 1371.
60. GG transcript: "entirely apolitical," p. 1336; later in the trial, pp. 1900–1903; disingenuously: p. 1901; proud, pp. 1346, 1903; no regrets, p. 1345; "a very simple question," p. 1840 (for similar examples, see pp. 1845–1846, 1850). Burks (1968) reported on Ginzburg's testimony for the *New York Times*.
61. GG transcript: calmly denied, p. 1711; more lucidly, pp. 1707–1708; Boroson's background, pp. 1646–1648; could appropriately comment, p. 1705; no hint, pp. 1662–1664; on Adorno, pp. 1693–1695, and Chapter 2.
62. Boroson in GG transcript: homosexual, pp. 1243–1247; no psychologist had reviewed, pp. 1715–1716; Erikson, pp. 1697, 1713–1714; key parts, p. 1247.
63. GG transcript: "whatever that is," p. 2230; Goldwater objected, pp. 788–789; Erikson's follow-up letter, p. 1730; "under oath," p. 1723; defensive, pp. 1724–1726; "didn't prepare," p. 1728.
64. Steinberg in GG transcript: constitutional history, pp. 2170–2171; let them decide, p. 2169; separate the real issues, pp. 2171–2172.
65. Foot injury: Goldwater to Robb, May 27, 1968, and Ruth Luff to Goldwater, May 29, 1968, both in BG Papers, 52:15. Robb in GG transcript: "lacking in excitement," p. 2190; fit the definition, pp. 2190–2225, esp. 2225; admitted as much, pp. 2225–2227; recklessness, p. 2238; bitter conclusion, pp. 2229–2254 (quotes are on pp. 2239, 2253).
66. Many attorneys: "Fact, Fiction, Doubt & Barry" (1968). Unruffled: Goldwater to A. Lawrence Chickering III of the *National Review*, May 19, 1968, in BG Papers, 52:15. Offered the best chance: Goldwater to R. Wallace Brewster, May 21, 1968, in BG Papers, 52:15.
67. Instructed by Judge Tyler: GG transcript, pp. 2297–2298. Nearly empty: Mayer (2010b). Suggested to some: see Hugo Black's dissent in *Ginzburg v. Goldwater* (1970).
68. "LOONEY": supporter to Goldwater, May 25, 1968, in BG Papers, 52:15. "TOO BAD": Supporter to Goldwater, May 25, 1968, in BG Papers, 52:15. The "LOONEY" reference is to the case of John Armstrong Chaloner (1862–1935), who famously spent years fighting an involuntary commitment in New York.
69. "VINDICATED": newspaper clipping in BG Papers, AP Wire Service, n.d. [circa May 25, 1968], 52:15. "Will never forget it": Goldwater to Robb, May 27, 1968, in BG Papers, 52:10. Years later: Goldwater to Roger Robb, December 12, 1972, in BG Papers, 52:19.
70. Goldwater had shown: Gruhl (1980), p. 510. In his view: GG transcript, p. 822. Political weapon: cf. Rosenberg (1986). Conservative legal movement: see Teles (2008).
71. Nothing inherently political: GG transcript, p. 820. Moral obligation: GG transcript, pp. 29–30, 39. Vowed to take, almost buoyant: photo and text in "Ginzburg Loses Again" (1968).

4 GINZBURG, GOLDWATER, AND THE SUPREME COURT

1. Barry Goldwater to Roger Robb, May 27, 1968, in BG Papers, 52:15.
2. "Arrogant – or worse": quoted in Driver (2012). "Leaning toward": Dean and Goldwater (2008), p. 163.
3. Kalman (2017).
4. Hentoff (1966), p. 295.
5. National Advisory Commission on Civil Disorders (1968).
6. The Ginzburg papers contain many examples.
7. "Just finished": supporter to Goldwater, May 15, 1968, in BG Papers, 52:15. "Enclosed" and "It is gratifying": supporter to Goldwater and BG reply, June 21, 1968, and July 12, 1968, respectively, in BG Papers, 52:16.
8. Buckley (1968): n.d. but likely late May 1968, in BG Papers, 52:16. "Goldwater's Victory," *Greenville Sun*, n.d. but likely June 1968, in BG Papers, 52:16.
9. "I want this to go to the Supreme Court": Goldwater to Robb, June 11, 1968, in BG Papers, 52:16. "Lying, cheating document": John Wilson to Goldwater, October 31, 1969, in BG Papers, 52:17.
10. Vietnam War casualties: National Archives. *Laugh-In* and *The Virginian*: Edgerton (2007), pp. 267, 197.
11. "Judge Roger Robb of U.S. Appeals Court Dies" (1985); Phelps (1970); Mayer (2010d). "Combative": "John Wilson Dies" (1986).
12. Reitman (1966); Powe (2010).
13. *Ginzburg v. United States*, p. 12.
14. Friedman (1966/1967), p. 74.
15. *Ginzburg v. United States*, esp. p. 7.
16. Widely protested: Friedman (1966/1967). Playboy advertising: *Playboy Interviews* (1966), p. 293. Harlan: *Ginzburg v. United States*.
17. Technically *Goldwater v. Ginzburg* was now known by slightly different names as it moved through the appellate courts (*Barry M. Goldwater, Plaintiff-Appellee* v. *Ralph Ginzburg, Defendant-Appellant* . . . .[1969]) and as it was considered for a writ of certiorari by the Supreme Court (*Ginzburg v. Goldwater*, 396 U.S. 1049 [1970]).
18. *Curtis* v. *Butts* and *Associated Press* v. *Walker*: Barbas (2017), p. 243; *Curtis Publishing Co.* v. *Butts* (1967); Phelps (1970). *Hill*: Barbas (2017), esp. pp. 242–243. Some experts believed: Barbas (2017), p. 194.
19. Black on *Sullivan*: quoted in Hall and Urofsky (2011), p. 180.
20. Wilson to Goldwater, October 31, 1969, in BG Papers, 52:17.
21. *Stanley v. Georgia*. Kalman (2017); Thomas I. Emerson, "Freedom of the Press under the Burger Court," in Blasi (1983), pp. 1–27.
22. Lewis (1964/1989), pp. 41–42, 27–30; John Wilson to Goldwater, October 31, 1969, in BG Papers, 52:17.
23. Black dissent: *Ginzburg v. Goldwater*, 396 U.S. 1049 (1970).
24. "Black day": Phelps (1970). Witch hunt: Hentoff (1966), p. 309.
25. Conservative legend: Dean and Goldwater (2008), pp. 145–176. Second time: Phelps (1970). Once the victory was in hand, Goldwater raised the issue of Douglas's failure to

recuse himself from the *Fact* case. He wrote to Robert Griffin, the Senate minority whip (Goldwater to Robert Griffin, January 26, 1970, in BG Papers, 52:18). Griffin referred the issue to members of the House of Representatives, "where any proceedings looking toward impeachment would have to be commenced, as you know" (Griffin to Goldwater, February 10, 1970, in BG Papers, 52:18). Douglas was never impeached.

26. Goldwater to Hon. Roger Robb, US Court of Appeals, Washington, DC, February 1, 1972, in BG Papers, 52:18.

27. *Goldwater* v. *Ginzburg* was one of several cases in the aftermath of *Sullivan* that probed the limits of, and developed the operational implications of, the new libel doctrine (Barbas 2017).

28. Stage check: photo, circa 1970, Ginzburg family archives. Boroson (n.d.) said that the court ordered Ginzburg and *Fact* to pay the $75,000; of the additional $1 awarded to Goldwater by the jury, Boroson's share was only 33 cents. The $1, he recalled, was also paid by Ginzburg (Warren Boroson interview with the author). The total amount Ginzburg eventually paid to Goldwater, including costs and interest, was actually $92,307; see Arthur J. Levy to David H. Marion, Esq., April 2, 1970, in BG Papers, 52:18.

5 "TO PROTECT PUBLIC FIGURES": THE APA AND THE GOLDWATER RULE

1. APA Archives, box 100226, folder 255.

2. Treatments of the APA's internal ethics process are scarce. Martin-Joy (2017a) and (2017b), from which some of the material in this chapter is drawn, show how the APA has interpreted the Goldwater Rule over the decades, focusing on ethics committee opinions and ethics task force reports. Lazarus (2000), an APA insider, uses internal documents to give an overview of APA ethics policy after World War II; Post (2002) draws on APA documents to trace evolving disagreements on the Rule and to argue that the Rule is baffling.

3. Movies: Gabbard and Gabbard (1999), pp. 107–164; "pseudoscientists" quote is on p. 146. *Myth of Mental Illness*: Szasz (1960/1974).

4. Predicted: Hofstadter (1964/1979). Ever more success: Schulman (2001).

5. The APA's drive for internal reorganization: Summary Report of the Special Session of the Council of the American Psychiatric Association, Airlie House, September 11–13, 1964, APA Archives, box 100219, folders 211–212, esp. pp. 15–25; "guidelines," p. 12. This report reviewed the APA's committee structure as of 1964 and declared it "in the main sorely deficient" (p. 23). Evolution of the APA's ethics code: Lazarus (2000).

6. General practitioner: Ludmerer (1999). Specialty societies: American College of Neurology (n.d.); American College of Cardiology (n.d.). "History of American psychiatry": American Psychiatric Association (1944), p. xi. New identity of the psychiatrist: Henry Alden Bunker, "American Psychiatry as a Specialty," in American Psychiatric Association (1944), pp. 479–505.

7. John E. Schowalter, "Child Psychiatry Comes of Age," in Menninger and Nemiah (2000), p. 466; Seymour L. Halleck, "Forensic Psychiatry after World War II," in Menninger and

Nemiah (2000), pp. 517–542; American Association of Directors of Psychiatry Residency Training (n.d. [circa 2010]); Davis (1990).

8. Davis (1990). The ABA's Model Rules were not completely new, but they replaced an earlier code of legal ethics (Davis 1990, p. 166). "Watershed": Cohen, Davis, and Elliston (2009), pp. 10–14, 67.

9. Cohen et al. (2009), p. 11; Brenan (2018).

10. Now known as section 7.3, the Rule was originally listed in section 10.

11. Hard to please: Kazin (1962). Heartless specialization: Coles (1960). Szasz: Norman Dain, "Antipsychiatry," in Menninger and Nemiah (2000), pp. 283–286. Literal-minded: Szasz (1960/1974), pp. xiii–xvi. "Much anguish": Sabshin (2008), pp. 48–49; Dain (2000); Hallek (2000), p. 526.

12. Minutes of the Special Meeting of [the APA] Council, Airlie House, Warrenton, Virginia, September 13, 1964, p. 17, APA Archives, box 100219, folder 210.

13. Poverty: Minutes, Special Meeting of [the APA] Council, September 11, 12, and 13, 1964, Airlie House, APA Archives, box 100219, folder 210, p. 15. Social problems: Summary Report of the Special Session of the Council of the American Psychiatric Association, Airlie House, September 11–13, 1964, APA Archives, box 100219, folder 211–212, pp. 14–15.

14. Ervin: Kirby (n.d.); Ervin (1964). Prudhomme: quoted in Stewart (2019).

15. "Prevention of war": APA Council, Task Force I, Summary [of] AM Session, September 13, 1964, p. 3, APA Archives, box 100219, folder 210. Walter Barton had once suggested that the APA expand its role in issuing position statements on current topics, but he made clear that he was referring to issues such as drug abuse and care for the elderly – and pointedly not to political events such as "the Berlin crisis" (Barton 1961).

16. APA Council, Task Force I, Summary [of] AM Session, September 13, 1964, p. 3, APA Archives, box 100219, folder 210.

17. Gail Barton interview.

18. Minutes of the Special Meeting of [the APA] Council, Airlie House, Warrenton, Virginia, September 13, 1964, p. 12, in APA Archives, box 100219, folder 210.

19. Biography: Barton (1967) and (1974). Menninger: Barton (1967), p. 19. Personal view: Gail Barton interview. Barton, whose family was of German descent, was born as Walter Bartush. With World War II imminent, he decided that it would be wise to change the German-sounding family name to Barton, and he did so with the aim of advancing his career (Gail Barton interview).

20. Barton letter: quoted in American Psychiatric Association (1976), p. 1. Golden Rule: Gail Barton interview with author.

21. "Is Barry Goldwater Psychologically Fit to Be President of the United States?" (1964).

22. Minutes of the Special Meeting of [the APA] Council, Airlie House, Warrenton, Virginia, September 13, 1964, p. 12, in APA Archives, box 100219, folder 210.

23. "To the great embarrassment": quoted in American Psychiatric Association (1976), pp. 1–2. "DISAPPROVING": quoted in "*Avant Garde*'s Malicious Mischief," item 22A in Medical Director's Report on Administrative Matters, APA Executive Committee

minutes, February 24, 1968, in APA Archives, box 100224, folder 240, pp. 20–21; quote is on p. 21. The AMA issued a stern press release as well; see news release, American Medical Association, undated but stamped as sent out on October 8, 1964, in APsaA Papers.

24. *Time*: quoted by Walter Barton in medical director's summation, APA Council, October 31–November 1, 1964, Part II, p. 9, in APA Archives, box 100219, folders 211–212.

25. Much later, in discussing the Goldwater Rule, Appelbaum (2017) made this point about risks to the public.

26. For a contemporary approximation of this reasoning – explaining how political expression must be balanced by the consideration of "maintaining an alliance" with the current presidential administration in order to keep a seat at the table – see Oquendo (2017).

27. Ludmerer (1999): massive and vast new stream, pp. 139–259; "astounding," p. 222; boomed financially, p. 226; demand, pp. 163–168. Medicare and Medicaid: Dallek (1998), pp. 203–211.

28. Minutes of the APA Council, October 31–November 1, 1964, Part II, p. 7, in APA Archives, box 100219, folders 211–212; Draft of Resolution for the APA Council from the Commission on Insurance, October 31, 1964, in APA Archives, box 100219, folders 211–212.

29. Guidelines for Psychiatrists: Problems in Confidentiality, Draft Statement for Consideration by the Board of Trustees, Item 9, in APA Archives, box 100226, folder 255.

30. Executive Committee Meeting, February 24, 1968, Item 13: Reference Committee, in APA Archives, box 100224, folder 240.

31. Gerald N. Grob, "Mental Health Policy in Late Twentieth-Century America," in Menninger and Nemiah (2000), pp. 233–234.

32. Vera Williams for the editors of *Avant Garde* magazine, to "Dear Doctor," n.d. [January 1968], Ex FG 1, WHCF [White House Central File], Box 17, LBJ Library.

33. Richard A. Baddour to Lyndon Johnson, January 20, 1968; Samuel Lowy letter to *Avant-Garde*, January 23, 1968, both in Ex FG 1, WHCF, Box 17, LBJ Library.

34. Fred Panzer to W. Marvin Watson, February 1, 1968, Ex FG 1, WHCF, Box 17, LBJ Library.

35. Lyndon B. Johnson, dictated memo in response to appointments secretary James R. Jones's memo to W. Marvin Watson, February 1, 1968, 9 PM, Ex FG 1, WHCF, Box 17, LBJ Library.

36. King: *Playboy Interviews*, p. 380. In 1964, psychiatrist Heinz Kohut, president of the American Psychoanalytic Association, raised the identical question in relation to *Fact*: whether responding publicly would merely give Ginzburg's survey more publicity.

37. Identification of "Harry": Liza Talbot, digital archivist at LBJ Library, e-mail to author, February 5, 2016.

38. James R. Jones to W. Marvin Watson, February 2, 1968, Ex FG 1, WHCF, Box 17, LBJ Library.

39. Annotation on James R. Jones memo to W. Marvin Watson, February 2, 1968, Ex FG 1, WHCF, Box 17, LBJ Library.

40. James R. Jones to W. Marvin Watson, February 2, 1968; Shoemaker memo to George Christian, February 16, 1968; both in Ex FG 1, WHCF, Box 17, LBJ Library.

41. *Avant Garde*'s cover letter: Vera Williams, "Dear Doctor," n.d., in BG Papers, 52:15. It was Coover: Goldwater to Darrell Coover, American Medical Association, Washington, DC, February 13, 1968, in BG Papers 52:15. "Maybe he will join us": Roger Robb to Goldwater, February 16, 1968, in BG Papers, 52:15; see also Robb to Goldwater, March 8, 1968, in BG Papers 52:15.

42. Barry Goldwater to Dr. Howard M. Cohen, January 27, 1969, in BG Papers, 52:17.

43. "*Avant Garde*'s Malicious Mischief," Executive Committee Meeting of February 24, 1968, item 22-A, p. 20, APA Archives, box 100224, folder 240.

44. Robinson (1968); "R.L.R" was identified as Robinson in an e-mail from APA archivist Deena Gorland to the author, June 12, 2018. AMA: APA Executive Committee Minutes, February 24, 1968, pp. 20–21, APA Archives, box 100224, folder 240.

45. "*Avant Garde*'s Malicious Mischief," Executive Committee Meeting of February 24, 1968, item 22-A, p. 21, APA Archives, box 100224, folder 240.

46. Bartholomew W. Hogan, MD, APA Deputy Medical Director, to Robert G. Garber, February 28, 1968, in APA Archives, box 10024, folder 240.

47. The *Fact* libel trial had not yet revealed Ginzburg's alterations of the 1964 survey responses, but the APA had little reason to trust him at this point.

48. Robert S. Gerber to three APA members, separate letters dated March 1, 1968, APA Archives, box 10024, folder 240. I have elected not to disclose the names of the members.

49. Gary R. Edgerton, "A Great Awakening: Prime Time for Network Television – 1964–1975," in Edgerton (2007), pp. 264–266; quote is on p. 265.

50. Burks (1968). Ginzburg – under oath in GG transcript, pp. 1913–1915, and as reported by Burks the next day – claimed that most psychiatrists included in the *Avant Garde* survey believed Johnson was fit for office.

51. Drescher (2007), p. 49.

52. Talbott on Kolb: Pritchard (2006). "Thoughtful": Drescher (2007), p. 49. Notably, it was Kolb who seconded the APA executive committee motion in February 1968 to ask APA members "what they wrote [about Johnson to *Avant Garde*] ... and the bases of their statements." Thus even the staunchest advocates for what became the Goldwater Rule were not necessarily conservative on political issues.

53. Drescher (2007). Protests over homosexuality as diagnosis: John O. Beahrs, "The Cultural Impact of Psychiatry: The Question of Regressive Effects," in Menninger and Nemiah (2000), p. 329; Gittings (2007), p. xvii; Bears (2000), p. 329.

54. "Attendance" and "Minutes: Organization Meeting of the Board of Trustees, American Psychiatric Association, Thursday, May 10, 1973," in APA Archives, box 100231, folder 296. At the May 10 meeting, the sole female trustee in attendance was Henriette R. Klein.

55. Barton (1987), p. 197; Lawrence C. Kolb et al., "The National Institute of Mental Health: Its Influence on Psychiatry and the Nation's Mental Health," in Menninger and Nemiah (2000), pp. 207–214; Dallek (1998), pp. 204–211.

56. Reitman (1966), pp. 193–196; Ginzburg (1973), pp. 10–18, 33, including Arthur Miller quote on p. 13. "Here and now": Miller (1972).

57. APA president Perry C. Talkington, MD, to Lawrence S. Kubie, MD, February 28, 1973, APA Archives, box 100231, folders 295–296.

58. Media stories: Lazarus (2000), pp. 557–558. Barton to chair of ethics committee: Walter E. Barton to C. H. Hardin Branch, MD, February 28, 1973, in APA Archives, box 100231, folder 296.

59. "Minutes: Organization Meeting of the Board of Trustees, American Psychiatric Association, Thursday, May 10, 1973," in APA Archives, box 100231, folder 296, p. 14. Public safety: Lazarus (2000), p. 563.

60. Sabshin (2008), p. 47; "Executive Committee, September 13–14, 1975," APA Archives, box 100236, folder 333, p. 20.

61. Nixon (1978), p. 716.

62. Consensus, Wilbur Cohen: Grob (2000), pp. 234–235. "Not a happy camper," pen used by Kennedy: Gail Barton interview. Recognized: Nixon (1978), p. 764.

63. "Guidelines for Psychiatrists: Problems in Confidentiality, Draft Statement for Consideration by the Board of Trustees," Item 9 [December 1969], pp. 8–9, in APA Archives, box 100226, folder 255.

64. American Psychiatric Association (1973a), pp. 4–10.

65. "Attendance" and "Minutes: Organization Meeting of the Board of Trustees, American Psychiatric Association, Thursday, May 10, 1973," in APA Archives, box 100231, folder 296. The *Principles* were ratified by the incoming 1973–1974 board.

66. "Cannot legislate": quoted in Appelbaum (2017), p. 229. "Circumstances": Stone (2017).

67. American Psychiatric Association (1973b).

68. American Psychiatric Association (1973b), section 10.

69. The 1973 first edition of the *Principles* banned psychiatric *diagnosis* of public figures; in 1975, the wording was widened to cover all psychiatric comment (see later in this chapter) and a sentence was introduced about the appropriateness of making general educational comments to the media. In 1973, the Rule was listed in section 10 of the *Principles* because the AMA's principles at the time discussed a physician's responsibility to society in *its* section 10, but the AMA later reduced the number of core principles from 10 to 7. The Goldwater Rule then became section 7.3 of the revised *Principles*.

70. "Minutes: Organization Meeting of the Board of Trustees, American Psychiatric Association, Thursday, May 10, 1973," in APA Archives, box 100231, folder 296, p. 15.

71. "Ethical Matters," Item 10, Executive Committee, June 1973, in APA Archives, box 100231, folder 302; Finney et al. (1973).

72. "Board of Trustees – Item 7A, December 14–15, 1973, Report of the Committee on Ethics," in APA Archives, box 100232, folder 306 [p. 1].

73. All quotes from opinions of the APA ethics committee in the remainder of this chapter are taken from American Psychiatric Association (2016) and are discussed in greater detail in Martin-Joy (2017b).
74. Task force: American Psychiatric Association (1976); Mack (1976). Probing reflection: Coles (1973/1995).
75. Barton: Walter E. Barton to Drs. Robert A. Moore and Charles K. Hofling, September 26, 1973, in APA Archives, box 100232, folder 305. Ethics committee was flexible, exceptions: "Board of Trustees – Item 7A, December 14–15, 1973, Report of the Committee on Ethics," in APA Archives, box 100232, folder 306, p. 2. Plaintive note: "Report of the Ethics Committee to the APA Board of Trustees," December 14–15, 1974, Item 3-D, "Psychiatric Profiles," pp. 2–3, in APA Archives, box 100234, folder 321, pp. 2–3.
76. Barton and Barton (1984), pp. 109, 98. Stone: Gersen (2017), p. 3.
77. "Board of Trustees – Item 7A, December 14–15, 1973, Report of the Committee on Ethics," in APA Archives, box 100232, folder 306, p. 4.
78. Satisfied Goldwater: see note 42. Recommended: "Actions: APA Board of Trustees, December 13–14, 1974," in APA Archives, box 100234, folder 322, p. xvii. Compelled: "Report of the Ethics Committee to the APA Board of Trustees," December 14–15, 1974, in APA Archives, box 100234, folder 321, pp. 5–6.
79. Bloch and Chodoff (1981), pp. 55, 306–307.
80. Seymour L. Halleck, "Forensic Psychiatry after World War II," in Menninger and Nemiah (2000), p. 525.
81. Levine (2017).
82. "Discredit": Nelson (2018), p. 110. "Less sensitive": Tom Wicker, quoted in Lebovic (2016), p. 190.
83. Nixon (1978): "stunning," p. 900; *Daily News*, quoted on p. 900; debated, pp. 898–903.
84. Death in the afternoon, *USA Today*: Thorn (1987), pp. 67, 74. Watergate hearings: Gary R. Edgerton, "A Great Awakening: Prime Time for Network Television – 1964–1975," in Edgerton (2007), pp. 282–283.
85. Grunebaum: "Report of the Ethics Committee to the APA Board of Trustees," December 14–15, 1974, Item 3-D, "Psychiatric Profiles," pp. 2–3, and Addendum # 2: Principles of Medical Ethics with Annotations Especially Applicable to Psychiatry, 1975 Revision/Addendum," in APA Archives, box 100234, folder 321. Hitler's ghost was far from exorcized in the new era. In 1987, when psychiatrist Robert Jay Lifton published a psychological study of doctors who had participated in the Nazi genocide, he ended his book with a plea for its relevance in the era of nuclear warfare: "The Holocaust we have been examining can help us avoid the next one" (Lifton 1986), p. 503.
86. Psychology guidelines: Mayer (2010f); Grohol (2019); Elms (1994). Lazarus: quoted in Post (2002), p. 643.
87. Sacks, Virginia Tech: quoted in "Ethics Reminder Offered about 'Goldwater Rule' on Talking to Media" (2007).
88. On Post, see also Chapter 6. Brendel confirmed that the ethics committee views the psychological profiling of foreign leaders as a kind of "Post exception" to the Rule. For

an interpretation of the 2008 ethics committee opinion similar to Brendel's, see Appelbaum (2017).

89. APA Task Force on Ethics Annotations: Ghaemi (2012); American Psychiatric Association (2015), p. 12. "Cavalierly": quoted in Martin-Joy (2017b), p. 237. The quotations from the APA *Commentary on Ethics in Practice* (2015) are given as they appeared on the APA's website from December 2015 until at least the time I accessed the document in February 2017 for this book. By the fall of 2019, the crucial phrase – i.e., "diagnostic conclusions" – had curiously been replaced with its opposite – i.e., "no diagnostic conclusions" – and the new version had been labeled "copyedited 2017."

6 THE CIA AND THE WHITE HOUSE: ADVENTURES IN ASSESSMENT

1. "Excerpt from Individual Views of Senator Howard H. Baker, Jr.," to Senate Report No. 93–981, 93d Cong, 2 sess, "The Final Report of the Select Committee on Presidential Campaign Activities, U.S. Senate" [1974], in Senate Foreign Relations Committee (1975), p. 35. The chief psychiatrist, who testified before the Watergate Committee in an executive session on March 6, 1974, is not identified by name either in the Baker "Excerpt" or in the 1975 Foreign Relations Committee hearing, but other sources confirm it was John Malloy (see notes 12 and 14 below). In the hearing, Richard Helms, the CIA director, was questioned by the committee about the "Excerpt" and agreed that he had approved the creation of the Ellsberg profile (p. 32).

2. Omestad (1994), p. 121.

3. Post (2015), p. xvi.

4. Public exposure: "CIA Is Told to Mind P's & Q's" (1973); Wells (2001). Clear national security risk: Hunt (1974), p. 147; Liddy (1980), p. 158; Krogh (2007a), pp. 66, 68. "Discredited," "find out everything": Nixon (1978), p. 513; see also p. 842. In contrast to Nixon, Goldwater, though opposed to the Vietnam War himself, chatted amiably with antiwar protestors who sat down in protest in a Senate office building, including psychiatrist Robert Jay Lifton and his own former speechwriter Karl Hess. He would have been disappointed, Goldwater told Hess, if he had not seen him there (Hess 1999, p. 180).

5. Plumbers: House Subcommittee on Intelligence report (1973) and Nixon (1978), esp. pp. 513–514; the quote is from House Subcommittee on Intelligence report (1973), p. 8.

6. "A few days after": "CIA Is Told to Mind P's & Q's" (1973). Ehrlichman called "Pentagon Papers problem": House Subcommittee on Intelligence report (1973), pp. 5, 9–10. In the habit: House Subcommittee on Intelligence report (1973), p. 7; during investigation of the profiling incident, Helms sardonically testified that "It is only lately that it has become a crime to try to assist the President" (Central Intelligence Agency 1973–4, p. 155). Hunt suggested: Hunt (1974) and (2007). "Trying Ellsberg in public," "example must be made": Central Intelligence Agency (1973–4), pp. 5, 54. The CIA's report quotes Hunt's use of the phrase and parallels the version given in the Baker "Excerpt" in Senate Foreign Relations Committee (1975), p. 35.

7. Central Intelligence Agency (1973–4), p. 48; House Subcommittee on Intelligence report (1973), p. 9; Hunt (1974), pp. 162–163; Woodward (1987), 248–249; Ostrow and Toth (1981).

8. Could well be illegal: Wells (2001); House Subcommittee on Intelligence report (1973), pp. 2, 4, 7; O'Sullivan (2018), p. 97, quoting the report of the Senate Watergate Committee. On the Agency's charter or what Baker called its "legislative parameters," see the Baker "Excerpt," in Senate Foreign Relations Committee (1975), p. 35, as well as the 1973 exchange between Richard Helms and Senator Clifford Case, quoted and discussed in Senate Foreign Relations Committee (1975), p. 17. Surveillance of American citizens, Helms said, would be "a clear violation of what our charter was," i.e., would represent a domestic rather than a foreign mandate. At the time that Henry Osborn delivered Dr. John Tietjen's first Ellsberg profile to the White House, he stressed that "however this is used, the Agency should not become involved," an obscure statement that could be construed as implying an understanding of the line between foreign and domestic activities (Central Intelligence Agency 1973–4, p. 53). The CIA's internal report defended the Agency's actions as being within its charter (Central Intelligence Agency 1973–4, pp. 154–155).

9. On the release of the internal report, see "Judicial Watch Uncovers CIA Inspector General's 'Watergate History' Report" (2016) and Locker (2016). O'Sullivan (2018) was the first to make detailed use of the disclosures about the Ellsberg profile that resulted from the release of the CIA internal report in 2016; he covers much of the material I present in the first part of this chapter.

10. Helms's reservations, "highest White House level support": House Subcommittee on Intelligence report (1973), pp. 8–9. Young had worked for Henry Kissinger, who was reportedly a particular fan of psychological profiles; see Ehrlichman (1982), p. 404, and Central Intelligence Agency (1973–4), pp. 48–50; though Young made his accusation under affidavit, Kissinger denied having any role in the creation of the profile ("Kissinger Denies Any Role in C. I. A. Study of Ellsberg," 1974). Helms called Young, "reluctantly" deferred to him: Central Intelligence Agency (1973–4), p. 50. The date of Helms's call is not specified, but my reading of the internal report is that it happened before the assignment was given to the chief of psychiatry, the deputy chief, and Post. National security: The CIA inspector general's report on the incident framed the whole incident in terms of the grave threat to national security posed by the leak of the Pentagon Papers and emphasized the possibility that Ellsberg had been in touch with the Soviet Union (Central Intelligence Agency 1973–4, pp. 1–5).

11. "Accepted": Central Intelligence Agency (1973–4), p. 51. House Subcommittee on Intelligence report (1973), p. 9.

12. Hunter (1973) identified the titles held by Tietjen and Malloy in the CIA in her reporting on their testimony before a Senate appropriations subcommittee; see also Nobile (1976).

13. "Dr. Post," "needed": Central Intelligence Agency (1973–4), pp. 50–52. When I asked APA ethics committee chair Rebecca Brendel whether approval by a government agency was an adequate ethical basis for conducting a psychological profile without

interview and consent, she said such a profile cannot be done ethically without a valid authorization, but she agreed that authorization is not in itself sufficient: "Just because it's authorized doesn't mean a psychiatrist should [necessarily] do it."

14. Central Intelligence Agency (1973–4), pp. 51–53, 58. *New York Times* article: Nobile (1976). On Malloy as author, see also "CIA Is Told to Mind P's & Q's" (1973). Malloy affidavit and testimony: House Subcommittee on Intelligence hearings (1975). On Malloy's active role, see O'Sullivan (2018), pp. 96–102, 133–134. Tietjen, who died in 2015, testified along with Malloy before the House Subcommittee on Intelligence and gave a similar account.

15. "Cleared": Central Intelligence Agency (1973–4), pp. 52–53. Congressional accounts of how the CIA responded to the White House's request and created the profile may be found in the House Subcommittee on Intelligence report (1973), p. 9, and in the Baker "Excerpt," in Senate Foreign Relations Committee (1975), p. 35. These sources are similar to the account in the internal CIA report, but are more summary in nature; they do not mention Post or other CIA medical or psychiatric staff members by name. For other accounts, see the detailed evidence assembled by O'Sullivan (2018), "CIA Is Told to Mind P's & Q's" (1973), and the *New Republic* article by Walter Pincus (1974). Of note, the CIA had a copy of Pincus's article in its files (I accessed it on July 7, 2019, at www.cia.gov/library/readingroom/docs/CIA-RDP09T00207R001000020029-2.pdf). Though several popular books on Ellsberg and most memoirs by the participants cover the profiling episode (e.g., Hunt 1974; Wells 2001), I have been unable to find any discussion of it at all in the literature on psychiatric ethics.

16. Meeting of August 12 in Room 16: Central Intelligence Agency (1973–4), pp. 53–55. Post was out of town at the time of this meeting, so a colleague (name redacted, but likely the chief psychiatrist) went in his place. "Highest priority": House Subcommittee on Intelligence report (1973), p. 9. See also Pincus (1974) and Wells (2001), p. 492; for Ellsberg's treatment history, see Central Intelligence Agency (1973–4), p. 59. "Goldwater in 1964": O'Sullivan (2018), p. 99. Kissinger's own account (1979) is significantly different than any of the other sources. Apparently staying above the fray, Kissinger does not mention either Ellsberg or the Plumbers by name. Instead he makes a high-minded case against the "wholesale theft and unauthorized disclosure" that he believes the release of the Pentagon Papers represented. On the one hand, he acknowledges proudly that "I encouraged" Nixon to fight to prevent the Papers' disclosure. Yet Kissinger also takes care to dissociate himself from the steps "later taken" (it is not clear by whom) that involved "sordidness, puerility, and ineffectuality" – steps that he acknowledges brought down the Nixon administration but of which he claims to have been unaware (pp. 729–730; quotes are on p. 730). This account contradicts the claim Young made to the CIA in 1971 that he had Kissinger's support in his request for a profile of Ellsberg.

17. August 11 memo: Central Intelligence Agency (1973–4), p. 55. The CIA internal report doubts whether Young, Hunt, and Liddy could have seen the first profile before the August 12 meeting. Its reasoning relies on the fact that no one in the meeting

complained about the profile's contents and on the recollection by CIA security director Osborn that Young placed his call to him a few days *after* August 11 (the day the profile was delivered). But the CIA's report itself notes that the memorandum of dissatisfaction, written from Young and Krogh to Ehrlichman ("Pentagon Papers Project, Status report"), is dated August 11. A status report to the boss would be a plausible response to receiving the profile that day, and the action plan described to Ehrlichman outlines just the argument that Young, Liddy, and Hunt did in fact convey to the CIA the next day (Central Intelligence Agency 1973–4, pp. 53–55). According to O'Sullivan, Malloy complied during the August 12 meeting, asking for material on Ellsberg's early years.

18. Central Intelligence Agency (1973–4), pp. 57–58. Ehrlichman's initial account, which minimizes the approval he gave and denies that any burglary was planned, may be found in House Subcommittee on Intelligence report (1973), pp. 10–11.

19. Krogh (2007a), pp. 66, 68. "Feed that information": Ehrlichman (1982), p. 404. Liddy: Wells (2001), pp. 11–13. For the break-in, the Plumbers once again obtained assistance from the CIA, this time in the form of disguises and other help, although the Nedzi Committee report and the CIA internal report both portray the Plumbers as duping the Agency into unwitting participation. Ehrlichman, Liddy, and others were later convicted of conspiracy to violate Fielding's civil rights (Charlton 1974), though the burglary itself produced no useful information.

20. Central Intelligence Agency (1973–4), pp. 59, 61–63; "ethical and political considerations," p. 59.

21. Rethought: Central Intelligence Agency (1973–4), pp. 64–66. The emphasis on secrecy throughout was consistent with Helms's request at the time he delivered the second profile.

22. Central Intelligence Agency (1973–4), pp. 64–66; objected, p. 66. Ended up in, inaccurate impression: Baker "Excerpt," in Senate Foreign Relations Committee (1975), p. 35.

23. Delivered: House Subcommittee on Intelligence report (1973), p. 9; Central Intelligence Agency (1973–4), p. 68. Aware of the chief psychiatrist's objections: Baker "Excerpt," in Senate Foreign Relations Committee (1975), p. 35. Asked for secrecy, "glad": Central Intelligence Agency (1973–4), p. 67; Baker "Excerpt," in Senate Foreign Relations Committee (1975), p. 35.

24. "Discredit Ellsberg," failed to differentiate: Krogh (2007a), pp. 66, 62; see also Krogh (2007b). But it created: Central Intelligence Agency (1973–4), pp. 51, 59, 66. "Agency cooperated": Central Intelligence Agency (1973–4), pp. 15–16, 50. "Not proud": Central Intelligence Agency (1973–4), p. 69.

25. "Peculiar problems": CIA, quoted in House Subcommittee on Intelligence report (1973), p. 9. "Acted properly": Central Intelligence Agency (1973–4), p. 154. Nixon himself (1978, p. 514) equivocated on the break-in and his own possible responsibility for it.

26. Ellsberg (n.d. [circa 1973]); Ellsberg (2007), p. xiv.

27. "The Proposed Impeachment Article II" (1974). Made a contribution: Wells (2001), pp. 502–503.

28. Front page story: Arnold (1973). "Sonafabitching thief": quoted in Linder (2011). Communications office: Kneeland (1973). Now regarded him, went to the Oval Office: Goldberg (1995), pp. 281–282.

29. Revelations about CIA: Turner (2005); Hersch (1974); Johnson (1985/2015); Church Committee (1976a, 1976b). Operation CHAOS: Church Committee (1976), p. 75. "Clandestine relationships": Radosh (1976). On the antiwar movement and the CIA, see also Senate Foreign Relations Committee (1975), pp. 17–18, 23.

30. Cameron: Weinstein (1990); Remnick (1985). Headlines' "flap potential": Church Committee (1976a), pp. 15–17, 295. In 1990, in an act of great integrity, the APA published a history and personal indictment of the CIA-funded experiments conducted by the former APA president; the book was written by an APA member whose father was one of Cameron's victims (Weinstein 1990).

31. Vidal: Church Committee (1976b). Betrayal: DeYoung and Pincus (2007). "Few questions": Goldwater, in Joint Senate Hearing (1977). "Sensational," "impossible." Background and motives: Goldwater (1975).

32. Cf. Lebovic (2016), pp. 178–179, on journalists' acquiescence in adjusting "the flow of information" at government request.

33. "Mighty Worlitzer": Bernstein (1977). Bush: Turner (2005), p. 101. *I Spy*: Gary R. Edgerton, "A Great Awakening: Prime Time for Network Television – 1964–1975," in Edgerton (2007), pp. 241–242.

34. "Not brought to us for discussion": "Board of Trustees – Item 7A, December 14–15, 1973, Report of the Committee on Ethics," APA Archives, box 100232, folder 306, p. 2.

35. Nobile (1976). It is not clear if the APA declined to investigate or declined to censure Malloy.

36. The shah in the late 1970s: Sullivan (1978). "Depressed": Devlin and Jervis (1979). "Think anew": Omestad (1994), p. 118.

37. Post (2013); Turner (2005).

38. Carter (1982), p. 319.

39. Post (2013); Central Intelligence Agency (1977) and (1978).

40. Negotiating effort: Post (2013); Carter (2010), pp. 229–230. "Rich dividends": Carter (1982), p. 320. "Superb": Carlucci (1978). Turner: Omestad (1994).

41. PLO, animosity: Penney (2013). Carter (1982): devastated, pp. 269, 272; "had given his life," p. 271.

42. "Most difficult": Carter (1982), p. 459. Covert operation failed: Turner (2005), pp. 175–181. *Nightline*: Rosenfield (2016). Casey's priorities; McManus (1987); cf. Turner (2005), pp. 189–207. Woodward (1987): report and profile, pp. 94–95; plan for covert operations, pp. 97, 157–158; Casey's close relationship with Reagan, p. 25; "impressed," p. 249; "Nancy's closet," quoted on p. 441. *Los Angeles Times* article: Ostrow and Toth (1981). Deaths: Davis (1990).

43. Post admired: Dyson (2014), p. 672; Carey (2011). "Ethical Considerations": Post (2002); quotes are on p. 636. Profile: Omestad (1994). Invaded: Turner (2005), p. 213. Consulted: Post (2002) and (2015), pp. xii–xiii.

44. Post (2002).

45. 2015 panel: Martin-Joy (2015); Appelbaum (2017). Post took: Post (2015), pp. xvi–xvii; see also Chapter 4. In his 2002 article, Post emphasizes the Rule's "unequivocal" wording and suggests that he viewed profiling for the CIA and FBI as prohibited by the Rule (p. 640); in his 2015 book, he emphasizes that the APA's rules gave him comfort while he worked for the CIA but raised problems once he left (p. xvi).

46. Post (2002): gratefully received and "would have been unethical," p. 637; "not contributing," p. 643. The incident is also covered in Post (2008), pp. xii–xiii.

47. A partial list of foreign leaders profiled by the CIA or the Department of Defense since 1964 includes Leonid Brezhnev of the Soviet Union (Omestad 1994, p. 118); Menachem Begin, Moshe Dayan, and Ezer Weizmann of Israel (Carey 2011; entries in CIA electronic reading room); Anwar el-Sadat and Muhammed Kamil of Egypt (Carey 2011); Ayatollah Khomeini of Iran (Omestad 1994, p. 118); Saddam Hussein of Iraq (Omestad 1994, p. 112), Muammar el-Quaddafi of Libya (Ostrow and Toth 1987); Ratu Mara of Fiji (entry in CIA electronic reading room); Jean-Bertrand Aristide of Haiti (Carey 2011); Kim Jong-Il of North Korea (Carey 2011); Hugo Chavez of Venezuela (Carey 2011); and Vladimir Putin of Russia (Bush 2010). For a popular overview, see Gibson (2015). The CIA's profiles were widely read and respected despite concerns about their limitations; in contrast, biographical profiles produced by the Defense Department's Defense Intelligence Agency (DIA) were produced by a rotating staff and were, the Church Committee found, regarded as low-quality products by their readers in the government (Church Committee 1976b, pp. 350–351).

7 FUROR: THE DEBATE OVER DONALD TRUMP

1. In Lee (2017), pp. 11, 12. Rebecca Brendel, the chair of the APA ethics committee, reviewed this quote and told me that the ethics committee fundamentally disagrees with the argument that "psychiatrists who have not examined an individual are in the best position to know" about that person's mental health.

2. Inauguration: Black (2018), p. 149; Cox et al. (2017). "Inability": Nelson (2018), pp. 2–3. Conservative writer: Black (2018), pp. 151, 212.

3. "Trump: A Billion-Dollar Empire and an Ego to Match" (1987). Much later, IRS information obtained by the *New York Times* suggested Trump was losing a massive amount of money at the time of the *Newsweek* interview and that he continued to do so most years for decades to come (Buettner and Craig 2019).

4. Tax break, "Screw back": "Trump: A Billion-Dollar Empire and an Ego to Match" (1987); Black (2018), pp. 7–9.

5. "Never surrender": Black (2018), p. 6. Jews and McCarthy: Cohn (1968), pp. 248–249.

6. "Elastic ethics": Bonventre (1979). Advice to countersue and 50th wealthiest: Black (2018), pp. 6, 15. Tax abatement: Zion (1988), pp. 211–212, 267–268. "If you need": Bonventre (1979). "I'm not running": "Trump: A Billion-Dollar Empire and an Ego to Match" (1987); cf. Black (2018), p. 20.

7. Gary R. Edgerton, "The Sky's the Limit: Satellites, Cable, and the Reinvention of Television – 1976–1991," in Edgerton (2007), pp. 297–302.

8. Jimmie L. Reeves and Michael M. Epstein, "The Changing Face of Television: Turner Broadcasting System," in Edgerton (2007), pp. 323–339.

9. Gary R. Edgerton, "The Business of America Is Show Business: U.S. TV in Global Context – 1992–Present," in Edgerton (2007), pp. 367–371, 410, 425.

10. Stroud (2011), pp. 7, 9; Hamilton (2016). Stroud makes the case that such "partisan selective exposure" or "likeminded news use" is complex but may have advantages, including moving citizens to participate in politics and thus potentially serving as a check on government power (pp. 8–10).

11. Black (2018), pp. 10–14; quote is on pp. 13–14.

12. Carolyn Gunnis, "The Hell That Black People Live": Trump's Reports to Journalists on Urban Conditions," in Gutsche (2018), pp. 140–155.

13. "Build the wall": Transcript of Donald Trump's Immigration Speech (2016). "I just start": Transcript: Donald Trump's Taped Comments about Women (2016).

14. Bernstein: Kellner (2016), p. 98, n. 21. Kellner (2016), pp. 20, 29–39, 95. Kellner acknowledges that Trump "is not Hitler" but says the analysis of authoritarian populism is still useful in understanding him.

15. Schlafly, Martin, and Decker (2016), p. ix; *National Review*. Levy (2016). Cato Institute: Gottfried and Fleming (1988), pp. 103–104.

16. Arrogant: Adams (2016). Election results: Krieg (2016). 2016 election results: Pam Creedon, "Media Narratives of Gender in the Contentious Conservative Age of Trump," in Gutsche (2018), p. 163; Al Cross, "'Stop Overlooking Us!': Missed Intersections of Trump, Media, and Rural America," in Gutsche (2018), pp. 234–235, and figure 12.3.

17. Krieg (2016). Unsupported by evidence: Black (2018), p. 213; Nelson (2018), p. 111; Kathleen Bartzen Culver, "Trump, Democracy, and the Extension of Journalism Ethics," in Gutsche (2018), p. 286. Urgent message: Oquendo (2016).

18. "American will start winning again": Black (2018), p. 150. Breitbart: the phrases are chapter titles from Pollak and Schweikart (2017). *What Happened*: Clinton (2017). Women's March: Chenoweth and Pressman (2017). "Exhibitionism": Black (2018), pp. 153–154; quote is on p. 154.

19. What would happen?: Judith Herman interview.

20. Herman letter: Greene (2016); Judith Herman interview. "Fruitless": Herman, in Lee et al. (2017), p. 3; Bruk (2017).

21. Thirty-five mental health professionals: Dodes and Schachter (2017). "Repeated failure": Herman and Lifton (2017). Forty-one thousand signatures: Gartner (2017).

22. Lee interview with author.

23. Lee et al. (2017); Judith Herman interview.

24. On several occasions in past years, Herman served as a guest lecturer on trauma in a seminar on adult development that I codirected at Harvard Longwood.

25. American Psychiatric Association (2017).

26. Board of Trustees of the American Psychiatric Association to Bandy X. Lee, Judith L. Herman, and Robert Jay Lifton, March 23, 2019; copy provided to the author by Bandy X. Lee.

27. Liberalization: see Martin-Joy (2017b). Rebecca Brendel told me she had chaired the group that produced the *APA Commentary on Ethics in Practice* (2015) and said the document's section on comment on public figures was not intended as a liberalization of the Rule.

28. Reversed the liberalizing trend: Martin-Joy (2017b). "Radical expansion": Lee (2017), p. 11. "Gag order" and variations on the phrase: Lee (2017), p. 11, and interview; "Rescind": Glass (2017a); Lee et al. (2018). "Questionable": Herman and Lee (2017), p. 5.

29. Brendel (2017).

30. Resignations: Glass (2017a); Leonard Glass interview. "I would take that": Glass to chair of APA ethics committee and to Maria Oquendo, president of the APA, n.d. [circa April 2017], copy provided to the author by Leonard Glass. Vida said that the Southern California Psychiatric Society informed her in 2017 that it was conducting "a review of allegations of unethical conduct" against her; she felt betrayed by the APA and resigned in disgust (Begley 2018; see also Dodes and Schachter 2017). Bandy Lee had resigned previously from the APA, but for unrelated reasons: she felt that the pharmaceutical industry exerted undue influence on the organization (Lee interview). Judith Herman and Robert Jay Lifton remain Distinguished Life Fellows.

31. American Psychiatric Association (2017).

32. Herman and Lee (2017), p. 1; Glass (2017b), p. 155.

33. The Yale conference (Lee et al. 2017) and the book (Lee 2017) make similar arguments. But the talks documented in the conference transcript appear aimed at mental health care professionals, while the book contributions are more simplistic and appear aimed at a popular audience.

34. "Possibly": Lee, "Introduction," in Lee (2017), p. 11. Criticized: Lee (2017), p. 11.

35. See note 48 below.

36. Herman and Lee: "Prologue," in Lee (2017); quotes are on pp. 2, 3, 4, 6. Psychiatrist and violence expert James Gilligan also emphasized the importance of warning potential victims when a leader is dangerous (Lee 2017, pp. 170–180, esp. p. 177).

37. "Sustaining," "witnessing professional": Robert Jay Lifton, "Foreword," in Lee (2017).

38. Herman and Lee, "Preface," in Lee (2017), p. 6.

39. "When they get better," "I am here": Dike, in Lee et al. (2017), pp. 2, 1. Brought back: Rebecca Brendel and Anita Everett interviews with the author. "We were interested": Brendel interview.

40. *Newsweek*: Dodes and Schachter (2017). *National Review*: Siegel (2018). "Propaganda": Moffic (2017). Special panel: Dotinga (2017). Reviews: Kroll (2018); Stone (2018). Press release: American Psychiatric Association (2017c).

41. "Irresponsible," "tabloid psychiatry," risks of political involvement, Twenty-Fifth Amendment: Lieberman (2017). Another commentator: Pouncey (2018). "Misguided and dangerous": Lieberman (2018c). Tweets: Lieberman (2018a) and (2018d). See also Lieberman (2018b).

42. Jeffrey Lieberman interview.

43. "Unravel": Karni (2018)."Deluded": Limbaugh (2018). Contrary to Limbaugh's implication, psychiatric training involves completion of an MD degree and then a residency in

psychiatry, not a "degree in psychiatry." When a white supremacist and a conservative group repeated the charge that Lee lacked a medical license, the Internet fact-checker snopes.com interviewed Lee and determined that the charge was false (snopes.com 2018). "Unacceptable": APA (2018a).

44. "Involuntary Committed," "Preposterous": Godfrey (2018). Judith Herman told me that the idea of involuntarily committing a president was "naïve" (Herman interview).

45. The overall account and quotes in this paragraph: Lee interview with author. Lee's article of June 2018 (Lee 2018) is consistent with the evolution in her role that she described to me in the interview.

46. "Probably will never," "duty to act": Lee interview with author. Kavanaugh: "Mental Health Experts Demand Psychological Evaluation of Kavanaugh for Drinking, Instability" (2018). On the Goldwater Rule, Lee differentiated her position from that of Claire Pouncey (2018) by emphasizing that the dangerousness criteria needed to be met for comment; she saw Pouncey as advocating for comment when there is merely a public health benefit (Lee interview).

47. In fact, in the first published edition of the *Principles* (American Psychiatric Association 1973b), the board of trustees prohibited only diagnosis; the ban was widened in 1975 to include all comment. The claim by Lee and others that the Rule was expanded in the March 2017 opinion is complex: it is strictly speaking not true of the official text of section 7.3. The APA's formal ban on wider psychiatric comment was long-standing, as was its history of less formal public concern. An APA press release in 1964, for example, referred broadly to psychiatric opinions and not only to diagnosis. At the same time, many observers thought there was a new tone of rigidity in the March 2017 opinion; some previous committee opinions had suggested greater flexibility to some readers (Martin-Joy 2017b). Also of note, an ethics committee opinion represents the APA's interpretation of board policy, but it does not have the same official standing as a section of the *Principles*.

48. Lee, Herman, and Lifton, "An Open Letter to the American Psychiatric Association: Silence v. Bearing Witness: An Ethical Question" (n.d. [February 12, 2018]), APA (2018b).

49. "Came to expect," shifted to consulting role: Lifton interview with author. Letter of mid-2018: Lee (2018); Begley (2018); Glass (2018), Robert Jay Lifton and Judith Herman to Anita Everett [president of APA], June 28, 2018; copy provided by Judith Herman; Bandy Lee interview; Leonard Glass interview. Unanswered: Judith Herman interview and e-mail dated February 6, 2019; Leonard Glass interview. Herman told me that the June 2018 letter was only one of several letters to the APA by her, Lee, and/or Lifton that the organization never answered. Glass said that significant contributions to the June proposal were made by Ed Fisher, Howard Corvitz, and Lance Dodes, then were discussed with Herman, Lee, Lifton, and Thomas Singer.

50. Rebecca Brendel interview.

51. Anita Smith Everett e-mail to the author, July 19, 2019; Rebecca Brendel interview.

52. Impeachment, immigration, North Korea: Nelson (2018), pp. 132–144, 61–63, 123–127. Running for president: Overby (2019).

53. Kristol: Nolte (2018). *National Review.* "Trump Hits Back at *National Review* Attack" (2016). First year: McLaughlin (2018a) and (2018b). Biography: Black (2018), pp. 3, 20.
54. "Enemy of the people": Black (2017); Nordlinger (2018). "Out of business": Grynbaum (2018). Moonves: quoted in Bond (2016). Trump bump: Pam Creedon, "Media Narratives of Gender in the Contentious Conservative Age of Trump," in Gutsche (2018), p. 157.
55. Trump promised: Grynbaum (2018). Gorsuch: Borchers (2017). Thomas: Liptak (2019). Scalia: Stone (2011); Staab (2006). Nunes: Israel (2019).
56. Four to eight hours of cable news, MSNBC: Nelson (2018), p. 105. Baldwin: Showalter (2019).
57. "Sick": on Megyn Kelly, quoted in Creedon, in Gutsche (2018), p. 160; on Democrats, Scott (2019). "WITCH HUNT": Trump (2018), also quoted in Scott (2019).
58. Baker (2019).
59. Higgins (2019). "Not well": Da Silva (2019).
60. APA tweet, January 24, 2018: https://twitter.com/APAPsychiatric/status/9562213803 82650368. Frustrating: Judith Herman interview; Leonard Glass interview.
61. APA membership, advocacy: Levin (2018); Schwartz (2018). "Push back": Moran (2019). African American member: Stewart (2019); Stewart served as APA president in 2018–19. "Ethics Corner": Zilber (2018). APA actions: Levin (2018); lawsuit, Richmond (2018); children at the border, Richmond (2019); stigma as a tactic, American Psychiatric Association (2017b); LGBTQ rights, National LGBTQ Task Force (2019).
62. Twenty-Fifth Amendment: McCabe (2019). Cohen: Sommerfeldt (2019). Mueller: Fleishman (2019). Comedian: Corden (2019); Mount Rushmore: Moritz-Rabson (2019).
63. "Exoneration," victory lap: Scott (2019). "Treasonous things": quoted in Jalonick (2019). Legality: Lee interview, March 30, 2019. "Mendacity": see Ganeva (2019). Jerrold M. Post's *Dangerous Charisma: The Political Psychology of Donald Trump and his Followers* (New York: Pegasus Books, 2019) appeared after my book was in Press. Impeachment inquiry: Cheney et al. (2019). Lee announced: Leonard (2019).

CONCLUSION: ON HISTORY, ETHICS, AND PLURALISM

1. Quoted in Lemann (2019), p. 124.
2. See the survey of mental health professionals reported in Moffic (2018).
3. Brennan: quoted in Lewis (1991), p. 143. Sullivan, like *Brown* v. *Board* (1954), showed boldness and newness, and in that way is a world apart from the decisions that build on a slow accretion of similar decisions in making new law. This bold or *de novo* quality of *Sullivan*'s reasoning is part of what appeared to bother Justice Thomas (Liptak 2019).
4. Lifton (2017), in Lee (2017), p. xix.
5. Teles (2008).
6. Max Horkheimer and Samuel Flowerman, "Foreword to Studies in Prejudice," in Adorno et al. (1950), p. v.

7. James Gilligan, "The Issue Is Dangerousness, Not Mental Illness," in Lee (2017), p. 171; Weber (1918).

8. Gilligan: Lee et al. (2017), p. 171.

9. On the corrupting influence of the media setting, see Levine (2017).

10. Kris and Speier (1944); Erik H. Erikson, "On Nazi Mentality," in Erikson (1987), pp. 341–345.

11. On the speed and ease with which supposedly confidential government information in the foreign policy domain can be leaked to the press, see, for example, the comments of Hubert Humphrey and Richard Helms in Senate Foreign Relations Committee (1975), pp. 10–11, 30.

12. Watergate investigations: Lebovic (2016), pp. 205–206. Cold War classification: Lebovic (2016), pp. 133–135, 164–189.

13. "A popular Government": Madison (1822). *Principles*: American Psychiatric Association (2013), p. 9.

14. See, for example, Kroll and Pouncey (2016); Martin-Joy (2017b). In the political sphere, some conservative writers appear to understand the Rule as banning all comment in all circumstances; see "Democrats Planning Town Hall to Attack President Trump's Mental Health" (2019).

15. The March 2017 ethics committee opinion is an exception. The APA's recent language: American Psychiatric Association (2017a).

16. When I spoke with Rebecca Brendel, she suggested that exceptions might be "better termed 'beyond the scope' or 'not covered by' the rule."

17. Conly (2013): "What is good for them," p. 125; perfectionism, pp. 100–125; on Locke, p. 111; Eliot quote, epigraph to her book. On coercive paternalism, see also Plaxton (2013) and Sunstein (2019).

18. Plaxton (2013): Hart quote, p. 460; on Feinberg, pp. 461–462.

19. Nussbaum (1986/2001): "simplify," p. 51; *Antigone*, pp. 54–63; "moral imagination," p. 57; "plurality," p. 83.

20. For the sake of the profession: Martin-Joy, Vijapura, and Carey (2014); Appelbaum (2017).

21. Maritain (1961): "have to live together," p. 17; on absolutists, pp. 22–23; on relativists, p. 16; "*mutual grasp*," p. 25; "real though imperfect": p. 26; "these diverse outlooks," pp. 34–35; fairness, p. 29.

22. "Forced to choose principles that are fair to all," liberty of conscience: Nussbaum (2008), p. 57. "Comprehensive doctrines": Rawls (1993/2005), pp. 58ff. "Reasonable pluralism": Rawls (1997), p. 441. "Inevitably differ": Dreben (2003), p. 318.

23. Rawls (1993/2005), p. 37; cf. Dreben (2003), p. 318.

24. Rawls (1993/2005): "Political conception of justice," p. 11; "overlapping consensus," p. 144. Advantages of fairness and exclusion of the unreasonable: Rawls (1993/2005), pp. 143–144; Rawls (1997), pp. 482–483.

25. Oppressive majorities: Rawls (1993/2005), p. 37; Dreben (2003), p. 318. Continuity and stability as the result of adequate overlapping consensus and reasonable pluralism: Rawls (1993/2005), pp. 38–40, 65–66. Rawls intended his system to apply to the most

basic structure of society and politics, but I believe it can be usefully applied to the functioning of professional organizations as well.

26. Rawls (1993/2005), p. 144.

27. Nussbaum (2008): "periodic attacks," p. 4; Maritain's tolerance, pp. 23–24; "mutually respectful civil peace," "preciousness and vulnerability" of conscience, "intimate searching": pp. 36–37. Nussbaum deepens and complicates the Rawlsian argument in her book *Frontiers of Justice* (2006).

28. Quoted in Dotinga (2017).

29. I am a member of APsaA.

30. See Burness E. Moore, MD, to Robert L. Robinson of American Psychiatric Association, October 6, 1964, and many other letters, in APsaA Papers. Sent its statement: Helen Fischer to [APsaA] Executive Committee, October 9, 1964, in APsaA Papers.

31. Heinz Kohut to APsaA Executive Committee, "The Fact Magazine Affair" [memo], September 15, 1964, in APsaA Papers.

32. Heinz Kohut to Warren Boroson, July 30, 1964, in APsaA Papers.

33. Heinz Kohut to APsaA Executive Committee, "The Fact Magazine Affair" [memo], September 15, 1964, in APsaA Papers.

34. Burness E. Moore to Executive Committee, "Fact Magazine Affair" [memo], September 21, 1964, in APsaA Papers.

35. American Psychoanalytic Association, "A Statement on the Use of Psychiatric Opinions in the Political Realm," October 5, 1964, in APsaA Papers.

36. American Psychoanalytic Association (2012). In his 2017 letter of concern to APA president Maria Oquendo, Leonard Glass said: "If the APA had [merely] advised its members to exercise such caution, I would take that as prudent advice and not object. But to establish that it is an ethical violation to comment on matters in the public sphere . . . is entirely excessive, intrusive, unnecessary, and insulting." Glass also made the point that APA members are presumably competent and well trained, so that it is "offensive" to gag them (Glass to Maria Oquendo, n.d. [2017], copy provided to the author by Leonard Glass).

37. My suggestion also resembles that of Kroll and Pouncey (2016).

38. Herman and Lee (2017), p. 2; American Psychiatric Association (2013).

39. Cooper's (2016) context is an exploration of the psychoanalyst's inevitable mourning for the incomplete and limited nature of psychoanalytic treatment, or what Melanie Klein called the "depressive position."

APPENDIX: THE GOLDWATER RULE IN 1973 AND TODAY

1. American Psychiatric Association (1973b) and (2013). The change from "diagnosis" to "professional opinion" first occurred in 1975.

Works Cited

ARCHIVES

I visited the American Psychiatric Association (APA) archives, the Boston Psychoanalytic Society and Institute (BPSI) archives in Newton, Massachusetts, and the Ralph Ginzburg archives in person, but also supplemented these visits with electronic requests. I consulted the Goldwater papers, the American Psychoanalytic Association (APsaA) papers, and material at the LBJ Library entirely by remote means, relying on the graciousness of the archives' staff in sending me scanned copies of archival material.

The transcript of *Goldwater* v. *Ginzburg* records in depth a fascinating and dramatic staging of a great conflict of ideas. Throughout, I have silently regularized the stenographer's spelling, capitalization, indenting, and line breaks, and have silently corrected any obvious typographical errors. In substantial quoted passages, I have also replaced the transcript's designations "Q" and "A" with the name of the speakers involved in the exchange. The greater part of the transcript consists of testimony given in the district court trial in New York City in May 1968. The attorneys also read into the trial record considerable portions of earlier depositions by Ginzburg and Goldwater (see, for example, GG transcript, pp. 1336–1493). The attorneys then cross-examined witnesses "live" about their earlier depositions. For the reader's convenience, except as noted, I have treated the depositions and the "live" testimony as one continuous sequence, which is how the material appears in the transcript.

ORIGINAL INTERVIEWS

For convenience in the text, I use "interview" as shorthand for any of the following: in-person interview, phone interview, e-mails, and/or letters, including comments on draft chapters. Specifics for each interviewee follow:

Barton, Gail, MD (Walter E. Barton's daughter). Three phone interviews and letter, June and July 2019.
Boroson, Warren. Phone interview and e-mails, May and June 2019.

Brendel, Rebecca Weintraub, MD (chair of the APA ethics committee). Phone interview and e-mails, July and August 2019.

Erbé, Bonnie Ginzburg (daughter of Ralph Ginzburg). Phone interview and e-mail, June 2019.

Everett, Anita Smith, MD (president of the APA, 2017–18). Letter of July 19, 2019.

Glass, Leonard L., MD. Phone interview and e-mails, April, May, and June 2019.

Herman, Judith Lewis, MD. Personal interview, March 1, 2019; e-mails, February, April, and June 2019.

Kuhta, Lark (daughter of Ralph Ginzburg). E-mails, May and June 2019.

Lee, Bandy X., MD. Personal interview, April 17, 2019; phone interview and e-mails, March, April, May, and June 2019.

Levin, Saul, MD (APA medical director). Phone interview and e-mail, July 2019.

Lieberman, Jeffrey A., MD (former APA president). E-mails, July 2019.

Lifton, Robert Jay, MD. Phone interview and e-mails, June and July 2019.

WORKS CITED

Adams, Myra (2016). How the Clinton Victory Party Went from Coronation to Despair. *Washington Examiner.* November 12, 2016. Accessed on February 3, 2019, at www.washingtonexaminer.com/how-the-clinton-victory-party-went-fr om-coronation-to-despair.

Adorno, Theodore W., Else Frenkel-Brunswik, Daniel J. Levinson, and R. Nevitt Sanford, in collaboration with Betty Aron, Maria Hertz Levinson, and William Morrow (1950). *The Authoritarian Personality.* New York: Harper & Brothers.

Against Trump. *National Review.* January 22, 2016. Accessed at www.nationalre view.com/2016/01/donald-trump-conservative-movement-menace/.

Aldridge, John W. (1966). *Time to Murder and Create: The Contemporary Novel in Crisis.* New York: David McKay.

Alumni Association of the City College of New York (2007). Ralph Ginzburg: Class of 1949, Inducted 2007. Alumni Association of the City College of New York [website]. Accessed on September 1, 2018, at www.ccnyalumni.org/alumni-rela tions/affiliates/communications-alumni/communications-hall-of-fame/348-gi nzburg-ralph–1949.

American Association of Directors of Psychiatry Residency Training (n.d. [circa 2010]). AADPRT Celebrates 40 Years [poster]. Accessed on November 26, 2018, at www.aadprt.org/application/files/9714/3932/0886/AADPRT_40_P oster_final.pdf.

American College of Cardiology (n.d.). Our History [web page]. Accessed on November 26, 2018, at www.acc.org/about-acc/our-history.

American College of Neurology (n.d.). History of the American Academy of Neurology [web page]. Accessed on November 2, 2018, at www.aan.com/AA N-Resources/Details/about-the-aan/history/.

American Psychiatric Association (1944). *One Hundred Years of American Psychiatry*. New York: Published for the APA by Columbia University Press.

American Psychiatric Association (1973a). 126th Annual Meeting, May 7–11, 1973, Honolulu, Hawaii [program]. APA Archives.

American Psychiatric Association (1973b). *The Principles of Medical Ethics with Annotations Especially Applicable to Psychiatry: 1973*. Reprinted from *American Journal of Psychiatry*, September 1973. Copy in APA Archives.

American Psychiatric Association (1976). *The Psychiatrist as Psychohistorian*. Task Force Report 11 (June). Accessed on August 4, 2019, at www.psychiatry.org/psychiatrists/search-directories-databases/library-and-archive/task-force-reports.

American Psychiatric Association (2013). *The Principles of Medical Ethics with Annotations Especially Applicable to Psychiatry, 2013 Edition*. Accessed on July 7, 2019, at www.psychiatry.org/psychiatrists/practice/ethics.

American Psychiatric Association (2015). *APA Commentary on Ethics in Practice*. Accessed on August 4, 2019, at www.psychiatry.org/psychiatrists/practice/ethics.

American Psychiatric Association (2016a). *Opinions of the Ethics Committee on the Principles of Medical Ethics with Annotations Especially Applicable to Psychiatry, 2016*. Accessed on April 30, 2017, at www.psychiatry.org/psychiatrists/practice/ethics.

American Psychiatric Association (2016b). Breaking the Goldwater Rule Is Irresponsible, Stigmatizing, Unethical [tweet from @apapsychiatric]. August 3, 2016. Accessed on August 4, 2019, at https://twitter.com/APAPsychiatric/status/760853784033492997.

American Psychiatric Association (2017a). American Psychiatric Association Ethics Committee Opinion. Issued March 15, 2017. Accessed on March 18, 2017, at www.psychiatry.org/news-room/apa-blogs/apa-blog/2017/03/apa-remains-committed-to-supporting-goldwater-rule/.

American Psychiatric Association (2017b). Position Statement on Use of Stigma as a Political Tactic. Approved by the Board of Trustees July 2017. Accessed on April 28, 2019, at www.psychiatry.org/FileLibrary/About-APA.

American Psychiatric Association (2017c). APA's Goldwater Rule Remains a Guiding Principle for Physician Members [press release]. October 6, 2017. Accessed on March 2, 2019, at www.psychiatry.org/newsroom/news-releases/apa-goldwater-rule-remains-a-guiding-principle-for-physician-members.

American Psychiatric Association (2018a). APA Calls for End to "Armchair" Psychiatry. January 9, 2018. Accessed on April 6, 2019, at www.psychiatry.org/newsroom/news-releases/apa-calls-for-end-to-armchair-psychiatry.

American Psychiatric Association (2018b). Board of Trustees of the American Psychiatric Association to Lee, Herman, and Lifton. March 23, 2019.

American Psychiatric Association (2019). APA Statement Opposing Separation of Children from Parents at the Border [press release]. May 30, 2018. Accessed on March 2, 2019, at www.psychiatry.org/newsroom/news-releases/apa-statement-opposing-separation-of-children-from-parents-at-the-border.

American Psychoanalytic Association (2012). Position Statement regarding Psychoanalysts' Providing Commentary on Public Figures. Accessed on

February 22, 2019, at www.apsa.org/sites/default/files/2012%20Position%20 Statement%20Regarding%20Psychoanalysts.pdf.

Anthony, Rey [Maxine Serett] (1960). *The Housewife's Handbook on Selective Promiscuity*. New York: Documentary Books.

Appelbaum, Paul S. (2017). Reflections on the Goldwater Rule. *Journal of the American Academy of Psychiatry and the Law* 45 (2), pp. 228–232.

Arendt, Hannah (1963). *Eichmann in Jerusalem: A Report on the Banality of Evil*. New York: Viking.

Arnold, Martin (1973). New Trial Barred. *New York Times*. May 11, 1973, pp. 1, 14.

Avant Garde (1968–71). New York: Avant-Garde Media.

Baker, Peter (2019). Trump Declares a National Emergency, and Provokes a Constitutional Clash. *New York Times*. February 15, 2019. Accessed on March 2, 2019, at www.nytimes.com/2019/02/15/us/politics/national-emer gency-trump.html.

Barbas, Samantha (2017). *Newsworthy: The Supreme Court Battle over Privacy and Press Freedom*. Stanford, CA: Stanford University Press.

Barclay, Eliza (2018). The Psychiatrist Who Briefed Congress on Trump's Mental State: This Is "An Emergency." *Vox* [online]. Updated January 6, 2018. Accessed on January 27, 2019, at www.vox.com/science-and-health/2018/1/5/16770060 /trump-mental-health-psychiatrist-25th-amendment.

Barry M. Goldwater, Plaintiff-Appellee, v. *Ralph Ginzburg, Defendant-Appellant* . . . . (1969). 414 F.2d 324 (2d Cir. 1969) [appellate court decision on *Fact*, July 18, 1969]. Accessed on March 2, 2019, at https://law.justia.com/cases/federal/a ppellate-courts/F2/414/324/84727/.

Barton, Walter E. (1961). The President's Page. *American Journal of Psychiatry* 118 (5) (November), pp. 463–464.

Barton, Walter E. (1967). Untitled contribution to *Memorial for William C. Menninger* [memorial service, New York, December 14, 1966]. Made possible by friends in the Group for the Advancement of Psychiatry and the Menninger Foundation. New York: Printed by Clarke & Way, pp. 18–21.

Barton, Walter E. (1987). *The History and Influence of the American Psychiatric Association*. Washington, DC: American Psychiatric Press.

Barton, Walter E., and Gail M. Barton (1984). *Ethics and Law in Mental Health Administration*. No publisher listed [New York: International Universities Press].

Begley, Sharon (2018). Psychiatrists Call for Rollback of Policy Banning Discussion of Public Figures' Mental Health. *Stat* [online]. June 28, 2018. Accessed on April 14, 2019, at www.statnews.com/2018/06/28/psychiatrists-goldwater-rule-rollback/.

Benedek, Therese (1952). Personality Development. In Franz Alexander and Helen Ross, eds., *Dynamic Psychiatry*. Chicago: University of Chicago Press, pp. 63–113.

Bernstein, Carl (1977). The CIA and the Media. *Rolling Stone*. October 20, 1977. Accessed on January 15, 2019, at http://carlbernstein.com/magazine_ cia_and_media.php.

Black, Conrad (2017). Trump and the "Enemy of the People." *National Review* [online]. February 21, 2017. Accessed on February 3, 2019, at www.nationalre view.com/2017/02/trump-media-enemy-people/.

Black, Conrad (2018). *Donald J. Trump: A President Like No Other*. Washington, DC: Regnery Publishing.

Blasi, Vincent, ed. (1983). *The Burger Court: The Counter-Revolution That Wasn't*. New Haven, CT: Yale University Press.

Bloch, Sidney, and Paul Chodoff (1981). *Psychiatric Ethics*. Oxford: Oxford University Press.

Bond, Paul (2016). Leslie Moonves on Donald Trump: "It May Not Be Good for America, but It's Damn Good for CBS." *Hollywood Reporter* [online]. Posted February 29, 2016. Accessed on January 26, 2019, at www.hollywoodreporter.com/news/leslie-moonves-donald-trump-may–871464.

Bonventre, Peter, with Tony Fuller (1979). Cohn for the Defense. *Newsweek*. April 2, 1979, p. 90.

Borchers, Callum (2016). Donald Trump Vowed to "Open Up" Libel Laws to Make Suing the Media Easier. Can He Do That? *Washington Post*. Accessed on December 30, 2018, at www.washingtonpost.com/news/the-fix/wp/2016/02/26/donald-trump-vows-to-open-up-libel-laws-to-make-suing-the-media-easier-heres-how-he-could-do-it/?noredirect=on&utm_term=.c54c0c10d533.

Borchers, Callum (2017). "Change Libel Laws"? Trump Doesn't Seem Serious. *Washington Post*. March 30, 2017. Accessed on December 30, 2018, at www.washingtonpost.com/news/the-fix/wp/2017/03/30/change-libel-laws-trump-doesnt-seem-serious/?utm_term=.66a7b8470d94.

Boroson, Warren (1964a). Untitled draft [draft 1 of "Goldwater: The Man and the Menace" and trial exhibit I in *Goldwater* v. *Ginzburg*, registered on June 15, 1966]. In Ginzburg Papers, box 1, folder 20.

Boroson, Warren (1964b). "Barry Goldwater: The Unconscious of a Conservative" [draft 2 of "Goldwater: The Man and the Menace" and trial exhibit H in *Goldwater* v. *Ginzburg*, registered on June 15, 1966]. In Ginzburg Papers, box 1, folder 19.

Boroson, Warren (1964c). What Psychiatrists Say about Goldwater. *Fact* 1 (5) (September–October 1964), pp. 24–64.

Boroson, Warren (1967). George Romney: Man and Mormon. *Fact* 4 (3) (May–June), pp 2–13.

Boroson, Warren (2008). The Goldwater Lawsuit. *Warrenboroson.blogspot.com* [blog]. Posted May 9, 2008. Accessed on August 4, 2019, at http://warrenboroson.blogspot.com/2008_05_01_archive.html.

Boroson, Warren (n.d.). Why Barry Goldwater Sued Me for $2 Million. Unpublished manuscript provided by Warren Boroson.

Boyer, Paul (1985/1994). *By the Bomb's Early Light: American Thought and Culture at the Dawn of the Atomic Age*. With a New Preface by the Author. Chapel Hill: University of North Carolina Press.

Bradlee, Ben (1995). *A Good Life: Newspapering and Other Adventures*. New York: Simon & Schuster.

Brendel, Rebecca (2017). The Goldwater Rule Is Still Relevant. *Psychiatric Times*. July 20, 2017. Accessed on August 5, 2019, at www.psychiatrictimes.com/couch-crisis/goldwater-rule-still-relevant.

Brenan, Megan (2018). Nurses Again Outpace Other Professions for Honesty, Ethics. Gallup [website]. December 20, 2018. Accessed on January 1, 2019, at https://news.gallup.com/poll/245597/nurses-again-outpace-professions-hon esty-ethics.aspx.

Bridges, Linda, and John R. Coyne Jr. (2007). *Strictly Right: William F. Buckley, Jr. and the American Conservative Movement.* Hoboken, NJ: Wiley.

Brinkley, Alan (1998). *Liberalism and Its Discontents.* Cambridge, MA: Harvard University Press.

Brinkley, Alan (2010). *The Publisher: Henry Luce and His American Century.* New York: Knopf.

Brown, J. Pat, B. C. D. Lipton, and Michael Morisy, eds. (2018). *Writers under Surveillance: The FBI Files.* Cambridge, MA: MIT Press.

Bruk, Diana (2017). Here's the Full Transcript of Gloria Steinem's Historic Women's March Speech. *Elle* [online]. January 21, 2017. Accessed on January 27, 2019, at www.elle.com/culture/news/a42331/gloria-steinem-wo mens-march-speech/.

Buckley, William F. (n.d. [1968]). Goldwater against Ginzburg [article, *National Review*]. Copy in PPBG 52:16.

Buckley, William F. (2008). *Flying High: Remembering Barry Goldwater.* New York: Basic Books.

Buettner, Russ, and Susanne Craig (2019). Trump's Tax Figures Show Huge Losses. *Boston Globe.* May 8, 2019, pp. A1, A7.

Burks, Edward C. (1968). "Ginzburg Likens 'Fact' to Crusade: Defends Article as 'Historical Contribution.'" *New York Times.* May 23, 1968, p. 27.

Bush, George W. (2010). *Decision Points.* New York: Crown Publishers.

Cannell, Michael (2017). *Incendiary: The Psychiatrist, the Mad Bomber, and the Invention of Criminal Profiling.* New York: Minotaur Books.

Carey, Benedict (2005). An Early Wartime Profile Depicts a Tormented Hitler. *New York Times.* March 31, 2005. Accessed on December 30, 2018, at www.nyti mes.com/2005/03/31/science/an-early-wartime-profile-depicts-a-tormented- hitler.html.

Carey, Benedict (2011). Teasing Out Policy Insight from a Character Profile. *New York Times.* March 28, 2011. Accessed on January 20, 2019, at www.nytimes .com/2011/03/29/science/29psych.html.

Carlucci, Frank C. (1978). Briefing Papers for Camp David. Frank C. Carlucci to Deputy Director for National Foreign Assessment, September 26, 1978 [CIA internal memorandum]. Accessed on August 5, 2019, at www.cia.gov/library/ readingroom/docs/1978–09-26a.pdf.

Carter, David (2004). *Stonewall: The Riots That Sparked the Gay Revolution.* New York: St. Martin's Press.

Carter, Jimmy (1982). *Keeping Faith: Memoirs of a President.* New York: Bantam Books.

Carter, Jimmy (2010). *White House Diary.* New York: Farrar, Straus and Giroux.

Central Intelligence Agency (1973–4). CIA Watergate History [unpublished draft report prepared by the CIA's Office of the Inspector General]. Accessed on March 17, 2018, at https://ia601204.us.archive.org/6/items/CIAWatergateH istory/Working%20Draft%20-%20CIA%20Watergate%20History.pdf.

Central Intelligence Agency (1977). Leadership Profile: Menachem Begin [redacted version]. July 7, 1977. Accessed on October 16, 2016, at www.cia.go v/library/readingroom/docs/1977–07-07.pdf.

Central Intelligence Agency (1978). Leadership Profile: Anwar al-Sadat [redacted version]. August 23, 1978. Accessed on October 16, 2016, at www .cia.gov/library/readingroom/docs/1978–08-23b.pdf.

Charlton, Linda (1974). Ehrlichman Is Convicted of Plot and Perjury in Ellsberg Break In. *New York Times.* July 13, 1974. Accessed on July 8, 2019, at www.nyti mes.com/1974/07/13/archives/ehrlichman-is-convicted-of-plot-and-perjury-in-ellsberg-breakin.html.

Chenoweth, Erica, and Jeremy Pressman (2017). This Is What We Learned by Counting the Women's Marches. *Washington Post.* February 7, 2017. Accessed on February 2, 2019, at www.washingtonpost.com/news/monkey-cage/wp/2017/02/07/this-is-what-we-learned-by-counting-the-womens-marches/?utm_term=.14fc316c67c2.

Cheney, Kyle et al. (2019). "Betrayal of His Oath of Office": Pelosi Opens Impeachment Inquiry. *Politico.* Posted September 24, 2019. Accessed on November 11, 2019, at www.politico.com/story/2019/09/24/donald-trump-impeachment-congress-1509360.

CIA Is Told to Mind P's & Q's. *The Evening Star and Daily News* (Washington, DC). May 10, 1973 [declassified copy in CIA's files]. Accessed on January 21, 2019, at www.cia.gov/library/readingroom/docs/CIA-RDP84-00161R000400210014-2.pdf.

Church Committee [US Senate Select Committee on Intelligence Activities within the United States] (1976a/2007). *Intelligence Activities and the Rights of Americans: 1976 US Senate Report on Illegal Wiretaps and Domestic Spying by the FBI, CIA, and NSA.* Reprinted, St. Petersburg, FL: Red and Black Publishing.

Church Committee (1976b). *Foreign and Military Intelligence, Book I: Final Report of the Select Committee to Study Government Operations with Respect to Intelligence Activities.* US Senate, Report # 94–755, 94th Congress, 2d Session. Marked as "Bequest of Gore Vidal," with marginal markings and underlining. Cambridge, MA: Houghton Library, Harvard University.

Clinton, Hillary Rodham (2017). *What Happened.* New York: Simon & Schuster.

Cohen, Elliot D., and Michael Davis, with Frederick A. Elliston (2009). *Ethics and the Legal Profession.* Second Edition. Amherst, NY: Prometheus Books.

Cohn, Roy M. (1968). *McCarthy.* New York: New American Library.

Coles, Robert (1960/1995). A Young Psychiatrist Looks at His Profession. Reprinted in *The Mind's Fate: A Psychiatrist Looks at His Profession.* Second Edition. Boston: Little Brown, pp. 5–13.

Coles, Robert (1973/1995). On Psychohistory. Reprinted in *The Mind's Fate: A Psychiatrist Looks at His Profession.* Second Edition. Boston: Little Brown, pp. 259–294.

Completing Our Mobilization. *Psychiatry* 5 (February, May, August, November, 1942), pp. 263–282.

Conklin, William R. (1950). Psychiatrist Lists Chambers' Phases; Charges Twelve Symptoms of Psychopathic Personality. *New York Times.* January 7, 1950.

Accessed on December 30, 2018, at www.nytimes.com/1950/01/07/archives/ psychiatrist-lists-chambers-phases-charges-twelve-symptoms-of.html.

Conly, Sarah (2013). *Against Autonomy: Justifying Coercive Paternalism*. Cambridge: Cambridge University Press.

Cook, Richard M. (2007). *Alfred Kazin: A Biography*. New Haven, CT: Yale University Press.

Cooke, Brian K. et al. (2017). The Risks and Responsible Roles for Psychiatrists Who Interact with the Media. *Journal of the American Academy of Psychiatry and the Law* 42, pp. 459–468. Accessed on August 5, 2019, at www.jaapl.org/content/ 42/4/459.full.

Cooper, Steven H. (2016). *The Analyst's Experience of the Depressive Position: The Melancholic Errand of Psychoanalysis*. London and New York: Routledge.

Corden, James (2019). The President Was So Presidential on President's Day. *Late Late Show* [CBS]. February 19, 2019. Accessed on March 31, 2019, at www .cbs.com/shows/late-late-show/video/LutDFBwxdxMHkGC_ZKo7Fus91p1zw ubh/the-president-was-so-presidential-on-president-s-day/.

Corliss, Richard (2006). My Favorite Pornographer. *Time* [online]. July 15, 2006. Accessed on September 3, 2018, at http://content.time.com/time/arts/arti cle/0,8599,1214904–1,00.html.

Cox, James Woodrow et al. (2017). Inauguration Day 2017: Pomp and Chaos Collide as Trump Becomes President. *Washington Post*. January 20, 2017. Accessed on February 3, 2019, at www.washingtonpost.com/news/local/wp/ 2017/01/20/inauguration-day-2017-washington-prepares-for-celebration-pro tests-and-donald-trump/?utm_term=.e257aaa827c2.

The Counterpuncher. *Time*. September 20, 1968, p. 20.

Cuneo, Ernest (1966). Obscenity Law Violated . . . . . . Court Decision Lauded. *Amarillo* [Texas] *Daily News*. April 11. Accessed on September 22, 2018, at https://newspaperarchive.com/amarillo-daily-news-apr-11–1966-p–12/.

Curtis Publishing Co. v. *Butts*, 388 U.S. 130 (1967). Accessed on September 30, 2018, at https://supreme.justia.com/cases/federal/us/388/130/.

Da Silva, Chantal (2019). "Former Bush Ethics Czar Tells MSNBC That Donald Trump Is 'Not Well at All, Mentally . . . He's Having a Hissy Fit.'" *Newsweek* [online]. Posted February 19, 2019. Accessed on February 19, 2019, at www .newsweek.com/former-bush-ethics-czar-tells-msnbc-donald-trump-not-well-al l-mentallyhes–1335084.

Dallek, Robert (1998). *Flawed Giant: Lyndon Johnson and His Times, 1961–1973*. New York: Oxford University Press.

Danto, Elizabeth Ann (2012). "Have You No Shame" – American Redbaiting of Europe's Psychoanalysts. In Joy Damousi and Mariano Ben Plotkin, eds., *Psychoanalysis and Politics: Histories of Psychoanalysis under Conditions of Restricted Political Freedom*. New York: Oxford University Press, pp. 213–231.

Davies, David R. (2006). *The Postwar Decline of American Newspapers, 1945–1965*. Westport, CT: Praeger.

Davis, Brian L. (1990). *Quaddafi, Terrorism, and the Origins of the U.S. Attack on Libya*. New York: Praeger.

Davis, Michael (1990). The Ethics Boom: What and Why. *Centennial Review* 34 (2) (Spring), pp. 163–186.

de Toledano, Ralph (2005). I Witness. *The American Conservative* [online]. February 14, 2005. Accessed on December 30, 2018, at www.theamericancon servative.com/articles/i-witness/.

Dean, John W., and Barry M. Goldwater Jr. (2008). *Pure Goldwater*. New York: Palgrave Macmillan.

Delmont, Matthew (2016). When Jackie Robinson Confronted a Trump-Like Candidate. *The Atlantic*. March 19, 2016. Accessed on January 26, 2019, at www.theatlantic.com/politics/archive/2016/03/goldwater-jackie-robin son/474498/.

Democrats Planning Town Hall to Attack President Trump's Mental Health. *OAN: One America News Network*. June 10, 2019. Accessed on June 11, 2019, at www.oann.com/democrats-planning-town-hall-to-attack-president-trumps-me ntal-health/.

Devlin, John F., and Robert L. Jervis (1979). Analysis of NFAC's Performance on Iran's Domestic Crisis, Mid-1977–7 November 1978. 15 June 1979 [top secret internal report for National Foreign Assessment Center] [redacted version]. Accessed on August 5, 2019, at www.cia.gov/library/readingroom/docs/CIA-RDP86B00269R001100110003-4.pdf.

DeYoung, Karen, and Walter Pincus (2007). CIA Releases Files on Past Misdeeds. *Washington Post*. June 27, 2007. Accessed on January 20, 2019, at www.washingtonpost.com/wp-dyn/content/article/2007/06/26/AR2007062600861.html.

Dodes, Lance (2017). "The Most Dangerous Man in the World": Trump Is Violent, Immature and Insecure, Psych Experts Say. *Newsweek*. September 27, 2017. Accessed on February 3, 2019, at www.newsweek.com/2017/10/06/tru mp-most-dangerous-man-world-psychologists-671182.html.

Dodes, Lance, and Joseph Schachter (2017). Mental Health Professionals Warn about Trump [letter]. *New York Times*. February 13, 2017. Accessed on April 28, 2019, at www.nytimes.com/2017/02/13/opinion/mental-health-profession als-warn-about-trump.html.

Dotinga, Randy (2017). Trump Presidency Prompts Goldwater Rule Debate at APA. *Clinical Psychiatry News*. May 23, 2017. Accessed on September 2, 2018, at www.mdedge.com/psychiatry/article/138795/practice-management/trump-presidency-prompts-goldwater-rule-debate-apa.

Dreben, Burton (2003). On Rawls and Political Liberalism. In Samuel Freeman, ed., *The Cambridge Companion to Rawls*. Cambridge: Cambridge University Press, pp. 316–346.

Drescher, Jack (2007). An Interview with Lawrence Hartmann, MD. In Jack Drescher and Joseph Merlino, eds., *American Psychiatry and Homosexuality: An Oral History*. New York: Haworth Press, pp. 45–61.

Dr. Henry W. Brosin, 94, Authority on Psychiatry. *Chicago Tribune*. July 25, 1999. Accessed on November 25, 2018, at www.chicagotribune.com/news/ct-xp m-1999–07-25–9907250312-story.html.

Driver, Justin (2012). The Constitutional Conservatism of the Warren Court. *California Law Review* 100 (5) (October), pp. 1101–1711.

Dyson, Stephen Benedict (2014). Origins of the Psychological Profiling of Political Leaders: The US Office of Strategic Services and Adolf Hitler. *Intelligence and National Security* 29 (5), pp. 654–674.

Edgerton, Gary R., ed. (2007). *The Columbia History of American Television*. New York: Columbia University Press.

Edwards, Lee (2018). How One Man Invented the Conservative Movement. The Heritage Foundation [website]. February 27, 2018. Accessed on September 22, 2018, at www.heritage.org/conservatism/commentary/how-one-man-inven ted-the-conservative-movement.

Ehrlichman, John (1982). *Witness to Power: The Nixon Years*. New York: Simon & Schuster.

Ellsberg, Daniel (2002). *Secrets: A Memoir of Vietnam and the Pentagon Papers*. New York: Viking.

Ellsberg, Daniel (n.d. [circa 1973]). Letter on Behalf of the Indochina Peace Campaign [redacted version in CIA files]. Accessed on August 6, 2019, at www .cia.gov/library/readingroom/docs/CIA-RDP90-00806R000100500010-4.pdf.

Ellsberg, Daniel (2007). Foreword. In Egil Krogh, *Integrity: Good People, Bad Choices, and Life Lessons from the White House*. With Matthew Krogh. New York: PublicAffairs.

Elms, Alan C. (1994). *Uncovering Lives: The Uneasy Alliance of Biography and Psychology*. New York and Oxford: Oxford University Press.

Erikson, Erik H. (1942). Hitler's Imagery and German Youth. *Psychiatry* 5 (February–November), pp. 475–493.

Erikson, Erik H. (1950/1996). A Conviction Born of Judiciousness. *Psychoanalysis and Contemporary Thought* 19 (2), pp. 277–282. Accessed on December 2, 2018, at www.pep-web.org/document.php?id=pct.019.0277a&type=hitlist&num=5& query=zone1%2Cparagraphs%7Czone2%2Cparagraphs%7Cauthor%2CEriks on%2C+Erik+H.%7Cauthorexact%2Ctrue#hit1.

Erikson, Erik H. (1950/1963). *Childhood and Society*. Second Edition: Revised and Enlarged. New York: Norton.

Erikson, Erik H. (1958). *Young Man Luther: A Study in Psychoanalysis and History*. New York: Norton.

Erikson, Erik H. (1987). *A Way of Looking at Things: Selected Papers from 1930 to 1980*. Edited by Stephen Schlein. New York: Norton.

Eros (1962). Volume 1, nos. 1–4. New York: Eros Magazine, Inc.

Ervin, Sam (1964). Letter to Betty Richardson, March 25, 1964, in Senator Sam Ervin and the 1964 Civil Rights Act. [Website of Sam Ervin Papers, Southern Historical Collection, University of North Carolina at Chapel Hill.] Accessed on January 3, 2019, at http://ervin062.web.unc.edu/historical-context/biogra phy-sam-ervin–2/.

Ethics Reminder Offered about "Goldwater Rule" on Talking to Media. *Psychiatric News*. Published online May 18, 2007. Accessed on January 13, 2019, at https:// psychnews.psychiatryonline.org/doi/full/10.1176/pn.42.10.0002.

Fact (1964–7). Volumes 1–4. New York: Fact Magazine, Inc.

Fact, Fiction, Doubt & Barry. *Time*. May 17, 1968, pp. 52, 57.

Fahmy, Mohamed Fadel (2016). 30 Years Later, Questions Remain over Sadat Killing, Peace with Israel. Updated October 6, 2011. Accessed on March 16, 2019, at www .cnn.com/2011/10/06/world/meast/egypt-sadat-assassination/index.html.

Feibel, Adelaide, and Hailey Fuchs (2018). Yale Psychiatrist Faces Threats. *Yale Daily News* [online]. January 16, 2018. Accessed on January 20, 2019, at https://yaledai lynews.com/blog/2018/01/16/yale-psychiatrist-faces-threats/.

Filene, Peter (2001). "Cold War Culture" Doesn't Say It All. In Peter J. Kuznick and James Gilbert, eds., *Rethinking Cold War Culture*. Washington, DC: Smithsonian Institution Press, pp. 156–174.

Finney, Joseph C. et al. (1973). Phases of Psychopathology after Assassination. *American Journal of Psychiatry* 130 (12) (December), pp. 1379–1380.

Fleishman, Glenn (2019). Robert Mueller Grand Jury Gets More Time to Consider Evidence, Issue Indictments. *Fortune.* January 4, 2019. Accessed on August 5, 2019, at http://fortune.com/2019/01/04/mueller-special-counsel-trump-grand-jury-extension/.

Frank, L. J. (2018). NPJ Book Review: *The Housewife's Handbook on Selective Promiscuity.* Definitive Edition by Rey Anthony (2012). *NPJ: An Evolving Architecture of the Human Voice.* Posted January 5, 2018. Accessed on August 5, 2019, at www.narrativepathsjournal.com/npj-book-review-the-housewifes-han dbook-on-selective-promiscuity-definitive-edition-by-rey-anthony–2012/.

Freud, Sigmund (1908). Character and Anal Eroticism. *Standard Edition of the Psychological Works of Sigmund Freud.* Volume 9. London: Hogarth Press.

Friedman, Lawrence J. (1990). *Menninger: The Family and the Clinic.* New York: Knopf.

Friedman, Lawrence J. (1999). *Identity's Architect: A Biography of Erik H. Erikson.* New York: Scribner.

Friedman, Lawrence J., assisted by Anke M. Schreiber (2013). *The Lives of Erich Fromm: Love's Prophet.* New York: Columbia University Press.

Friedman, Leon (1966/1967). The Ginzburg Decision and the Law. *The American Scholar* 36 (1) (Winter), pp. 71–91.

Friedman, Richard A. (2008). Role of Physicians and Mental Health Professionals in Discussions of Public Figures. *JAMA* 300 (11), pp. 1348–1350.

Fromm, Erich (1941). *Escape from Freedom.* New York: Rinehart & Company.

Fromm, Erich (1955). *The Sane Society.* New York: Holt, Rinehart and Winston.

Frosch, Stephen (2016). Theorizing Anti-Semitism in the Wake of the Nazi Holocaust. In Matt Ffytche and Daniel Pick, eds., *Psychoanalysis in the Age of Totalitarianism.* London and New York: Routledge, pp. 29–41.

Gabbard, Glen O., and Krin Gabbard (1999). *Psychiatry and the Cinema.* Second Edition. Washington, DC: American Psychiatric Press.

Ganeva, Tana (2019). A Yale Psychiatrist Explains How Donald Trump's Mental Incapacity Was Exposed by Robert Mueller. *Salon.* May 7, 2019. Accessed on May 8, 2019, at www.salon.com/2019/05/07/a-yale-psychiatrist-explains-how-donald-trumps-mental-incapacity-was-exposed-by-robert-mueller_partner/.

Gartner, John (2017). Why Trump Is Dangerously Unfit to Be President. Reported in Hal Brown, "Exclusive: Dr. John Gartner's Speech to Yale Duty to Warn Conference on Trump's Mental Unfitness" [online post]. *Daily Kos.* April 23, 2017. Accessed on January 27, 2019, at www.dailykos.com/stories/2017/4/23/1655450/-Exclusive-Dr-John-Gartner-s-speech-to-Yale-Duty-to-Warn-Conference-on-Trump-s-mental-unfitness.

Ghaemi, Nassir (2012). Psychiatrists Can Speak Too: Understanding the Goldwater Rule. Posted September 16, 2012. Accessed on March 16, 2019, at www.psychologytoday.com/intl/blog/mood-swings/201209/psychiatrists-can-speak-too.

Gilson, Dave (2015). The CIA's Secret Psychological Profiles of Dictators and World Leaders Are Amazing. *Mother Jones*. Posted February 11, 2015. Accessed on November 11, 2019, at www.motherjones.com/politics/2015/02/cia-psychological-profiles-hitler-castro-putin-saddam/.

Ginzburg, Ralph (1958). *An Unhurried View of Erotica*. New York: Helmsman Press.

Ginzburg, Ralph (1962). Portrait of a Genius as a Young Chess Master. *Harper's*, January. Accessed on September 3, 2018, at http://bobbyfischer.net/bobby04.html.

Ginzburg, Ralph (1962/1988). *100 Years of Lynchings*. Reprinted by Black Classics Press.

Ginzburg, Ralph (1964). Goldwater: The Man and the Menace. *Fact* 1 (5) (September–October), pp. 3–22 [published version].

Ginzburg, Ralph (1973). *Castrated: My Eight Months in Prison*. New York: Avant Garde Books.

Ginzburg Loses Again. *Time*. May 31, 1968, p. 41.

Ginzburg v. Goldwater, 396 U.S. 1049 (1970) [US Supreme Court's denial of Ginzburg's petition for writ of certiorari; includes dissent by Justice Black, January 26, 1970]. Accessed on August 22, 2018, at https://supreme.justia.com/cases/federal/us/396/1049/.

Ginzburg v. United States, 383 U.S. 463 (1966) [US Supreme Court decision in *Eros* case]. Accessed on September 1, 2018, at https://supreme.justia.com/cases/federal/us/383/463/.

Gittings, Barbara (2007). Preface: Show and Tell. In Jack Drescher and Joseph Merlino, eds., *American Psychiatry and Homosexuality: An Oral History*. New York: Haworth Press, pp. xv–xx.

Glass, Leonard L. (2017a). Dealing with American Psychiatry's Gag Rule. *Psychiatric Times*. July 20, 2017. Accessed on January 27, 2019, at www.psychiatrictimes.com/couch-crisis/dealing-american-psychiatrys-gag-rule.

Glass, Leonard L. (2017b). Should Psychiatrists Refrain from Commenting on Trump's Psychology? In Bandy X. Lee, ed., *The Dangerous Case of Donald Trump: 27 Psychiatrists and Mental Health Experts Assess a President*. New York: St. Martin's Press, pp. 151–159.

Glass, Leonard L. (2018). The Goldwater Rule Is Broken. Here's How to Fix It. *Stat*. June 28, 2018. Accessed on June 15, 2019, at www.statnews.com/2018/06/28/goldwater-rule-broken-psychiatrists/.

Godfrey, Elaine (2018). The Psychiatrist Telling Congress Trump Could Be Involuntarily Committed. *The Atlantic*. January 12, 2018. Accessed on January 27, 2019, at www.theatlantic.com/politics/archive/2018/01/bandy-lee/550193/.

Goldberg, Robert A. (1995). *Barry Goldwater*. New Haven, CT, and London: Yale University Press.

Goldwater, Barry M. (1960). *The Conscience of a Conservative*. Shepherdsville, KY: Victor Publishing Company.

Goldwater, Barry M. (1964). Goldwater's 1964 Acceptance Speech. Accessed on September 3, 2018, at www.washingtonpost.com/wp-srv/politics/daily/ma y98/goldwaterspeech.htm.

Goldwater, Barry M. (1975). Media's Rush-to-Judgment Helps Cripple CIA. *Human Events* 35 (39) (September 27), p. 9.

Goldwater v. *Ginzburg* (1968) [district court trial, Southern District of New York]. See "G v G transcript," in Abbreviations.

Goldwater, Barry M., with Jack Casserly (1988). *Goldwater.* New York: Doubleday.

Gottfried, Paul, and Thomas Fleming (1988). *The Conservative Movement.* Boston: Twayne Publishers.

Graetz, Michael J., and Linda Greenhouse (2016). *The Burger Court and the Rise of the Judicial Right.* New York: Simon & Schuster.

Gray, Christopher (2006). Building the Halls Where History Would Echo. *New York Times.* May 7, 2006.

Greene, Richard (2016). Is Donald Trump Mentally Ill? 3 Professors of Psychiatry Ask President Obama to Conduct "A Full Medical and Neuropsychiatric Evaluation." *Huffington Post* [online]. December 12, 2016. Accessed on August 5, 2019, at www.huffingtonpost.com/richard-greene/is-donald-trump-mentally_b_13693174.html.

Grohol, John M. (2019). What the Media Get Wrong about the Goldwater Rule. *PsychCentral* [online]. Updated April 15, 2019. Accessed on April 21, 2019, at https://psychcentral.com/blog/what-the-media-get-wrong-about-the-goldwa ter-rule/.

Grove Press, Inc. v. *Christenberry,* 175 F. Supp. 488 (S.D.N.Y. 1959) [*Lady Chatterley's Lover* case]. Accessed on September 1, 2019, at https://law.justia.com/cases/ federal/district-courts/FSupp/175/488/1382008/.

Gruhl, John (1980). The Supreme Court's Impact on the Law of Libel: Compliance by Lower Federal Courts. *Western Political Quarterly* 33 (4) (December), pp. 502–519.

Grynbaum, Michael M. (2018). Trump Renews Pledge to "Take a Strong Look" at Libel Laws. *New York Times.* January 10, 2018. Accessed on January 26, 2019, at www.nytimes.com/2018/01/10/business/media/trump-libel-laws.html.

Gutsche, Robert E., Jr., ed. (2018). *The Trump Presidency, Journalism, and Democracy.* New York and London: Routledge.

Hall, Kermit L., and Melvin I. Urofsky (2011). New York Times *v.* Sullivan: *Civil Rights, Libel Law, and the Free Press.* Lawrence: University Press of Kansas.

Hamedy, Saba, and Caitlan Collins (2018). Trump Tweets "WITCH HUNT" Following His Attacks on Mueller. CNN. Accessed on December 30, 2018, at www.cnn.com/2018/03/19/politics/donald-trump-witch-hunt-tweet/index .html.

Hamilton, Jay (2016). *Democracy's Detectives: The Economics of Investigative Journalism.* Cambridge, MA: Harvard University Press.

Harris B. Steinberg Dies at 57; Noted Criminal Defense Lawyer. *New York Times,* June 5, 1969, p. 47.

Hart, H. L. A. (1963). *Law, Liberty, and Morality*. Stanford, CA: Stanford University Press.

Heidenry, John (1997). *What Wild Ecstasy: The Rise and Fall of the Sexual Revolution*. New York: Simon & Schuster.

Heller, Steven (2006). Ralph Ginzburg, 76, Dies; Publisher in Obscenity Case. *New York Times*. July 7, 2006. Accessed on June 13, 2018, at www.nytimes.com/2006/07/07/us/07ginzburg.html.

Hentoff, Nat (1966/1967). Ralph Ginzburg. Reprinted in *Playboy Interviews*. Selected by the Editors of *Playboy*. Chicago: Playboy Press, pp. 284–309.

Herman, Ellen (1995). *The Romance of American Psychology: Political Culture in the Age of Experts*. Berkeley: University of California Press.

Herman, Judith Lewis, and Bandy X. Lee (2017). Prologue: Professions and Politics. In Bandy X. Lee, ed., *The Dangerous Case of Donald Trump: 27 Psychiatrists and Mental Health Experts Assess a President*. New York: St. Martin's Press, pp. 1–10.

Herman, Judith Lewis, and Robert Jay Lifton (2017). "Protect Us from This Dangerous President," 2 Psychiatrists Say. *New York Times* [letter]. March 8, 2017. Accessed on January 27, 2019, at www.nytimes.com/2017/03/08/opinion/protect-us-from-this-dangerous-president-2-psychiatrists-say.html.

Hersch, Seymour M. (1974). Clifford Favors a Special Inquiry into C.I.A. "Spying." *New York Times*. December 26, 1974, pp. 1, 46.

Herzog, Dagmar (2017). *Cold War Freud: Psychoanalysis in an Age of Catastrophes*. Cambridge, MA: Cambridge University Press.

Hess, Karl (1999). *Mostly on the Edge: An Autobiography*. Edited by Karl Hess Jr. Amherst, NY: Prometheus Books.

Higgins, Tucker (2019). Lawsuits Challenging Trump's National Emergency Declaration Use His Words against Him. *CNBC* [online]. Posted February 19, 2019. Accessed on February 19, 2019, at www.cnbc.com/2019/02/19/trumps-words-used-against-him-in-national-emergency-lawsuits.html.

Hoffman, Louise E. (1992). American Psychologists and Wartime Research on Germany, 1941–1945. *American Psychologist* 47 (2) (February), pp. 264–273.

Hofstadter, Richard (1954/1979). The Pseudo-Conservative Revolt. Reprinted in *The Paranoid Style in American Politics and Other Essays*. Reprinted, Chicago: University of Chicago Press, 1979, pp. 41–65.

Hofstadter, Richard (1964/1979). Goldwater and Pseudo-conservative Politics. Reprinted in *The Paranoid Style in American Politics and Other Essays*. Reprinted, Chicago: University of Chicago Press, 1979, pp. 93–141.

Horney, Karen (1937/1964). *The Neurotic Personality of Our Time*. New York: Norton.

Hossbach, Friedrich (1937). Hossbach Memorandum [November 10, 1937]. The Avalon Project: Documents in Law, History, and Diplomacy. Yale Law School, Lillian Goldman Law Library [website]. Accessed on January 5, 2019, at http://avalon.law.yale.edu/imt/hossbach.asp.

Hulten, Charles M. (1958). The Impact of Senator Joseph McCarthy on the Press of the United States. *Gazette* 4 (1), pp. 11–20.

Hunt, E. Howard (1974). *Undercover: Memoirs of an American Secret Agent.* New York: Berkley Publishing Corporation.

Hunt, E. Howard (2007). *American Spy: My Secret History in the CIA, Watergate, and Beyond.* Hoboken, NJ: Wiley.

Hunter, Marjorie (1974). C.I.A. Doctors Say Ellsberg Is First American Given "Personality Assessment." *New York Times.* May 11, 1973. Accessed on July 13, 2019, at www.nytimes.com/1973/05/11/archives/cia-doctors-say-ellsberg-is-first-american-given-personality.html.

Hurley, Richard (2009). Medicine and the Media: The Chilling Effect of English Libel Law. *BMJ: British Medical Journal* 339 (7728) (October 31), p. 1006.

Is Barry Goldwater Psychologically Fit to Be President of the United States? *New York Times* [advertisement], September 19, 1964, p. 56.

Israel, Jerold H. (1966). *Elfbrandt v. Russell:* The Demise of the Loyalty Oath. *Sup Ct Review* 1966, 193–252. Accessed on December 25, 2018, at https://reposi tory.law.umich.edu/cgi/viewcontent.cgi?referer=https://search.yahoo.com/ &httpsredir=1&article=1557&context=articles.

Israel, Josh (2019). Trump Defender Alan Dershowitz Says Devin Nunes Has "No Case at All" against Twitter. Think Progress [online]. March 20, 2019. Accessed on March 20, 2019, at https://thinkprogress.org/alan-dershowitz-devin-nunes-has-no-case-twitter-6c17595b892c/.

Isserman, Maurice, and Michael Kazin (2000). *America Divided: The Civil Wars of the 1960s.* New York: Oxford University Press.

Jalonick, Mary Clare (2019). President Trump Says Opponents Did "Treasonous Things" and Vows Investigation of His Own. *Time* [online]. March 25, 2019. Accessed on August 5, 2019, at www.youtube.com/watch?v=OuyMMsA7vu0.

Jamieson, Kathleen Hall (1984). *Packaging the Presidency: A History and Criticism of Presidential Campaign Advertising.* New York: Oxford University Press.

Jackson, Kenneth T. (1985). *Crabgrass Frontier: The Suburbanization of the United States.* New York: Oxford University Press.

Jay, Martin (1973/1996). *The Dialectical Imagination: A History of the Frankfurt School and the Institute of Social Research, 1923–1950.* Berkeley: University of California Press.

John, Richard R., and Jonathan Silberstein-Loeb (2015). *Making News: The Political Economy of Journalism in Britain and America from the Glorious Revolution to the Internet.* Oxford: Oxford University Press.

John Wilson Dies; Top Trial Lawyer. *New York Times.* May 21, 1986. Accessed on September 30, 2018, at www.nytimes.com/1986/05/21/obituaries/john-wil son-dies-top-trial-lawyer.html.

Johnson, David K. (2004). *The Lavender Scare: The Cold War Persecution of Gays and Lesbians in the Federal Government.* Chicago: University of Chicago Press.

Johnson, Loch K. (1985/2015). *A Season of Inquiry Revisited.* Lawrence: University of Kansas Press.

Jordan, Ken (1997). Barney Rosset, the Art of Publishing No 2. *The Paris Review,* issue 145 (Winter). Accessed on September 1, 2018, at www.theparisreview.or g/interviews/1187/barney-rosset-the-art-of-publishing-no-2-barney-rosset.

Judge Roger Robb of U.S. Appeals Court Dies. *New York Times*. December 21, 1985. Accessed on November 11, 2018, at www.nytimes.com/1985/12/21/us/judge-roger-robb-of-us-appeals-court-dies.html.

Judicial Watch Uncovers CIA Inspector General's "Watergate History" Report. Judicialwatch.org. August 30, 2016. Accessed on July 6, 2019, at www.judicial watch.org/press-room/press-releases/judicial-watch-uncovers-cia-inspector-generals-watergate-history-report/.

Kalman, Laura (2017). *The Long Reach of the Sixties: LBJ, Nixon, and the Making of the Contemporary Supreme Court*. New York: Oxford University Press.

Kane, Peter E (1983). Public Figure Libel after *Sullivan: Goldwater v. Ginzburg. Free Speech Yearbook* 22 (1), pp. 43–50.

Kaplan, Fred (2009). The Day Obscenity Became Art. *New York Times*, July 20, 2009. Accessed on September 1, 2018, at www.nytimes.com/2009/07/21/opinion/21kaplan.html.

Karni, Annie (2018). Washington's Growing Obsession: The 25th Amendment. *Politico.com*. January 3, 2018. Accessed on April 13, 2019, at www.politico.com/story/2018/01/03/trump-25th-amendment-mental-health–322625.

Kashani, Tony, and Benjamin Frymer, eds. (2013). *Lost in Media: The Ethics of Everyday Life*. New York: Peter Lang.

Kassam, Ashifa (2018). "He's Done Quite Well": Why Conrad Black Thinks Trump Is What the US Needs. *Guardian* [online]. Posted July 18, 2018. Accessed on February 2, 2019, at www.theguardian.com/business/2018/jul/18/conrad-black-trump-book-support-pardon.

Kazin, Alfred (1962). *Contemporaries*. Boston: Little, Brown.

Kazin, Alfred (2011). *Alfred Kazin's Journals*. Selected and Edited by Richard M. Cook. New Haven, CT: Yale University Press.

Kearns, Doris (1976/1977). *Lyndon Johnson and the American Dream*. Reprinted, New York: Signet/New American Library.

Kellner, Douglas (2016). *American Nightmare: Donald Trump, Media Spectacle, and Authoritarian Populism*. Rotterdam/Boston/Taipei: Sense Publishers.

Kelly, Jacques (2005). Jerome D. Frank, 95, Psychiatry Professor at Johns Hopkins. *Baltimore Sun*. March 15, 2005. Accessed on February 24, 2019, at www.baltimoresun.com/news/bs-xpm-2005–03-15–0503150100-story.html.

Kershaw, Ian (2000). *Hitler: 1936–45: Nemesis*. London: Penguin.

Khrushchev in Budapest. *New York Times*. December 3, 1959, p. 36.

Kirby, Alex (n.d.). Biography of Sam Ervin. In Senator Sam Ervin and the 1964 Civil Rights Act. [Website of Sam Ervin Papers, Southern Historical Collection, University of North Carolina at Chapel Hill.] Accessed on January 3, 2019, at http://ervin062.web.unc.edu/historical-context/biography-sam-ervin–2/.

Kirkpatrick, David D. (2004). *National Review* Founder Says It's Time to Leave Stage. *New York Times*. June 29, 2004. Accessed on September 2, 2018, at www.nytimes.com/2004/06/29/us/national-review-founder-says-it-s-time-to-leave-stage.html.

Kissinger Denies Any Role in C. I. A. Study of Ellsberg (1973). *New York Times*. September 27, 1973, pp. 1, 30.

Kissinger, Henry (1979). *The White House Years*. Boston: Little, Brown.

Klarman, Michael J. (2004). *From Jim Crow to Civil Rights: The Supreme Court and the Struggle for Racial Equality.* Oxford: Oxford University Press.

Klarman, Michael J. (2013). *From the Closet to the Altar: Courts, Backlash, and the Struggle for Same-Sex Marriage.* New York: Oxford University Press.

Kluckhohn, Clyde (1944). Psychiatry and Anthropology. In American Psychiatric Association, *One Hundred Years of American Psychiatry.* New York: Published for the American Psychiatric Association by Columbia University, pp. 588–618.

Kneeland, Douglas E. (1973). White House Officials and David Eisenhower Continue President's Attack on the News Media. *New York Times.* October 31, 1973, p. 23.

Krieg, Gregory (2016). It's Official: Clinton Swamps Trump in Popular Vote. *CNN Politics* [online]. December 22, 2016. Accessed on March 20, 2019, at www.cnn.com/2016/12/21/politics/donald-trump-hillary-clinton-popular-vote-final-count/index.html.

Kris, Ernst, and Hans Speier (1944). *German Radio Propaganda: Report on Home Broadcasts during the War.* London and New York: Oxford University Press.

Krogh, Egil (2007a). *Integrity: Good People, Bad Choices, and Life Lessons from the White House.* With Matthew Krogh. New York: PublicAffairs.

Krogh, Egil (2007b). The Break-In That History Forgot. *New York Times.* June 30, 2007, p. A17.

Kroll, Jerome L. (2018). The Dangerous Case of Donald Trump: 27 Psychiatrists and Mental Health Experts Assess a President [review]. *Journal of the American Academy of Psychiatry and the Law* 46 (2) (June), pp. 267–271.

Kroll, Jerome L., and Claire Pouncey (2016). The Ethics of APA's Goldwater Rule. *Journal of the American Academy of Psychiatry and the Law* 44 (2) (June), pp. 226–235.

Langer, Walter C. (n.d. [1943]). *A Psychological Analysis of Adolph Hitler: His Life and Legend.* Copy # 4 of 100 [Walter Langer's personal copy of his report to the OSS, typed and bound manuscript, with minor handwritten corrections and letter of bequest]. Collection of Houghton Library, Harvard University.

Langer, Walter C. (1972). *The Mind of Adolf Hitler: The Secret Wartime Report.* New York: Basic Books.

Langer, Walter C., and Sanford Gifford (1978). An American Analyst in Vienna during the Anschluss, 1936–1938. *Journal of the History of the Behavioral Sciences* 14, pp. 37–54.

Lazarus, Jeremy (2000). Ethics in the American Psychiatric Association after World War II. In Roy W. Menninger and John C. Nemiah, eds., *American Psychiatry after World War II: 1944–1994.* Washington, DC: American Psychiatric Press, pp. 545–568.

Lebovic, Sam (2016). *Free Speech and Unfree News: The Paradox of Press Freedom in America.* Cambridge, MA: Harvard University Press.

Lee, Bandy X. (2018). Psychiatrists Challenge a Gag Order. *Psychology Today.* Posted July 16, 2018. Accessed on April 14, 2019, at www.psychologytoday.com/us/blog/psychiatry-in-society/201807/psychiatrists-challenge-gag-order.

Lee, Bandy X., ed. (2017). *The Dangerous Case of Donald Trump: 27 Psychiatrists and Mental Health Experts Assess a President*. New York: St. Martin's Press.

Lee, Bandy X., Judith L. Herman, and Robert Jay Lifton (2018). "An Open Letter to the American Psychiatric Association: Silence v. Bearing Witness: An Ethical Question," n.d. [February 12, 2018], undated copy provided to the author by Bandy X. Lee; Board of Trustees of the American Psychiatric Association to Lee, Herman, and Lifton [reply], March 23, 2019, copy provided to the author by Bandy X. Lee.

Lee, Bandy X. et al. (2017). Does Professional Responsibility Include a Duty to Warn? [transcript of the Yale Duty to Warn Conference, Yale School of Medicine, April 20, 2017]. Accessed on January 27, 2019, at https://static.ma cmillan.com/static/duty-to-warn-conference-transcript.pdf.

Lemann, Nicholas (2019). A Historian and His Publics. In David Greenberg et al., eds., *Alan Brinkley: A Life in History*. New York: Columbia University Press, pp. 120–125.

Leonard, Kimberly (2019). "Mental Instability": Psychiatrists Who Called Trump Dangerous Want to Testify on Impeachment. *Washington Examiner*. Posted November 8, 2019. Accessed on November 10, 2019, at www.washingtonexami ner.com/policy/healthcare/psychiatrists-who-called-trump-dangerous-seek-to-testify-in-impeachment-hearings.

Levin, Aaron (n.d.). Goldwater Rule's Origins Based on Long-Ago Controversy [reprint from *Psychiatric News*]. Accessed on August 20, 2018, at www.psy chiatry.org/newsroom/goldwater-rule.

Levin, Saul (2018). Report of the CEO and Medical Director. *American Journal of Psychiatry*. Published online July 1, 2018. Accessed on January 12, 2019, at https://ajp-psychiatryonline-org.ezp-prod1.hul.harvard.edu/doi/full/10.11 76/appi.ajp.2018.1750702.

Levine, Meredith (2017). Journalism Ethics and the Goldwater Rule in a "Post-truth" Media World. *Journal of the American Academy of Psychiatry and the Law* 45 (2), pp. 241–248.

Levy, Gabrielle (2016). It's On: *National Review*, 22 Conservatives Openly Denounce Trump. *U.S. News & World Report* [online]. January 2016, p. 1. Accessed on January 26, 2019, at www.usnews.com/news/articles/2016–01-22 /its-on-national-review-22-conservatives-openly-denounce-trump.

Lewis, Anthony (1964/1989). *Gideon's Trumpet*. New York: Vintage/Random House.

Lewis, Anthony (1991). *Make No Law: The Sullivan Case and the First Amendment*. New York: Random House.

Liddy, G. Gordon (1980). *Will: The Autobiography of G. Gordon Liddy*. New York: St. Martin's Press.

Lieberman, Jeffrey A. (2017). The Dangerous Case of Psychiatrists Writing about the POTUS's Mental Health. *Psychiatric News*. Published online, November 15, 2017. Accessed on January 26, 2019, at https://psychnews.psychiatryonline.org/doi/full/10.1176/appi.pn.2017.11b13.

Lieberman, Jeffrey A. (2018a). [Tweets of January 6, 2018, on Bandy Lee] Accessed on January 26, 2019, at https://twitter.com/DrJlieberman/status/949872134310055936.

Lieberman, Jeffrey A. (2018b). Maybe Trump Is Not Mentally Ill. Maybe He's Just a Jerk. *New York Times.* January 12, 2018. Accessed on July 22, 2019, at www.nytimes .com/2018/01/12/opinion/trump-mentally-ill.html.

Lieberman, Jeffrey A. (2018c). Psychiatrists Diagnosing the President – Moral Imperative or Ethical Violation? [letter]. *NEJM* 378 (5), pp. 483–484.

Lieberman, Jeffrey A. (2018d). [Tweet of February 26, 2018: "Lee n her band . . . ."] Accessed on March 16, 2019, at https://twitter.com/DrJlieberman/status/968237286235152384.

Lifton, Robert Jay (1972). The Man Who Wanted to Live Forever [review of Walter C. Langer's *The Mind of Adolf Hitler*]. *New York Times.* December 31, 1972. Accessed on December 30, 3018, at www.nytimes.com/1972/12/31/archives/the-mind-of-adolf-hitler-by-walter-c-langer-foreword-by-william-l-l.html.

Lifton, Robert Jay (1986). *The Nazi Doctors: Medical Killing and the Psychology of Genocide.* New York: Basic Books.

Limbaugh, Rush (2018). *Newsweek:* Trump Can End Human Species. Rushlimbaugh.com. January 8, 2018. Accessed on February 24, 2019, at www.rushlimbaugh.com/daily/2018/01/08/newsweek-trump-can-end-human-species/.

Linder, Douglas O. (2011). The Pentagon Papers (Daniel Ellsberg) Trial: An Account. Accessed on November 9, 2019, at http://law2.umkc.edu/faculty/projects/ftrials/ellsberg/ellsbergaccount.html?source=post_page.

Lintelman, Ryan (2018). In 1968, When Nixon Said "Sock It to Me" on "Laugh-In," TV Was Never Quite the Same Again. January 19, 2018. Smithsonian.com. Accessed on October 19, 2019, at www.smithsonianmag.com/smithsonian-institution/1968-when-nixon-said-sock-it-me-laugh-tv-was-never-quite-same-again-180967869/

Liptak, Adam (2019). Justice Clarence Thomas Calls for Reconsideration of Landmark Libel Ruling. *New York Times.* February 19, 2019. Accessed on February 24, 2019, at www.nytimes.com/2019/02/19/us/politics/clarence-thomas-first-amendment-libel.html.

Locker, Ray (2016). CIA Director Misled FBI about How Agency Spied on Pentagon Papers Leaker. *USA Today.* August 31, 2016. Accessed on March 17, 2018, at www.usatoday.com/story/news/politics/2016/08/31/cia-helms-fbi-pentagon-papers/89642908/.

Ludmerer, Kenneth M. (1999). *Time to Heal: American Medical Education from the Turn of the Century to the Era of Managed Care.* Oxford: Oxford University Press.

Lunbeck, Elizabeth (2018). Thinking Psychoanalytically (and Historically) about the State of the Nation: 1938, 2018. Nemetz Lecture, Boston Psychoanalytic Society and Institute.

Mack, John E. (1976). *T. E. Lawrence: A Prince of Our Disorder.* Boston: Little, Brown.

Madison, James (1822). Letter to W. T. Barry. Accessed on May 3, 2019, at http://press-pubs.uchicago.edu/founders/documents/v1ch18s35.html.

Mailer, Norman (1964). In the Red Light. *New York Post.* May 27, 1964. Reprinted in Mailer, *Cannibals and Christians.* New York: Dial Press, 1966.

Mailer, Norman (1968/1996). *Miami and the Siege of Chicago: An Informal History of the Republican and Democratic Conventions of 1968.* New York: Random House.
Mailer, Norman (2014). *Selected Letters of Norman Mailer.* Edited by J. Michael Lennon. New York: Random House.
Malloy, Bernard M. (1975). Affidavit. In House Subcommittee on Intelligence Hearings, pp. 33–35. Accessed on July 23, 2018, at https://babel.hathitrust.or g/cgi/pt?id=mdp.39015082037170&view=1up&seq=41.
Mandler, Peter (2016). Totalitarianism and Cultural Relativism: The Dilemma of the Neo-Freudians. In Matt Ffytche and Daniel Pick, eds., *Psychoanalysis in the Age of Totalitarianism.* London and New York: Routledge, pp. 102–113.
Mann, Robert (2011). *Daisy Petals and Mushroom Clouds: LBJ, Barry Goldwater, and the Ad That Changed American Politics.* Baton Rouge: Louisiana State University Press.
Maritain, Jacques (1961). Truth and Human Fellowship. In *On the Use of Philosophy: Three Essays.* Princeton, NJ: Princeton University Press.
Martin Luther King. Reprinted in *Playboy Interviews.* Selected by the Editors of *Playboy.* Chicago: Playboy Press, 1967, pp. 346–383.
Martin-Joy, John (2015). Images in Psychiatry: *Goldwater* v. *Ginzburg. American Journal of Psychiatry* 172 (8), pp. 729–730.
Martin-Joy, John (2017a). Introduction to the Special Section on the Goldwater Rule. *Journal of the American Academy of Psychiatry and the Law* 45 (2), pp. 223–227.
Martin-Joy, John (2017b). Interpreting the Goldwater Rule. *Journal of the American Academy of Psychiatry and the Law* 45 (2), pp. 233–240.
Martin-Joy, John, Sagar Vijapura, and Jonathan E. Carey (2014). Politics, Psychiatry, & the Goldwater Rule: An Interview with Michael Dukakis [excerpts from a videotaped interview]. Accessed on March 2, 2019, at www .scattergoodethics.org/revisiting-the-goldwater-rule. The clip and a transcript of the full interview are on deposit in the archives of the Boston Psychoanalytic Society and Institute in Newton, MA.
Martin-Joy, John et al. (2015). Ethical Perspectives on the Psychiatric Evaluation of Public Figures. Invited Forum, American Psychiatric Association Annual Meeting, Toronto, Ontario. May 18, 2015.
Mayer, Jane (2017). Should Psychiatrists Speak Out against Trump? *The New Yorker.* May 27, 2017. Accessed on January 17, 2019, at www.newyorker.co m/magazine/2017/05/22/should-psychiatrists-speak-out-against-trump.
Mayer, John D. (2009a). Libel, in *Fact:* The 1,189 Psychiatrists. *Psychology Today.* Posted on August 9, 2009. Accessed on May 6, 2019, at www.psychologytoday .com/us/blog/the-personality-analyst/200908/libel-in-factthe-1189-psychiatrists.
Mayer, John D. (2009b). Libel in *Fact* ... The Storm Clouds Gather. *Psychology Today.* Posted on August 16, 2009. Accessed on August 5, 2019, at www.psycho logytoday.com/us/blog/the-personality-analyst/200908/libel-in-factthe-stor m-clouds-gather.
Mayer, John D. (2009c). Libel, in *Fact:* Lawyering Up. *Psychology Today.* Posted on August 24, 2009. Accessed on May 6, 2019, at www.google.com/amp/s/www

.psychologytoday.com/us/blog/the-personality-analyst/200908/libel-in-fact-l awyering%3Famp.

Mayer, John D. (2009d). Libel in *Fact*: Did Senator Goldwater Suffer a Nervous Breakdown? *Psychology Today*. Posted on September 6, 2009. Accessed on May 6, 2019, at www.google.com/amp/s/www.psychologytoday.com/us/blog/the-p ersonality-analyst/200909/libel-in-fact-did-senator-goldwater-suffer-nervous-b reakdown%3Famp.

Mayer, John D. (2009e). Libel in *Fact* Magazine: Judging Sarah Palin vs. Judging Barry Goldwater. *Psychology Today*. Posted on November 29, 2009. Accessed on June 13, 2019, at www.psychologytoday.com/us/blog/the-personality-analyst/ 200911/libel-in-fact-magazine-judging-sarah-palin-vs-judging-barry.

Mayer, John D. (2009f). Libel in *Fact* Magazine: Judging Goldwater by Psychological Theory. *Psychology Today*. Posted on December 13, 2009. Accessed on June 13, 2019, at www.psychologytoday.com/us/blog/the-person ality-analyst/200912/libel-in-fact-magazine-judging-goldwater-psychological-theory.

Mayer, John D. (2010a). Libel in *Fact* Magazine: Instructions to the Jury. *Psychology Today*. Posted on February 21, 2010. Accessed on March 16, 2019, at www.psy chologytoday.com/us/blog/the-personality-analyst/201002/libel-in-fact-mag azine-instructions-the-jury.

Mayer, John D. (2010b). Libel in *Fact* Magazine: The Verdict. Posted on February 28, 2010. Accessed on April 28, 2019, at www.psychologytoday.co m/us/blog/the-personality-analyst/201002/libel-in-fact-magazine-the-verdict.

Mayer, John D. (2010c). The *Fact* Libel Trial: Was the Verdict the Right One? *Psychology Today*. Posted on March 21, 2010. Accessed on August 5, 2019, at www.psychologytoday.com/us/blog/the-personality-analyst/201003/the-fact-libel-trial-was-the-verdict-the-right-one.

Mayer, John D. (2010d). The *Fact* Magazine Libel Trial: Onto [*sic*] the Supreme Court. *Psychology Today*. Posted on March 28, 2010. Accessed on August 6, 2019, at www.psychologytoday.com/us/blog/the-personality-analyst/201003/the-fa ct-magazine-libel-trial-the-supreme-court.

Mayer, John D. (2010e). The *Fact* Magazine Libel Trial: Where Are They Now? *Psychology Today*. Posted on April 25, 2010. Accessed on August 11, 2018, at www.psychologytoday.com/us/blog/the-personality-analyst/201004/the-fact-magazine-libel-trial-where-are-they-now.

Mayer, John D. (2010f). The APA's Ethics Code and Personality Analysis at a Distance. *Psychology Today*. Posted June 27, 2010. Accessed on January 13, 2019, at www.psychologytoday.com/us/blog/the-personality-analyst/201006/ the-apas-ethics-code-and-personality-analysis-distance.

McCabe, Andrew G. (2019). *The Threat: How the FBI Protects America in the Age of Terror and Trump*. New York: St. Martin's Press.

McCarthy, Joseph (1951). Drew Pearson: Speech of Hon. Joseph R. McCarthy of Wisconsin in the Senate of the United States, December 15, 1950. In *"Confusing Freedom of the Press with Prostitution of the Press" – "License to Poison and Pollute the Waterholes of Information": Speeches of Hon. Joseph R. McCarthy of Wisconsin in the*

Senate of the United States, December 15, 19, 1950, and January 5, 1951. Not printed at government expense. Washington, DC: US Printing Office, 1951, pp. 3–22.

McLaughlin, Dan (2018a). Trump's First Year: First, the Good News. *National Review* [online]. January 26, 2018. Accessed on February 2, 2019, at www.na tionalreview.com/2018/01/donald-trump-first-year-accomplishments–2/.

McLaughlin, Dan (2018b). Trump's First Year: The Bad News. *National Review* [online]. January 27, 2018. Accessed on February 2, 2019, at www.nationalre view.com/2018/01/trump-administration-first-year-office-bad-news-politics-perception/.

McManus, Doyle (1987). Case and Woodward: Who Used Whom? [review of Bob Woodward's *Veil*]. *Los Angeles Times.* October 11, 1987. Accessed on January 21, 2019, at http://articles.latimes.com/1987–10-11/books/bk-13227_1_bob-woodward.

McNamara, Robert S. (1969). Introduction. In Robert F. Kennedy, *Thirteen Days: A Memoir of the Cuban Missile Crisis.* New York: Norton, pp. 13–16.

Memorial for William C. Menninger: Wednesday, December 14, 1966, New York Academy of Medicine (1967). New York: Printed by Clarke & Way, Inc.

Mendes, Elizabeth (2011). In U.S., Fear of Big Government at Near-Record Level. Gallup [website]. December 12, 2011. Accessed on January 1, 2019, at https://news.gallup.com/poll/151490/fear-big-government-near-record-level.aspx.

Menninger, Roy W., and John C. Nemiah (2000). *American Psychiatry after World War II (1944–1994).* Washington, DC: American Psychiatric Press.

Mental Health Experts Demand Psychological Evaluation of Kavanaugh for Drinking, Instability [interview with Amy Goodman]. *Democracy Now!* [online]. October 3, 2018. Accessed on March 16, 2019, at www.democracy now.org/2018/10/3/mental_health_experts_demand_psychological_assessment.

Mettler, Katie (2017). The Day Anti-Vietnam War Protesters Tried to Levitate the Pentagon. *Washington Post.* October 19, 2017. Accessed on September 29, 2018, at www.washingtonpost.com/news/retropolis/wp/2017/10/19/the-day-anti-vi etnam-war-protesters-tried-to-levitate-the-pentagon/?utm_term=.a6f9e73186f9.

Miller, Arthur (1987). *Timebends: A Life.* New York: Grove Press.

Miller, Merle (1972). Ralph Ginzburg, Middlesex, N. J., and the First Amendment. *New York Times.* April 30, 1972. Accessed on September 3, 2018, at www.nytimes.com/1972/04/30/archives/ralph-ginzburg-middlesex-nj-and-the-first-amendment-ralph-ginzburg.html.

Moffic, H. Steven (2017). Psychiatric Diagnoses of Public Figures. *Psychiatric Times.* March 2, 2017. Accessed on January 27, 2019, at www.psychiatrictimes .com/couch-crisis/psychiatric-diagnoses-public-figures.

Moffic, H. Steven (2018). What Our Goldwater Rule Poll May Be Telling Us. *Psychiatric Times.* March 19, 2018. Accessed on March 19, 2018, at www.psychia trictimes.com/couch-crisis/what-our-goldwater-rule-poll-may-be-telling-us.

Moran, Mark (2019). BBRF Head Responds to *New York Times* on Psychiatric Research Comments. *Psychiatric News* 54 (1) (January 4), p. 5.

Moritz-Rabson, Daniel (2019). Sinclair Media Commentator Floats Putting Donald Trump's Face on Mount Rushmore in Segment Run on 50 Stations. *Newsweek* [online]. February 20, 2019. Accessed on March 10, 2019, at www.newsweek.com/ sinclair-media-trump-face-mount-rushmore–1337754.

Müller, Knuth (2016). Psychoanalysis and American Intelligence since 1945. In Matt Ffytche and Daniel Pick, eds., *Psychoanalysis in the Age of Totalitarianism.* London and New York: Routledge, pp. 148–162.

Murray, Henry A. (1943). Analysis of the Personality of Adolf Hitler. In Law Collections: Donovan Nuremberg Trials Collection, Cornell University Law Library website. Accessed on December 1, 2018, at http://hydrastg.library.cor nell.edu/fedora/objects/nur:01134/datastreams/pdf/content.

Nash, George H. (1976). *The Conservative Intellectual Movement in America since 1945.* New York: Basic Books.

National Advisory Commission on Civil Disorders [Kerner Commission] (1968). Report of the National Advisory Commission on Civil Disorders – Summary of Report. Accessed on October 20, 2019, at www.eisenhowerfoundation.org/do cs/kerner.pdf.

National Archives (2008). Vietnam War U.S. Military Fatal Casualty Statistics. Accessed on September 29, 2018, at www.archives.gov/research/military/viet nam-war/casualty-statistics.

Naughton, James M. (1972). Nixon Disclosure on Health Asked. *New York Times.* July 27, 1972, p. 1.

Navasky, Victor (1980). *Naming Names.* New York: Viking.

Nelson, Michael (2018). *Trump's First Year.* Charlottesville: University of Virginia Press.

New,Michael J. (2008). *Pure Goldwater* [review of Dean and Goldwater 2008]. *National Review.* June 10, 2008. Accessed on September 22, 2018, at www.natio nalreview.com/2008/06/pure-goldwater-michael-j-new/.

Newman, Roger K. (1994). *Hugo Black: A Biography.* New York: Pantheon.

Nicholson, Ian (2011). "Shocking" Masculinity: Stanley Milgram, "Obedience to Authority," and the "Crisis of Manhood" in Cold War America. *Isis* 102 (2), pp. 238–268.

Nixon, Richard M. (1978). *RN: The Memoirs of Richard Nixon.* New York: Grosset and Dunlap.

Nobile, Philip (1976). A Controversial Discipline. *New York Times.* October 10, 1976. Accessed on July 13, 2019, at www.nytimes.com/1976/10/10/archives/ a-controversial-discipline.html.

Nolte, John (2018). Trump Attacks "Pathetic" *Weekly Standard.* Breitbart [online]. December 15, 2018. Accessed on February 3, 2019, at www.breit bart.com/the-media/2018/12/15/nolte-donald-trump-mocks-pathetic-weekl y-standard/.

Nordlinger, Jay (2018). Enemies and Anthems. *National Review.* June 26, 2018. Accessed on February 3, 2019, at www.nationalreview.com/corner/enemies-a nd-anthems/.

Nussbaum, Martha C. (1986/2001). *The Fragility of Goodness: Luck and Ethics in Greek Tragedy and Philosophy.* Revised Edition. Cambridge: Cambridge University Press.

Nussbaum, Martha C. (2006). *Frontiers of Justice: Disability, Nationality, Species Membership.* Cambridge, MA: Harvard University Press.

Nussbaum, Martha C. (2008). *Liberty of Conscience: In Defense of America's Tradition of Religious Equality.* New York: Basic Books.

Omestad, Thomas (1994). Psychology and the CIA: Leaders on the Couch. *Foreign Policy* 95, pp. 105–122.

Oquendo, Maria A. (2016). The How and Why of Working Closely with the Country's Leadership. *Psychiatric News.* Posted on November 28, 2016. Accessed on June 15, 2019, at https://psychnews.psychiatryonline.org/doi/10.1176/appi .pn.2016.12a18.

Oquendo, Maria A. (2017). APA's Methodical Approach to Communication. *Psychiatric News.* Posted on February 23, 2017. Accessed on June 15, 2019, at https://psychnews.psychiatryonline.org/doi/10.1176/appi.pn.2017.3a24.

Ostrow, Ronald J. and Robert C. Toth (1981). CIA Psychological Profile [word missing] Kadafi as Insecure [sanitized version in CIA files]. *Los Angeles Times.* December 18, 1981. Accessed on March 16, 2019, at www.cia.gov/library/read ingroom/docs/CIA-RDP90-00552R000605720005-8.pdf.

O'Sullivan, Shane (2018). *Dirty Tricks: Nixon, Watergate, and the CIA.* New York: Hot Books.

Overby, Peter (2019). Democratic Hopefuls Complete to Spurn Establishment Cash. NPR [online]. February 2, 2019. Accessed on February 3, 2019, at www .npr.org/2019/02/02/690156001/democratic-presidential-hopefuls-com pete-to-spurn-establishment-cash.

Overy, Richard (1999). Misjudging Hitler: A.J.P. Taylor and the Third Reich. In Gordon Martel, ed., *The Origins of the Second World War Reconsidered: A.J.P. Taylor and the Historians.* Second Edition. London and New York: Routledge, pp. 93–115.

Palma, Bethania (2018). Does the Psychiatrist Who "Diagnosed" President Trump Lack a License? *Snopes.com.* Posted on January 15, 2018. Accessed on February 24, 2019, at www.snopes.com/fact-check/does-psychiatrist-trump-la ck-license/.

Paschal, Olivia (2018). Trump's Tweets and the Creation of "Illusory Truth." *The Atlantic.* August 3, 2018. Accessed on December 20, 2018, at www.theatlantic .com/politics/archive/2018/08/how-trumps-witch-hunt-tweets-create-an-illu sory-truth/566693/.

Penney, Matthew T. (2013). CIA, Camp David, and U.S. Policy in the Middle East. In President Carter and the Role of Intelligence in the Camp David Accords, report of conference at Jimmy Carter Presidential Library, Atlanta, GA, November 13, 2013, pp. 7–13. Accessed on November 7, 2019, at www.cia.gov/ library/publications/international-relations/president-carter-and-the-camp-dav id-accords/Carter_CampDavid_Pub.pdf.

Percy, Walker (1991). *Signposts in a Strange Land,* ed. Patrick Samway. New York: Farrar, Straus and Giroux.

Perlstein, Rick (2001). *Before the Storm: Barry Goldwater and the Unmaking of the American Consensus.* New York: Hill and Wang.

Pew Research Center (2018). Newspapers Fact Sheet. Accessed on December 28, 2018, at www.journalism.org/fact-sheet/newspapers/.

Phelps, Robert H. (1970). Court Allows Goldwater Judgment to Stand. *New York Times.* January 27, 1970. Accessed on September 16, 2018, at www.nytimes.com/

1970/01/27/archives/court-allows-goldwater-judgment-to-stand-75000-libel-sui t-against.html.

Phillips-Fein, Kim (2009). *Invisible Hands: The Making of the Conservative Movement from the New Deal to Reagan.* New York: Norton.

Pincus, Walter (1974). Getting to the Bottom of the CIA Cover-Up. *The New Republic.* September 28, pp. 11–13.

Plaxton, Michael (2012). The Challenge of the Bad Man. *McGill Law Journal* 58 (2), pp. 451–480.

Playboy Interviews (1967). Selected by the Editors of *Playboy.* Chicago: Playboy Press.

Pollak, Joel B., and Larry Schweikart (2017). *How Trump Won: The Inside Story of a Revolution.* Washington, DC: Regnery Publishing.

Post, Jerrold M. (2002). Ethical Considerations in Psychiatric Profiling of Political Figures. *Psychiatric Clinics of North America* 25, pp. 635–646.

Post, Jerrold M., ed. (2003). *The Psychological Assessment of Political Leaders.* Ann Arbor: University of Michigan Press.

Post, Jerrold M. (2011). Qaddafi under Siege. *Foreign Policy.* March 15, 2011. Accessed on January 15, 2019, at https://foreignpolicy.com/2011/03/15/qad dafi-under-siege–2/.

Post, Jerrold M. (2013). Psychological Profiling in Support of the Camp David Summit. In President Carter and the Role of Intelligence in the Camp David Accords, report of conference at Jimmy Carter Presidential Library, Atlanta, GA, November 13, 2013. Accessed on October 12, 2016, at www.cia.gov/libra ry/publications/international-relations/president-carter-and-the-camp-david-accords/Carter_CampDavid_Pub.pdf.

Post, Jerrold M. (2015). *Narcissism and Politics: Dreams of Glory.* New York: Cambridge University Press.

Pouncey, Claire (2017). President Trump's Mental Health – Is It Morally Permissible for Psychiatrists to Comment? *NEJM* 378 (5), pp. 405–407.

Powe, L. A., Jr. (2010). The Obscenity Bargain: Ralph Ginzburg for Fanny Hill. *Journal of Supreme Court History* 35 (2) (July), pp. 166–176.

Pritchard, Bill (2006). Kolb Broke New Ground in Community Psychiatry. *Psychiatric News* 41 (24) (December 15), p. 14.

The Proposed Impeachment Article II. *New York Times.* July 30, 1974, page 1. Accessed on January 21, 2019, at www.nytimes.com/1974/07/30/archives/th e-proposed-impeachment-article-ii-article-ii.html.

Psychiatrist Will Menninger. *Time.* October 25, 1948. Cover and pp. 64–66, 69–72.

Publisher of *Eros* Plans New Journal. *New York Times,* January 13, 1964, p. 22.

Radosh, Ronald (1976). The Teacher as Scholar-Spy: The CIA and the Academy. *Change* 8 (7) (August), pp. 38–42, 64.

Rawls, John (1971/1999). *A Theory of Justice.* Revised Edition. Cambridge, MA: Harvard University Press.

Rawls, John (1993/2005). *Political Liberalism.* Expanded Edition. New York: Columbia University Press.

Rawls, John (1997). The Idea of Public Reason Revisited. In Rawls, *Political Liberalism.* Expanded Edition. New York: Columbia University Press, pp. 440–490.

Redden, Molly (2017). Effusive Hugh Hefner Tributes Ignore *Playboy* Founder's Dark Side. *Guardian.* Posted September 29, 2017. Accessed on August 31, 2018, at www.theguardian.com/media/2017/sep/28/hugh-hefner-playboy-foun der-91-dark-side.

Reich, Wilhelm (1933/1946). *The Mass Psychology of Fascism.* Third Edition. New York: Orgone Institute Press.

Reitman, Bob (1966). *Freedom on Trial: The Incredible Ordeal of Ralph Ginzburg.* San Diego, CA: Publishers Export Company.

Remnick, David (1985). 25 Years of Nightmares. *Washington Post.* July 28, 1985, p. F1.

Richmond, Linda M. (2018). APA Joins Lawsuit against Trump's "Skimpy" Plan Rule. *Psychiatric News* (October 19), p. 1.

Richmond, Linda M. (2019). First Step Act Is Start Toward Meaningful Prison Reform. *Psychiatric News* [online]. Posted January 25, 2019. Accessed on February 3, 2019, at https://psychnews.psychiatryonline.org/doi/full/10.117 6/appi.pn.2019.2a10.

Richmond, Linda M. (2019). APA Opposes Trump Administration Plan Targeting Psychiatric Drugs in Medicare. *Psychiatric News* 54 (6) (March 15), p. 1.

Roazen, Paul (1975/1992). *Freud and His Followers.* Reprinted, New York: Da Capo Press.

Robert S. Garber: Obituary. *Sarasota (Florida) Herald-Tribune.* December 8, 2005. Accessed on January 13, 2019, at www.legacy.com/obituaries/heraldtribune/ obituary.aspx?pid=86251303.

Robinson, Robert L. [writing as "R.L.R"] (1968). More Mischief Afoot. *Psychiatric News* (February), p. 2.

Robin, Corey (2011/2018). *The Reactionary Mind: Conservativism from Edmund Burke to Donald Trump.* Second Edition. Oxford: Oxford University Press.

Rosenberg, Norman L. (1986). *Protecting the Best Men: An Interpretive History of the Law of Libel.* Chapel Hill: University of North Carolina Press.

Rosenfield, Dylan (2016). The Portrayal of the Iranian Hostage Crisis by American Media and Its Effects on the Presidential Election of 1980. *Vanderbilt Historical Review* [online]. November 8, 2016. Accessed on January 21, 2019, at http://van derbilthistoricalreview.com/iranian-hostage-crisis/.

Roth v. *United States,* 354 U.S. 476 [US Supreme Court decision]. Accessed on September 1, 2018, at https://supreme.justia.com/cases/federal/us/354/47 6/case.html.

Rothman, Lily (2016). The Scathing Speech That Made Television History. *Time* [online]. May 9, 2016. Accessed on February 28, 2019, at http://time.com/4 315217/newton-minow-vast-wasteland-1961-speech/.

Sabshin, Melvin (2008). *Changing American Psychiatry: A Personal Perspective.* Washington, DC: American Psychiatric Publishing.

Shirer, William L. (1960). *The Rise and Fall of the Third Reich: A History of Nazi Germany* [mass market paperback edition]. Greenwich, CT: Fawcett Crest.

Schlafly, Phyllis, Ed Martin, and Brett M. Decker (2016). *The Conservative Case for Trump.* Washington, DC: Regnery Publishing.

Schlesinger, Arthur M. (1960). *Kennedy or Nixon: Does It Make Any Difference?* New York: Macmillan.

Schulman, Bruce J. (2001). *The Seventies: The Great Shift in American Culture, Society, and Politics.* New York: The Free Press.

Schumach, Murray. Lindsay Notes Progress in Times Square Cleanup. *New York Times*, April 18, 1973. Accessed on September 3, 2018, at www.nytimes.com/1973/04/18/archives/lindsay-notes-progressin-times-square-cleanup-he-pled ges-stepped-up.html.

Schwartz, Bruce (2018). Report of the Treasurer. *American Journal of Psychiatry.* Published online July 1, 2018. Accessed on January 12, 2019, at https://ajp-ps ychiatryonline-org.ezp-prod1.hul.harvard.edu/doi/full/10.1176/appi .ajp.2018.1750702.

Scott, Rachel (2019). President Trump Calls Democrats "Sick People," Takes Victory Lap on Mueller Report during Rally in Michigan. *ABC News* [online]. March 28, 2019. Accessed on March 31, 2019, at https://abcnews.go.com/Po litics/president-donald-trump-hold-campaign-rally-michigan-1st/story? id=61987526.

Shermer, Elizabeth Tandy (2008). Origins of the Conservative Ascendancy: Barry Goldwater's Early Senate Career and the De-legitimization of Organized Labor. *Journal of American History* 95 (3), pp. 678–709.

Sherwin, Martin J. (1975). *A World Destroyed: The Atomic Bomb and the Grand Alliance.* New York: Knopf.

Showalter, Monica (2019). Trump Makes Big Bully Alec Baldwin Cry Like a Baby. *American Thinker* [blog]. Accessed on February 19, 2019, at www.americanthin ker.com/blog/2019/02/trump_makes_big_bully_alec_baldwin_cry_like_a_ baby.html.

Siebert, Fred (n.d.). My mentors: Ralph Ginzburg[sic]. Fredseibert.com. Accessed on September 1, 2018, at http://fredseibert.com/post/184887226/ my-mentors-ralph-ginzburg.

Siegel, Marc (2018). President Trump and the Dangers of Armchair Psychiatry. *National Review* [online]. January 11, 2018. Accessed on January 20, 2019, at www .nationalreview.com/2018/01/trump-mental-health-armchair-psychiatry/.

A Sixteen-Year Hunt for New York's "Mad Bomber." NPR [online]. May 13, 2011. Accessed on February 28, 2019, at www.npr.org/2011/05/13/136287845/a-1 6-year-hunt-for-new-yorks-mad-bomber.

Smant, Kevin J. (2002). *Principles and Heresies: Frank S. Meyer and the Shaping of the Conservative Movement.* Wilmington, DE: ISI Books.

Staab, James B. (2006). *The Political Thought of Justice Antonin Scalia: A Hamiltonian on the Supreme Court.* Lanham, MD: Rowman & Littlefield.

Stabile, Carol A. (2018). *The Broadcast 41: Women and the Anti-Communist Blacklist.* London: Goldsmiths Press.

Stanley v. *Georgia* (1969). 394 U.S. 557. Accessed on September 16, 2018, at https://supreme.justia.com/cases/federal/us/394/557/.

Stein, Jacob A. (2001). Legal Spectator: Defamation. DC Bar [website]. Reprinted from *Washington Lawyer* (November 2001). Accessed on January 5, 2019, at www.dcbar.org/bar-resources/publications/washington-lawyer/arti cles/november-2001-legal-spectator.cfm.

Stevenson, Adlai (1962). UN Security Council Address on Soviet Missiles in Cuba. *American Rhetoric: Online Speech Bank.* Accessed on April 13, 2019, at www.americanrhetoric.com/speeches/adlaistevensonunitednationscuba .html.

Stewart, Althea (2019). 175 Years of Caring: A Celebration. *Psychiatric News* 54 (1) (January 4), p. 2.

Stickgold, Marc (2010). "The Hysteria of Our Times": Loyalty Oaths in California. Accessed via Golden Gate University School of Law, GGU Digital Commons on December 25, 2018, at https://digitalcommons.law.ggu.edu/cgi/viewcontent .cgi?referer=https://search.yahoo.com/&httpsredir=1&article=1175& context=pubs.

Stone, Alan (2018). The Psychiatrist's Goldwater Rule in the Trump Era [review of Lee et al. 2017]. *Lawfare.* April 19, 2018. Accessed on November 26, 2018, at https://lawfare.s3-us-west-2.amazonaws.com/staging/2018/Stone%20review .pdf.

Stone, Geoffrey R. (2011). Justice Scalia, Originalism, and the First Amendment. *Huffington Post.* Updated December 13, 2011. Accessed on February 24, 2019, at www.huffingtonpost.com/geoffrey-r-stone/justice-scalia-origina lis_b_1009944.html.

Strozier, Charles B. (2001). *Heinz Kohut: The Making of a Psychoanalyst.* New York: Farrar, Straus and Giroux.

Stroud, Natalie Jomini (2011). *Niche News: The Politics of News Choice.* Oxford University Press.

Sullivan, William (1978). Thinking the Unthinkable [cable to State Department]. November 9, 1978. Accessed on July 13, 2019, at https://assets.documentcloud .org/documents/5734181/National-Security-Archive-Doc-07-U-S-Embassy .pdf.

Sunstein, Cass R. (2019). *On Freedom.* Princeton, NJ: Princeton University Press.

Szasz, Thomas (1960/1974). *The Myth of Mental Illness.* Revised Edition. New York: Harper & Row.

Teles, Stephen M. (2008). *The Rise of the Conservative Legal Movement: The Battle for Control of the Law.* Princeton, NJ: Princeton University Press.

Thorn, William J. (1987). *Newspaper Circulation: Marketing the News.* With Mary Pat Pfeil. New York: Longman.

To the Right, March. *Time.* September 20, 1968, pp. 22–23.

Tolman v. *Underhill* (1952). 39 Cal. 2d 708. Accessed on December 25, 2018, at https://scocal.stanford.edu/opinion/tolman-v-underhill–32699.

Transcript of Donald Trump's Immigration Speech. *New York Times.* September 1, 2016. Accessed on February 2, 2019, at www.nytimes.com/2016 /09/02/us/politics/transcript-trump-immigration-speech.html.

Transcript: Donald Trump's Taped Comments about Women. *New York Times.* October 7, 2016. Accessed on February 3, 2019, at www.nytimes.com/2016/1 0/08/us/donald-trump-tape-transcript.html.

Truell, Peter (1998). Riding Shotgun for Wall Street; Combative Lawyer for Aggressive Brokers Is in Demand. *New York Times.* February 19, 1998. Accessed on August 12, 2018, at www.nytimes.com/1998/02/18/business/riding-shot gun-for-wall-street-combative-lawyer-for-aggressive-brokers-demand.html.

Trump: A Billion-Dollar Empire and an Ego to Match. *Newsweek* [cover story]. September 28, 1987. Accessed on January 26, 2019, at "The Other Time Trump Was Huge," www.newsweek.com/rise-trump–357533.

Trump Hits Back at *National Review* Attack: "It's a Dead Paper." *Fox News Insider* [online]. January 22, 2016. Accessed on February 3, 2019, at https://insider .foxnews.com/2016/01/22/donald-trump-responds-national-review-editorial-its-dying-paper.

Trump, Donald J. (2018). Tweet of April 10, 2018. Accessed on February 3, 2019, at https://twitter.com/realDonaldTrump/status/983662953894436864.

Trump, Ivana (2017). *Raising Trump.* New York: Gallery Books.

Two Definitions of Obscenity. *Time.* June 21, 1963, p. 25.

Turner, Stansfield (2005). *Burn before Reading: Presidents, CIA Directors, and Secret Intelligence.* New York: Hyperion.

UK Ministry of Justice (2013). Defamation Laws Take Effect [press release]. December 31, 2013. Accessed on November 18, 2018, at www.gov.uk/govern ment/news/defamation-laws-take-effect.

The Unconscious of a Conservative: A Special Issue on the Mind of Barry Goldwater. *Fact* 1 (5) (September–October, 1964).

US Census Bureau (2002). *Demographic Trends in the 20th Century.* Accessed on March 24, 2019, at www.census.gov/prod/2002pubs/censr-4.pdf.

United States v Ginzburg, 224 F. Supp. 129 (E.D. Pa. 1963) [district court opinion in *Eros* matter]. Accessed on September 1, 2018, at https://law.justia.com/cases/ federal/district-courts/FSupp/224/129/1558456/.

United States of America *v.* Ralph Ginzburg, Documentary Books, Inc., *Eros* Magazine, Inc. and Liaison News Letter, Inc., Appellants, 338 F.2d 12 (3rd Cir. 1964) [initial appeals court decision]. Accessed on September 1, 2018, at https://law.justia.com/cases/federal/appellate-courts/F2/338/12/333790/.

United States of America *v.* Ralph Ginzburg, Documentary Books, Inc., *Eros* Magazine, Inc., Liaison News Letter, Inc., Ralph Ginzburg, Appellant, 398 F.2d 52 (3d Cir. 1968) [later appeals court decision on Ginzburg's request for a rehearing of the case by the district court]. Accessed on September 1, 2018, at https://law.justia.com/cases/federal/appellate-courts/F2/398/52/29655/.

Upton, William J. (2011). Conservatives and Libertarians. *American Thinker.* Posted February 16, 2011. Accessed on December 2, 2018, at www.american thinker.com/articles/2011/02/conservatives_and_libertarians_1.html.

Waggoner, Walter H. (1981). Walter Langer Is Dead at 82; Wrote Secret Study of Hitler. *New York Times.* July 10, 1981. Accessed December 1, 2018, at www.nyti mes.com/1981/07/10/obituaries/walter-langer-is-dead-at-82-wrote-secret-stu dy-of-hitler.html.

Waite, Robert G. L. (1972). Afterward. In Walter C. Langer, *The Mind of Adolf Hitler: The Secret Wartime Report.* New York: Basic Books, pp. 217–238.

Walter Barton: A Job Well Done. *Psychiatric Services* 25 (9) (September 1974), pp. 577–579.

Waxman, Olivia B. (2017). Why the "Goldwater Rule" Keeps Psychiatrists from Diagnosing at a Distance. *Time.* July 27, 2017. Accessed on August 21, 2018, at https://news.yahoo.com/why-apos-goldwater-rule-apos-151536099.html;_ylt=

AwrE19ZvWEhd2uYaoRxXNyoA;_ylu=X3oDMTByOHZyb21tBGNvbG8DYmY xBHBvcwMxBHZ0aWQDBHNlYwNzcg–.

Weber, Max (1918/1989). Science as a Vocation. Translated by Michael John. In Peter Lassman and Irving Velody, eds., with Herminio Martins, *Max Weber's "Science as a Vocation."* London and Boston: Unwin Hyman, pp. 3–31.

Weinstein, Harvey (1990). *Psychiatry and the CIA: Victims of Mind Control.* Washington, DC: American Psychiatric Press.

Wells, Tom (2001). *Wild Man: The Life and Times of Daniel Ellsberg.* New York: Palgrave.

What Makes Marilyn? *Playboy* 1 (1) (December 1953), pp. 17–18.

White, Theodore H. (1965). *The Making of the President 1964.* New York: Atheneum.

Whitfield, Stephen J. (1988). *American Space, Jewish Time: Essays in Modern Culture and Politics.* Hamden, CT: Archon Books.

Whitmer, Caleb (2018). Seventy Years Ago, Whitaker Chambers Stood Courageously as a "Witness" against Totalitarian Propaganda. *The Federalist.* August 14, 2018. Accessed on December 30, 2018, at http://thefederalist.co m/2018/08/14/70-years-ago-whittaker-chambers-stood-courageously-witness-totalitarian-propaganda/.

Williams, Kevin (2000). Defaming Politicians: The Not So Common Law. *Modern Law Review* 63 (5) (September), pp. 748–756.

Wilson, Edmund (1944/1950). Thoughts on Being Bibliographed. In *Classics and Commercials: A Literary Chronicle of the Forties.* New York: Farrar, Straus and Giroux, pp. 105–120.

Woodward, Bob (1987). *Veil: The Secret Wars of the CIA 1981–1987.* New York: Simon & Schuster.

Zilber, Claire (2018). Psychiatry and Politics: Can They Mix? *Psychiatric News* (October 5), p. 4.

Zion, Sidney (1988). *The Autobiography of Roy Cohn.* Secaucus, NJ: Lyle Stuart.

Index

Anthony, Rey (Lillian Maxine Serett), 52, 54–55
APA. *See* American Psychiatric Association
APA Commentary on Ethics in Practice (American Psychiatric Association, 2015), 290
Appelbaum, Paul, 4–5, 207, 237–238
APsaA. *See* American Psychoanalytic Association
Arendt, Hannah, 64, 75
Arkin, Stanley, 97
Associated Press v. *Walker*, 127–128
Austria, 17–18
The Authoritarian Personality (Adorno), 38–39, 71–73, 117, 153
authoritarianism
    Fromm on, 22–23
    anal-sadistic character, 22–23, 74
    susceptibility to, 22–23
    Trump, D., and, alleged authoritarian populism of, 196
autonomy, limitations of, 245–247
Avant Garde (magazine), 100, 125
    survey about Johnson, by psychiatrists, 148–149, 150
    American Psychiatric Association response to, 151–153

Bachrach, Louis, 145
Baker, Howard, 172
Barbas, Samantha, 12, 71
Bar-Ilan, David, 97, 269, 273
Barton, Gail, 145, 146, 278
Barton, Walter E., 12, 29, 34, 68–69, 256
    American Psychiatric Association and, 144–147, 157, 158–159, 164, 278
    Menninger, W., as influence on, 144–145
Begin, Menachem, 185–186
Bell, Daniel, 50
Belli, Marvin, 156
Bernstein, Carl, 183, 196
Berryman, John, 35
Binger, Carl, 40
Black, Conrad, 217–218
Black, Hugo (Justice), 10, 48, 71, 128, 130, 227, 256
Blain, Daniel, 68–69, 141–142, 146, 160
Boroson, Warren, 12, 62, 63, 64, 266. *See also Fact*
    "Goldwater: The Man and the Menace," 66–73
    drafts by, 73–74, 75–76, 269–270

research sources for, 71–73, 74–75, 117
Goldwater v. *Ginzburg* and, 97, 121
Fascism and the legacy of Nazism and, 74–75
testimony of, 116–118
"What Psychiatrists Say about Goldwater" (survey), 67–68, 81
Bozell, L. Brent, Jr., 37, 42
Bradlee, Ben, 33
Brendel, Rebecca, 12–13, 171, 202–203, 207, 213–215, 246, 284–285
Brennan, William (Justice), 70–71, 126–127
Brinkley, Alan, 47, 55, 224
Broder, David, 89
Brosin, Henry W., 151
Brown, Pat, 66
Brown v. *Board of Education*, 11–12, 47–48
Brussel, James A., 40–41
Buchwald, Art, 89
Buckley, William F.
    on Ginzburg, R., 55–56, 96, 132
    on Goldwater, 41–42, 87–88
    Goldwater v. *Ginzburg* and, 91, 98, 123
    on Khrushchev, 43
Burger, Warren (Chief Justice), 97, 129
Burlingham, Dorothy, 23
Bush, George H. W., 184, 189
Butterfield, Alex, 168

Cameron, Ewen, 182–183
Carter, Jimmy, 185–186
    Central Intelligence Agency profiling under, 185–186
Case, Clifford, 284
Casey, William, 187–188
Castro, Fidel, 43
Central Intelligence Agency (CIA), profiling by, 5–6
    of Begin, 185–186
    of Ellsberg, 173, 284
        American Psychiatric Association response to, 184
    ethics of, 175–176, 179–181
    likely harm as result of, 180–181
    political purpose of, 173, 179–180
    source material for, 176–178
    ethical guidelines for, 188–191, 284–285
    of foreign leaders, history of, 288
    of Hussein, 189, 190
    of Khomeini, 185–186
    Post and, 172–173, 188–190
    public view of, 182–184

alleged housing discrimination by,
193–194
authoritarian populism and, 196
Cohn and, 193–194
conservative response to, 196–197,
217–218
Constitutional crisis under, 222–223
election campaign of, 195–197
alleged racist elements of, 196
media coverage of, 193
proposed reform of libel law,
218–219
public protests against, 198
2016 election of, 192
ethical questions about diagnosing
after, 1
unorthodox administrative practices of,
219–220
Trump, Donald, psychiatrists' comments
on, 199–218
American Psychiatric Association's
official response to, 201–209
Goldwater Rule and, 202–205, 211–212
ethics of, 1
by Lee, B., 192, 200, 204–206, 207–212
The Dangerous Case of Donald Trump, 9,
10, 204–205, 207, 208
meetings with Congress, 209–211
response of other mental health
professionals to Trump, 199
Trump, Fred, 193–194
Turner, Stansfield, 186
Twain, Mark, 6

An Unhurried View of Erotica (Ginzburg, R.),
51–54

Vida, Judith, 203, 290
Vidal, Gore, 183
Vietnam War, 10, 285

Wallace, George, 52, 79, 100
Warren, Earl (Chief Justice), 43, 48, 122,
126–127
Watergate affair
hearings on, 168
impeachment proceedings resulting
from, 181–182
"Plumbers" (White House staff), 174. *See
also* Hunt, Howard; Krogh, Egil;
Liddy, G. Gordon; Young, David
Watson, Marvin, 149,
150
Weber, Max, 229–230
Weinberger, Caspar, 158–159
Welch, Robert, 42
What Happened (Clinton, H.),
198
"What Psychiatrists Say about Goldwater"
(*Fact* magazine survey), 81
White, Theodore H., 87, 89
Why Not Victory? (Goldwater), 106
Wilson, Edmund, 33
Wilson, John, 124, 125
Wisner, Frank, 184
World War II. *See also* Hitler, Adolf; Nazism
American Psychoanalytic Association
during, 27–28
COI and, 19–20
Erikson and, 23–28
Langer and, 18–23
psychoanalysis and the war effort,
19–28
OSS and, 19–28

Young, David, 174, 175, 176,
179
Young Man Luther (Erikson), 1–2, 4, 26–27,
73

Zeneger, John Peter, 118